University
Of Dundee
UNIVERSITY LIBRARY

Date of Return

United States

Expansionism and

British North

America,

1775–1871

United

States

Expansionism

and

British

North

America,

1775–1871

Reginald C. Stuart

The University of

North Carolina Press

Chapel Hill and

London

©1988 The University of North Carolina Press

Manufactured in the United States of America

The paper in this book meets the guidelines for permanence
and durability of the Committee on Production Guidelines for
Book Longevity of the Council on Library Resources.

92 91 90 89 88   5 4 3 2 1

Library of Congress Cataloging-in-Publication Data

Stuart, Reginald C.

  United States expansionism and British North America,
ca. 1775–1871.

  Bibliography: p.
  Includes index.
  1. United States—Territorial expansion. 2. British
—North America—History—18th century. 3. British—
North America—History—19th century. 4. United
States—Relations—Great Britain. 5. Great Britain—
Relations—United States. I. Title.
E179.5.S85 1988 911'.73 87-25506
ISBN 0-8078-1767-8 (alk. paper)

TO JOHN K. MAHON

teacher, scholar, example, and friend

Contents

Maps

Preface

The United States and the colonies that would become Canada emerged with separate political identities in 1783. The recently acquired French colonies suddenly became British bases that could be used against the Americans instead of in their defense. After 1783, the Americans looked north to British North America, a string of provinces stretching from Nova Scotia through New Brunswick to Lower Canada and after the Constitutional Act of 1791, Upper Canada. Down to Confederation in 1867 and beyond, Americans increasingly dealt with these provincials in many spheres.

Research into the question of how Americans reacted to provincial developments in light of their own expansionism reveals a cluster of themes. First, an American-provincial borderland emerged after 1783 built around proximity, personal contacts arising from family ties, back-and-forth frontier migration, a broadly shared culture, similar institutions, and a network of growing economic links. Second, Americans gradually penetrated the provinces in demographic, commercial, ideological, and political ways. Third, many Americans came to believe in the eventual convergence of the states and the provinces, even while some talked about a separate Canadian destiny. The convergence thesis overshadowed periodic aggressive urges to wrest the provinces from British control, notwithstanding the frequently strident remarks by American editors and politicians during heated moments in Anglo-American relations. As my research developed, promoted by several papers presented at scholarly meetings, the second and third themes of penetration and convergence seemed inseparable.

This book therefore defines American expansionism broadly. Historians such as Norman A. Graebner, Frederick Merk, Richard Van Alstyne, and Albert Weinberg have argued that expansionism was an aggressive impulse for territorial aggrandizement based on commercial, security, and settlement interests. But as Reginald Horsman, James A. Field, Akira Iriye, Walter La Feber, William Appleman Williams, and others have suggested, American expansion meant more than greed for land and riches. Americans after 1783 developed a culture built around capitalistic, democratic, individualistic, and republican values. They also inherited aggressive British mercantilism and laissez-faire conceptions of the role of government in society. And regions within the United States developed variations on the overall culture, such as the slave South, commercial and industrial New England, and the agricultural Midwest. Each area defined national expansionism differently.

Many Americans became more aware of the provinces after 1783. Americans steadily exported ideas, domestic problems and quarrels, trade goods and money to the provinces in exchange for impressions, manufactured items, and raw materials. People moved back and forth across the frontier, both as travelers and settlers. The British provinces represented opportunity to a wide range of Americans. Occasionally, the provinces also seemed a menace because of the strong British military presence. And surprisingly often, the provincials were merely neighbors, "just upstairs," and the objects of a curiosity satisfied by simple tourism. For the most part, Americans looking toward the provinces for whatever reason no more exploited the provincials than they did their stateside neighbors.

This book therefore explores the cultural dynamics behind America's external relations with a particular group of foreigners—British North Americans, both French and Anglo-Saxon—on the northern frontier of the United States. American values as much as interests shaped perceptions of a similar, but foreign people. An Anglo-Saxon character dominated both societies between 1775 and 1871, despite a developing ethnic pluralism in the United States and the presence of significant minorities, French-Canadians and blacks, in both societies.

No work on American expansionism or on American-Canadian relations approaches either topic in this way. The extensive literature on American expansion rarely even mentions the British provinces. Reginald Horsman's perceptive treatment of racial attitudes and foreign policy, for example, scarcely refers to British North America despite Horsman's Anglo-Saxon theme and his probing of American anti-Catholicism. The present work therefore tries to fill gaps in the literature on American expansionism, American-Canadian relations, and American foreign policy in the nineteenth century.

Americans have historically found it difficult to step outside of themselves when judging others. And they have rarely realized how much their own values unconsciously smudged the lenses through which they viewed the world. Thus this book may serve those in each country who wish the other well.

Acknowledgments

Acknowledgments never shield an author's fallacies, faults, and flaws. Thus the ideas, observations, conclusions, and scholarship in this book are my responsibility. But many along the way have helped me, and their faith and generosity deserve recognition. To begin with, the University of Prince Edward Island's Senate Research Committee provided travel subsidies so that early phases of this study could be presented as conference papers. Another grant provided for the maps. UPEI also awarded a sabbatical leave and a wondrous word processor that vastly accelerated the task of writing. Dr. Betty Hall, formerly UPEI's research officer, coached me on grantsmanship. The Social Sciences and Humanities Research Council of Canada awarded successive two-year research grants for travel to various depositories in the United States and Canada, sundry supplies and services, and a research assistant, Ms. Helen Gill. Helen made sense out of my frequently ambiguous directions and waded through newspapers and other materials that J. Franklin Jameson aptly described as "low grade ore" for historians.

The staff in the depositories I consulted were unfailingly cheerful, helpful, and courteous. They rival the materials they care for as a resource for all writers. Several learned societes and other groups encouraged me by accepting my papers on their programs—the Canadian Historical Association, the Society for Historians of American Foreign Relations, the Organization of American Historians, and the National Bicentennial Committee of the Treaty of Paris in the United States.

I completed the manuscript while on sabbatical at the University of British Columbia. The History Department listened patiently in a colloquium, asked pertinent questions, and permitted me to lecture. The chair, Dr. Allen Tully, assisted in many matters. Mrs. Ann Yandel of the UBC library's Special Collections found me a home among her carrels. And Dean of Arts Robert Will let me use a word processor. The Open Learning Institute, with the kind help of Dean Ian Mugridge and Ms. Catherine Kerr, gave me access to their processors for early revisions. UPEI's processors and mainframe computer facilitated final editing and electronic transmission.

Last, many individuals read portions of the manuscript or preliminary papers and offered helpful suggestions. Lawrence Kaplan of Kent State University, Clifford Egan of the University of Houston, Ron Hatzenbuehler of Idaho State University, Robert Beisner of the American University, S. F. Wise of Carleton University, Russell Weigley of Temple University, George Rawlyk of Queens University, and last but foremost, Tom Spira of UPEI, all criticized my project and encouraged me. Lewis Bateman and the dedicated staff at the University of North Carolina Press have hammered my prose into shape and reminded me of what readers need to know. I only hope that the reception awarded this book will justify such a collective investment of energy, funds, and time.

Reginald C. Stuart
Charlottetown, P.E.I., Canada
1988

PART 1

The Era of

Defensive Expansion,

1775–1815

At the end of the War for Independence, despite its far-flung borders that stretched to the Mississippi River in the west, the United States was a small, economically weak, militarily slender power huddled between the Atlantic seaboard and the Appalachian mountains of North America. It was part of Europe's North Atlantic world, yet geographically remote from Europe's commercial, financial, industrial, and political centers.

European countries occupied parts of North America, however, and their influence touched the United States. Great Britain retained West Indian islands, Bermuda, and provinces on America's northern frontier that extended to the limits of the Great Lakes Basin in the continental interior. This meant an insecure northern border for the United States because the British occupied fur posts on American soil and controlled Indian tribes linked with the fur trade. And the provinces also harbored many loyalist refugees who had fled from the United States during and after the Revolution. Spain controlled Florida and the Louisiana territory. Thus Spain's capricious fingers rested on the throat of the Mississippi River, an increasingly important communications channel for Americans moving into the Ohio Valley after 1783. In addition, Spain held the Pacific Coast of North America, while England and Russia, by virtue of exploration and commercial activity, also sustained a Pacific presence by the end of the eighteenth century.

Internally, the United States had many potential fracture lines. The Confederation government struggled to gain control of western lands and to shape a national economy from what survived of the largely separate thirteen colonial economies. Production, trade, and finance gradually recovered from their postwar disruptions. The States grudgingly ceded their western claims to the Confederation government to form a national domain. And delegates hammered out a series of ordinances to transform portions of this territory into states that would be partners with the original thirteen. A major group of social and political dissenters had departed with the loyalist evacuations of 1783. Yet the loyalists remained politically contentious. The Treaty of Paris of 1783 theoretically allowed loyalists to recover lost property through legal action in state courts. But the states refused loyalists this privilege and in retaliation Great Britain held fur posts on American soil.

Americans had only begun to learn to live together instead of as a collection of English colonials. The War for Independence had created a foundation for union, but now Americans had to get to work on the upper stories of their nation. Problems on both American frontiers, international weakness, and what many revolutionary leaders saw as a dangerous tendency toward social anarchy, debt, and commercial chaos combined to produce the movement for a stronger central government that culminated in the Constitutional Convention at Philadelphia in the summer of 1787.

Through these immediate postwar years, politically active Americans were deeply concerned about national security. Both practical and ideological difficulties threatened the survival of the United States in what many saw as a hostile world. Republicanism had found a lonely and isolated home in America, and revolutionary leaders were determined that their political experiment should have the best possible chance of success. They were convinced that republicanism created favorable circumstances for human progress. At the same time, American farmers needed markets, merchantmen needed protection and free access to other countries, and frontiersmen needed defending. If the United States could not achieve external security and internal stability, republicanism would collapse and its American supporters would become pawns in Europe's games of power. The adoption of the Constitution of 1787 was a major step toward national security in the minds of the founding fathers.

The successful creation of a national government was only partly completed when new forces menaced national security. The wars of the French Revolution brought restrictions against overseas trade, and the impressment of seamen by the British an assault on national sovereignty. The governments of the Early National period pursued a tortuous route in their efforts to maintain international neutrality. They employed a combination of wishful thinking, economic coercion, diplomacy, and the limited use of military force, both on land and sea. The several wars between 1783 and 1815 played an important role in allowing the new nation to survive.

Many who considered themselves heirs to eighteenth-century ideas about politics saw a greater danger in domestic factionalism. It took some time for the idea of a legitimate opposition operating within a patriotic consensus to take hold in the American mind.

American leaders may not have accepted two-party politics as natural until the 1820s. But the first American party system of the 1790s nevertheless became a source of strength and union however much the two camps suspected each other of subversive intentions.

American expansionism during the Early National period occurred within this context. At the level of national policymaking, territorial expansion was primarily opportunistic and defensive. Another form of expansionism was undertaken by merchants who sought to extend commercial contacts and petitioned for federal support and protection in the form of legislation and even of military power when they encountered difficulties. But they did not intend that the flag follow their traders except on the flagstaffs of their vessels. Nor did they intend to spread direct political influence where their vessels called or their merchants established trading stations. Even if they had wanted to, such efforts were beyond the power of the American government. But leaders such as Thomas Jefferson, Alexander Hamilton, James Madison, and John Quincy Adams had a vision of America that reached beyond merely erecting outer barricades against foreign assault.

Continental migration patterns constituted a third form of expansionism. American settlers had moved into the Ohio Valley even during the Revolution. After 1783, they pushed against frontier Indian tribes from the Great Lakes to the Gulf of Mexico. American settlers spilled over national boundaries into the British provinces of Upper and Lower Canada, and into Spanish Florida and Louisiana. American policymakers extended unofficial support to an 1810 rebellion of the Florida settlers, but made no other direct political efforts to aid other countrymen settling outside the national boundaries, as in the British provinces, for example.

Territorial acquisitions came from cautiously limited ambitions linked with opportunities and a fundamentally defensive strategy for national security. The negotiators at Paris before 1783 had obtained generous boundaries, far more than the United States required for its population. But Benjamin Franklin, the most influential and perceptive American agent overseas, believed that Americans would eventually spread deep into North America. And many revolutionary leaders gazed westward when they thought of national development.

Specific acquisitions suggest the pattern of defensive territorial expansion. In 1802 Jefferson's government sought a small strip of land along the Mississippi River so that Ohio settlers could deposit their goods to await shipment to outside markets. But shifts in European politics produced an unexpected windfall in the vast and undefined Louisiana. Jefferson did think in terms of American exploitation of the interior, even to the Pacific Coast, as his sponsorship of the Lewis and Clark expedition before his government learned of the Louisiana Purchase indicates. He also talked about an empire of liberty in North America. But he was not clear whether this would be several countries under one government, or a loose affiliation of independent republics. During the War of 1812, James Madison's administration had limited territorial ambitions, if any. Madison and his secretary of state, James Monroe, would have kept Upper Canada if American armies had ejected British power. But the British remained. Few, apart from Westerners, had territorial ambitions in the North, and their principal goal was to sever British links with the Indians in the Old Northwest.

American expansionism in the Early National period therefore had three fundamental components. First, merchants had particular interests in free trade and in expanding opportunities now that they could no longer circulate within the British Empire. Second, western settlers wanted access to the Gulf of Mexico down the Mississippi River and frontiers secure against what they saw as the Indian "menace." These restless and ambitious frontiersmen also wanted to move where they chose, and for the most part were able to do so. Both British and Spanish officials became alarmed at the influx of Americans. They considered them potentially disloyal elements that would eventually rebel against colonial rule and seek annexation to the United States. Third, successive administrations wanted international respectability and secure borders for the United States.

Each of these three fundamental elements of expansionism contributed to a diversity of American perceptions of the British provinces. Most Americans below the northern tier of states were unaware of a series of borderlands that began to form after 1783 from Halifax, Nova Scotia, to Sandwich, on the Detroit River. Most Americans perceived the northern provinces through the veils of ambition, fear, and prejudice. American officials, for example, saw the provinces as an enemy base. Policymakers therefore sought to eject the British from the Northwest Posts they had retained since 1783. They also sought to define and secure boundaries, and sever the British links with Indian tribes on American soil. American settlers and merchants, on the other hand, saw the provinces, not as a threat, but as a source of opportunity. The former migrated into the eastern townships of Lower Canada, across the St. Lawrence, Niagara, and Detroit rivers into Upper Canada, and even in small numbers into the maritime provinces of Nova Scotia and New Brunswick.

Northern merchants sought access to borderland markets and resources. In Halifax, New England entrepreneurs saw a backdoor to the coveted West Indian market. Farmers along the northern border were cut off from the centers of American economic activity. Their natural outlets lay through British territory with Montreal as their entrepôt. For certain groups of Americans, the provinces provided opportunity of another kind—free land, or the chance to join friends and relatives who had left during the War for Independence.

American borderlanders began to see the provincials as neighbors as the British regime in the provinces began to be distinguished from the people it ruled. The provincials were also potential recruits to American republicanism, or at least this was the belief of many in the United States on the eve of the War of 1812. Proximity, cultural similarity, kinship, and economic links encouraged this view. For still others, the provinces were an object of curiosity. Yankee travelers visited to see for themselves how the provincials lived and what they were like. Finally, the provinces offered a refuge to some Americans. Quakers sojourned in Nova Scotia, Moravian Indians and their missionary leaders fled to the Thames Valley in Upper Canada, and a few Dunkards and former Whiskey Rebels of 1794 also found a refuge outside of, but nearby the United States.

These various perceptions solidified in American thinking during the Early National period, and carried through to Canadian Confederation in 1867 and beyond. They constitute the pattern of American views of British North America after 1783 and provide in turn a framework for understanding how national expansion of the United States intertwined with the development of Canadian history. Most Americans were indifferent to the provinces, but many were not. Those who were informed and interested provide a window on American national behavior between 1783 and 1871.

Chapter 1.
Revolutionary
Expansionism
and the
Provinces

*The union is yet incomplete, and will
be so, until the inhabitants of all the
territory from Cape Breton to the
Mississippi are included in it: while
Great Britain possesses Canada and
West Florida, she will be continually
setting the Indians upon us, and
while she holds the harbors of Augustine and Halifax, especially the
latter, we shall not be able to protect
our trade or coasts from her depredations, at least for many years to
come.*
—*George Mason to
Richard Henry Lee,
21 July 1778*

After the fall of Quebec in 1759, American colonials began to celebrate Britain's triumph in the Great War for Empire. In a 1760 sermon on the victories, the Reverend John Mellon of Lancaster recalled the long, dreary, and violent history of French-English relations in North America. But only recently the French had been swept away from the northern border; the Spanish had been ejected from the southern. The war had been just, Mellon declared, and God had smiled. America could look forward to safe frontiers, the spread of the true gospel among the Indians, new land for settlement, the growth of British dominions, peaceful trade, and an end to wars.[1]

George Mason's letter and John Mellon's sermon suggest the early pattern of American perceptions of the northern borderlands, whether in British or French hands. Except for the brief interlude between the Treaty of 1763 that confirmed British mastery of North America and the opening campaigns of the War of Independence, Americans saw the north as an enemy base. Before 1763, Britain's national and imperial rival, and the deadly enemy of all Protestants, Roman Catholic France, had garrisoned the strongholds. After 1775, British officials and their troops threatened the colonial rebellion from this northern base. In both cases, enemy agents sought to enlist Indian allies to slaughter American frontiersmen. Sallies from northern bases also imperiled American coastal settlements and shipping. Finally, both the British and the French used their northern colonies as bases to vie with the Americans for resources nominally controlled by the Indians—land, transportation routes, and furs.

This fear of a northern enemy base became associated with a countervailing perception. The provinces represented opportunity. During the colonial era, these opportunities were agrarian and commercial. Who controlled the territory did not matter as long as Americans had free access. New England merchants, for example, traded briskly with the French at Louisbourg and in Acadia, whether peace or war prevailed between the home countries across the Atlantic. The frontiersmen wanted only to be left alone to carve out new homesteads. Finally, as Mellon hinted, the northern provinces offered religious opportunities—the occasion to spread the true Protestant gospel.

These northern provinces lay on the fringes of the American frontier and consequently New Yorkers and New Englanders in particular had been aware of the opportunities they offered for many years. New England merchants and fishermen had only a short voyage to the Bay of Fundy or a slightly longer one beyond to the waters off Cape Breton, St. John's Island (later Prince Edward Island), and Newfoundland. For New Yorkers, the journey to the northern provinces was more difficult and dangerous. Yet the ancient invasion route down the Champlain Valley was also a commercial highway that had tempted entrepreneurial spirits even in the 1760s. Half-pay British officers and American merchants trekked north to seek patrimonies and penetrate the Montreal fur trade. By 1776 they formed a small but vocal group in Canadian provincial affairs, with southern contacts.

Mellon's and Mason's remarks, however, did not cover all facets of the American perception of the northern provinces. Perceptions varied with circumstances and individuals. For example, the provinces provided both refugees and a refuge. After 1755, refugee Acadians landed in Massachusetts from the Annapolis expulsion. In the 1760s, however, New Englanders migrated to the Annapolis area in Nova Scotia to farm or speculate in land. The provincials themselves were also objects of conquest, forced recruits either to

British imperialism in the 1760s or to United States democratic republicanism after 1776. In other words, on this occasion provincials were potential Americans, even though they were products of an alien, even enemy, society and culture.

Revolutionary Americans have a historical reputation as aggressive conquerors casting covetous glances at Canada and Nova Scotia. Even before declaring independence, colonial revolutionaries launched a struggle for a fourteenth colony. Although Canada became both a political and military target, misadventure, bad luck, and later fear that France might regain Canada, combined to thwart American designs and insure Canadian survival as a British province.[2] The 1775 invasion was a strategic defense with only overtones of imperial ambition. "Manifest Destiny" has been wrenched from its nineteenth-century context to explain how expansionistic revolutionaries thought about British provinces other than the rebellious thirteen. Although a few of the revolutionaries hinted at territorial ambitions, most saw the 1775 expedition as an effort to guard against future wars.[3]

Were expansionism and the American Revolution functionally interrelated? The natural law Revolutionary leaders so frequently cited sanctioned an outward thrust. As self-appointed guardians of liberty, Americans inevitably looked beyond their as yet undefined borders to extend their sanctuary of freedom. At the same time, economic impulses arising in colonial times stimulated a search for markets and materials. Agrarian ideals, republican ideology, strategic necessities, and a belief that the Revolution was incomplete without the other mainland colonies combined to draw revolutionary minds north.[4]

The story of United States expansionism and the British North American provinces began during the revolutionary period. Great Britain's 1774 Quebec Act riveted revolutionary attention on the special nature of Canada as a province under British, rather than French control. This act defined Canada as a Roman Catholic aggressor that had thrust into the Ohio Valley, a region some Americans coveted for future exploitation. Americans also heard rumors of British plans to mobilize their new French subjects to subdue American resistance to Parliament's decrees.

The events of 1774 and 1775 suggest that the Continental Congress sanctioned, but did not initiate a military invasion of Canada.

The rebels had not yet become revolutionaries seeking independence. Sam Adams, ever ready to believe the worst about Great Britain, persuaded fellow Massachusetts radicals that a dangerous British base lay to the north. Alarmed, the Boston Committee of Correspondence sent John Brown on a harrowing mid-winter trek to contact former French colonists and forestall British influence even before the armed clashes at Lexington and Concord in April of 1775. Brown's mission was discouraging. While he sought support in Montreal on the basis of common interest, continental agents spread propaganda leaflets in the countryside that threatened invasion and reprisals if the French helped the British. And the Americans could neither disguise nor overcome their obvious religious bigotry toward Roman Catholics.

By May 1775, the British had reportedly sent French-Canadian militia to attack Americans near St. Johns and were allegedly recruiting Indians as allies. The northern menace swelled in rebel imaginations. Montreal and Quebec were enemy bastions once again. But the rebel radicals were not quite certain how to view Canada's French population.

Continental leadership advertised for support against the British in its 1774 overture to Quebec and "the colonies of St. John's, Nova Scotia, Georgia, East and West Florida, who have not deputies to represent them in this Congress." On 24 October, Congress endorsed Brown's mission with the Canadian letter. This letter recited the justice of resistance to Parliament's authority, asserted the identity of purpose and interest among all the North American colonies, and asked Canadians not to rebel independently. Rather, the letter urged Canadians to "unite with us in one social compact, formed on the generous principles of equal liberty, and cemented by such an exchange of beneficial and endearing officers as to render it perpetual." Congress advised the Canadians to meet in their towns, organize a provincial congress, and dispatch delegates to meet in Philadelphia in May of the following year. The Congress pretended that the Canadians were simply fellow colonials with a similar interest, political outlook, and social structure.[5]

After the British-colonial armed clashes farther south, events such as Ethan Allen's seizure of Fort Ticonderoga again drew Congress's strategic attention north. Viewed from the south end of the Champlain Valley, Canada seemed an obvious base from which the

British would launch expeditions against the rebellion. At the same time, Continental leaders persuaded themselves that the French-Canadians might still join the Revolution. A mixture of strategic perceptions and an eagerness for continental solidarity against the British therefore persuaded Congress to support a substantial expedition against British power in Canada. This dual view of Canada as a British base on the one hand, and as a source of potential recruits on the other, accounts for the ambivalent character of Congress's policy toward Canada during the War for Independence.

Although the Canadians failed to respond as favorably as Congress had hoped, radical leaders continued to pretend that the Canadians were merely fellow colonists who would see reason if properly persuaded. Congress proposed more letters to the French-Canadians. But on 17 May 1775, Congress ordered a boycott of the colonies that had not yet agreed to resist Parliament. Next, New Yorkers took a few British outposts close to Montreal. The New York Assembly hastened to explain this aggressive initiative to the French-Canadians. "Our only intention, is, to prevent any hostile incursions upon us, by the troops in your province."[6] The New Yorkers insisted that their attack was defensive.

Congress's policy was still unclear. Was Canada a potential recruit to be wooed or a British base to be conquered? It seemed to be both. Congress collected intelligence on French-Canadian opinion and on 29 May again appealed to its "fellow subjects" who bore the "yoke of oppression." Homes, families, lands, religion, nothing was safe under British rule. Congress supported New York's explanation for aggression with a creativity that spilled into fiction. The British forts and supplies in the Champlain Valley "were intended to annoy us, and to cut off that friendly intercourse and communication, which has been hitherto subsisting between you and us." There was no need for alarm. "We yet entertain hopes of your uniting with us in the defence of our common liberty." Again, however, threats and appeals coexisted. American sympathy would yield to contempt and anger if the French-Canadians did not stand with their southern neighbors against Britain.[7]

The American radicals had tried to accommodate their dual view of Canada by distinguishing between British rulers and their French-Canadian subjects. On 1 June 1775 Congress resolved that "no expedition or incursion ought to be undertaken or made, by any colony, or body of colonists, against or into Canada." These orders went to Ethan Allen at Ticonderoga, and after translation, north to reassure the French-Canadians. Less than four weeks later, however, President John Hancock of Congress wrote to George Washington that he had instructed General Philip Schuyler to march north and seize British installations as far as Montreal, "if he finds it practicable, and not Disagreeable to the Canadians." Military necessity and Allen's action elasticized the boundaries of defensive expansion.

Busy at Cambridge managing the siege of Boston, Washington doubted that the Canadians would join the American military effort. But he issued a softer, more diplomatic letter to Quebec than Congress's virtual broadsides. Washington flattered the Canadians as "enlightened, generous, and virtuous," in short, good potential republicans. He begged for union to pursue a "free Government," but issued no threats. The army invading Canada under General Schuyler was "not to plunder, but to protect you; to animate and bring forth into Action those sentiments of Freedom you have declared."[8] Others—Ethan Allen and the New Hampshire legislature, for example—sent similar letters, although they had no real grounds for supposing the Canadians would be receptive to their overtures. But this gesture clearly reflects the distinction they drew between the British and their provincial subjects.

As the rebellion gathered military, political, and emotional headway, Americans came to believe more firmly that the Canadians favored their cause. Testimony by those who claimed to know, along with written reports from the New York frontier, suggested strong French-Canadian sympathy with revolutionary goals. This intelligence and the desire to deny the British use of their Canadian base persuaded Washington to mount a reinforcing expedition to Quebec, by way of the Kennebec River in the Maine district of Massachusetts. Benedict Arnold was in command and had a perilous march through a tangled wilderness in wretched weather. Washington and Congress expected both Schuyler and Arnold to test opinion and conciliate the Canadians as they went. The invasion might also persuade the Indians to remain neutral. But the friendship of the French-Canadians was crucial. If the Canadians were either "averse" or unwilling to accept the Americans, then Schuyler and Arnold were to withdraw.[9] Washington knew that Congress could not hold Canada by force of arms alone.

Washington sounds very much like the leader of a national army in these letters. The rebellion and invasion also sustained the momentum for independence that grew in Congress over the winter of 1775–76. Launching a war of conquest against a neighboring province, whatever the rationale, drew a solid line between colonial and British authority. Despite radical claims to the contrary, reconciliation with Parliament and the Crown had become almost impossible.

The invading armies trudged north. General Richard Montgomery took over when Schuyler became too ill to continue. Montgomery found sympathy but limited commitment in the Richelieu River Valley. After his victories at Chambly and St. John, however, the Canadians became openly cooperative. Ethan Allen's prediction that a successful invasion would lead the French to throw off any allegiance to Britain seemed correct. Montreal fell, and General Guy Carleton fled down the St. Lawrence River to Quebec City. Montgomery followed and Arnold joined him with the survivors of his march through Maine to lay siege to the British defenses. But then, winter, exhaustion, dwindling financial and material resources, Carleton's stubborn defense, Quebec's sturdy walls, a balky American army, and the failure of more than a trickle of Canadians to swell the rebel ranks produced disaster. Montgomery died in an assault, and Arnold was seriously wounded. The weakened army remained around Quebec, but withdrew after British reinforcements arrived in the spring. The gamble had failed. Canada remained a British base.

Congress continued to woo the French-Canadians even though there was little cause for encouragement. The views of such American leaders as General Wooster that the French were near savages who followed the prevailing military wind did not make their conciliatory efforts easier. Anti-Catholic tirades were stopped nonetheless.[10] Furthermore, Congress selected Benjamin Franklin, Charles Carroll, Samuel Chase, and John Carroll, a Catholic clergyman, to travel north and salvage the situation.[11] Once in Canada they found little to cheer them. Old fears of American anti-Catholicism and the failed invasion kept the Canadians away. The Canadians even began to appear dangerous, likely to support Carleton. Moses Hazen, one of the few prominent English Canadians to join and fight with the Americans, concluded that the French now supported the British crown. Charles Carroll and Franklin returned south shortly and the mission collapsed.[12] The Revolution's agents developed a different political view of the provinces than their leaders farther south.

Washington continued to hope that Canada could be added to "complete our union," but realized that French-Canadians would not take up arms in the continental cause. Congress remained optimistic after the Declaration of Independence. The committee on the Articles of Confederation stated that "Canada acceding to this Confederation, and entirely joining in the measures of the United Colonies, shall be admitted into the same." Congress preratified Canada as a member of the union. The Articles were then translated into French and dispatched north. American fantasies about French-Canadian recruits died hard. By 1783 these illusions existed only in the Articles of Confederation.[13]

Canada still remained a dangerous British base. Richard Henry Lee warned that the "Ministerial dependence on Canada is so great, that no object can be of greater importance to North America than to defeat them there." If the colonials could even hold at the falls on the Richelieu River, "we thereby effectually cut off all communications with the upper Country, or Western Indians, and prevent the West Indies from receiving supplies." The loss of Canada was not merely the loss of territory, President of Congress Henry Laurens wrote to John Thomas. "The whole frontier of the New England and New-York Governments will be exposed, not only to the ravages of the Indians, but also to the British forces."[14]

The course of the war now shaped American perceptions of Canada. The British prepared to invade. Frontier fears of the Indians resurfaced to grip revolutionary imaginations when Joseph Brant declared his support of Great Britain. In addition, refugees hounded out of their homes and communities for refusing to support rebellion began to collect in makeshift borderland settlements and organize into auxiliary British units. Loyalist leaders such as John Johnson in Quebec and Walter Butler in the Niagara region became terrible names to New Yorkers. The war on the northern frontier degenerated into a protracted, savage, indecisive series of raids and counterraids even as General John Burgoyne's expedition down the Champlain Valley ended in Britain's first military disaster in the fall of 1777.

Despite Burgoyne's surrender, the revolutionaries could not do more than defend their northern frontier. But in 1778, after the Franco-American treaty of alliance, interest in a new Canadian invasion quickened. Surely now the French-Canadians, however they felt about the Americans, would rally behind an invading army led by a notable and attractive French leader such as the Marquis de Lafayette.

Lafayette agreed to lead an expedition, and Congress's Board of War began its planning in January 1778. Gouverneur Morris suggested that Lafayette as commander of the enterprise would evoke positive memories of old allegiances for the Canadians. Congress appointed French officers to recruit in Canada for the same reason. But few Americans were truly enthusiastic about renewed northern expansion.

General Philip Schuyler, who had reason to know, believed that the operation would be difficult. Experience suggested that the American militia would be certain to plunder and alienate the French-Canadians, officers from old France notwithstanding. Colonel John Laurens wrote to his father, Henry Laurens, that the resources would go better elsewhere. The elder Laurens agreed and was against the projected invasion. John Jay of New York thought that if the effort succeeded, well and good. "If not Congress will be taught a useful lesson." Washington disliked it also. Eliphalet Dyer, a member of Congress, called it a "wild plan." Others feared that if the invasion succeeded, France would retain Canada and the United States would be no better off than if the British controlled it. Once again ambivalent when it came to its Canadian policy, Congress instructed Lafayette to withdraw if he found no clear evidence of Canadian support.[15]

Meanwhile, preparations for the expedition went ahead slowly, when at all. High-sounding resolutions notwithstanding, Lafayette discovered that his "army" was little more than a skeleton force with few supplies and fewer funds. By 1778, Congress could scarcely hold a war effort together, much less launch an invasion. Only a core of committed patriots and aid from the French sustained the struggle for independence. By March, John Henry told Governor Thomas Johnson of Maryland not to fear that the expedition against Canada would proceed. He pointed out that winter approached, and few preparations had been made. Besides, American interests dictated that energies be concentrated on strengthening Washington's military hand.[16] As Henry Laurens noted, the invasion was over before it began. Congressmen even began to deny earlier interest in the idea. On 14 March, Congress officially ordered the Canada expedition "suspended."[17]

Military, political, and diplomatic factors foredoomed the expedition. British military pressure provided the main rationale. Congress explained to the disappointed Lafayette that the plan had been advanced while the Americans anticipated a British "evacuation of all the Posts they held in these States." But the British remained, so "prudence therefore dictates that the arms of America should be employed in expelling the Enemy from her own shores" before liberating a "neighbouring Province."[18]

Did Congress dissemble, or was this a convenient pretext to suspend its ambition of making Canada the fourteenth colony? In either case, Canada was still a British base from which Loyalists and Indians battered the New York frontier. General John Sullivan even foresaw a large and powerful colony eventually emerging in the north. A British Canada would be a base to menace the United States. He urged an immediate invasion to expel Britain and prevent future war. In France, Benjamin Franklin prodded his diplomatic counterparts from Britain on the issue of Canada, although neither his colleagues nor Congress would pursue the province at the expense of peace or independence.[19]

The American view of Nova Scotia, at the time a separate British province, underwent a similar evolution. But the background relationships were somewhat different from those with Canada. Nova Scotia was on the northern flank of the New England expansion, and the frontier always represented opportunity to settlers. This frontier was both on the land and the sea. As early as the 1670s, New Hampshire fishermen sailed north for the season in Cape Breton and Newfoundland waters. By 1700, these seemed richer than New England fisheries. By the 1750s, trade in lumber opened between Portsmouth, New Hampshire, and Halifax. New Englanders also migrated to northern Vermont, New Hampshire, and the Maine district of Massachusetts. By 1760, settlers had reached the western shore of the tip of Penobscot Bay. By 1776, the area from the Penobscot to what became the Nova Scotia border had 15,000 people.[20]

After the British victory in 1763, Louisbourg was no longer an enemy base. Clashes between proprietors and tenants in many New

England towns provided a pool of people who saw in migration to Nova Scotia an opportunity for farming or fishing. Governor Charles Lawrence advertised for settlers as early as October of 1758. Between 1759 and 1765, some 5,000 migrated, mostly from Connecticut and Rhode Island. Massachusetts sent few farmers, although her fishermen settled onto Nova Scotia's southern shore. This flow slowed in the mid-1760s. British migrants to Nova Scotia now came directly from the old country. But even with this shift, the Nova Scotia population in 1776 was about one-half Yankee. These settlers maintained close personal, family, and economic ties with New England. Produce for export from farms, fish, lumbering, and the St. John River trade all moved through Boston, not Halifax.

Britain held tight political control over Nova Scotia. The province remained royal throughout the War of Independence. Halifax was a naval base of rising importance, and during the controversies preceding independence, was to be the new venue for trying accused violators of the Navigation Acts. Sam Adams, James Otis, and other New England radicals, saw Nova Scotians as an ideologically unworthy people, and the province as conservative, despotic, and overly dependent upon the crown. They did not pay it much heed, and apart from the settlers around Machias, Maine, few saw Nova Scotia as a likely fourteenth (or fifteenth) province.

Although not as sophisticated a society as the New England colonies, Nova Scotia was nevertheless sufficiently developed to be divided about the quest for independence that emerged in the southern colonies between 1763 and 1776.[21] Halifax officials supported the crown, and the military easily dominated the population in the immediate vicinity of the city. Merchants appear to have been equivocal, supporting resistance, but taking a conservative stance about rebellion. The many small and isolated settlements scattered around the Bay of Fundy shores, whatever their views, could not easily act together or even communicate among themselves. They were part of the first American-provincial borderland, and their feelings were as much torn as in any colony. Settlers in Cumberland County in the Chignecto land neck, for example, largely favored the rebels. But many Nova Scotians wanted to be neutral, as the Massachusetts General Court discovered from petitions sent by settlers between the Penobscot and St. Croix rivers. New England privateers, frequently indistinguishable from pirates in their ferocious rapacity, likely extinguished much Nova Scotian sympathy for the Revolution between 1775 and 1783.²²

Machias became the core of a drive to recruit Nova Scotia for the revolution. The Reverend James Lyon and two refugees from the Chignecto region, Jonathan Eddy and John Allan, proposed an invasion to the Massachusetts legislature. The Massachusetts government had already invited the eastern Indians to join the rebellion and turned to George Washington for advice. At the time, Washington had already committed his resources to the Canada expedition. Perhaps this explains why he argued that an invasion of Nova Scotia contradicted the principle of defense that motivated the Americans.

Whatever Washington's actual thoughts, the revolutionaries lacked the means to launch a third invasion north in the late summer of 1775. Consequently, Massachusetts and the Continental Congress were indifferent to the Machias proposal, but reconsidered briefly when settlers in the Passamaquoddy region of Nova Scotia petitioned to form a local committee of safety and "be admitted into the Association of the North Americans, for the preservation of their rights and liberties." Congress dispatched agents to gauge Nova Scotia opinion, although these men were more actively engaged in spying on British defenses. Despite this action, and continued concern about Indian neutrality, neither Congress nor George Washington took any substantive action through 1775 or 1776.²³

In the meantime, the Machias rebels seized the initiative. In August of 1775 a foray captured the British fort (with its garrison of four) at the mouth of the St. John River. But Eddy and Allan planned more than a mere raid. They recruited among local rebels and the Nova Scotia refugees. The results were unencouraging, too much so for Allan, but by the late summer of 1776, Eddy led an invasion to wrest Nova Scotia from British control. He believed that the majority of Nova Scotians would rally to the Continental cause once British power had been humbled. The recruits seem to have had mixed motives. Some were motivated by republicanism, but others joined for revenge against loyalist neighbors who had turned them into refugees. Still others simply sought loot.²⁴

Once in Nova Scotia, Eddy's force of eighty men attracted few recruits. Nova Scotians wanted neutrality. Eddy nevertheless besieged Fort Cumberland, the old French Fort Beausejour, on the Chignecto land neck, in November. The British routed him. This dismal defeat, but more importantly the failure to recruit local French and ex-Yankees, convinced Allan and others that Nova Scotia was not a likely candidate for the American union after all. Mirroring the thoughts of those on New York's northern frontier, Allan argued for resources to defend his region and keep the Indians neutral. In August of 1777, George Stillman, one of Allan's colleagues, wrote to Congress's Board of War. "When we view Machias as a valuable frontier town, a proper Retreat for the Indians, and a barrier to all our eastern Country, its importance to the State rises in our esteem a greater Excitement for Defending it."[25] But defending this frontier remained a low priority for Congress and Massachusetts. Only when America demanded access to the Atlantic fisheries during the peace conference did the province come into focus once again.

The War for Independence generated an ugly American perception of Nova Scotians and the other Maritime provincials. Rebels, especially those on privateers, viewed the entire region as the home of loyalists and therefore an open hunting ground. These men bullied, pillaged, raided, ravaged, and stole indiscriminately. No one was safe, regardless of status or professed sentiments. The privateers ignored safe conduct passes no matter what the signature and seal. This raiding brought extensive suffering to Maritime provincials, and did force the British to devote military resources to improve defenses. Massachusetts abandoned all interest in further invasions of Nova Scotia and wanted the raiding to stop to prevent British retaliation. The privateers persisted, even though they had little impact on the overall war effort, and brought the counterraids Massachusetts feared. In 1779, the British seized Castine, established a base, and routed a Massachusetts fleet sent to dislodge them. The privateers also drove Nova Scotians firmly into loyalism.[26]

Other Americans sought to maintain prewar contacts with family, friends, and business associates in the provinces. John Allan, for example, kept his eye on personal opportunities. He corresponded with friends in Nova Scotia, but concluded that the constant movement back and forth to New England had damaged the revolutionary cause by passing intelligence to the enemy. People going to

Nova Scotia to settle private business and trading vessels plying the coast constituted a spy network.[27]

The Americans and the British worked out informal agreements for the exchange of prisoners, so cartel vessels sailed between Boston and Halifax. Massachusetts also received, but rejected summarily, petitions from Nova Scotians who wanted to trade in Boston and Marblehead for provisions. Authorities viewed those Nova Scotians who did come as spies. On 24 January 1782, the legislature even denied passes "to any person or persons of what description soever to carry goods to Nova Scotia or any place in possession of the enemy . . . on any pretence whatever."[28] It is difficult to determine how serious a problem this traffic was because, between the privateers and British control over maritime waters, little unmolested trade remained along the North Atlantic coast by 1782.

A handful of Americans persisted in the illusion that Nova Scotia could be added to the union. Some thought that the French alliance might alter Nova Scotian sympathies, or provide fresh opportunities for conquest, depending upon the fortunes of war. But for most, Nova Scotia was a British base and a loyalist refuge.[29] The only likely chance for a major northeastern military effort came in 1779, when the British seized Castine as a forward base against New England privateers, as a loyalist refuge, and perhaps as a bargaining token for the peace talks. After the Americans failed to dislodge the British, a bitter local civil war erupted in the vicinity.[30] Massachusetts now had a military problem, rather than a military-political opportunity. The British and loyalists remained in Castine until the general British evacuation of American territory in 1784. Then, they only went as far north as St. Andrews, at the mouth of the St. Croix River.

The revolutionaries' approach to Canada and Nova Scotia suggests the complexity and ambiguity of American views of the British North American provinces that would develop after 1783. Provincials seemed potential recruits for the cause of republican independence, but the provinces themselves were British bases. In addition, some believed that private opportunities lay to the north. New England fishermen saw the waters near the shores of the Northumberland Strait, Cape Breton, and Newfoundland as opportunities as well. The Maritime region had coal, furs, and lumber into the bargain. And fishing was a cover for smuggling into the French possessions of St. Pierre and Miquelon. John Allan combined all these themes in his view of Nova Scotia. So did Moses Hazen, a recruit to the invading American army under Richard Montgomery in 1775.

By 1775, Benjamin Faneuil and Joshua Winslow, two Boston merchants, had extensive northern Maritime interests. War only suspended the development of northern trade possibilities for these Americans. After 1783, land speculators, merchants, and fishermen moved back into the Maritimes and Canada, ignoring as best they could the new political boundary. They resurrected the development of the two borderland regions that had begun to emerge before the Revolution—the Bay of Fundy and the Champlain Valley.[31] American expansionism therefore had personal and commercial as well as political and ideological themes.

The pursuit of northern opportunities existed even during the war. After 1778, Generals Henry Clinton and Frederick Haldimand offered free trade to Vermonters, hoping to pry one region away from the United States. Ethan Allen's family, among others, proved happy to service personal and local economic interests, whatever their commitment to republicanism and American independence. Quebec exports of barrel staves, oak timbers, and potash all rose during the war as a result. The suppliers were all in Vermont. Vermont contractors even fed British troops colonial beef. David S. Franks, who joined General Montgomery's forces after the capture of Montreal, speculated in gold and currency between Montreal and the United States as a sideline to his revolutionary military career. Moses Hazen understood the political and strategic need to conquer Canada, but also knew that conquest would allow him to redeem his land holdings, forfeited to the British when he joined Montgomery's army. As Charles Carroll traveled north to persuade Canadians to enlist in the American cause, he jotted down Philip Schuyler's comment about building a waterway to link New York and Canada. Champlain Valley lands would surely rise in value as north-south trade developed.[32] American views of Canada during the War for Independence mixed defensive strategy, ideological expansion, and entrepreneurship.

The provinces were also a refuge for the loyalists. The British, the loyalists themselves, and the revolutionaries all understood this. Once the attempts to conquer Canada and Nova Scotia had failed, the British bases and loyalist sanctuaries were secure. From the first controversies, through the British evacuations, and even after American independence, loyalists found a refuge in the north against patriot persecution.

Perhaps 50,000 loyalists fled to what remained of British North America between 1776 and 1784. A few trickled north even before General Howe's evacuation of Boston in 1776, when 1,100 refugees landed in primitive Halifax. Although Nova Scotia and Canada both had reputations for bad weather, New England loyalists believed that the lands around the Bay of Fundy were similar to their own. Most left with no more than rumor to encourage them. Younger loyalists were more optimistic about starting over than the older, established people. But the loyalists soon adopted an aphorism about their northern refuge—"To Hell or Halifax."[33]

The loyalists moved into a wilderness. Some, such as Joel Stone, read that Nova Scotia was "an asylum of freedom and safety." The loyalist perception was best summarized in a 1783 Shakespearean parody.

> To go—or not to go—is that the question?
> Whether 'tis best to trust the inclement sky
> That scowls indignant oe'r the cheary Bay
> Of Funday and Cape Sables rocks and shoals,
> And seek our new domains in Scotia wilds,
> Barren and bare; or stay among the rebels.
>
> .   .   .   .
>
> Hard choice! Stay, let me think,-To explore our way,
> Thro' raging seas, to Scotia's rocky coast,
> At this dire season of this direful year.
> Where scarce the sun affords the cheerful ray;

The final argument was widely convincing.

> Then let us fly, nor trust a war of words
> Where British arms and Tory arts have failed
> T'effect our purpose. On bleak Roseway's shores,
> Let's lose our fears, for no bold Whig will dare
> With sword or law to persecute us there.[34]

In the northern states, the bitter border war left vivid memories and fears for the future because of British links with the Indians. And because such infamous Tory leaders as Walter Butler and John

Johnson found refuge in the provinces, along with less belligerent loyalists, the stereotype of the provinces as an enemy base continued. The loyalists thus contributed to the view of the provinces as an enemy base and as a refuge. In the future, however, the motivation and composition of the refugees would change dramatically. Borderland bitterness faded through the 1780s and 1790s, and other Americans migrated across the frontier in search of land, relatives, former friends and neighbors, financial opportunities, and even a refuge from persecution within the United States.

If the provinces were an asylum for loyalists, they were also a source of refugees. Jonathan Eddy led some of his Nova Scotia neighbors to Machias even before the rebellion evolved into a war for independence and Eddy launched his expedition against Fort Cumberland. In Canada, landowner and entrepreneur Moses Hazen joined Montgomery's army and stumped the countryside for other recruits. When the invasions of Nova Scotia and Canada failed, Eddy and Hazen led their followers, often accompanied by their families, in the train of the retreating armies. All were now outlaws, their property lost to the Crown as punishment for treason.[35]

Once uprooted, neither the republican nor the loyalist refugees could easily return to their homelands. So they sought compensation from the governments they had supported. Hazen, Eddy, and other leaders petitioned Congress and the state legislatures as soon as they landed in the United States. Although the legislators were unflaggingly sympathetic, for many years the refugees had little beyond sympathy to console them for their losses. Congress referred Nova Scotia refugee claims to Massachusetts and granted territory in the west, along Lake Erie. Massachusetts refused to help Eddy. The western lands were poor, and hostile Indians made the area dangerous. The Canadian refugees remained unsettled for nearly twenty years. By the time suitable lands were assigned, many had died.[36]

Congressional leaders and their diplomats overseas in the peace talks in Paris opposed compensating the loyalists for their losses in the War for Independence. They were, however, divided about America's future relationship with the provinces. Canada had an alien population—French and Catholic—onto which was grafted large numbers of Anglo-Saxon loyalists. New York was the state primarily concerned about relations with Canada because of fur-trading interests and the idea of Canada as an enemy base. Nova Scotia was overwhelmingly loyalist by 1783. New Englanders had particular interests in the provincial maritimes because of past family and economic connections. Congress and the diplomats had to reconcile those interests and bargain with Britain about other matters as well. In the United States, some supported acquiring the provinces, but never at the expense of independence and an end to the war.[37]

Some revolutionary leaders coveted Nova Scotia in particular. Gouverneur Morris, on the committee to draft peace instructions, was clear about that, and so was Elbridge Gerry. John Adams argued, "As long as Great Britain Shall have Canada Nova Scotia, and the Floridas, or any of them So long will Great Britain be the Enemy of the United States, let her disguise it as much as she will."[38] William Whipple from New Hampshire asserted that in addition to independence, America should insist that Britain "quit all pretensions to Canada and Nova Scotia." But in February of 1779 Congress decided not to require the concession of Nova Scotia although they also declared that the United States should not trade a bid for that province for access to the Newfoundland fisheries.[39]

Few saw Nova Scotia as having intrinsic value. Adams's perception was primarily strategic. Great Britain was America's only enemy. Remove her from the northern border, and the United States would have a peaceful future. Other potential antagonists were the distance of an ocean away. But Adams also had an eye on the fisheries. New Englanders in the coastal towns where fishing was important wanted access to provincial maritime waters, and the right to land and dry fish on the beaches. Even Virginians, such as Richard Henry Lee, believed that the northern fisheries would be the basis of America's future maritime power. Some, however, did not think that the United States had any legitimate claims to Nova Scotia.[40]

In the negotiations, Americans placed priority on gaining independence and fishing rights; next came a secure border with Canada and Nova Scotia; and last, if miracles occurred, cession of Nova Scotia to the United States. Congress made these goals clear. "When the boundaries of the United States were declared to be ultimata, it was not thought advisable to continue the war merely to obtain territory as far as the St. John's River; but that the dividing line of Massachusetts and Nova Scotia was to be consigned to future settlement." Americans were prepared to see Nova Scotia remain British for the indefinite future. Americans such as Samuel Cooper took the sanguine attitude that it did not matter. All the remaining British provinces would eventually join the United States anyway, and as American power grew, any future war would see their early conquest.[41] This position forecast a major future theme in American perceptions of British North America—faith in an eventual convergence between the provinces and the United States.

Regarding Canada, additional factors such as interest in the fur trade, western lands, and interior navigation complicated American perceptions. James Lovell, among others, thought that the United States should insist upon Canada.[42] The legalistic George Mason wanted to draw careful interior boundaries to reduce British influence over the Indian tribes. But the Quebec Act of 1774 established Canada's borders, and only old colonial charters could provide the basis for a challenge. Mason concluded, "And unless the United States conquer Canada by Force of Arms, what Claims have we upon it?" Another policymaker, John Jay, was principally interested in extensive western boundaries along the proclamation line of Canada and down the Mississippi River. The United States needed navigation from the Gulf of St. Lawrence to the Gulf of Mexico, but not more land from Canada.[43]

American diplomats in Paris nudged the British to cede Canada, but echoed Jay's position. When Americans talked about their "Rising Glory," as Philip Freneau would, they meant the West. As a territorial force, American expansionism had a westward, but not a northward gaze. Franklin, apparently the most ardent for Canada, knew that the United States had leverage for territory in the unsettled west, but not in the north where British troops were in firm control. Besides, the British offered generous terms to pry the Americans away from their French ally. As a result, the United States received ample western territory. Franklin could therefore suggest that the British compensate the loyalists for their losses with Canadian land, and the diplomats told Robert Livingston that the boundaries they established were the best that the United States could hope for.[44]

Other priorities along with political and military necessity convinced American policymakers to accept the borders with Canada and Nova Scotia. The United States in 1783 was bankrupt and its

economy exhausted. The country needed time for domestic reconstruction and to gain international recognition. Because the invasions of Canada and Nova Scotia failed and the provincials refused
to join the rebels, Americans had to accept Britain and her provincials as neighbors.

Although America was unable to gratify her expansionistic desires, the principal themes of the relationship between America and
British North America had emerged by 1783. First, the provinces
contained enemy bases, now manned by Great Britain instead of
France. This dictated a defensive expansion for secure borders. Second, the provinces contained potential recruits to the American
union. This suggested a push to enlarge republicanism. Third, the
provinces offered opportunities in furs, farming, fishing, lumbering and trade, and few Americans anticipated any serious difficulty
in developing the northern frontier. Fourth, the provinces offered
a refuge for discontented Americans right on America's northern
frontier. British military power reinforced the paper border and
blunted calls for northward territorial aggrandizement that punctuated the era of defensive expansion. Demographic, commercial, or
intellectual movement, on the other hand, could easily occur. Law-
ful immigrants, merchants, and printed matter freely passed the
frontier. There was, however, far more to the relationship between
American expansionism and the British North American provinces
than mere territorial and ideological ambition, as the ensuing decades would show.

Chapter 2.

Northern

Expansion

and the

Provinces

The difference between the American and the British side, in every attribute of individual and natural improvement, must strike the most superficial eye. It is flattering to our national pride, and to the cause of republican government. . . . The politics of Upper Canada are tempestuous. A great majority of the people prefer the American government, and on the firing of the first gun would unite their destinies with ours. The Irish and emigrants from the United States are opposed to the Scotch, who have monopolized the government.
—De Witt Clinton, 1808

*I*n 1783 the United States was a new nation, lacking cohesiveness and seeking international security, domestic stability, ideological acceptance, and economic prosperity. America's complex expansionism flowed from these forces and was never simply a grab for territory. Outward impulses had cultural, demographic, economic, and politically defensive elements. And during the Early National period, much of this expansionism was to deflect external pressures or to secure the national domain against foreign intervention, particularly from Great Britain.

As near neighbors, the largely unsettled and undeveloped northern British provinces were more closely intertwined in their expansionist ambitions than most Americans realized. Americans who observed and wrote about the provinces in the Early National period often reacted in simple ways. Frequently, they ventilated their Anglophobia, as De Witt Clinton did. On the other hand, some appraised what they saw with sober and open minds.

Few early American leaders had a better grasp of the subtleties of the American-provincial relationship than Alexander Hamilton. Inevitably, he thought, Americans would move northward to impinge upon relations with Great Britain. He saw the value of the fur trade for New York and for the United States as a whole. Furthermore, he saw the benefits of conciliation. Many loyalists remained in New York after 1783. American persecution would produce bitterness, hatred, and more refugees. Finally, Nova Scotia, "by its position will become a competitor with us among other things in that branch of commerce in which our navigation and navy will essentially depend. I mean the fisheries."[1]

Hamilton understood the essential interests, actual and potential, that the United States shared with the British provinces. He also knew that Canada could well grow, and that the British would maintain forces there that might menace the United States. This meant that Americans would be forced to garrison the northern frontier and keep peace with the Indians. British proximity to northern settlers created other difficulties. Hamilton warned the New York Assembly that if it frustrated Vermont's bid for statehood, Vermonters might leave the union. "Connections have *already* been formed with the British in Canada. We have the strongest evidence that negotiations have been carried on between that government and the leaders of the people in Vermont."[2] The United States were not yet a nation. Despite republican ideology and the War for Independence, aggravated individual and local interests might still reject the government of the Constitution.

As president, George Washington appointed Hamilton as the first secretary of the treasury under the government of the Constitution. Hamilton's circle of correspondents widened, and he learned a great deal more about American contacts with the provinces as a result. He assured George Beckwith, the British envoy with whom he shared much about his government's plans and problems, that the administration had no territorial ambitions to the north. American-provincial relations nevertheless became increasingly intricate.

Hamilton had his hands full. To begin with, he had to contend with Nova Scotia and New Brunswick counterfeiters circulating bogus bank bills in Boston. He had to negotiate with the British who wanted a regular mail service through New York. There were frauds in the pickled fish trade between Boston and Nova Scotia. American fishermen smuggled openly in Maritime waters in defiance of American revenue laws. The British had persuaded disgruntled Nantucket whalers to move to Halifax, a loss to American enterprise. Finally, contraband furs cost the Treasury revenue. Hamilton therefore organized customs collectors for the entire northern frontier as far as the Lake Champlain region. He created the Passa-maquoddy District in 1789, with a Nova Scotia refugee as the first collector.[3] In between posts, customs officers had to patrol a massive and largely unsettled northern frontier.

Even after he left the federal government, Hamilton followed America's relationship with the provinces. He corresponded with frontier agents to spy out British activity as far away as Detroit and Michilimackinac, the old fur post where Lakes Huron, Michigan, and Superior came together. He traced British links with the Indians in the fur trade and defended the treaty John Jay had negotiated with the British in 1794 on the grounds that it stabilized the northern borderland and permitted an access to the provinces that would benefit the United States in the long run. According to Hamilton, the United States could never prevent borderland smuggling and the attendant loss of national revenue. However, if Americans could penetrate provincial markets, they would outstrip the British, who could not compete with Americans. So free trade would promote "good neighbourhood between the U[nited] States and the bordering British territories and consequently . . . a good understanding with Great Britain conducing to the security of our peace." American-provincial relations, in short, bore directly on Anglo-American relations.[4]

Hamilton was especially conscious of America's northern expansion after 1783. This expansion took several forms. New Englanders sought to reestablish commercial contacts with Nova Scotia settlements formed long before the Revolution. They also discovered new markets among many of the loyalist refugees who could not support themselves on the stony Maritime soils. New England fishermen, looking for their accustomed harvest in Atlantic waters, now crossed an international boundary. They also sailed farther north, working the Gulf of St. Lawrence after passing the Strait of Canso between Cape Breton and the Nova Scotia peninsula.

Apart from a resumption of north-south commercial contacts, New Englanders, as frontier migrants, moved up the coast of Maine to found small settlements along the American side of Passama-quoddy Bay in the 1790s. The founders of St. Andrews, New Brunswick, came from Castine, on the north shore of the Penobscot River. These refugees had stopped at Castine during the Revolution, thinking that they had reached the edge of future British territory.

But the Treaty of Paris established the boundary at the St. Croix River, so they moved again, dismantling homes and shops, which they shipped and reassembled in their new location. They maintained family and mercantile contacts with coastal towns in the Maine portion of Massachusetts. Lumber was a cash crop of immediate value both locally, and in the United States.

Going the other way, Nova Scotia sympathizers with the Revolution founded Lubec, Maine, across a narrow strait from Campobello Island, and sustained old contacts to the north. Other Americans and provincials moved up the St. Croix Valley to farm and log. They settled on Moose Island, founding the town of Eastport, which soon became a notorious smuggling center. New England's commercial and settlement frontier intermeshed with the new provinces of Nova Scotia and New Brunswick. This created a Maritime borderland community, built around common economic interests, family ties, and cultural heritage.[5]

New Englanders migrated northwestward as well as northward. They moved into Vermont and across the Champlain Valley to New York. In 1791, Vermont had 85,000 people. By 1800, the population had risen to 154,000, and by 1810 it was 218,000. Much of this was in the south, but migrants filtered up both sides of Lake Champlain to number 143,800 in the valley by 1810. From New York and Vermont, settlers penetrated the forests along the southern shore of the St. Lawrence River. By 1800, 24,000 whites lived west of the Hudson River in New York. Land speculators acquired large tracts and promoted further settlement.

Some companies were genuine borderland ventures. John Butler, John Johnson, and other British provincials joined American Benjamin Barton to form the Niagara Genesee Company in 1787. Northern New York had been a battleground during the War for Independence, and state authorities were eager to establish a populated defensive buffer against the presumed vengeful loyalist refugees and British to the north. Alexander Macomb bought most of what became St. Lawrence County in 1787. Macomb had made a fortune in furs as a partner of John Jacob Astor. Other well-connected speculators, such as William Constable and Robert Morris, promoted settlement for their own profit. Not all succeeded personally, but western New York grew. By 1812, some 40,000 settlers were scattered along the northern border with eastern Upper Canada.[6]

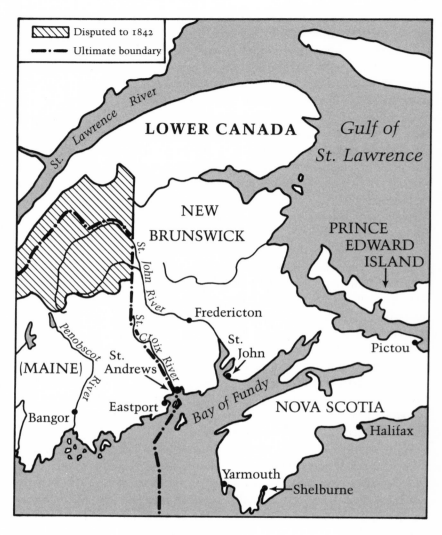

MAP 1. *Maritime Borderlands, ca. 1800*

Migrating Americans also drifted up into Lower and Upper Canada. Some 15,000 New Englanders went into the Eastern Townships of Lower Canada, for example. Artisans, entrepreneurs, and merchants accompanied the land seekers exploiting the British government's liberal terms. Americans founded provincial stage lines and hostelries, while lumbermen, masons, saddlers, and tailors found employment. American merchants settled in Montreal and established networks with friends and relatives in the United States. Horatio Gates came from Massachusetts and helped his father transport goods down Lake Champlain and the Richelieu River. He joined with Charles Bancroft in Montreal's import-export trade. When the War of 1812 erupted, he remained, took a loyalty oath to the crown, and died a prominent and wealthy man, one of the founders of the Bank of Montreal. Many others went to Upper Canada, west of the Ottawa River. The northern shore of Lake Ontario and Lake Erie offered a climate familiar to these New Englanders and New Yorkers, fertile soils as well as old friends and relatives. Some, such as Quakers, Dunkards, Mennonites, went seeking refuge, and after 1794, they were joined by participants of the failed Whiskey Rebellion.

The lakes and rivers offered easy communications. Montreal and British garrisons provided steady and accessible markets. It did not take long for an extensive commerce to develop along north-south lines through Rouses Point, New York, and St. Johns, Lower Canada, to Montreal. Travelers and goods went by both water and land. As early as 1795, shipwrights had built a thirty-ton sloop at Burlington with false bulkheads that swiftly acquired a reputation for smuggling. Settlements near the frontier sought Vermont's permission to raise funds to build or maintain roads. One Burlington tavern owner, to welcome both Americans and provincials, put likenesses of George Washington and Horatio Nelson on opposite sides of his sign.[7]

Authorities on the provincial side doubted the loyalty of these American immigrants, who were often dubbed "late loyalists." Despite British fears, however, they were not advance agents of an American empire seeking to eject British rule from North America, although subsequent events made such a construction of their actions possible. These people were frontier migrants seeking to better themselves or to find a refuge. Liberal land terms and an open border were the attractions, not ideological fervor against loyalists and monarchism.

This expansion of American settlement northward followed lines of geographic accessibility. As Americans moved onto the northern New York frontier, they became isolated from the mainstream of national life to the south. They naturally looked to the provinces for markets and supplies and for services in some cases. They formed over time a genuine borderland where local loyalties based on human relations, survival, and self-interest often transcended allegiance to a distant national government. National policymakers and politicians not from borderland constituencies knew little about this development. For them, the provinces constituted competitive market centers along a line of old Tory and British settlements and military bases.

Political leaders of the Early National period generally ignored the provinces. James Monroe, Thomas Jefferson's protégé, suggested a more focused view than most. Based on travel to the Great Lakes and Montreal in 1784, he urged Jefferson to have the American government make Canada as expensive a possession as possible for the British, even to the point of refusing provincial trade. A policy of pressure might weaken Britain's hold, and the provinces could merge with the United States. James Madison at first dismissed the provinces as a possible supplier of the British West Indies. The British colonies seemed dependent upon American produce. Jefferson's and Madison's foreign policy recommendations from 1793 to 1812 rested on the belief that economic coercion could compel Britain to yield to the United States in international disputes. Jefferson himself disregarded the provinces or the borderland until the Embargo of 1807–9. Perhaps Western dissidents felt encouraged by the British presence in Canada. Perhaps the United States might subvert provincial loyalties to Great Britain. "Tories" lived there, but Jefferson agreed with Monroe that over time the provincials might even join the United States.[8]

Albert Gallatin, Jefferson's and Madison's Treasury Secretary, had less hazy views. He read customs reports from the northern frontier that informed him about this borderland. He also asked John Jacob Astor, the New York fur merchant with Montreal partners, to compile an extensive study on provincial development. But even Gallatin failed to appreciate the political implications of borderland settlement and growth, as his recommendations for military preparations in 1807 made clear.

Anglo-American tensions ran high that summer. A British man-of-war, the *Leopard*, fired broadsides into the American frigate *Chesapeake* because the American captain refused to permit a British search for alleged deserters. If an Anglo-American war erupted, Canada was an obvious target. Gallatin assumed that the northern states would cheerfully provide volunteers for expeditions to conquer the provinces. He assumed, in short, borderland support for national foreign policy. The Jefferson administration did not put borderland loyalties to the test on this occasion, but it did with the Embargo, to its great embarrassment.[9]

Early National leaders sustained the earlier view that the provinces were a British base. Consequently, they remained intensely suspicious of Great Britain in the decades following the Treaty of Paris. Those who became Federalists when the party system first sorted itself out in the 1790s had milder views than their opponents, the Jeffersonian Republicans. But all believed that they had humiliated Great Britain in the War for Independence, and that Britain would seek revenge at the first opportunity. She would use the Indians to wage a proxy war on frontiersmen and control the fur trade. Proof lay in the British refusal to evacuate the Northwest Posts. They also feared Britain would bar Americans from trade with her colonies. In actuality, British leaders strove to regain ascendancy on the high seas after 1783, protect the West Indies markets and supply, and maintain the navy through the merchant marine and fisheries. Despite American suspicions, the loyalists did not form a coherent lobby counseling revenge, however many offices they held. London policymakers sought to defend existing holdings in North America and control the Indians in Canada to avoid a war between the natives and the Americans.

But the speeches of Guy Carleton, Lord Dorchester, impulsive anti-American British officers on the frontier (John Graves Simcoe wanted to meet George Washington in single combat with swords), and scheming British-Indian traders confirmed American suspicions. These developments, coupled with the presence of redcoats on American soil in the Northwest Posts, drew American attention to the northern boundary and stimulated a policy of defensive expansion.

Secretary of State Edmond Randolph, reflecting American alarm and Anglophobia, stressed British interference in American territory time and again to John Jay, who went to England to avert a war over maritime and border issues in 1793 and 1794. "We cannot add upon *proof*," Randolph wrote. "British influence has been tampering with the people of Kentucky and of the neighbourhood of Pittsburgh, to seduce them from the United States, or to encourage them in a revolt against the general Government." Jay achieved a timetable for British evacuation of the Northwest Posts. But to the disgust of many Americans, he also granted the British trading privileges with the Indians on American soil. His treaty passed the Senate, but outraged Jefferson and Madison, who denounced the Jay Treaty when James Monroe and William Pinkney were in London in 1806 and 1807 trying to revise Anglo-American commercial and border arrangements. However these men felt about annexing the provinces, they wanted British influence removed from American soil. The failure to settle this issue contributed to the deterioration of Anglo-American relations before 1812. American leaders could not help but see the provinces as a British base, and this view shaped the course of Anglo-American diplomacy.[10]

Westerners in Kentucky, Ohio, and Michigan feared that the British would sally from their provincial bases to foment a frontier Indian uprising. For this reason, settlers in the Old Northwest were by no means eager for war in 1811 and 1812. From 1783 forward, they had been eager to sever British links with the tribes on American soil. Northwest territorial governor Arthur St. Clair also reported rumors of British agents promising support for Kentucky separatists in 1788. Touring his region in 1791, St. Clair reported that the British had a stranglehold on the Indian trade through Michilimackinac and along the western waterways to Upper Canada. Throughout, frontier officials ignored America's own contributions to Indian hostility. They blamed the British for misrepresenting American intentions, supplying the Indians with weapons, and urging the tribes to slaughter frontiersmen.

Alexander Hamilton had warned the British diplomatic representative in the United States, George Hammond, that if Britain were unable to control the Indians, she would be blamed for whatever happened, and that is precisely the way it worked out. Because of their Anglophobia, Americans refused to believe that the Indians acted on their own. There were separate issues here, as Hamilton recognized, but most Americans saw trade and frontier raids as parts of a British plot to control the Northwest and exclude the United States. If the British took Detroit, William Hull noted in 1811, they would once again have the run of the Northwest.[11]

Not all points along the northern frontier felt the need to assume a defensive military posture. The American-provincial borderland developed several distinct geographic components during the period of northern expansion after 1783. The Maritime region developed first, revolving economically around fishing, lumbering, and trade. It dated from the pre-Revolutionary years. Farmers and lumbermen settled the St. Croix Valley in the 1780s and 1790s. The Champlain Valley, settled in the 1790s, evolved next. North-south communications links and a local economy characterized this borderland. The land necks and river banks of the St. Lawrence River–Great Lakes Basin to the Detroit frontier constituted the third borderland, which was first settled in the 1800s.

Americans looking north had, depending upon their location, ambivalent views of the provinces. The Indian problem meant nothing to Maritimers and was of less importance in the Champlain Valley than farther west. For settlers in western New York along the St. Lawrence and Niagara rivers, the Indian problem was contingent on an Anglo-American war. Farther west, however, Americans were torn. On the one hand, they disliked British links with the Indians and sought to expel British traders from American soil. On the other hand, they realized that aggressive action would surely produce the war and slaughter they feared. The Indian "menace" took precedence with Westerners, as General Anthony Wayne symbolically demonstrated when he marched up and berated British troops in Fort Miami after his victory at the Battle of Fallen Timbers in 1795.

American officials simultaneously pursued defensive expansionism in the Old Northwest and worked out agreements with British authorities in the provinces. In July of 1783, Baron von Steuben visited Montreal to arrange the withdrawal of the British from the Northwest Posts, mostly on New York's soil—Ogdensburg, Oswego, Niagara, Presque Isle, Sandusky—and Detroit and Michilimackinac in the far northwest. The British retained these posts after 1783 to control the frontier fur trade and the Indians. At the same time,

Britain dabbled with the idea of an Indian buffer state along the northern frontier. This project finally died in the negotiations that produced the Treaty of Ghent in 1814.

In the crisis of 1793, the possibility of an Anglo-American war generated a military interest in the provinces. Jeffersonian Republicans believed that the American militia could conquer the Canadas if war erupted, but the Federalists argued that conquest would require considerable exertion. When the British evacuated the Northwest Posts three years later, American military strength was barely sufficient to pacify the tribes and too slight to take possession of all the posts simultaneously. An American officer visited Quebec to ask Lord Dorchester to delay the British departure in some cases. Nevertheless, with the enactment of the Jay Treaty the American government took a major step in its principal northern objective of gaining defensive control over the frontier. In 1802, James Madison was satisfied that the St. Croix boundary was fixed. Now, he wrote to America's representative in London, Rufus King, an Anglo-American boundary had to be drawn as far as Lake of the Woods. Anglo-American relations regarding the northern border suggested an indefinite sharing of North America.[12]

The British presence in the provinces generated other awkward diplomatic situations for the American government. In 1790, for example, the Spanish seized English traders in Vancouver Island's Nootka Sound, on the far west coast of North America. Washington's cabinet met to discuss the prospect of the British marching overland from Canada to attack Spanish Louisiana. The issue remained hypothetical because Spain capitulated under British pressure. But Europeans with North American colonies might still use their bases adjacent to the United States to assault one another in wartime, a clear danger for any American government.

General James Wilkinson's double game in the southwest on the Spanish frontier was a variation on this theme. His northern counterparts are less famous, but Vermonters engaged in several similar separatist schemes. Settlers on the eastern shore of Lake Champlain had early contacts with the British in Montreal. The Allen family was deeply involved in speculation in the New Hampshire grants that eventually became the state of Vermont. In 1785, Ira Allen arrived at Quebec with a commission from Vermont's government to negotiate free trade with the British. In 1788, Ethan

Allen hinted that Vermonters would resist American aggression and might even return to the British fold. Levi Allen represented himself to Lord Sydney as a virtual minister plenipotentiary. These feelers brought no direct results, but suggested the political implications of British proximity.[13]

The outbreak of war in Europe in 1792 renewed the threat of Vermont separatism. The flamboyant representative of the French Girondist government, Edmond Genet, arrived in the United States to stimulate American privateering ventures and expeditions against the New World possessions of his country's enemies, Britain and Spain. He even encouraged Vermonters to invade Lower Canada to liberate the French from British rule. The Allens, and Matthew Lyon, a rising Vermont Jeffersonian Republican, responded enthusiastically. American anger against Britain had flared along the border because of West Indies seizures and alleged British influence with the Indians. Local Jeffersonian political societies called for an end to British rule in Canada. But George Washington's administration insisted on a neutrality that Vermont adventurism was too weak to challenge.[14]

The Allens participated in one final separatist plot involving Vermont and Lower Canada. In 1796, Ira Allen took part in a French scheme to smuggle arms to the French in Canada and foment a rebellion against British rule. French agents tried to recruit American merchants with Montreal business connections to act on their behalf. One of these, William Barnard of Deerfield, Massachusetts, suspected only the machinations of a business rival, so he betrayed them to American authorities, who informed the British. In Lower Canada, the British arrested two brothers from Rhode Island and David McLane and Thomas Butterfield of Vermont on sedition charges. McLane was hanged, drawn, and quartered for his efforts. In Britain itself the scheme exploded when authorities seized the arms shipment en route. Allen claimed that the weapons were destined for the Vermont militia. John Adams and Timothy Pickering were skeptical, but accepted Vermont Governor Martin Chittenden's assurances that the militia indeed required arms, and Allen had bought them from France as a speculative venture to recoup financial embarrassment.

The seizure and arrests ended whatever plot existed, which may have included Allen's fanciful dream of establishing a separate republic between the British provinces and the United States. Because of the atmosphere created by the Quasi-War with France, which arose in 1797 from French seizures of American vessels in the West Indies, most Vermonters were quite unsympathetic with this plan. So was the Federalist government of John Adams. Friends and enemies changed caps with astonishing ease in the fast-moving era of the French Revolution.[15]

The Allens pursued their own ambitions, reflecting and exploiting Vermont's maverick political character as a part of the broader frontier separatism that periodically plagued the United States in the Early National period. These episodes illustrate the clash of interests between the American borderland and the rest of the nation. American northern development was not necessarily an extension of national policies or objectives.

The New England–Maritimes borderland established the pattern in the 1780s. Sir Guy Carleton's fleets arrived in Nova Scotia through 1783 to deposit sad cargoes of loyalist refugees who scattered through makeshift hamlets along the shores of the Bay of Fundy and the Atlantic Ocean. The numbers of these refugees far exceeded the ability of local agriculture or stores to feed them, and outstripped available supplies of building materials. The British had no choice but to turn to Yankee merchants to prevent what was already a tragedy for the loyalists from becoming a disaster. The Navigation Acts prohibited trade, but British officials granted licenses under the authority of Royal proclamations. Sixty-eight such decrees specified exempted items until Halifax became a free port in 1818. Once the immediate crisis had passed in 1783 and 1784, American merchantmen brought to Halifax not only products for local consumption but also surpluses for export to the West Indies. When Britain created the separate province of New Brunswick in 1785, Americans traded in St. John as well. From both ports they carried back grindstones from Maritime quarries and gypsum for use as fertilizer, as well as specie, fish, furs, and manufactured goods.[16]

The lack of overall regulations annoyed the New Englanders and Maritimers, but their trade nevertheless flourished. The settlers who moved into the St. Croix Valley in the 1800s shipped goods and logs across the boundary at will and served the export markets of Halifax, St. John, and overseas. New England papers reported not only on the commercial link with the Maritimes, but provincial political news as well. In 1806, James Madison suggested open trade with greater freedom for American vessels but admitted that this would only benefit the United States. Halifax had already become an American entrepôt to the West Indies, even if the Navigation Acts officially excluded Yankee vessels. But Madison and other policymakers during this period did not realize to what extent the Maritime borderland had become a world of its own.[17]

Maritime merchantmen often carried extra goods for personal trading when they sailed south as did American fishermen who worked provincial waters. This so-called "schooner trade" was continuous and extended to smuggling, a natural product of the Maritime borderland's growth and the intimacy of the Passamaquoddy Bay waters. If governments, provincial, imperial, state, or federal, tried to control the trade for revenue or retaliate against regulations imposed by the other side, the locals ignored the law. Despite the efforts of the various governments, Moose Island became a major center for Bay contraband.[18]

Wilderness and low but rugged mountains separated the St. Croix Valley and the Maritimes from the next major borderland region, the Champlain Valley. Here, American northward expansion followed a similar pattern. In 1787, Lord Dorchester opened the border. Despite clashes and uncertainties until the Jay Treaty was concluded, Americans in the valley traded north, not south. The Richelieu River, Montreal, and the St. Lawrence River constituted their outlet during the ice-free season. Roads south were primitive and unable to carry the bulky produce of the frontier—foodstuffs, timber, pot and pearl ashes—to American markets. Only fur pelts were sufficiently valuable to repay the overland cartage.

John Jacob Astor began his fortune in the New York borderland in 1786 and 1787. He developed contacts with Montreal fur traders by 1788, advertising "Canada Furs" for sale in a New York City paper that October. Careful to obey local laws, he nevertheless ignored the international boundary. He also speculated in land in both New York and Lower Canada as he diversified on his way to becoming America's first millionaire. Astor was part of America's northward commercial expansion and stood aside from both ideology and politics. Ira Allen, by contrast, combined business with political dabbling.[19]

As the population in the valley thickened in the 1790s, the north-south trade developed accordingly. Vermonters drove cattle south to Boston and New York, but Montreal offered higher profits. In 1800, Vermont exports had a value of $57,267. By 1804–5, this figure was $169,402, and up to $204,285 by 1806–7. Vermonters responded eagerly to Britain's liberal trade terms, aimed at driving the northern United States from the rest of the country. Loyalists and British garrisons provided most of the market for Vermont foodstuffs, timber, and the pot and pearl ashes. Rafts went down Lake Champlain and the Richelieu River laden with produce. As in the Maritime borderland, much smuggling accompanied the regular trade. Rouses Point was the Lake Champlain equivalent of Eastport. Furs, wine, tea, tobacco, brandy, and salt were the principal smuggled commodities. The arrival of a customs collector in Vermont in 1791 made little difference. Trade through the British customshouse at St. John listed thirty-two commodities between September 1794 and May 1795 valued at £17,300. By 1800 the records showed seventy commodities and a value of £88,900. After 1796, manufactured goods, especially tobacco products, became increasingly important and constituted one-half of the Champlain trade route to Canada by 1807.

After 1794, the balance of trade favored the United States by a substantial margin each year. Roads improved, and travel increased and became easier. The journey from New York City to Montreal dropped from sixteen days in 1793 to one week in 1809. Local industry, such as tanneries, paper, grist and saw mills, carding machines, and Matthew Lyon's ironworks served markets on both sides of the boundary. As in the Maritimes, geography produced a true borderland region, straddling the American-provincial boundary, linking the people through business, friendship, and family ties. And if local problems arose, the governors of Lower Canada and Vermont often solved them locally rather than going through higher political and diplomatic channels.[20]

The northern New York frontier along the St. Lawrence River and the Great Lakes developed later than the Champlain Valley, and the borderland networks emerged mostly where the lakes came together, as at the Niagara and Detroit rivers. Prior to the War of 1812, the farther west and the more rudimentary the local settlements and economies, the more important the American fear of

British influence with the Indians tended to be. Montreal was nevertheless an important entrepôt for northern New Yorkers, as New York City merchants well understood. And American frontier migration to Upper Canada had created some of the same cross-border bonds as had developed farther east. Trade moved east-west along the lakes and rivers. Land speculators were active throughout what became the border counties of New York. But not until the first decade of the nineteenth century did settlers migrate in sufficient numbers to create commercial centers.

All the river and lake towns on the American side had only a few hundred people by 1805, but as soon as the settlements passed subsistence stage, they set themselves up as trading centers. For example, the British had kept Americans out of the vicinity of Oswego and Ogdensburg, which were among the Northwest Posts, but by 1803 Oswego had already acquired a commercial importance as a lake port. Its contacts were principally with Montreal. By 1810, eleven vessels moved from Oswego along Lake Ontario routes, engaged partly in the salt trade. Other American produce went east in provincial vessels for foreign markets. De Witt Clinton, on a reconnaissance for the Erie Canal route, reported that the previous year, over 28,000 barrels of salt and $536,000 in merchandise had moved out of Oswego, bound for Canada. Coastal vessels ran from Oswego to Lewiston and Queenston by 1806. Salt boats moved laboriously down treacherous streams to reach the St. Lawrence.

By 1811, Ogdensburg, the site of another Northwest Post, had only fifty houses. The New England origins of most of these settlers meant that they were largely Federalist in political orientation and pro-British because of their economic links. These links went beyond mere business. The Ogden family had a loyalist branch in Montreal. Nonetheless, although the backcountry remained largely empty, the first road from Ogdensburg was cut straight to the St. Lawrence River. Most of the settlement clustered along the riverfront, and it was the scene of socializing and intermarriage between Americans and provincials. The St. Lawrence River was a highway north and south, as well as east and west.[21]

In 1805, moving into Lake Ontario from the St. Lawrence River settlements to the Niagara River region was a little like moving back in time. The early settlers on the Niagara frontier were loyalists who intermarried with Americans. The settlements appeared crude, with local subsistence economies dependent upon water transport down the lakes. Furs, skins, military stores, some fish and lumber, and household goods constituted the cargoes of vessels on Lake Erie as well as Ontario. Land speculators struggled to attract buyers. Peter Porter pioneered a portage business across the Niagara peninsula in an effort to drive out the British carriers. The provincials had better organization, finance, and roads, and American carriers therefore faced stiff competition. The British had a steamboat on Lake Ontario in 1809. At the same time, Americans built and sold schooners to the British. Land companies became active in the late 1790s and by 1806, the village of Buffalo, consisting of a few houses, had appeared. In 1811, Porter used political influence, however, to have the American customshouse located in Black Rock instead of Buffalo. The Barton family first came to the region in 1787, driving cattle and sheep from western New Jersey to sell to the British. A younger Barton later linked with Porter, who was also a land speculator and Erie Canal promoter, to found hydraulic works, carding machines and mills, tanneries, a rope walk, and a grist mill.[22]

The economy of this borderland region was distinctly rudimentary. Even so, by 1798 settlers in the Holland Purchase region exported lumber, potash, and a few provisions to Montreal. Joseph Ellicott, the principal proprietor of the land, approved. The sooner trade developed, the sooner his buyers would be able to pay off their debts. A minor tourist traffic augmented the local economy. Already, travelers struggled through the wilderness to gaze at Niagara Falls. American John Vanderlyn painted the falls in 1801–2, and a hostelry for the shelter of tourists had appeared at Niagara as early as 1799, although the British side generally offered much better accommodations than the Americans could muster. Dr. Cyrenius Chapin, the area's first physician, settled in Canada and worked both sides of the Niagara River. So by 1810, a borderland emerged in the Niagara region to stand alongside its more easterly counterparts.[23]

Americans believed in the future of this region. Settlers by the score came from both sides of the boundary after 1800. Michael Smith, a Baptist clergyman from Pennsylvania who settled in Upper Canada in 1808, concluded that exports in wheat, flour, potash, and timber had risen swiftly by the eve of the War of 1812. The early promoters of what became the Erie Canal also eyed the growing farms.

These men, including De Witt Clinton, Peter B. Porter, Stephen Van Rensselaer, and Gouverneur Morris, foresaw a rich development in the Great Lakes Basin in the near future. People would not care by which waterway their goods and supplies traveled. "But the political connexion, which would probably result from a commercial connexion, certainly deserves the consideration of intelligent men." The canal promoters cast themselves in that role and prophesied the convergence thesis of eventual American-provincial union. In their 1811 report, they noted that American goods went north at British invitation. Wherever De Witt Clinton encountered traders on his trek to Niagara, such as at Hanford on the Genesee River, they dealt through Montreal. Clinton sneered at provincial politics, but respected genuine economic rivals. Consequently, the promoters argued against a canal terminus on Lake Ontario because, rather than siphon trade from the lakes basin south to the benefit of New York City, it would draw New York state's trade north to the benefit of Montreal.[24]

The farthest borderland region from population centers was in Ohio and Michigan, near the westernmost portion of Upper Canada. Here visitors found only tiny, scattered settlements. Agriculture was bare subsistence, and the only commercial activity the fur trade, which the British monopolized through their contacts with the northwestern Indians. General Anthony Wayne noted in 1795 how the Northwest Company agents freely roamed American territory. He added that the settlers were mostly French, and of doubtful loyalty. Americans expanded defensively into this region, to assert control over the far reaches of the national domain. Forts were important centers for commerce, settlers, and soldiers alike.

By 1799, Detroit had only three hundred rude houses and narrow dirty streets under the protecting walls of the fort. Three years earlier, the Americans had been unready to take over Detroit from the British, the terms of Jay's Treaty notwithstanding. Links with the provinces were also weak. Moravian missionaries had established colonies of Ohio Indians along the River Thames in Upper Canada in the 1790s. Troops and a few French Canadians held over from the fur trade around Detroit were the only whites in Michigan when it became an organized territory in 1805. The Americans did not really consolidate their control of this region in the next few years as the opening campaigns of the War of 1812 would reveal. It was little wonder that the Americans thought defensively about their farthest frontier in the Great Lakes Basin.[25]

Overall American trade with the provinces in the Early National period was small, however important it was to the people of the borderland. Because the United States only loosely controlled its outer fringes, government officials were not even certain what went on there. Furs moved freely in the Far Northwest unknown to the Treasury Department except through largely anecdotal reports by travelers, army officers, and government officers. Much informal bartering occurred along the borderlands along with organized smuggling. The internal trade of the United States prior to 1814 was dominantly local, and the borderland segments sustained the pattern of local economies. As these borderland regions developed, some Americans were persuaded that the provinces were evolving into distinct societies as well as British bases.[26]

The problems in Anglo-American relations after 1805 made many Americans in the government and elsewhere more conscious of these borderlands. In 1807, Thomas Jefferson's administration called for a trade embargo to coerce Great Britain into accepting the American position on neutral trade and impressments. This put the national government in conflict with the borderlands, which thereupon revealed a power to influence national policy that neither their inhabitants nor Washington officials had dreamed of.

While northward migrants were carving out homes and enterprises in the American-provincial borderlands and establishing communication links along North American waterways both coastal and interior, Washington policymakers strove to cope with the difficulties of national survival in a world at war. The French Revolution had spilled over the boundaries of France in 1792 and almost immediately touched the United States because France's principal enemy became Great Britain. Except for a brief interlude during the Peace of Amiens, in 1802–3, the Anglo-French war dominated international politics in the Atlantic world for over two decades. The British practice of impressment touched Americans on the high seas and in foreign ports. The British Orders in Council and the economic warfare both France and Britain employed between 1803 and 1812 resulted in serious shipping losses to the United States, not to mention affronts to national pride.[27]

After the *Chesapeake-Leopard* encounter of 1807, Jefferson and Madison determined on a trade embargo as a simultaneously protective and coercive measure. If it failed to affect British policy, the administration could still move toward military force. But withal, the embargo would demonstrate how Republicans should conduct foreign affairs—attempt peaceful coercion, rely upon the virtue of the citizenry, and avoid armed force until all other measures had failed. Both Jefferson and Madison overestimated the extent to which Britain and her colonies depended upon American supplies, and they overestimated as well the national discipline of their own countrymen when confronted with a policy that worked against local self-interest. At the same time, they underestimated how important the defeat of Napoleon had become to Great Britain. British policymakers, their arrogance notwithstanding, were prepared to hazard an unwanted conflict with the United States rather than risk losing the war against Napoleon.

The Jefferson administration and its majority supporters in Congress established the Embargo incrementally. In December of 1807, Congress enacted the previously suspended Non-Importation Act of 1806. Next, Jefferson's cabinet expanded the concept, and Republican majorities passed a total embargo on ocean trade 21 December 1807.[28] Through 1808, supplementary acts closed loopholes or provided for enforcement because of the persistent, even defiant, borderland evasions after the Jefferson administration severed trade between the northern states and the provinces. At times, this defiance approached insurrection. Throughout 1808 the Republican Party lost ground in northern counties on both state and national levels. The partisan furor the Embargo produced ripped into the next congressional session and created the cloud under which Jefferson departed the presidency in March of 1809.[29] The story of the Embargo's failure is complex, but the borderland interests contributed a major share to the frustration of national policy.

The original Embargo Act prohibited ocean trade. New England shipmasters, however, simply sailed where they wished once clear of port. Congress next closed down coastal trade to stop evasions, but state governors could issue special licenses to service outlying ports. Massachusetts's Governor James Sullivan signed many for ports in Maine. Shortly, shipments to Maine by far exceeded what the locals could have consumed on their own. The surplus wound up in the provinces. New England Federalism joined forces with the

New England–Maritimes borderland's trading interests to nullify the Embargo.

Coastal trade from Boston in 1808 doubled that of 1807. Overall movement of vessels in the port rose by just over 14 percent. Federal agents in Boston and Portland were unable to immobilize smugglers. Halifax recorded seventy-six vessels from American ports paying duties, fourteen of which were of American registry. In 1807, 108 out of 176 vessels landing at Halifax were American-registered. In 1808, fourteen of sixty-four vessels flew a Yankee flag. The Embargo failed to strain the ability of the British to supply their West Indies colonies, largely because of the widespread evasions in the New England–Maritimes borderland region.

The British eagerly encouraged attempts to bypass the Embargo. They offered high prices for timber and foodstuffs and issued special proclamations to attract New England traders. Passamaquoddy Bay became a bustling waterway. British carriers awaited smuggled cargoes at St. Andrews and Grand Manaan. Moose Island and Eastport throve. Over 150,000 barrels of flour were transported to Nova Scotia and New Brunswick ports in 1808, where they brought twice their Maine prices. Smugglers stockpiled goods for illegal shipments along the beaches. The customs collector was overwhelmed, despite having at his command a sloop, a frigate, several gunboats, their crews, and a detachment of regular infantry. The profits of the illegal trade were too high, and the Passamaquoddy Bay waters were too intimate. British vessels maneuvered to protect smugglers from revenue boats. Some of the men the collector hired to watch for smugglers took bribes or smuggled themselves. Patriotism was the only commodity discounted. Arrests, seizures, and convictions occurred occasionally, but a mob released one party of smugglers arrested after a shoot-out with American authorities. And capture was no deterrent, despite a growing list of cases in United States District Courts concerning Embargo violations in 1808. Often, juries simply found in favor of the accused. Shipmasters became inventive regarding the vagaries of storms and the activities of pirates that had driven them off course or forced them to break the law.[30]

The Champlain Valley was similarly bustling with commercial activity in 1808. Valley people ignored the Embargo at first, assuming that it applied only to ocean trade. British agent John Henry, on his way through Swanton, Vermont, on one of several intelligence gathering trips to New York and New England, noted in February 1808 that "the roads are covered with sleighs and the whole country seems employed in conveying their produce beyond the line of separation." Valley people were adept smugglers at any time. Vermont lumbermen continued to send rafts down the lake and the Richelieu River. The act of 12 March 1808 ostensibly closed the border, but evasions continued. On 16 April, Burlington, Vermont residents convened to denounce the "Land Embargo" while the local press attacked federal policy. Vermonters harassed customs officers, and judges and juries hesitated to convict captured smugglers. People left goods on the Alburg peninsula, where provincials later picked them up. Provincials would also cross the boundary, leave money, and help themselves to cattle and swine on an honor system. Supplies were placed on hillsides and rolled north. Smugglers cut new roads and warned that they would fight any who opposed them. *The Black Snake*, a well-known contraband vessel, worked the obscure inlets of Missiquoi Bay. In August of 1808 its crew resisted a militia arrest and killed three men. Only one of the captured lawbreakers was executed.[31]

Reports of these evasions flooded the desk of Albert Gallatin, secretary of the treasury. Gallatin had the unenviable responsibility for enforcing the Embargo. The wholesale defiance astonished him, but he failed to grasp the significance of the borderland outlook. Instead, he blamed lax customs officers, Federalist partisans who encouraged defiance of national law, unreliable borderland militia, local politicians afraid to enforce unpopular laws, and weak federal courts. A "love of gain" had nullified the law, Gallatin wrote to Jefferson. The Embargo was so unpopular that "truly friendly characters were afraid to act." Regulars and gunboats would be needed on Lake Champlain. By July 1808, Gallatin wrote again about the stream of violations all along the borderland. "As to judicial redress there is very little hope. For, a few days ago, a Republican jury, notwithstanding the charge of Judge Sailly and the efforts of the attorney, have refused to find bills against the Canadians made prisoners after resistance on board one of the rafts which they were forcibly carrying away across the line on Lake Champlain."[32]

Patriotism and profit exerted opposite pulls on the borderland. Local federal officers blamed all the trouble on "Tories" and Federalists. But this was a naive oversimplification meant to excuse ineffectiveness. Jefferson put evasions down to defective legislation, greed, British temptations, and Federalist plotting, all of which combined to subvert the virtue of ordinarily good, republican citizens. Gallatin referred to the "criminal party rage of the Federalists and Tories," although he was more aware than Jefferson by the middle of 1808 of the borderland mentality. Both agreed that only rigid enforcement measures could salvage the Embargo as a diplomatic weapon. Jefferson proclaimed an insurrection in the Champlain Valley, but town meetings in Vermont defied him. Customs officers, judges, juries, all increasingly condoned smuggling. Often the goods seized in evidence vanished from federal storerooms. Desperate collectors hired thugs as enforcers who used their new immunity to help employees smuggle on the side.[33] Enforcement was hopeless.

Along the St. Lawrence and in the lake ports the story was the same. Gallatin concluded that opposition at Oswego had become insurrection by August. Only federal troops had prevented one armed party from rescuing confiscated barrels of flour. Ogdensburg became for Montreal what Eastport was for Halifax. Montreal merchants offered high prices for pot and pearl ashes, one of the few cash crops available to north country borderlanders. New York Governor Daniel Tompkins was reluctant to use the militia to police civilians, although he sent a detachment to Oswego to assist the federal collector. New Yorkers resented their government forcing citizens in the militia to police their neighbors. Customs officers were threatened, some resigned, and a few were murdered.

Passing through Oswego in 1810 on his way to the Niagara region, De Witt Clinton noted that "the embargo enriched the frontier settlements, and the impediments to a free intercourse with Canada became very unpopular. In this place there was a combination to resist the execution of the Embargo laws. The collector was menaced, and his life jeapordized; and he is now harassed with suits for refusing clearance for vessels to go to Sacketts Harbor, with potash, &c." Through it all, the shipments to Montreal continued. Sackett's Harbor, Oswego, and Cape Vincent became contraband centers in western New York. Smugglers built roads to avoid patrols and reach the St. Lawrence to ship their goods. One from Brownville to Fisher's Landing became known as the "Embargo Road." In February of 1809, John Jacob Astor estimated that

75 percent of all potash, 20 percent of all flour, and much of the timber, lard, and beef in Montreal came from the United States.[34]

The Niagara frontier duplicated the pattern already established eastward to Passamaquoddy Bay. Joseph Ellicott, a Republican and land speculator in the Genessee tract, found that the Embargo hurt his sales and reduced the local cash supply. But smuggling restored the balance. Montreal merchants dispatched vessels directly to the Holland Land Purchase region to obtain foodstuffs and potash. Ellicott was pleased. Local farmers selling on the Montreal market received cash to pay their mortgages. Informers risked personal violence, if discovered. William Duane passed a letter from Ezekiel Hill in Buffalo to Jefferson: "Smuggling is carried on from Lewiston to Canada to a considerable extent, and disgusting and humiliating as the practice is to every feeling that is American, it is almost as publicly transacted as any common avocation." Good Republican Hill accused the lax customs officers of being closet Federalists.[35]

Only an army along the border and a fleet along the shorelines could have prevented smuggling in the borderland from Eastport to Buffalo. Jefferson eventually concluded that it could not be stopped, although he presented draconian enforcement measures to Congress in January of 1809 that made some representatives shudder. The Embargo cost the Republican Party seats at both national and state levels. Matthew Lyon, formerly of Vermont, but by 1808 in Kentucky, told his constituents that the Embargo had produced great distress among farmers without damaging Britain's ability to supply the West Indies. Wilson Cary Nicholas, a Virginia Republican and intimate of Jefferson, noted that "many vessels escaped from New England. Immense quantities of American produce, not only of the neighboring states, but also of the cotton and tobacco of the south, were collected in Canada, ready to be shipped to G. Britain, as soon as the St. Lawrence should be free from ice."[36]

As Jefferson stood down from the presidency to make way for James Madison, the Republicans and Congress sought a dignified substitute. How much the smuggling eroded the Embargo's effectiveness is uncertain. Without doubt, enforcing the Embargo because of the violations became a major political liability for the Republicans by 1809. The administration had counted on a national consensus behind its policies, partisan opposition notwithstanding.

Defiance of the Embargo on the borderlands exploded the fallacy of this expectation. Even the milder Non-Intercourse Act produced defiance. Smuggling continued on the borderlands. Customs collectors were warned to watch for false manifest entries and illegal goods entering on back roads. As far as controlling borderland trade was concerned, local habits and interests, distant federal authority, poor enforcement, and the vagaries of personalities in public offices sustained on a lower level all the difficulties that the Embargo exposed.[37] Individualistic Americans had produced borderland networks strong enough to defy national interest and law.

Northward expansion after 1783 had created the American-provincial borderlands. Frontier migration had followed geographic channels apparent during the colonial and revolutionary periods. Local commercial interests accompanied the movement of peoples into northern Maine, Vermont, and New York. As the demographic expansion carved settlements from the northern wilds and local economies developed beyond subsistence level, the borderlanders reached out to export what surpluses they could produce and import finished goods, both necessaries and luxuries. Difficulties of travel between the borderland regions and the centers of American political and economic activity, except along the New England coast, turned these borderlanders toward provincial waterways and entrepôts, especially Montreal. Anglo-American difficulties over trade to the West Indies made Halifax a backdoor entrepôt for New Englanders. Complex local relationships and trading patterns evolved.

American federal authority attempted to control this movement, establishing customs districts and collectors at ports in all the borderland regions. Officials found American-provincial trade habits well established. In the Far Northwest, in Michigan and Ohio, federal agents acted tentatively because these regions were almost beyond the reach of effective national authority. Only after the region had been secured through military action and diplomatic agreement between 1811 and 1815, did settlers move in substantial numbers into the western Great Lakes Basin. At that time, American expansion created the fifth major American-provincial borderland region, that between Upper Canada and Michigan Territory.

The reaction of Thomas Jefferson's administration to defiance of the Embargo suggests how little most national politicians, or most

Americans for that matter, knew about the American-provincial borderlands. Federalist conspiracies and greed only partly persuaded borderlanders to defy the Embargo. Local self-interests and a sense of cross-border community worked against national allegiance. Family and friendship ties reinforced economic linkages to produce the borderland mentality, a product of American frontier expansion where the people from one society intermingled with the people of another. For American leaders in the Early National period, the provinces were principally British bases. For American borderlanders they were neighbors, markets, relatives, and friends.

Chapter 3.
Expansionism
and the War
of 1812

Geography is a useful part of knowledge. The first objects ought to be, to become well acquainted with the country in which we live, the second those countries most contiguous to us. The British Provinces of Upper and Lower Canada are of the second description—being neighbors to us, we feel more interest in their situation, than we do in countries more remote. Indeed the crisis appears to be approaching, when the U[nited] States will be more interested in that country, than they have been heretofore.
—National Intelligencer,
12 February 1812

Anglophobe and Jeffersonian-Republican patriot Hezekiah Niles founded his *Weekly Register* in September of 1811 to support congressional militants arguing for a policy of war against Great Britain. Niles's prejudices became near obsessions and went beyond a staunch American Republican's detestation of the British monarchy. He carried to extremes the widespread American tendency to see Great Britain as an international bully. For Niles, scheming British statesmen would go to any lengths to smother American development. They supplied and prodded the Indians in the Northwest to murder American frontiersmen. They kidnapped American citizens on the high seas. They stifled American overseas commerce. Force was the only policy they would understand.

But how could Americans apply force against the British? England was the world's mightiest military power, despite her deep engagement with France. The answer to America's strategic dilemma lay in the British North American provinces. Seize them and Britain would be humbled.

Niles, like so many others, believed that his country was under siege. He thought defensively when he suggested invading Canada.

And, although Quebec and other strong points would prove stubborn, he thought that all the United States had to do was "give the word" and "American emigrants as well as the dissatisfied French descendants" would rise up and overthrow British rule. He expected only feeble provincial resistance.

Consequently, he followed British military preparations in the provinces closely. Canadians had been warning their American friends along the frontier of impending danger "in the most interesting and affectionate manner" that proved their disenchantment. As the decision for war approached in May of 1812, Niles anticipated that "Upper Canada, at least, would be immediately and completely in our possession. The Pandora boxes at Amherstburg and Malden would be closed, and all the causes of the present murders of the savages would cease, for they make neither guns nor gunpowder."[1]

In this, as in other respects, Anglophobia not only defined America's problems, but suggested their solutions. And Anglophobia colored Niles's initial view of the provinces and his interpretation of the war. The British remained an evil enemy. *Register* reporting during the War of 1812 at times resembles a boy's own adventure. The quest was simple and just. Heroes and villains loomed larger than life over the northern battlefields. Victory was glorious. Defeat was ignominious and flowed from treachery. Provincial property was rich, "justly attributed to the activity and enterprise of the American farmers, who, from grants of crown lands, have been induced to settle in great numbers." The "inhuman" British had a "horde of remorseless savages" as allies. The subjugated French would surely refuse to serve their cynical masters. Even British settlers had to be drafted to defend the Crown's honor because "large bodies" of people balked at military service. Given how little most Americans knew about the provinces in 1811 and 1812, such opinions seemed logical, however fantastic they were in fact. After General William Hull's surrender of Detroit, Niles argued that with "a leader of honor and capacity" Malden and Upper Canada would fall. "The wilderness, the scene of savage barbarity, shall howl with the groans of the murderers, in just retribution for their crimes."[2]

War has a way of dispelling illusions while creating others. Images of victorious promenades into the citadels of the enemy fade with time and experience. As Karl von Clausewitz knew, in war everything seems simple, yet everything is enormously difficult. Defeating the British in the provinces would not prove easy. The provincials did not rise as one to declare their deliverance when American troops stepped over the border. British regulars were tough in battle, Americans less valorous than the myth of the embattled farmers of the Revolution suggested, and military plans seemed to go awry with alarming frequency.

In the course of reporting the war, Niles collected much information about the provinces that neither he nor his readers knew before. He printed articles on provincial geography, settlement patterns, history, economic activity, government, politics, and events. Niles tended to lump all of Britain's New World holdings in one package at first. So Barbados stood alongside Upper Canada and Nova Scotia as parts of British America. But, gradually, the various provinces developed distinctive identities. Niles said little about the Maritimes, except to report the movement of vessels and troops. He focused mostly on Lower and Upper Canada, reflecting the locale of the campaigns. New England's position as a nearly neutral buffer in the northeast quarter and Montreal's role as the source of most provincial news also shaped his perspective. And, like other editors of the time, Niles clipped and reprinted relentlessly to fill his pages.

So he extracted an account of Quebec from George Heriot's *Travels in Canada*, took articles from the *Montreal Herald*, assembled from various sources geographic descriptions of the Canadas, and passed along vital statistics on trade, people, and towns. Americans could read the provincial militia draft law, the 10 July 1812 regulation affecting resident Americans, and various speeches by British officials. Along with a narrative on the borderland campaigns, Niles traced the fate of Americans trapped in the provinces because of the war. He deplored both lukewarm American patriotism and smuggling. Although many Americans living in the provinces, pressed by British regulations and in fear for their lives and property, did become refugees when war erupted, illegal cross-border trade also flourished along the borderland. In October of 1812 Niles called for an investigation of 500 wagonloads of goods from Canada passing through Saratoga, New York. He doubted that these belonged to American citizens. He observed in the summer of 1813 that "the Treasury Department must be put upon the war establishment—

the whinings of the dealers have been so much attended to, that smuggling and treason have almost passed for virtues."[3]

As the war dragged on, Niles's enthusiasm for provincial conquest cooled. The campaigns along the land necks and river regions of the borderland had been disappointing, at best. The Americans did achieve a major objective when William Henry Harrison's army smashed the combined force of British and Indians, killing the dreaded Tecumseh in the process, at the Battle of the Thames in October of 1813. They also redeemed the disgraces of Detroit and Queenston Heights. But Niles ceased to parade his truculence and seemed matter-of-fact about the return of peace, although his Anglophobia never faded. For Niles, the British remained jealous of American mercantile success and English books in America represented a cultural imperialism. Furthermore, the British monarchy seemed a satanic force in world affairs. For all that, after 1815 Niles reported dispassionately on American-provincial trade and British efforts to attract English, Scottish, and Irish settlers. Over time he conveyed the sense of an emerging provincial society, although he usually reflected that the provincials would likely do far better if they voluntarily joined the United States.[4]

If he remained prejudiced, Niles also remained interested. The war had educated him about the North American provinces. As he had freely confessed, he knew nothing about them before 1811. But by reading Heriot's *Travels*, clippings from provincial papers, British documents, and the reports of American settlers and soldiers who had crossed the frontier, he discovered that the provinces were more than a British base for launching attacks on the United States. Separate societies were emerging along the northern American border. Niles represented many Americans in this respect, just as he did in his defensive expansionism. Contrary to expectation, provincials of French and American origins had not joined the invaders from the republic to the south. Partisan, strategic, personal, or administrative failings aside, conquest proved impossible, except for a restricted occupation of the western part of Upper Canada. For all his Anglophobia, Niles accepted the failure of the peace treaty to annex the provinces to the United States.

Niles's own ambiguities about the provinces in the War of 1812 reflected the overall American perspective. Some were aggressive expansionists. Others saw the provinces merely as a theater for combat.[5] Some Northern politicians and editors wanted to conquer the provinces. But New York was divided on the matter, and New England representatives railed against conquest right through the War of 1812. Southerners had little interest in annexing the provinces, and Westerners focused on Upper Canada because they believed that Britain sponsored Indian atrocities in the Old Northwest.[6] For James Madison's administration, the provinces were a convenient source of leverage to apply pressure on Great Britain to rescind the constricting Orders in Council and cease impressing American seamen.[7] American arms did not do well enough, however, to give him much more than a bargaining token.[8]

Defensive expansionism had been the central theme of American foreign policy in the Early National period as it related to British North America until the end of the War of 1812. American expansionists had only vaguely defined demographic, commercial, territorial, and strategic objectives as far as the provinces were concerned. By the congressional session of 1811 and 1812, many American politicians, especially in the Northern and Western states, had begun to talk themselves into arguing for seizing the provinces to force the British to abandon the Orders in Council and impressment. The ongoing Anglo-American crisis produced a defensive reflex that linked the provinces and territorial expansion by conquest in the minds of those supporting a policy of war by 1812.

Fragments of this view emerged prior to the war congress. In 1807, for example, Tennessean Arthur Campbell ventilated his feelings to Thomas Jefferson over the *Chesapeake-Leopard* affair. "It will be a sublime spectacle to spread liberty and civilization in that vast country, Canada." In 1810, Henry Clay harangued his fellow congressmen about the need for positive action against Britain. "The conquest of Canada is in your power," he thundered. "I verily believe, that the militia of Kentucky are alone competent to place Montreal and Upper Canada at your feet." Clay's aim was not the acquisition of territory. Taking the provinces would wound British pride, "extinguish the torch that lights up savage warfare," acquire the fur trade, and stop borderland smuggling. Annexation would, therefore, resolve a combination of economic, ideological, and political problems.[9]

Madison listed these same arguments when he asked Congress for war 1 June 1812. He justified a policy of force in the intellectual currency of eighteenth-century statesmen, reciting grievances, American forbearance and entreaties, and the arrogance and aggression of a country that already waged war against the United States.[10] He knew that Congress would respond favorably, although he overestimated the national unity that would flow from taking action to defend his country's interests.

Madison was largely silent about the provinces once the war began. In August of 1812, he ventured that military prospects in Upper Canada seemed bright. New England opposition had compromised the mobilization of national resources, but the eventual occupation of Montreal was crucial for severing British contacts with the Indians. After Hull's surrender of Detroit, Madison urged William Dearborn, the new northern commander, to dominate western waters, trading posts, and Indians. In addition, the United States must hold Canada "as a hostage for peace & justice."[11] But did this mean permanent annexation of the provinces, as the Federalists and later the British, would insist, or was Madison advancing the only feasible strategy for pressing Britain's government? Members of Madison's cabinet occasionally seemed more explicit, but were equally obscure and inconsistent. From the administration's perspective, views shifted according to two interrelated dynamics—first the Anglo-American diplomatic crisis, and second the fortunes of the war once the campaigns were under way.

The government's order to the northern commanders was emphatic enough. William Hull read that he was to take Malden, opposite Detroit, "and extend your conquests as circumstances may justify." Vice-President Elbridge Gerry spoke in the Senate in 1813. "If the war should continue, the Canadas will be rendered independent" of the British, who would then be unable to attack American borders through their Indian proxies.[12] James Monroe, in many respects a driving force in the administration's war effort, suggested that "in case of war it might be necessary to invade Canada, not as an object of the war, but as a means to bring it to a satisfactory conclusion." If the British refused to capitulate and thereby prolonged the struggle, and the United States captured Canada, it would not be easy "to relinquish Territory which had been conquered." Hull's surrender at Detroit both infuriated and inspired Monroe. "We must efface the stain before we make peace, & that may give us Canada." Monroe wrote to the chairman of the Senate

Military Committee, George W. Campbell, that "before this time next year the honor & interest of the United States require that the British forces be driven into Quebec and Halifax, and be taken there if possible."[13]

Monroe seems to have been playing events as they came, however, because his enthusiasm ebbed and flowed and always had a reflexive quality. The war was to stop Indian harassment on the northern flank and stop impressment. In episodic charge of the War Department, Monroe took a special interest in the military plans for conquering the provinces. But this was a defensive expansionism arising from the circumstances of war rather than an effort to translate a territorial and political ambition into reality.

His tone with America's peace commissioners, appointed shortly after the war began, is perhaps most revealing in this regard. In the spring of 1813, keeping Canadian traders out of the United States, building a naval force on the Great Lakes, and restoring territory on the basis of prewar holdings were the three objectives the United States sought to include in any treaty. By June, the war was going better. Monroe now argued: "That these provinces will be severed from Great Britain at no distant day, by their own career, may be fairly presumed. . . . These considerations shew that her interest well understood, is in favor of a separation at the present time." He expected, however, that Britain and the United States would share North America in the foreseeable future. The British dismissed the argument that their provinces might seek independence and advanced their own territorial claims for an Indian buffer state in the borderland. Monroe seems to have indulged in wishful thinking rather than expressed a carefully conceived policy.[14]

The American peace commissioners conscientiously reflected this defensive policy in their discussions among themselves and with the British. They undoubtedly wanted to see American arms succeed in the provinces. But was this because they wanted to add the provinces to the United States? Or, did they want to humble Great Britain and force a concession on impressment? Or, did they simply want to prove that the United States would stand up for its self-defined international rights?

They probably would have argued for keeping the provinces if American armies had been triumphant. On the other hand, John Quincy Adams was clear enough in November of 1812. "The Acquisition of Canada, however, was not, and could not be the object of this war. I do not suppose it is expected that we should keep it, if we were now to take it." He did believe that eventually there would be an American-provincial merger. But the power of historical evolution, not arms, would produce it. More specifically, Adams and James A. Bayard wanted an arrangement on the future use of the fisheries. William Crawford and Henry Clay were primarily interested in settling the impressment issue and staving off the British diplomatic attempt to create an Indian buffer state in the Old Northwest. All repudiated William Hull's and Alexander Smyth's bombastic declarations and hoped that this "would effectually remove the impression that the annexation of Canada to the United States was the declared object of their Government."[15]

Of course, the American diplomats would be expected to insist on this view. They would by virtue of their mission defend the purity of their country's motives, deny the government's aggressive intentions, and insist upon the justice of the war from the American standpoint. The fortunes of war also affected their emphasis, given a twist by the delays that bedeviled transatlantic communications in the early nineteenth century. The war would by 1814 drive hopes of provincial conquest to the fringes of American imaginations. At the same time, American policymakers accepted a continued British presence in North America (being unable to do anything about it) and wanted to stop the war.

Indeed, Madison was willing to negotiate from the summer of 1812, suggesting that territorial expansion was only a byproduct of the British refusal to yield on impressment. The Treaty of Ghent restored peace, defined boundaries, shared the fisheries, and established methods for settling future disputes. The treaty marked a return to the status quo ante bellum and rested on the assumption of an indefinite Anglo-American sharing of North America. Defending the American policy during the war, Treasury Secretary Alexander Dallas insisted that the Americans had fought in Canada to deny British control of maritime trade and to stop Indian raids on the frontier. "The military occupation of Upper Canada was, therefore, deemed indispensable to the safety of that frontier, in the earliest movements of the war, independent of all views of extending the territorial boundary of the United States." Only in Canada could the United States grapple with the British over these issues, and the proclamations by invading American commanders should be considered "unauthorized and disapproved . . . infractions of the positive instructions, which had been given, for the conduct of the war in Canada."[16] The Madison administration insisted that its expansionism was defensive and flowed from political and strategic circumstances.

The apparent union between the British and the Indians in the Old Northwest outraged Westerners. Editors, politicians, and settlers believed that the British waged a war against them by proxy to control the fur trade and push back settlement. One Tennessee paper called for the expulsion of all British power from North America to pacify the frontier. But even this expansionist outburst was defensive, to pacify the frontier and secure the border, not gather more land under the American flag. Northwest settlers, although many felt exposed and vulnerable, saw the War of 1812 as a continuation of the Indian war that began the previous year. Conquest of Upper Canada would destroy British influence with the Indians. Ohioans focused naturally on Fort Malden, the seat of British-Indian trade in the upper Great Lakes Basin. Furthermore, many believed, as did the governor of Michigan Territory, William Hull, that in event of war, many Upper Canadians would sympathize with the United States, would not fight, and might even welcome an American invasion.[17]

William Henry Harrison, a western hero after his victory at the Battle of Fallen Timbers, concentrated on the Indian menace. His correspondents feared that the British were intent on conquering the Old Northwest using the Indians. Harrison's reaction, because his goal was to remove this threat, was essentially defensive, although he planned for offensive operations while accumulating the strength to carry them out. In command after Hull's surrender, Harrison noted in December of 1812 that he had to take Malden to recover Detroit and take the "adjacent part of Upper Canada." He slowly prepared for the 1813 campaign with a virtual carte blanche from the government "to recover the ground that had been lost & to conquer upon Canada." The Americans first had to seize control of Lake Erie. Oliver Hazard Perry's victory paved the way for Harrison's advance on Detroit and Upper Canada. This strategy produced the ultimately successful Thames Valley campaign.[18]

After that, Harrison seemed to lose enthusiasm for the war. He quarreled with Secretary of War John Armstrong, spent a quiet winter, and resigned from the army in 1814. Much of his army then traveled by water and short marches down Lake Erie, across the Niagara peninsula, and down Lake Ontario to Sackett's Harbor for campaigning under Generals James Wilkinson and Wade Hampton. To be sure, had Montreal fallen, British resistance from there west would have collapsed, and if Harrison was disinterested in further active campaigning, other westerners were not. Thomas Posey, for example, told the Indiana legislature that it would be prudent policy to conquer Upper Canada at least and Lower Canada if possible. America would make the provincials an independent people, if not part of the union.[19]

The desire to annex the provinces was concentrated in the territories of Ohio and Michigan and the states of Kentucky and Tennessee. And military commanders displayed great enthusiasm for such a campaign. Andrew Jackson, for example, told volunteers on the eve of the war that the United States sought "some indemnity for past injuries, some security against future aggressions, by the conquest of all the British dominions upon the continent of North America." Although William Hull was no less enthusiastic, his proclamation upon landing in Upper Canada promised the provincials "the invaluable blessing of Civil, Political, & Religious Liberty, and their necessary result, individual, and general, prosperity." Colonel Lewis Cass, seething over Hull's later surrender of Detroit, noted that the army had landed in Canada "with an ardent zeal and stimulated with the hope of conquest." He ventured that had Hull defeated Isaac Brock's command of British regulars, provincial militia, and Indian allies, "the whole country would have been open to us, and the object of our expedition gloriously and successfully obtained."[20]

Some Americans expressed a recurrent enthusiasm for conquering the provinces throughout the war, despite the disappointing military efforts to achieve this goal. After the Thames River victory in October of 1813, the *Philadelphia Enquirer*, for example, declared that "Kingston will be ours. We shall again meet our enemy, and he will again be ours. From Kingston to Montreal we can pass down the St. Lawrence in 2 or 3 days in boats, and Montreal is ours."[21] This had the ring of rhetoric designed for local consumption and did not reflect national views. By this time, neither the administration nor Congress could muster any interest in anything except ending the war on honorable terms.

For all their desire to take Canada, Westerners, like other Americans, seemed remarkably satisfied with the results of the war in 1814. The Battle of the Thames completed what the Battle of Tippecanoe had begun. With Tecumseh dead, native military power was finally broken in the Northwest, and that was the principal western objective in the War of 1812. Rhetorical claims to the contrary, western expansionism in the Old Northwest was largely internal and defensive as far as the provinces were concerned. The nature of the war dictated an offensive strategy against Upper and Lower Canada. Any resulting territorial expansion would have been a by-product of the war and not the achievement of an original objective.

The opposition, however, believed that the Madison administration was bent on conquest. As early as 1810, John Stanley of North Carolina denounced those dreamers who talked about invading Canada and Nova Scotia as a means of retaliating against Britain. Even if successful, Americans would, in his opinion, acquire only a barren land with an undesirable population. Trying to assimilate this territory, given its mix of population, would only "extend the grounds of jealousies and disagreement" within the Union. Federalists were convinced that Madison had embarked on an unjust war of conquest to save himself and his party. They saw Great Britain as a bastion of order against the anarchy and tyranny of Napoleon. John Lowell, in an 1812 pamphlet, labeled Madison as a crypto-Jacobin. Even if American arms won, the campaigns would be costly, the land was bleak, and the French population constituted a danger. "For it ought to be known that every Louisianian and Canadian is at heart as well as by habits a Frenchman."[22] For many Federalists in the War of 1812, France and Napoleon, not Great Britain and George III, were America's true enemies.

In the House, John Randolph of Roanoke, spokesman for the Rump Tertium Quids, pounded the Madison administration for its unjust war of conquest. On every occasion, Federalists echoed his remarks. Daniel Webster believed that Madison would sustain the war until he had "made more attempts on the Canadian Provinces." As these men spoke and wrote, they revealed ignorance and old prejudices about the provinces and their people. They frequently dismissed the land as barren and the French Canadians as an "illiterate, uninformed people, devoted by the nature of their religion to their clergy." French Canadians could never become proper Americans. Some Republicans shared such views. Matthew Lyon flatly opposed conquest. Richard Rush wrote privately to John Adams that the conquest of Canada posed ideological and ethnic problems for the states: "admit that we have conquered it. As a republic we cannot hold it as a vassal province; and as a member of the Union, what can be expected from a representation in Congress composed of Englishmen and Frenchmen?"[23] Perhaps it was just a reflection of a war that had gone sour, but neither the provinces nor the provincials seemed promising recruits for a republican federation.

On the whole, regardless of partisanship or location, few Americans saw the provinces as an asset. The fur trade had value, as did navigation of the St. Lawrence River, but what of the rest? Henry Clay, even in January of 1812, disclaimed an interest in conquest because the provinces offered so little. Nathaniel Macon summarized the mélange of assertions and impressions about the provinces in American minds during the War of 1812.

> But these Canadians are surely a most uncommon people. At one time they are our brothers, friends, and associates; at another, they are French refugees and old Tories. Their country, too, must be something like themselves. At one time it is so valuable that Great Britain will never part with it, and at another it is so poor that it would be a curse to the United States; at one time the whole nation cannot take it; at another, a single State, and that not a large one, can take it with ease.[24]

The Americans best informed about the provinces lived in the borderlands, from the Maritimes to the Detroit frontier. They generally had grave misgivings about the advent of hostilities in 1812 and rarely displayed much enthusiasm for conquest. At the same time, they readily defended against a British invasion of their homeland. The war disrupted their relations with the provincials just across the frontier and made trade not merely illegal but dangerous. Congress prohibited exports to the provinces and trade with any part of the British Empire by a bill of 6 July 1812. But members of Congress and the administration knew that Americans would defy national regulations to maintain trade with the provinces.[25] And that is precisely what happened all along the frontier, despite the best efforts of treasury officers and the military.

The New England–Maritimes borderland around the Bay of Fundy allowed the greatest possibilities for maintaining near normal trade relations. For one thing, New England was virtually neutral. No land campaigns occurred east of the Champlain Valley, although many New Englanders enlisted in federal regiments and fought on the northern frontier farther west. Some New England recruits, however, spent part of the war patrolling the Maine–New Brunswick border to stop their friends and neighbors from running supplies to the British. This illegal trade provided a safety valve for those bitterly opposed to the war, and it was profitable as well.

Halifax prices for American produce rose steadily through the war. Yankee captains easily obtained safe-passage licenses from British naval officers. Americans traded these documents openly, like bills of credit, on New York, Philadelphia, and Boston exchanges. Customs officers based in New England ports supplied Halifax merchants with similar licenses, at least until British Admiral Warren tightened the blockade in 1814. So British manufactured goods continued to enter the United States through much of the war.

At the beginning of the war, local pressure in Eastport, Maine, forced the removal of an army officer who had pursued the Passamaquoddy Bay smugglers too zealously. Settlers in the St. Croix Valley held a meeting, decided that nothing would be served by warring on one another, and declared a local truce for the duration of the conflict. Yankees even supplied British military contractors in Halifax, and New England fishermen found licenses freely available from Nova Scotia and New Brunswick authorities. American–Nova Scotian trade rose after hostilities officially began, and plaster of paris, a bulky cargo, continued to flow through Boston to American markets. The numbers of small New England vessels in the coasting trade rose steadily between 1812 and 1814, although they dropped in 1815. American vessels in the cod fisheries decreased during the war, but still numbered over 17,000 in 1814. The British navy protected smugglers who eluded Boston's loyal federal agents. And when Britain tightened the coastal blockade in 1814, her forces occupied eastern Maine and set up a customs post at Castine, where they found locals freely willing to swear loyalty to King George III and stay in business. Actual smuggling may have declined, but Yankee merchants frequently followed "captured" cargoes to Halifax, where they secured prompt redress for their "losses." New Englanders often paid for illegal British goods in cash, and Christopher Gore noted to Rufus King in 1814 that nearly $2 million had left two Boston banks alone as payment for British government bills during June and July.[26]

Farther west, the Champlain Valley people responded to the war in much the same way. Vermonters feared a British invasion, but the Republican state legislature stood behind Madison's policy. An initial stab at local neutrality by an armistice between Generals Sir George Prevost and Henry Dearborn broke down when the Madison administration insisted that its military commander in the region get on with the war. In 1813, however, the Federalists triumphed and worked to reestablish borderland contacts despite the campaigns being planned and waged in the area. The state legislature repealed the act prohibiting trade. British commissioners soon crossed the border to purchase supplies when the large stock of American exports acquired just before war opened ran low. Provincial merchants continued to trade bills on the New York exchanges. American army contractors roaming the Champlain Valley found that supplies flowed north because the British in Montreal paid better than Washington's agents. At the start of the war, some thirty-five American merchants in Montreal had taken an oath of allegiance to the Crown so that they could remain in Lower Canada and carry on business.

Smugglers clashed with treasury agents, and the militia, supposedly acting as border police, often conspired in contraband operations. When General George Izard led regulars into the Champlain Valley in 1814, he was outraged over this traffic. Illegal commerce flourished. "The road to St. Regis is covered with droves of cattle, and the river with rafts destined for the enemy." Government officials were helpless. "On the eastern side of Lake Champlain, the high roads are found insufficient for the supplies of cattle which are pouring into Canada. . . . Nothing but a cordon of troops from the French mills to Lake Memphremagog could effectively check the evil."[27]

The story was the same across the lake in New York. Local producers and businessmen who had resented the Embargo resent-

Steamer route, 1809–15 ••••••••
Boundary •—•—•—•

Ottawa River

UPPER CANADA

Prescott

Kingston

LAKE ONTARIO

Sackett's
Harbor

York

Fort
George

Fort Oswego

Fort Niagara

Hamilton

Fort Erie

Buffalo

NEW YORK

*LAKE
ERIE*

Erie

PENNSYLVANIA

MAP 2. *New York–Lake Champlain Borderlands, ca. 1812*

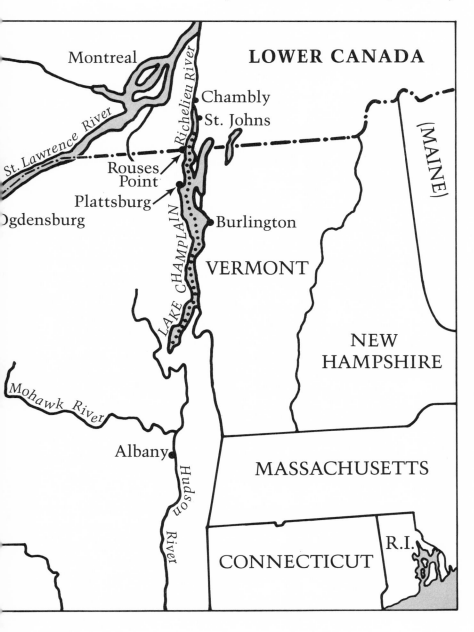

ed the war for the same reason. For many, borderland needs outweighed national loyalty when it came to controlling frontier
traffic and trade with the enemy. The valley smuggling network
reached far into the United States. One chain linked Moses and
Guy Catlin, Burlington merchants, with Lynde Catlin and John Jacob Astor in New York City—and C. P. Van Ness, the Vermont
customs collector. Other merchants hired the services of Ramon
Manzuco, who ran a ship across the line on the lakes under the
neutral Spanish flag to protect contraband cargoes, a device Bay of
Fundy smugglers also used during the war. Bogus privateers on the
lake "captured" cargoes for shipment south. Astor maintained his
lucrative fur trade, albeit at a reduced level. In July 1812, he removed his pelts personally and, in 1813, sent up an agent who collected nearly 50,000 additional furs for export. Even as federal
troops gathered around Plattsburgh in 1814 for what became one of
the final campaigns of the war along the northern frontier, illegal
traffic continued. One military patrol caught some smugglers, but
civilian authorities released the accused and jailed the officer of the
arresting detail for exceeding his authority.[28]

New York borderland defiance of federal law limited the effectiveness of Madison's policy of war. The St. Lawrence economy depended upon access to Montreal, and upstate New Yorkers had no
enthusiasm for invading their neighbors and relations. Neither side
could count on the loyalty of the locals. Congressional representatives from northern New York opposed the war, despite Governor
Daniel Tompkins's support for Madison. The militia responded
largely because locals feared a British and Indian attack. Americans
in Buffalo and other lake settlements also foresaw bombardment
from British ships.

Ogdensburg provided a case study in borderland ambiguity about
the war. In late February of 1812, the British captured Ogdensburg.
Provincials crossed on the ice and, reinforced by American looters,
plundered the town. Federalist houses generally escaped harm. Because of this experience Ogdensburgers resisted having American
troops stationed among them for fear of being a target again. And
Ogdensburg's economic interests led to the resumption of trade
with the provinces. David Parish, a prominent local businessman
and banker, openly opposed the war and conducted a brisk trade
with the British through agents on both sides of the frontier. Parish's nephew, John Ross, wrote in July of 1813 that "it is incredible

what quantities of cattle & sheep are driven into Canada. We can hardly get any for love or money; the day before yesterday upwards of 100 oxen went through Prescott, yesterday about 200." Feelings of enmity were short-lived and began to dissolve even before hostilities ceased. Friendships renewed. Even British officers visited Ogdensburg, not to fight, but to shop and dine. Visitors went back and forth across the river and provincials picked up tea and other supplies unobtainable in the provinces because of wartime shortages. Borderland New Yorkers' dislike of the war had political ramifications as well. In 1813, every northern county except one voted Federalist.[29]

The Niagara frontier was sparsely settled by 1812, isolated, with few roads and a poorly developed economy. Exports went across the frontier to the provincials, who supplied finished goods and supplies. Although the Holland Land Company had laid out Buffalo by 1803, seven years later the town only had about 500 people. Like the St. Lawrence Valley, the Niagara region hosted furious, but indecisive campaigns between 1812 and 1814. Local ambivalence emerged almost at once. In the fall of 1812, Buffalo Federalists met at Ralph Pomeroy's hotel to denounce the war. A riot ensued when Republicans accused the Federalists of toryism. In a sense, the charge was accurate, for many had friends and relatives as well as business contacts across the river in Upper Canada.

Some American settlers on the provincial side returned to the United States and enlisted with, or supported in other ways, the invading forces. But not all on the American side welcomed General Alexander Smyth's bombastic proclamation to the "Soldiers of the Army of the Center" on 17 November 1812 about conquering the provinces and transforming them into states. For one thing, the neighboring Indians would likely side with the British, and frontiersmen from the St. Lawrence to Detroit feared the explosion of brutal warfare as a result. Besides, naval control of the lakes would determine local military supremacy, and the Americans had no naval power around Niagara in 1812. Apart from the formal campaigns, local raids provoked reprisals and much destruction. The Americans torched Newark in December of 1813. British retaliation was swift. By the end of the war, Buffalo was largely cinders, the worst scarred of any borderland town, and its people rejoiced when news of the Treaty of Ghent arrived.[30]

Farther west, American settlers near the provinces had an even more rudimentary existence than those around Niagara. There was much more enthusiasm for invasions in Ohio and Michigan, despite fears of Indian attacks and concern about local military vulnerability. Ohio congressmen saw the provinces as strategic targets, but had reservations about the coming of the war. In their opinion, the Indians would ravage isolated frontier settlements immediately, before Ohio could organize a defensive force. But Westerners believed that if they could end British intrigues among the Indians, the frontier would be pacified forever. This view compounded the feelings created by competition with the British over the fur trade in the Great Lakes Basin.

The Far Northwest was also ambivalent. Michiganers had little ambition for conquest, despite William Hull's initial proclamation and Lewis Cass's histrionic fuming when Hull surrendered. Most Michiganers felt vulnerable. They too knew that the Indians would side with the British. The few Americans in Wisconsin, where settlement on both sides was so sparse as not to deserve the name, agreed. Local American interests revolved around control of the fur trade.[31] Expansionism for Northwesterners meant internal growth and control of the Indians and the fur trade, not the addition of provincial territory to the union.

Some congressmen in Washington seemed strident at times, and even ambitious to conquer the provinces. But the context of the speeches and the circumstances of their delivery show that defenders of the Madison administration's policy had a defensive outlook. The Indian problem in the Northwest was a major motivation for the war. Henry Clay stated that "in making the war effective, conquest may become necessary; but this does not change the character of the war—there may be no other way of operating upon our enemy but by taking possession of her provinces which adjoin us." He may have dissembled for partisan and popular consumption, but Clay later stressed that the provinces had become a target because they constituted a base for the British war on American settlers. Clay would have retained the provinces only if the United States had occupied them, but he insisted that the war had not been for conquest.[32]

Other war Republicans had similar views. John C. Calhoun defended the strategy of attacking the provinces, because it was the only feasible way to press Great Britain. In January of 1814, Parry

Humphreys from Tennessee summarized what many Republicans in Congress had come to believe. A defensive war demanded military offensives. "The conquest of Canada, and the expulsion of the English power from the American continent, would operate most powerfully in depriving the enemy of the means of annoying our commerce and preying upon our citizens.[33] Madison had defended American rights on both maritime and inland frontiers. The provinces were a convenient target, a hostage to be used to settle other issues.

Americans removed from the borderland rarely thought of the provinces as other than British bases. Even along the boundary, settlers feared British control over the tribes from Montreal west. The British also represented a vestigial monarchism in North America that some Americans wanted to erase. But a defensive expansion for future security was a far more common theme. The *Military Monitor and American Register*, which was founded solely to record the war, saw provincial annexation as "indemnity for past injuries, security against future aggression." Like Niles's *Register*, the *Monitor* began to print descriptive articles on the provinces along with battle news. In December of 1812, the *Monitor* argued that "the conquest of upper Canada is essentially necessary" to force the British "to accept peace on equitable terms." The editors educated themselves and their readers about the provinces. Some thought that it would be enough if the British left the provincials to decide for themselves independence or annexation to the United States. Conquering and ruling the provinces as dependencies was out of the question.[34]

Many papers denounced Republican policy, echoing congressional opposition to the war of conquest. The *New England Palladium and Commercial Advertiser* carried extensive provincial news during the war, more than before 1812. Again, the press served an educational role, reporting not merely military news, but information about provincial social life and commerce. The *Raleigh Minerva*'s editor supported the war effort, but argued that South Carolinians, whatever their rage against Great Britain, had no desire "to make foreign conquests and to spill the blood of neighboring brethren." Nor did the *Minerva* criticize the New York militia that refused to cross into the provinces. Its position was that citizens served to defend the United States, not to invade others. In New York itself, a volunteer unit wrote to Madison that although it was ready for war, "we feel no ambition for foreign conquest."[35]

Few Americans considered the future of the British North American provinces beyond the war. Those who had a longer view thought that eventually they might peacefully evolve toward union with the United States. As the war progressed, or rather, failed to progress for Americans, conquest became unlikely, whether intended or not. Yet some argued that the provinces were historically and geographically intertwined with the United States. John Quincy Adams projected a unified Anglo-Saxon North America. For James Monroe, "these provinces will be severed from Great Britain at no distant day, by their own career." A "Backwoodsman" wrote to the *Monitor* that if the provinces became independent, they would probably become part of the United States as a natural consequence of events.[36] Neither Manifest Destiny nor national conceit, such views reflected a dawning conviction in a process of historical evolution that would separate North America from Europe and the past.

Many had expected that the Americans who settled in the provinces prior to the war would view the invaders as liberators and flock to the American colors. That prospect certainly worried British officials, and many former Americans did enlist in or assisted the invading armies. Yet many former Americans remained neutral, fearing British retaliation because of their origins and suspected sympathies. Some left the provinces rather than risk loss of liberty or life. A portion of those who remained actively supported the Crown.[37]

Americans had responded variously as they learned more about the provinces during the war. A kaleidoscope of views resulted. Americans simply had no consensus about their present or future relationship with the British North American provinces as they waged a limited war to defend national security against the threat posed by Great Britain.

Whatever their views, the reluctant warriors of 1812 welcomed the return of peace in 1815. In some respects, the Treaty of Ghent suggested that Americans anticipated an indefinite sharing of North America with the British provincials, because differences over boundaries, trade, and the fisheries were postponed for future settlement. Even so, the Reverend Alexander McLeod, a noted New York minister and supporter of the Madison administration, believed that the provincials had learned the "benefits of peace with the United States." Provincial loyalty to Great Britain would likely decline, while an interest in republican independence would grow. John Quincy Adams took a geopolitical view. "The lakes of Canada may be considered as having made their debut upon the political scene."[38] Henceforward, he asserted, American interests would have a continental as well as Atlantic orientation.

Once the war was over, American analysts fixed on the theme of defensive security that had generated support for military action in the first place. Congressional speeches stressed the redemption of national honor. Politicians let the rhetoric flow but had no sense of chagrin at the failure to conquer the provinces. Contemporary histories of the war stressed that the mere act of fighting had renewed national self-respect. Samuel Perkins, who had been hostile to the Madison administration, wrote that "European nations now see that America has both the spirit and the means of defence, and her government the ability to call them into action." Perkins also portrayed the provincials as real people, with justifiable loyalties and a viable society. Samuel White, who spent some time in Montreal, Beaufort, and Halifax as a prisoner in 1814, appended a detailed geographical and social description of the two Canadas to his narrative. White, along with travelers, politicians, the readers of the *Weekly Register* and the *Monitor*, and the soldiers, learned a good deal about the provinces because of the war.[39] For its part, the government left the war behind. The Senate ratified the Treaty of Ghent quickly and easily, although Congress quibbled over compensation for provincial volunteers who had lost their property to the Crown.[40]

After 1815, the international political and military environment that had dominated North Atlantic affairs since 1793 abruptly changed. Having defeated Napoleon, Britain no longer needed impressment to man her navy or trade restrictions to strangle her continental enemy. Britain did not abandon the claim that she had the right to impress at will, but ceased to apply the policy. Americans remained suspicious of British intentions in North America, but attention shifted farther west and to the south by the 1830s. National security remained an issue, but the northern frontier stabilized after the defeat of the northwestern Indians, and surveyors fixed the American-provincial boundary between 1815 and 1846. If the provinces remained hostages to British good behavior, American coastal residents pointed out that their towns and cities were hostages to American good behavior. An aggressive movement north would surely provoke a naval retaliation difficult to deflect. Congress recognized this standoff and voted funds over the next half-century to increase the navy and construct fortifications at strategic points ranging from Maine in the north to the Dry Tortugas and Pensacola in the Gulf of Mexico.

The limited war of 1812, fought by James Madison and the Republicans to defend national honor, secure the northern frontier and the oceans, and sustain republican ideology, was over. If the results of the war were largely psychological, this was fitting, because attitudes of mind had generated the conflict in the first place. Proximity and the belief that the British used the provinces as a base to thwart American settlement in the northwest had stimulated Americans to attack the provinces. But what seemed like territorial expansionism actually arose from a defensive mentality, not from ambitions for conquest and annexation.

American expansionism had become a complex force since 1783, with commercial, demographic, diplomatic, ideological, political, and territorial elements. As the old revolutionary generation slipped from national power, a new age began for the United States. The concerns of the next generation would affect the provinces in both old and new ways after 1815. The War of 1812 represented a transition in successive phases of the impact of American expansionism on the British North American provinces.

PART 2

The Era of

Manifest Destiny,

1815–1860

New elements crept into American expansionism after the War of 1812. The defensive reflex of the Early National period survived, but American expansionism acquired a more aggressive and impulsive thrust. A shifting international context that affected British foreign policy, the evolution of the American party system, social changes, economic growth, fresh definitions of America's national destiny, and even technological innovations combined to transform the nature of American expansionism.

To begin with, the international context overseas and in North America changed dramatically after 1815. The Napoleonic Wars were over. Overt British assaults on American honor and trade therefore vanished. The War of 1812 was the direct consequence of America's frustrated pursuit of neutrality in a world of war. James Madison's administration had sustained Thomas Jefferson's defensive diplomacy. The very decision to go to war was fundamentally defensive. Although at the last moment, Britain had withdrawn the Orders in Council, events had developed a momentum that Madison and his supporters were unwilling to contest. At the same time, the war became a national catharsis, venting a decade of frustration and fury over what many Americans saw as British arrogance and hostility.

With Napoleon in exile, the Treaty of Ghent restored the status quo. Outstanding Anglo-American problems either reverted to bilateral diplomacy or to joint commissions of arbitration for settlement. As a consequence, the sense of the provinces as an enemy base dimmed. Even so, a residue of suspicion and a reflex Anglophobia remained to dog American policymakers for decades. Fear of British designs in Texas, Mexico, California, and the Pacific littoral partly stimulated the American westward drive between 1815 and 1854. But a declining British commitment to North America permitted diplomacy to dissolve most Anglo-American problems. Emotional surges, as in the Maine–New Brunswick boundary dispute, the provincial rebellions of 1837, or the Oregon controversy in 1846, could not deflect a strengthening Anglo-American diplomatic accord.

Other European powers with North American interests played almost no role in the fate of the accord. France had no influence in North American affairs after 1815. Spain's empire withered. John

Quincy Adams acquired East Florida and a block of interior territory in the Transcontinental Treaty of 1819. After Mexican independence in 1823, Spain retained only a few Caribbean islands. The
United States now confronted an independent, but weak, republic
to the south and southwest. Russia's few interests on the Pacific
Coast were mercantile, feeble, and the end of a long, thin line of
commitment and communications. The United States became almost by default the dominant North American power, free from
overseas interference and without significant European competitors
in the New World, except for a passive Britain in the north.

American domestic politics shifted as the revolutionary generation faded from national politics. The men in power after 1815
were very young during the Revolution. The preeminent statesman
of the time, John Quincy Adams, remembered his mother taking
him by the hand to watch the British bombardment of Boston in
1775. The first party system, the Federalist-Jeffersonian partisanship, crumbled by 1815. Politics entered the mildly misnamed Era
of Good Feelings under James Monroe's presidency. One party prevailed, but before long personal ambitions and new disagreements
produced factions. The Missouri Compromise of 1820 and the arrival of Andrew Jackson on the national political scene exploded
the illusion of harmony. And once again expansionism became intertwined with partisanship, even though the second party system
proved to be as much oriented around power and personalities as
around issues and ideology.

As regional interests coalesced, distinct versions of American expansionism emerged in New England, the South, and other sections
of the nation. New England merchantmen were active in the Pacific
Northwest and the China trade by 1800. Over time, Yankees acquired ambitions for the ports of San Diego, San Francisco, and
Puget Sound to develop the trade of the Pacific and the Orient.
Their imaginations transformed the trickle of trade between America and the Far East into a river of commerce with the United States
as Asia's entrepôt to Europe. These ambitions joined others in fuel-
ing the drive to the Pacific Coast, splitting Oregon with the British along the forty-ninth parallel, and fostering President James K.
Polk's objective of acquiring California from Mexico in 1844. By the
1840s, New England merchants allied themselves with local manu-

facturers and railroad promoters to form a powerful lobby for national economic expansion and development.

Southerners had different ideas about national expansion. In the 1820s, Southerners moved into the Lower Mississippi Valley to spread their cotton culture. Technological innovations in harvesting and manufacturing had created a rapidly growing textile industry in England and at home. But this expansion had limits because of the nature of the slave system, the fragility of the cotton plant, and the practical implications of geography. Cotton stopped on the fringes of the arid Great Plains. Northern and Western opposition to the expansion of slavery up the Mississippi Valley led some Southerners to look at Central America, Cuba, and even South America as regions for possible future development. By 1854, the slave owner's identification with expansion and the South's opposition to a national economic program led by an activist federal government split the Democratic Party and created the party system of the 1850s. But before 1854, Southern expansion had produced tangible territorial results. Americans in Texas rebelled against Mexican rule in 1836 and created a separate republic. After a brief independence, Texas joined the United States in 1845. Southerners also strongly supported the 1846 war against Mexico, convincing themselves that they would gain access to new territory suitable for slavery from an American victory.

Southerners wanted new land because they believed that slavery must expand or else shrivel and die. They defended this institution on cultural as well as economic and constitutional grounds, but their ability to balance the objective of sustaining slavery with their goal of controlling the Democratic Party faltered in the 1850s. The South became more cohesive because of its exaggerated fears of abolitionists and free soilers, and the resulting sectional rift paralyzed the ability of the United States to admit more territories into the Union.

In the North, migrants filled in around the Great Lakes and Upper Mississippi Valley. But settlers looked farther west as well. Frontier fur traders and entrepreneurs were the first to venture regularly up the Missouri Valley and across the Rockies to the Pacific Coast. Then missionaries and a handful of settlers trekked to Oregon in the 1830s. Next, larger numbers journeyed across the

Oregon Trail, with some breaking off to cross the Sierra Nevada Mountains to California in the 1840s. Simultaneously, the Mormons escaped persecution by migrating to Utah, their wilderness Zion. Under Mexican sovereignty when the Mormons planned their exodus, Utah soon became American territory with the Treaty of Guadalupe Hidalgo that ended the Mexican War. Although not by design a part of America's expansion—Mormon purpose was to escape America—the Mormons under Brigham Young soon developed expansionist designs of their own, projecting colonies down the Colorado River and into Nevada and California, as well as north into Idaho. Other motivations besides commercial interests led large groups of Americans to acquire and settle lands not part of the United States in 1815.

During the 1840s, the divisions of the two-party system made the Democrats the party of continentalism. New states of the union emerged. Political expansion followed territorial acquisition, commercial ambitions, and demographic movement. Between 1815 and 1860, the American economy itself underwent dramatic growth as a result of the nation's westward movement. This economic expansion had important implications for America's external relations. Entrepreneurship characterized America's antebellum period. It is true that Americans did not suddenly become entrepreneurs after 1815. After all, the dream of free enterprise had driven Englishmen across the Atlantic in the seventeenth and eighteenth centuries. But the pursuit of commerce and economic growth after the War of 1812 went far beyond what colonials or the founding fathers had envisioned. Acquisitiveness, ambition, and the knack for applying technology to manufacturing and transportation transformed the United States into the leading economic power after Great Britain. Although this growth was gradual, with booms and busts, in the antebellum period, it was real and profound. And manufacturing, along with increased food production for export, was crucial to the development of a growing global network linked by American merchantmen. These economic changes had important ramifications for relations with the British North American provinces.

The demographic, political, and territorial changes that characterized American expansionism after 1815 did not affect the provinces directly. Americans along the northern tier of states no longer spilled over the border. The British restricted American immigration to the provinces, fearing a swift dilution of their power if they did not. Concomitantly, they encouraged emigration from Great Britain and Ireland, much of which, to British chagrin, simply filtered into the United States. Finally, residual Anglophobia deterred American migrants from crossing the border.

At the same time, a complex American-provincial economic network developed. Local trade flourished all along the borderland where pockets of Americans and provincials had easy contact. This trade was both legal and recorded as well as illicit. Smuggling occurred in the dead of night in small boats on lakes, bays, and rivers, or over back roads far from the gaze of customs officers from either government.

The Northern states were settled thickly and swiftly after 1815, and a transportation system linked the economies of these new regions to the union. This network inevitably ensnared provincials, even as the St. Lawrence River served as a communications channel for many Americans in the Great Lakes Basin. The Erie Canal promoters, the Great Lakes carriers, and Northwestern railroads saw themselves as national benefactors and continental agents. They soon had a cross-border clientele. The provinces were one region among several that produced goods for carriers and hence profits. The British provinces represented economic opportunity. Editors, officials, politicians, travelers, and writers generally concurred that eventual American-provincial convergence would result from these connections. Many also speculated about an independent British North America. In this sense, "continentalism" took the form of confidence in the flow of history. It was a fancy, rather than a policy to be pursued.

Americans who talked about the British provinces regretted the survival of monarchical power in North America. But many claimed to have observed some movement from British despotism to democratic and republican forms. The reality of British power, however, led Americans to accept the continued British presence, despite inflammatory speeches and editorials during moments of stress in Anglo-American diplomatic relations. Americans placed their faith in the proximity of the United States to the provinces, their infectious example of material progress, and their democratic and republican forms of government. In time the provincials would seek independent self-government and remove the colonial officials, the established and landed churches, and the restrictions on trade imposed by their British rulers.

Americans believed that the march of history implied convergence with the provinces. They therefore applauded the rebellions of 1837 as the advent of republicanism. And Britain's decision to throw the provinces onto the world economy with the abolition of the Corn Laws in 1846 seemed another step toward inevitable continental union. Peace also survived because the compass of Manifest Destiny pointed west and southwest, not north, despite the use of the term "continentalism." Finally, no American administration from James Monroe's presidency to James Buchanan's stirred up Anglo-American difficulties. Even the blustering James K. Polk wanted a compromise over Oregon.

At the same time, Americans learned a great deal about the provinces between 1815 and 1850. Entrepreneurs sought markets, sources of raw materials, places to invest, and goods to carry and trade. A few settlers emigrated. Curious travelers came in growing numbers to produce a borderland tourist industry in the summer months. The provinces also became a refuge once again, this time for runaway slaves, and, during the Civil War, for Northern deserters, rebels who escaped from Union prison camps near the border, and for Confederates who used provincial border towns as bases for raids into Union territory. America's civil war, therefore, focused attention on the provinces. Renewed scrutiny modified old impressions. American perceptions of the provinces revealed that the United States had moved into a national adolescence. It had developed a worldview that included more than its original republican inheritance, yet it continued to judge other peoples by American cultural values, standards, and expectations.

Chapter 4. Manifest Destiny and Provincial Boundaries

> *Geographic position, kindred interests, language and laws, sympathy of origin and destiny, to say nothing of the oppressions of a hard-hearted step mother, must ultimately, sooner or later, place the Canadas under the Aegis of this empire.*
>
> —New York Evening Post, *1835*

*J*ohn L. O'Sullivan, who coined the phrase that politicians and historians have used to characterize mid-nineteenth-century expansionism—Manifest Destiny—argued that God had granted Americans use of the North American continent. The inherent virtues of agrarianism, American entrepreneurship, republican institutions, and a conviction that European countries would eventually retreat from North America reinforced the idea that the United States would extend its superior civilization throughout the continent. Manifest Destiny implied not simply territorial growth, but sanctified ideology and institutions.

The idea of Manifest Destiny was not without its precursors. James Monroe had mused about fusing Anglo-Saxon North America during the War of 1812. When John Quincy Adams hinted at American continental dominion, he meant something like O'Sullivan's concept. But O'Sullivan expressed a far more strident nationalism. And he hinted at America's millennial role, an idea with wide appeal in the nineteenth century.

O'Sullivan began his journalistic career with the *United States Magazine and Democratic Review* during the Panic of 1837. These were exciting times. American troops pursued the Seminole Indians in Florida. Prairie traders wound along the Santa Fe Trail and missionaries settled in Oregon. Southern and Western frontiersmen helped Texans establish an independent republic. The rebellions in Lower and Upper Canada seemed to imply another republican surge. During those years Americans were moving geographically and developing ideologically. A patriotic spirit and commercial optimism flourished despite the panic.

O'Sullivan was a child of the times. He was well educated, a staunch Republican, something of a literary man, and subject to grandiose political visions. He had a naïve faith in democracy's power to steer human nature toward social perfection and believed that the United States was destined to guarantee freedom to the world. He also had a strong sense of Anglo-Saxon superiority. This mélange of views and his turgid, fanciful rhetorical flights make him seem quaint. But he provides a clear window on his times. His magazine survived for years, although he wandered from journalism to Caribbean filibustering in the 1850s, to Confederate sympathizing in the 1860s. He died in obscurity.[1]

The Anglo-American disputes that punctuated United States foreign policy after 1815 inflamed O'Sullivan's nationalism. But his common sense survived. He sympathized with the provincial rebels of 1837–38, but stressed that they must determine their own political destiny. He warned against American intervention. Although he suggested that war with England was possible because of British intransigence in the disputed northeastern boundary between Maine and New Brunswick, his sense of Anglo-Saxon unity made the mere thought morally and intellectually repugnant.

> But war!—between the two nations of the earth the most closely knit together by the bands of a common origin, language, and literature—the extent, intimacy and importance of their commercial intercourse—the proximity of their possessions upon this continent—their close intellectual association, and their peculiar and sacred relations to the cause of civilization and freedom! It cannot be.[2]

O'Sullivan understood provincial political questions and as an American republican disliked British colonial rule. He denied that Anglo-French racial antagonism had caused the rebellions of 1837. British misrule inevitably sparked resistance, and O'Sullivan believed that a provincial majority would support independence. Britain should recognize that blocking provincial political progress was futile. Whether the provinces became independent or part of the United States, all would benefit. He argued that Lord Durham's report was liberal and important to Americans, and a positive step for their provincial neighbors.[3]

Despite his strident expansionism, O'Sullivan saw provincials as junior partners, not victims, in an Anglo-Saxon Manifest Destiny.

He believed, vaguely echoing John Quincy Adams, that many American republics would eventually emerge and flow together. The European idea of a balance of power could not apply in North America. Spanish America languished, and "whatever progress of population there may be for the British Canadas, is only for their own early severance of their present colonial relation to the little island three thousand miles across the Atlantic, soon to be followed by annexation, and destined to swell the still accumulating momentum of our progress."[4] But for all his urgent rhetoric, the man who invented Manifest Destiny saw only peaceful evolution toward an eventual American-provincial merger.

As a fervent Democrat, O'Sullivan reflected the partisan politics of the times. Debates raged over the admission of Texas. President James K. Polk headed an expansionist-minded Democratic Party. Ambition for Oregon accelerated as columns of settlers moved along "Pathfinder" John Charles Frémont's well-publicized trails. Polk's administration moved toward revoking the 1818 treaty of joint occupation with the British. But Northern Democratic and Whig antiexpansionists opposed the admission of new territory to the Union because of the rising controversy on the spread of slavery.

O'Sullivan captured the ambiguity of the American view of the provinces in the age of Manifest Destiny. Superficially, territorial expansionism rendered precise delineation of American-provincial boundaries superfluous. Why spend so much time and energy establishing and surveying boundaries if acquisition of the provinces were imminent? Yet, from 1815 to the 1850s, when aggressive administrations added territory to the south and west, British and American diplomats strove to settle boundary disputes. The three separate strands in American thinking about the provinces explain this paradox. These strands shifted in strength over time, but they helped to reconcile the opposing impulses toward expansionism and coexistence that characterized American policy toward the provincials.

To begin with, many Americans still saw the provinces as a British base. But Anglo-American agreements, an inchoate sense of Anglo-Saxon brotherhood, and American self-confidence combined to persuade many Americans that Great Britain would never use that base against the United States. Yet the British remained competitors for furs, the West Indies trade, and influence with the new Latin American countries, especially Mexico. Britain also remained active on America's Pacific Coast, touching the old fear about British encirclement that had arisen in the 1790s. American foreign policy, therefore, sustained its defensive cast in face of British designs in the New World and the Pacific Ocean.

The existence of the border settlements produced a second American perception of the provinces that was stronger than the fading sense of a British menace from the north. As the border was defined with increasing clarity between 1815 and 1850, successive American governments demonstrated that they expected to live with their British provincial neighbors indefinitely. Cordial relations were maintained with Britain. Presidents chose secretaries of state and diplomatic representatives who would get along in Britain, such as James Buchanan and Edward Everett, and, on the whole, amicable relations persisted between British ministers in Washington and succeeding administrations.

This willingness to negotiate produced the accord that began with drawing a definitive boundary after the War of 1812 and dividing the islands in Passamaquoddy Bay. The Webster-Ashburton Treaty of 1842 resolved the Maine–New Brunswick border dispute. Minor pieces of territory, such as a tip of land in the northern part of Lake Champlain and islands in the Detroit River, changed hands by mutual agreement. The compromise over Oregon in 1846 capped this process. Even so, possession of the San Juan Islands and navigation through the Strait of Juan de Fuca were not settled until the Treaty of Washington in 1871. Furthermore, the border was never undefended, as Canadian-American mythology insists. Provincials occasionally convinced themselves that an American invasion was imminent. This was alarmism, but as a result, the British proved more enthusiastic fortress builders than the Americans. Nonetheless, when crises arose, the two governments seemed determined to resolve their differences.[5]

The juxtaposition of Anglophobia and American respect for British power and achievement constituted the third strand of American thinking about the provinces during the era of Manifest Destiny. Congressional speeches, private letters, editorials, and pamphlets yield an alarming array of arrogant and inflammatory remarks about seizing the provinces, a reflection of the Anglophobia that had become a staple of American political life, especially among such groups as the Irish. At the same time, upper-class Americans sustained a constant admiration for Britain. And, as the British navy still dominated the seas and the crisis over slavery drew attention away from the North to the West and Southwest and the Caribbean and Central America, the political power of American Anglophobia diminished.[6]

Immediately after the War of 1812, many Americans believed that the British remained hostile to the United States. Anti-British feelings were strong along the Great Lakes land necks, where the war had been largely fought. Raids had devastated the Niagara area, but rebuilding occurred swiftly. Local friendships reemerged, and a growing commerce and prosperity eased borderland bitterness.

Lingering suspicion surfaced periodically nevertheless. The *Albany Argus* warned against reducing American border forces. The British could unleash their forces from the provinces at any time. In the *Buffalo Gazette*, "Horace" wanted to settle the frontier with veterans to "present a formidable barrier to the hostile inroads of a savage neighbor, and afford a permanent security to the interior." Anglophobia even persuaded some to jettison old republican prejudices against standing armies and argue for an enhanced regular force to deter Britain. Henry Clay reminded the House of Representatives of America's vast borders and "powerful nations coterminous on the whole frontier." Clay never seemed to want the provinces, but sought instead to pursue his so-called American System through commercial agreements with Great Britain that would include British North America.[7]

As Americans reopened contacts with the northwest Indian tribes after the war, they discovered that British agents still funneled furs to Montreal from Amherstburg, across from Detroit. Michiganers also remained uneasy because the British were slow to evacuate the posts they had taken during the war. Local officials wanted to import settlers as soon as possible and deport Indians. Lewis Cass used his military service as a springboard to become territorial governor, and he still considered Upper Canada as an enemy base. "The contiguity of these Indians to the British possessions in Canada, and the use which might be made of them, in the event of any future difficulties on this frontier" made removal of the tribes urgent. The legacy of the war, the vulnerability of the frontier, and continuing

British commercial activity in the Northwest, all sustained the old fear of the provinces as an enemy base well into the 1820s.[8]

After 1815, Americans read far more about provincial trade, politics, and settlement than they did about British schemes for revenge against the United States. British military activity slackened, despite the construction of a string of fortifications from St. Andrews to the Great Lakes. American newspapers began to refer to redcoats as symbols of despotic power or as colorful tourist attractions, rather than as a menacing army. In 1817, the *National Intelligencer* dismissed rumors of war with England as ridiculous. British troops in the provinces had become a "useless measure . . . in a time of profound peace." Arch-Anglophobe Hezekiah Niles reported that British fiscal retrenchment had reduced regiments and war vessels alike. No one could foresee the future, "but there is nothing in this part of the world, that indicates even a thought of an approaching war with the United States." British commercial regulations might chafe, Henry Clay noted, but could not "possibly lead to war." American observers saw the Rideau and Welland canals, which had defensive as well as commercial functions, primarily as a flattering imitation of republican economic progress. Provincials came to be seen as brother Anglo-Saxons seeking self-improvement.[9]

After 1815, many congressmen viewed the British more as commercial rivals than military ones. Although the British also controlled fisheries to which Americans assumed that they had a natural right, Americans were confident that they could dominate these grounds, not by force, but by marketing the fish at lower prices. At the same time, the Convention of 1818 showed that Americans were content to share the resource. Anglophobia remained common among editors and politicians, but this dislike assumed a ritual quality in the United States after 1815, unless an incident touched a concern close to national interests and security.[10]

Generally speaking, British and American authorities got on well together and approached difficulties in a spirit of compromise and cooperation rather than with ill-grace and truculence. The limitation of naval power on the Great Lakes was a case in point. The War of 1812 had drawn the attention of many Americans north. John Quincy Adams wrote: "The lakes of Canada may be considered as having in the late war made their debut upon the political scene.

They are, if I mistake not, destined at no distant period to perform upon that theatre a still more conspicuous part." Adams in part fulfilled his own prophecy by having Richard Rush negotiate to limit naval forces on the lakes. The Rush-Bagot Agreement of 1817 did not lead to automatic and complete naval disarmament in the region, because both sides raised force levels during tense times. But after 1817, each accepted the good faith and good intentions of the other regarding warships on the Great Lakes.[11]

Over time, the Americans relaxed their defenses on the northern frontier. Few troops stood along the St. Lawrence River or the lake shores. In 1817, of 7,616 officers and men in northern posts, 4,355 were scattered along the border from Green Bay and Michilimackinac, on the Maine coast, and at interior points in New England, New York, and Pennsylvania. Between 1816 and 1829 Congress appropriated $8.25 million for coastal fortifications from Maine to the Dry Tortugas in the Gulf of Mexico, but only just over $200,000 went to the northern border. Americans had put three years' work and $113,000 into a fort on Rouses Point at the north end of Lake Champlain when border surveyors discovered in 1818 that it stood on the provincial side of the line. The Americans abandoned it. By 1825, most of America's fresh water naval establishment had been sold or broken up. Brigadier General John Wool recommended against spending even "one dollar for the erection of permanent fortifications on our Northern and Western Frontier." As secretary of war in 1836, Lewis Cass saw no danger from the north and recommended only minimal works to control Lake Champlain.[12]

Cass reflected the rising confidence Americans had in their own military power. The growing population of the northwest provided the basic sense of security, and the United States devoted only limited resources to fortify the frontier. When a brief, small provincial foray near Buffalo during the border troubles in 1838 generated local fears of an invasion to come, American force levels were so low that federal authorities had to rely on militia and a handful of regular officers to control the turbulent frontier. Eventually, the War Department scraped together a few units to support the officers. But after 1841, work stalled on new forts at Detroit and Buffalo, and by 1860 Army engineers reported the neglect and decay of all the borderland fortifications. Although Confederate raiders based in Canada during the Civil War renewed fears of a menace from the

north, American work on border forts had stopped completely by
1871.

The United States never built up its military forces in the North
between 1815 and 1871, and no government pursued a policy of
force against the British North American provinces. Only a few
individuals even suggested a strong or militant policy. In 1818, for
example, Judge A. B. Woodward, a former governor of Michigan and
noted Anglophobe, wrote to John Quincy Adams that "it is the
duty of the American administration to make a serious effort to
obtain the whole of the British possessions on this continent by
negotiation." Henry Dearborn tried to persuade Daniel Webster in
1830 that the United States should seek to purchase the provinces.
Dearborn had politics as well as future profits in mind. The North
would gain strength in Congress from four new states "to counter-
balance the growing states of the northwest." But Woodward and
Dearborn both spoke of acquisition by negotiation.[13]

During the Oregon uproar, some genuine militancy erupted. But
even here, motives were typically mixed. Citizens in Detroit petitioned the government to balance Texas with the provinces. *Niles'
Register* trumpeted, "*If we are to fight*, why then, we had better
fight for all of Canada and of Nova Scotia too. The prize must
be made something worth fighting for." But Niles's point was that
by itself, Oregon was not worth the trouble. Lieutenant Matthew
Maury of the United States Navy wanted a Great Lakes force poised
to conquer western Upper Canada in the event of an Anglo-American war. Maury made his case because he thought in strategic, not
political or ideological terms. His tone was abrupt, urgent, assured,
but his assumptions were faulty. "There is nothing to prevent us
from conquering and annexing the 'State of Toronto.' The people in
it would be glad to join the Union." The equally deluded *New York
Evening Post* argued that "the Canadas are ripe for rebellion, and
the single states of Ohio and New York could reduce them to sub-
jection in six weeks." Such echoes of prewar boasting alarmed com-
merce-conscious Whig papers and earned sharp rebuttals. The *Baltimore American* mockingly called Americans to liberate Niagara
Falls. "If the Gulf of Mexico is to be regarded as 'our sea' . . . certainly the great lakes ought to be our lakes and the St. Lawrence
our river."[14]

In 1845, a war with Mexico seemed far more likely to American expansionists than a conflict with England. Polk focused on pressuring Mexico to release California. Once under way, the Mexican War swallowed material as well as emotional resources. When controversy arose about the future of slavery in any lands taken from Mexico, Americans discovered that Manifest Destiny could provoke paralyzing and divisive internal crises. Some Northerners looked toward expansion into the provinces as a way of restoring national balance. Frustration over the Kansas-Nebraska issue in 1854 prompted the *New York Tribune* to write that "Expansion in the direction of the north star—expansion for the purpose of union with more than two millions of liberty-loving, slavery-hating people . . . is not a prospect to cry out against at the present moment. To 'extend the area of freedom,' not in hollow cant, but in sober earnest, does not . . . strike us as very dreadful."[15]

Manifest Destiny more typically seemed to include the provinces when diplomatic crises with Britain aggravated American tempers. In October of 1851, Zachary Taylor's administration feared a possible Anglo-American clash over the Atlantic fisheries. The *New York Times* suggested that "the policy adopted by the British government in relation to the fishery business is calculated to remove any delicate scruples we have about wedding our coy neighbor at the North." Americans were acquisitive by nature and haughty foreigners courted danger. "Let our British friends at the North make us unpleasantly sensible of their existence; let them stand one moment in the way of the national prosperity and obvious destiny, and there is no telling how soon we [may] swallow them, headland and inland, lake, river and town."[16]

The annexation movement that slowly gathered momentum in the provinces after 1846 encouraged those who foresaw the United States governing the entire continent. Free traders in Great Britain were able to vote out the Corn Laws that had granted provincials a protected market for their agricultural produce. This created momentary commercial panic in the provinces, especially among Montreal merchants. Staring at depression and ruin, they decided that only annexation to the United States would lead them out of the economic crisis that Britain had caused them.

American consuls in the provinces found in the annexation movement an opportunity to accelerate American-provincial convergence. Moving primarily in commercial circles, which supplied the core of the annexation movement, the consuls saw what they wanted to see. They reported a veritable provincial groundswell for union with the United States. Americans visiting Montreal and Toronto gained similarly distorted impressions about the strength of provincial annexationism because they had few contacts with the bulk of the provincial population. New York newspapers committed similar errors. The Montreal "Annexation Manifesto" of 1849 therefore evoked great American enthusiasm. The *New York Tribune* established an "Annexation Correspondent" in Montreal to follow developments. All overlooked provincial British patriotism and antirepublicanism.[17]

Americans misread provincial loyalties because they mistook resemblances for shared values. Americans pictured the provincials as Anglo-Saxons who held similar economic and political convictions. *Niles' Register*, for example, misread provincial disputes over the bill to compensate citizens for losses during the rebellions of 1837–38. Niles believed that discontent over the bill forecast Canadian independence. After all, the English provincials were just like Americans, "intelligent, active, enterprising, desirous of making the most of the country's great natural resources, and ready to appropriate money for the construction of canals, roads and bridges, and the diffusion of education." Progress and agitation might combine in a call upon Americans "to add another State to the Union."[18] Niles, like many Americans, utterly misunderstood provincial loyalties as well as the anti-Americanism that arose from the invasions of 1812–14.

American views were less aggressive than boastful. The belief in North America's historical evolution followed from America's own national experience rather than from an understanding of the provinces. This circumstance produced a spate of shortsighted pronouncements. Any peaceful American-provincial fusion produced by the annexation movement would be consummated, as the Vermont legislature resolved, "with the consent of the British Government and of the people of Canada, and upon just and honorable terms." The New York legislature agreed, linking annexation with Anglo-Saxonism, American ideology, economics, and the slavery debate. Annexation would reunite us into one family, and make citizens of a brave, industrious, and intelligent people who are now our brethren in interest and language. It would save this country the expense of maintaining a line of customs houses and fortifications 3,500 miles in extent, and give to the whole continent the blessing of free and unmolested trade. It would secure the preponderance of free institutions in this Union, and it would unite under one republican Government all the people and all the territory between the Atlantic and the Pacific, and the Gulf of Mexico and the Arctic Ocean.[19]

Senator D. S. Dickinson of New York, speaking on America's political and commercial future, portrayed North America as a single geographic entity that would become a global economic nexus. A single political structure would emerge, in his view, from the "influences of law more potent than those which prescribe artificial boundaries."[20] Dickinson pinpointed a central theme in American expansionism. Despite the high-flown rhetoric and imagery, Dickinson believed that political union between the provinces and the United States must not be forced.

In the 1840s and 1850s, America's sectional controversy poisoned debates over expansion, no matter what the geographic region or the people in question. The *Washington Union* linked Cuban and provincial annexation, but noted that neither could occur until after the colonials had secured their own independence. *De Bow's Review* in 1850 attributed provincial interest in union to Anglo-French ethnic antagonism and political jealousy. The silent majority of Americans probably favored provincial annexation, but those speaking out, such as Northern newspapers, voiced only free-soil sympathies and commercial ambitions, a fact that did not escape Southern commentators. "If . . . we of the South can believe, that the North desire the annexation of Canada only as an amplitude of our grand and glorious republic, without reference to the question of slavery, we shall open our arms for the reception of a sister who has cast off the rags of monarchy, and comes to our bosom clad in the heavenly livery of republicanism." Sectionalism had muddied the clear struggle between monarchism and republicanism in the American mind. Charles Sumner wrote to English friends that ultimately, the provinces would enter the American union. In addition, "the annexation of that colony to the United States would redress the balance which has been turned in favor of slavery by the annexation of Texas." But he believed also that all parties must consent.[21]

Behind the strident expansionistic stance lay the political and intellectual subtleties that had evolved in the American mind since the Revolution. The *New York Herald* had a reputation for relentless expansionism. Yet, the *Herald* insisted that the United States would never solicit Canadian annexation. The American belief in self-determination, along with respect for British power and a desire for good Anglo-American relations, made Americans refrain from taking actual steps to achieve annexation of the provinces, in marked contrast to the way they lunged ahead to acquire Mexican lands. True to their own ideology, Americans considered mutual consent a vital prerequisite to union with the provinces.[22]

Manifest Destiny had begun to come apart by 1850 under the pressure of political and economic realities. The self-assigned national right to govern North America because of ideological superiority and divine sanction broke into sectional fragments. During the Mexican War, racial prejudice and moral opposition to the war defeated those who sought the annexation of all Mexico. Adding Texas and Oregon to the Union was one thing. After all, Americans had settled those regions and these expatriates sought to sustain republican institutions. And even if the South was more interested in Texas than Oregon, and midwesterners took a reverse view, commercial forces, logic, national ideology, and politics could at least weld a temporary Democratic compromise behind James K. Polk's policy of limited territorial expansion.

The Compromise of 1850 generated a controversy that revealed how territorial acquisitions threatened party and national unity. Polk's diplomatic objectives had exacerbated a national problem. The American destiny did not seem so manifest in the 1850s. Southern expansionists sought a separate destiny in Central America and the Caribbean and viewed possible Canadian annexation as a free-soil plot to control the national government.

Nonetheless, there were many efforts to maintain the momentum of expansion. Franklin Pierce and the Young America movement momentarily sustained Manifest Destiny. Stephen A. Douglas, like many 1850s expansionists, wanted to develop the west and link it with the eastern states. Although a Democrat, Douglas leaned toward exponents of an American commercial empire. Secretary of State William L. Marcy of New York coveted the Hawaiian Islands. William Henry Seward envisioned a vast trade network stretching between Europe and the Orient.[23] This shift toward commercial, rather than territorial expansionism is evident in America's attitude toward the provinces. By 1859 the *New York Times* doubted that annexation of the provinces would be beneficial. The United States currently had enough troubles from its territories, and the *Times* insisted that relations with the provinces should be commercial and social, not political. The *Times* did not even care "whether Canada shall declare her independence."[24]

At the same time, many Americans believed that common language, origins, tastes, habits, interests, and similarity of institutions would produce the eventual union of the provinces and the United States. After 1846, the response to provincial annexationism, reflections on provincial development, and the place of British North America in the ideology of American expansionism during the era of Manifest Destiny all suggest this. The American mission was social and political regeneration according to republican principles, or so its champions maintained.

During the Mexican War, nativist opponents of the all-Mexico drive insisted that non-Anglo-Saxons could never benefit from the American system. These were lesser peoples, unable to understand democracy. This viewpoint explains why English-French antagonism in the provinces attracted American attention. Americans generally viewed the French-Canadians as inferior because of their Roman Catholic religion and peasant culture. The French seemed static. But the Catholic population was not a problem as it had been in Mexico. Anglo-Saxon provincials would overwhelm and assimilate the French, level them upwards as it were, as Americans themselves had done with the French in Louisiana.[25] Because they believed that the English provincials had similar, if not identical, values and ambitions and moved on a parallel historical track, nativists never objected to an eventual provincial-American convergence. Even monarchy would ultimately succumb to North America's democratic destiny.[26]

Literary figures echoed this theme. Upper Canada's "prosperity as a nation will be its ruin as a province. The stronger it grows, the weaker it will become, as a dependency of Britain," Joseph Sansom wrote in 1820. Introducing Thomas Chandler Haliburton's work on Nova Scotia to American readers, Caleb Upham noted that provincials and Americans came from the same origins. Inevitably, the provinces would become independent "and the whole continent, from the Gulf of Mexico to the coast of Labrador, [will] present the unbroken outline of one compact empire of friendly and confederated states."[27]

Others saw the provincials as Americans by geographic location and therefore inclination. Surely they bristled under rule by a distant empire. A reviewer of Joseph Bouchette's two-volume work on the provinces concluded that as more immigrants embittered by Great Britain arrived, they would erode British authority. At the same time, many writers argued that Americans must learn more about the provincials, cultivate them, and encourage their eventual entry into the United States.[28]

This belief in an eventual American-provincial convergence was what some contemporaries and later scholars characterized as the fruit-drop theory of empire. This theory was built upon a sense of historical inevitability. As Parke Godwin noted in 1854, "the fruit of it will fall into our hands when it is ripe, without an officious shaking of the tree. Cuba will be ours, and Canada and Mexico too—if we want them—in due season, and without the wicked imperative of war."[29] The American sense of Manifest Destiny that evolved after the War of 1812 was more than mere imperialism—the rule of alien lands and peoples for profit—and meant more than the annexation of contiguous territory. Americans believed in self-determination, and popular constitutional arguments denied the federal government the license to seize foreign territory at will.

The American example, not conquest, would persuade neighboring peoples to adopt republicanism. The American destiny was manifest by its very success, as Edward Everett argued flamboyantly. Loyalist historian Lorenzo Sabine believed that historical evolution favored provincial independence. The old Jeffersonian Republican editor William Duane agreed. America's progress would tease the provincials beyond endurance. Joining the United States would end forever the French-English clash. Upper and Lower Canada would become mere states, and their ethnic antagonism would dissolve in a federal political structure.[30]

In contrast to the debate over the future of lands taken from Mexico, a broad consensus emerged about the future of the British North American provinces and the United States. By the 1830s Americans had accepted an indefinite sharing of North America with the provincials under the protection of their powerful British rulers. American policy toward the provinces did not display the aggressive thrust implied by Manifest Destiny. The ideological champions of American continentalism believed that eventually the forces of history and nature would erase the boundary between the United States and the provinces. In the meantime, it was perfectly sensible to define the border with Great Britain, which they did in a series of agreements between 1815 and 1871.

American-provincial boundary settlements were of course Anglo-American agreements. Because of the east-to-west settlement patterns these agreements followed the path of westward movement. In each case, American and British agents worked out compromises. Disputed ownership of the islands in Passamaquoddy Bay came first. The Treaty of Ghent prescribed arbitration. In 1819, the British finally left Eastport, which they had occupied early during the War of 1812 and maintained as a trading center between the Maritime provinces and New England. In 1835, a minor controversy over Indian Stream settlement, along the Lower Canada–New Hampshire border arose and quickly died. By contrast, the disputed Maine–New Brunswick border troubled British and American diplomats for many years. Negotiations, arbitrations, discussions, all foundered on Maine's refusal to permit the federal government to barter any of its land. Andrew Jackson even offered Maine a piece of Michigan in exchange for lands lost, but public pressure led Maine officials to reject this.[31]

Minor troubles occurred over timber cutting in 1825. The problem arose from borderlanders sharing frontier resources, local politics compounded by Maine's states' rights fervor, and a series of national governments in Washington unwilling to take action against a state that refused to abide by an international agreement. The federal government feared a border clash and had no desire at all for New Brunswick territory. Manifest Destiny was absent. Henry Clay, while secretary of state, sent up S. B. Barrell as a special agent to collect information on Americans arrested by New Brunswick authorities. Clay did not want local violence complicating affairs of state. Barrell found misunderstandings on both sides and produced a balanced report.[32]

The issue illustrated the problems for the creation of a national foreign policy caused by states' rights and the actions of borderlanders. The borderland was something of a world unto itself. Settlers worked lands and forests oblivious of the international implications of their actions and ambitions. They threatened bothersome officials from across the line, and they protested and petitioned for help when they ran into trouble. In this instance, both nations let the problem drop until Americans poked into the rich Aroostook Valley, where they clashed again with New Brunswick officials. This time the clash produced a bloodless "war" and an Anglo-American crisis by 1839. Several states supported Maine's stand on the high ground of rights and honor. The secretary of war dispatched Winfield Scott to restore peace and let the two governments settle the matter.[33] Although several suggested fortifying the area, congressmen thought this too warlike. Northern representatives, such as Daniel Webster, blanched at the thought of a borderland war.[34]

Officials at all levels in the United States scrambled to accommodate themselves to partisan stands. Whig journals and commercial interests opposed any precipitate action. President Martin Van Buren wanted to settle the matter, but wanted Maine in the Democratic camp. He had already alienated American borderlanders by pursuing neutrality in the provincial rebellions of 1837 and 1838. Webster and the British minister in Washington worked out an arrangement to let both sides retreat with grace. Maine's governor, John Fairfield, postured, yet tried to avoid violence. Winfield Scott soothed politicians, the public, and New Brunswick officials alike.

Daniel Webster was the real peacemaker. He planted stories in the Maine press with the help of Francis Smith, a local newspaperman and borderland entrepreneur with interests in a telegraph linking the provinces and the American Northeast. Webster used secret funds to create a network throughout Maine supporting compromise. A Whig sweep in 1840 reduced the militant voices in Maine's legislature. Webster invited Maine and Massachusetts officials to his negotiations with Lord Ashburton and worked to persuade the Senate when the treaty came forward. All the while, he argued that continued peace was necessary to recover from the depression of

1837. The Webster-Ashburton Treaty of 1842 thus resolved the American-provincial boundary from the St. Croix River to the St. Lawrence River. Americans were satisfied with the treaty and the boundary settlement. Together, they reinforced the Anglo-American détente that resolved a series of outstanding issues, despite lingering distrust, rivalry, and occasional diplomatic outbursts.[35]

The northeastern boundary settlement demonstrated that after 1815 Americans foresaw an indefinite sharing of North America with the British provincials. Administrations from James Monroe down through Andrew Jackson, Martin Van Buren, and John Tyler, despite continuing suspicions of British intentions, worked for a peaceful northern frontier, although, as in the case of Maine, they were forced to acknowledge states' rights as a powerful doctrine that could cost national political parties dearly. The realization that both the Americans and the British would suffer in the event of a rupture reinforced the cause of mutual accommodation. The provinces were vulnerable to any American assault. On the other hand, the British navy could maul American shipping and coastal regions. And a war would produce havoc in the borderlands, as Americans knew from the 1812–14 experience. The complex of ideas and forces behind Manifest Destiny reinforced the trend toward accommodation as did the sense of Anglo-Saxon commonality that slowly permeated American ruling circles, despite popular Anglophobia. The criminal extradition clause of the Webster-Ashburton Treaty, applying both to the provinces and the United States, underscored détente. Murderers, pirates, arsonists, forgers, and thieves could no longer find a ready refuge across the line. The treaty also stipulated shared use of the St. John River, with wood products crossing the border free of duties, and joint use of the Detroit River and the St. Lawrence River at the Long Sault Rapids and Barnhart Islands. Beyond that, it fixed the line from Lake Superior to Rainy Lake.[36]

To some extent, this was backing and filling. The convention of 1818 fixed the forty-ninth parallel as the dividing line from Lake of the Woods to the Rocky Mountains with joint occupation of the Oregon territory. John Quincy Adams wanted to confine the British north of that line and keep them away from the Mississippi River Basin. Joseph Sansom, traveling in Canada shortly after the War of 1812, remarked on the surveyors hard at work. The people of the borderland wanted the line fixed, and this was "of infinitely greater importance to the peace and welfare of the two countries than the possession of a few millions of useless acres on one side or the other." Newspapers, politicians, and travelers noted that the British took provincial development seriously in the 1820s. Throughout, writers and national leaders had approached the northeastern boundary question as a matter to be settled, not an excuse to press claims.[37] Manifest Destiny in its aggressive territorial form did not seem to apply to the determination of much of the provincial-American boundary.

Manifest Destiny was a factor, however, in the bid for Oregon. American claims rested upon Captain Robert Gray's discovery of the mouth of the Columbia River, the Lewis and Clark expedition, and John Jacob Astor's fur trading venture at the river mouth, Astoria. Actually, the entire coast north of California was open for competition, and American entrepreneurs were the first frontiersmen. These Yankee traders had no interest in land. They stopped in Oregon over one hundred times, but only to pick up otter furs for the China trade. Settlements, such as Astoria, were essentially factories, or trading stations. After the British ejected the Americans from Oregon's coast during the War of 1812, John Quincy Adams resurrected his country's claims at Ghent. After 1814, he sustained the American toehold in the Pacific Northwest.[38]

In the 1820s Representative John Floyd of Virginia spearheaded a modest effort to claim Oregon in Congress. A Kentuckian originally, Floyd had a grand westward vision, and wanted European power removed from the Western Hemisphere. He also knew William Clark, Thomas Hart Benton of Missouri, and some of the Astorians. Floyd's persistence succeeded only in bringing Oregon to the attention of Americans. Newspaper editors argued that the United States should one day possess the country, but Congress accepted John Quincy Adams's example and took no direct action. Congressmen were concerned that aggressive moves would violate the convention of 1818 and might unnecessarily antagonize the British at a time when the United States sought commercial access to other parts of the British Empire. Moreover, Oregon might threaten the integrity of the Union; many believed that the republic would disintegrate if it grew too large. Oregon, a continent away from most Americans, was of unproven value and might not yield much of a return for the effort to acquire it.[39]

In the 1830s, American missionaries established stations among the Indians in Oregon. Hall Kelley's publicity attracted a trickle of settlers and Benton's junior colleague from Missouri, Senator Lewis F. Linn, emerged as the next congressional champion. Then, "Oregon fever" struck. American migrants trekked to the distant Willamette Valley in the thousands and established a claim that the British could not ignore. The Hudson's Bay Company executed a planned withdrawal to the southern tip of Vancouver Island. The British effort to establish a countersettlement with the Puget Sound Agricultural Company failed. Now a powerful lobby favored canceling joint Anglo-American occupation of Oregon and partitioning the territory.[40]

Anglo-American discussions in 1818 had produced a tacit agreement to divide North America along the forty-ninth parallel to the Pacific. John Quincy Adams, who advised Richard Rush on the Pacific holdings prior to the Monroe Doctrine of 1823, could not imagine that any European country would settle in the Pacific Northwest. Although he wanted to press for a British cession up to fifty-one degrees, he accepted projecting the forty-ninth parallel to the Pacific. Not all American politicans were certain that the United States would ever expand that far, but doubts about an oversized republic subsided in the era of Manifest Destiny.

Oregon began to appear more promising than it had seemed at first glance, despite its reputation for perpetual rain. Albert Gallatin spoke with one of Astor's Columbia River agents and concluded that north of Puget Sound, the coast was bleak, but Puget Sound itself was a treasure. Captain Charles Wilkes, stopping there while on his Pacific charting expedition, waxed rhapsodic about the local wealth in fish, furs, and trees. The fur trade was dying by 1840, but many Americans still sought forests, harbors, and land.[41]

In 1835, Secretary of State John Forsyth sent William Slacum to Oregon as a special agent. Slacum went by sea and reported in 1837. The United States had to protect settlers and traders from the Hudson's Bay Company, which monopolized the Indian trade. Like Adams and Gallatin, Slacum believed that control of "Pugitt's" Sound was crucial. Thomas Hart Benton and other Democrats agreed. Apart from Slacum's dispatches, and the Wilkes reports, congressmen could consult a book by Robert Greenhow, a State Department translator and librarian. He argued that north of the forty-ninth parallel the land was rugged and barren, with sterile soils in small parcels unsuited for cultivation and "little prospect of the diffusion of the pure Anglo-Saxon race." Below that line Americans had a clear title by rights of discovery and occupation. American ideology explained the British presence in Oregon in terms of the historical struggle between the forces of tyranny, aristocracy, monopoly, restrictive land tenure, and state-imposed religion, and the forces of enlightened republicanism.[42]

Several forces lay behind the carefully defined American drive for Oregon. Some 5,000 settlers lived in the territory by 1845. North Pacific whaling interests and Pacific traders wanted Puget Sound, for once on the northwest coast, Americans looked farther west. The extreme Democratic expansionists called for all the territory up to the southern limit of the old Russian claim, fifty-four degrees, forty minutes. Polk blustered for the sake of party unity, but wavered in cabinet discussions, and accepted compromise. The United States was barely prepared for any war in 1846, let alone against mighty Britain. Few wanted to confront the British, whatever their views on the ongoing struggle between republicanism and monarchism in North America. Western extremists in the Senate demurred, but the Oregon treaty passed handily, 41 to 14.[43]

The Oregon Treaty and the boundary compromise both proved popular. Some papers expressed the oft-repeated conviction that the provinces would someday join the Union. The *North American Review* denounced the sense of crisis as trumped up. Anglo-Saxon unity demanded a peaceful settlement. War would be a disgrace. W. S. Allen wrote from St. Louis to Caleb Cushing that "the ties of common blood, language & laws, and of vast & varied mutual interests" forbade a conflict.[44]

The acquisition of Oregon was not part of any plan to eject the British from North America, even though Americans assumed that Great Britain would eventually leave. While reserving the right of expropriation, the United States even guaranteed the lands of the Puget Sound Agricultural Company between the Columbia River and the new boundary. The treaty was motivated by the desire to secure national commercial and security interests in the Pacific Northwest, to get along with the British, and to protect the American settlers who had migrated to the west coast. As other cross-boundary issues arose, American administrations approached them in the same spirit. The Oregon Treaty reinforced the détente established by the Webster-Ashburton Treaty.

On the whole, American authorities believed that the British acted in good faith and refused to manufacture incidents out of the complaints of citizens. James Buchanan told Richard Pakenham in 1846, for example, that provincial claims over timber rights in islands near Sault St. Marie should go to a Michigan court. Buchanan, who was well disposed toward the British, believed that courts on both sides of the boundary had rendered findings on the principles of justice and law, unswayed by patriotism. When provincials complained about Americans blocking navigation of the Richelieu River into Missiquoi Bay at the head of Lake Champlain, Buchanan sent the material to Governors John Young and Carlos Coolidge of New York and Vermont to settle, the matter "proceeding, as it does, from the subjects of a friendly power in a neighboring province." In 1850, the government decided to build a lighthouse on a reef in Lake Erie near the Niagara River. Congress appropriated funds to purchase the site, but after discussions, the British ceded it willingly.[45] Such diplomatic largesse was easy enough given the tiny interests at stake. But by 1846, if not by 1842, Anglo-American détente about sharing North America had emerged, whatever the rhetorical excesses of Manifest Destiny extremists.

Chapter 5.

The Provinces

and Antebellum

Entrepreneurs

Advantages too have resulted to our agricultural interests from the state of trade between Canada and our territories and States bordering on the St. Lawrence and the Lakes, which may prove more than equivalent to the loss sustained by the discrimination made to favor the trade of the northern colonies with the West Indies.
—Andrew Jackson, 1831

Secret Treasury Inspector T. L. Thompson was on a hunt in the summer of 1843. He traveled northern New York, crisscrossing the lakes and rivers to ferret out borderland smugglers.[1] The smugglers probably knew about him and others like him. After all, they had been plying borderland waters and backroads from the Bay of Fundy to Michilimackinac since 1783, even earlier counting illegal trade between English and French colonials. Unless Thompson was unusually skillful or fortunate, locals would soon know that a Washington agent was on the prowl. But Thompson took his detective's role to heart, tracing customs evaders by rumor and eavesdropping on the gossip of border towns, steamers, and markets. He was, nonetheless, inevitably doomed to frustration. From Alexander Hamilton forward, no knowledgeable observer of the borderland trade seriously expected laws, investigations, or snooping to do more than inconvenience those determined to smuggle along the American-provincial frontier.

Lax border customs officers around Rochester, New York, irritated Thompson. A lack of vigilance only encouraged the well-organized smugglers. On some occasions, Thompson masqueraded as a smuggler himself to test customs men, but aroused no suspicions at all. At Burlington, Vermont, the officers seemed more alert and thorough. Even so, legitimate businessmen everywhere smuggled for extra profit, using their reputations to camouflage contraband. Merchants at Buffalo and Rochester colluded to smuggle fine woolens and cottons. Captains of lake vessels falsified manifests and transferred goods at will. New York and Boston businessmen had extensive contacts in Canada and traveled back and forth regularly transporting goods illegally. At Rouses Point, at New York's northern end of Lake Champlain, ferrymen convoyed smugglers at night. Canadian officers had no better luck than Thompson and other American agents in suppressing contraband trade.[2]

The articles carried were often those that moved legitimately on the surface. Liquor, tea, tobacco, cottons and woolens, and leather goods crossed the border legally and illegally. American-provincial trade blossomed in the spring. The 1844 smuggling season opened in April, when the ice had cleared from the rivers and lakes, and Thompson expected a busy time. Buffalo and Niagara now seemed the favored locations, and he suspected many provincial traders along the Welland Canal because they were so well situated. Provincial growth created new markets for smugglers who moved into the provincial hinterland.

Thompson learned much—names, methods, locations, merchandise, prices, markets—but he was unable to translate this knowledge into an effective campaign against the lawbreakers. He exposed a few, who apparently retired, but others replaced them. As late as December, he was off for Montreal to observe smuggling over the frozen St. Lawrence River.[3]

Thompson's letters describe a flourishing borderland trade network from the Champlain Valley to the Niagara River banks. Had he gone to the Atlantic Coast, he would have found the same conditions there, along the St. Croix Valley and in the Bay of Fundy. Merchants in both the United States and the provinces worked a profitable business in legal and illegal trade. Smuggling had a long history. It developed along the frontier well before the War of 1812, contributed to the frustration of Jefferson's Embargo of 1807–8, and undermined James Madison's war effort against the British.

In short, there was nothing startling about this American-provincial trade, and that is the point. Treasury Department reports, the dispatches of American consuls in the provinces during the 1830s, the impressions of travelers, items in newspapers, and letters and speeches by leading politicians all suggest the expanding economic relationship between the United States and the provinces after 1815. American entrepreneurs, whether legitimate or not, looked north, and where laws prohibited trade, businessmen and speculators alike evaded or defied them.

Several historical developments stimulated borderland traffic. First the population of the borderland region mushroomed following the War of 1812. Americans no longer had free access to provincial lands after 1815, but fewer sought them, because the way to the American west was now clear. Before the Battle of Tippecanoe, the Indians in the Old Northwest had barred American settlement. But Tippecanoe and the death of Tecumseh at the Battle of the Thames in October 1814 broke Indian power in the region and severed tribal contacts with the British. Between 1790 and 1860, the center of gravity of the American population shifted westward, from near Baltimore, Maryland, to near Chillicothe, Ohio. In 1800, 7 percent of the population lived in the West. By 1820, this had reached 25 percent. Western New York, northern Ohio, and Michigan accordingly filled in.

Other developments accompanied this demographic shift. In northern New York, speculators and settlers moved back toward the border after the war and developed towns and farms along the St. Lawrence River and the lakeshores. Roads pushed south through the wilderness to replace the dirt trails of the prewar period. Cities such as Toledo, Cleveland, and Erie grew on the south shore of Lake Erie. Indiana and Illinois became states in 1816 and 1818; Michigan in 1837. After the Erie Canal opened in 1825, the cheaper rates benefited not only merchants and traders but also passengers and migrants. Inexpensive passage encouraged settlement.

Upper Canada also expanded after 1815, although not at the same rate, nor to the same level, as the adjacent states. As recent enemies, Americans were suspect and could not take up land grants until seven years after swearing a loyalty oath. Provincial conservatives remained hostile toward Americans, although their distrust was not likely shared by the bulk of the provincial population. The British tried to solve the problem of underpopulation of their North American provinces without wooing American immigrants. The end of the war in Europe encouraged some migrants to head for British North America. These new arrivals partially compensated for the loss of American settlers, although with the Indian defeat in the Old Northwest, the Yankee migration to Upper Canada would likely have slowed anyway.

From 1815 to 1825, about 90,000 settlers arrived in Nova Scotia and New Brunswick. Despite confused land policies, Upper Canada townships, such as Guelph and Goderich, appeared in the 1820s. The population of Upper Canada reached 150,000 in 1824 and 400,000 in 1838. The provincial economy proved erratic, unable to match the lurching, but generally prosperous economy in the United States. This strong economy, more plentiful and cheaper land, and higher wages attracted many provincials to the United States.

Americans contributed directly to provincial expansion after 1815, although not as farmers. Many invested or began businesses. Ohio iron makers came to Gosfield township in 1831. E. W. Hyman from Pennsylvania built a tannery at London in 1835. Many New York businessmen, such as J. B. Yates, of Chittenango, who financed part of the Welland Canal, saw the developing provinces as a good investment. American physicians, preachers, and educators migrated, either temporarily or permanently. Among the preachers, Methodists were active and successful.[4] Few Americans came to the Maritimes, although shipping records reveal a slow, steady drain of Maritime provincials to the United States between 1815 and 1838. Ulster Irish emigrating to New Brunswick walked over the border to settle in northern Maine. And American timber merchants moved into New Brunswick or speculated in New Brunswick lands. Consequently, the St. Croix Valley became a single socioeconomic region, the border notwithstanding.[5]

As settlements and local prosperity developed after 1815, transportation systems connected the borderland economy. North-south communication lines have always dominated American-Canadian relations, but the Great Lakes Basin was linked by a complex, interlocking system. Despite the ice that jammed the river for five months a year, the St. Lawrence River remained a significant trade route and Montreal an important entrepôt for Americans along the northern border west of the Champlain Valley, even after the Erie Canal opened. British and provincial leaders tried to improve this waterway. In 1829 they completed the Welland Canal with American financial and engineering help. And if they lived west of the Niagara land neck, Americans also used the Welland, as New York officials frequently noted.

The water transport network on the Great Lakes was particularly impressive. Before 1812, sailings on the Great Lakes were irregular. After 1815, timetables appeared. The first steamboat, *Walk-in-the-*

Water, was built in 1818 at Black Rock, near Buffalo. By 1827, fifty-three American vessels plied the upper lakes and scheduled steam-ships sailed the St. Lawrence River and Lake Ontario. By 1830, Midwestern canals carried the Northwest's produce to the lakes. In New York, the branch from Syracuse reached Oswego in 1828 and brought prosperity to that small, former fur port. By 1843, sixteen American and thirty-eight provincial steam vessels chugged back and forth. American tonnage on the lakes, however, tripled that of the provinces. By 1844, tonnage along the Erie Canal–Great Lakes route exceeded that on the Mississippi River. Both American and provincial borderlanders participated in America's national economy.[6]

Improved diplomatic relations provided new opportunities for American entrepreneurs in the provinces. A commercial convention in 1815 called for the mutual appointment of consuls in provincial and American ports. But American efforts to establish a comprehensive trade agreement with Great Britain failed. When American diplomat Jonathan Russell read the terms of the convention, he wondered why it did not regulate trade between the United States and British North America. Russell recalled Albert Gallatin's concern for such an arrangement, but decided that the British would come to terms eventually.[7] In common with other senior American politicians and statesmen, Russell believed that the United States would eventually dominate North America economically and diplomatically, as the Monroe Doctrine of 1823 suggested.

Anglo-American commerce remained unregulated. The colonial legend that enormous profits were to be had from the carrying and supply trade in the West Indies still bedazzled American states-men. This belief, as well as the assertion of interests in the guise of rights, led Americans to look south, not north, in economic negotiations with Great Britain. After the War of 1812, the British conceded ground slowly, reluctantly, and only partially. Provincial trade was only a secondary issue. Therefore, continued British protection of imperial trade, American retaliatory efforts in 1818, 1820, and 1823, and sporadic, unsuccessful diplomatic negotiations characterized American-provincial trade until 1830.

At the same time, even without trade agreements, the borderland reality guaranteed that trade across the northern frontier continued. Americans and provincials living near the line from the Maritimes to the Detroit frontier exchanged produce and goods no matter what the circumstances. Even during the War of 1812, the British interest in reinforcing New England's virtual neutrality and the occupation of Eastport and then Castine had imposed near-peacetime commercial conditions on the northeast coast until 1814. New England and New York exchange with the Maritimes had always been literally an extension of the northern American coasting trade.

After 1815, the New England fisheries remained a powerful interest and had a formidable champion in Secretary of State John Quincy Adams. Adams also pursued American access to the St. Lawrence River and provincial ports. For some time, however, many Americans saw the provinces merely as way stations in the West Indies trade. So for some traders, prying open provincial ports was synonymous with opening the West Indies. They viewed American-provincial business as a pawn in the larger game. In the 1820s, successive British and American acts closed and opened their North American ports to one another's vessels. Some stability ensued in 1825 when Halifax became a free port for Americans. Pictou and Sydney followed suit in 1828. All the while, smuggling satisfied local needs. Entrepreneurs on the Atlantic coast and along the interior borderland continued to exploit opportunities as they saw them, and ignored both Anglo-American agreements and boundaries.[8]

Congress collected data on American-provincial trade after the War of 1812 solely to bolster its negotiations with Great Britain. Import revenues from the provinces went from $62,154 in 1802 to a prewar high of $244,125 in 1807, then plummeted to $26,552 by 1813. But in 1815, revenues leaped to $1,386,620, about 50 percent of the duties on all goods imported from British colonies in North America including the West Indies. As the United States drew more from other British regions, the North American share of such revenues dropped to about 10 percent. American exports to the provinces, mostly destined for the West Indies by way of Halifax, rose in value to $1,396,815 in 1815 and $3,038,995 in 1819, or nearly three-quarters of all exports to all the British colonies. Although this income was only a small portion of government revenue, the increase was notable. In 1825, exports of $2,556,032 constituted about .06 percent of all exports to Great Britain, which received about 42 percent of America's total exports.[9] The British permitted many commodities, such as wood products, seeds and grains, provisions and livestock, skins, pot and pearl ashes, pig iron, and tallow, to enter the provinces duty free.

American efforts to export industrial products served regional economic interests and eventually pried the West Indies markets open. John Quincy Adams wanted free access in 1823 only for goods that could compete with provincial exports to the West Indies.[10] Henry Clay in 1817 spoke of reciprocity, but he clearly wanted access to the West Indies for American merchantmen and producers. The provinces, he insisted, could not be serious competitors in this trade. British efforts to exclude the Americans would drive up prices, render the supply irregular because of winter ice on the St. Lawrence, and lay the inland provinces open to harmful retaliation. By 1826, some congressmen became convinced that the provincial trade was as important as the trade with the British West Indies.

Conflicting seaboard and interior interests surfaced in the 1827 Anglo-American trade discussions. It seemed a reprise of the eve of the War of 1812. In the House of Representatives, Rollin Mallary of Vermont noted that commercial retaliation against Britain to open the West Indies would only ravage the interior trade. Churchill Cambreling of New York, on the other hand, saw the provinces as commercial enemies and the West Indies as allies. But Cambreling's colleague, Michael Hoffman, argued that two trades existed; open American navigation of the St. Lawrence River was the only link between them. Prohibit all border trade, and Americans in the northern frontier states would lose markets, neighbors, and family. Furthermore, as only an imaginary line separated Americans and provincials for many hundreds of miles, legislation in Hoffman's view could never block illegal trade, and even an army of collectors policing the border would only mean a greater number of corrupt officials, smugglers, and thieves.[11]

Senators agreed. The provinces were caught in the middle of Anglo-American competition. Several senators from northern states understood borderland integration and defended their constituents' interests. Ultimately, they sponsored a bill that would have prohibited nonintercourse with the provinces. This bill passed the House in 1827, but failed in the Senate. Anglo-American trade negotiations remained focused on the West Indies. But the debate exposed an American-provincial lobby based on the borderland with champions in the United States Congress.

Anglo-American trade relations began to stabilize in the late 1820s, despite the series of mutual recriminations, restrictions, and retaliations. The United States pursued freer trade with several European countries, such as the Hanseatic Republics. The British Empire was a mercantile prize that outstripped all others, and pursuit of a formal arrangement with Britain was part of America's overall commercial expansion dating from 1783. The free-trade movement that gathered momentum in Great Britain assisted the United States. So did doubts about the ultimate value of the colonies. Richard Rush reported from London that increasing numbers in Parliament attacked the colonial system. Britain was also on the verge of abolishing slavery within the empire. The West Indies declined in overall British trade, and the old planter lobby had become feeble.

At the same time, changing conditions implied that the growing provinces might become economically more valuable to Americans than the potential trade from free access to the West Indies. By 1843, the Chambly Canal opened on the upper Richelieu River. New canals bypassed the shoal waters of the upper Hudson River to connect lower New York with the Lake George–Lake Champlain system. Navigation was clear from New York City to the St. Lawrence River, which still served Americans in the Great Lakes Basin during ice-free months. Montreal and Quebec absorbed some American produce sent down the Great Lakes and through the Welland Canal. Northern Vermonters and New Yorkers, who had traded with the provincials since the 1780s and 1790s, were increasingly sensitive to any British curbs on borderland trade. American diplomats therefore married two objectives by trying to open both the West Indies and the North American provinces.

Andrew Jackson and the Democrats promised in the election of 1828 that they would secure access to the British colonies where Adams and Clay had failed. Actually, Jackson merely continued the Adams-Clay policy, which in turn had sustained old American ambitions dating from the Confederation. Louis McLane opened talks with Lord Aberdeen's government in November of 1829. Jackson's diplomats conceded that the provinces should have special privileges in the West Indies trade, but threatened economic retaliation against them nevertheless. Americans believed that once restrictions were removed, they would easily eclipse the provincials as suppliers. In 1830, the British relented. The West Indies came open to American vessels. An old sore in Anglo-American relations was allowed to heal with important implications for American-provincial commerce.[12]

The crucial American legislation regarding provincial trade came 2 March 1831. Jackson had sent Congress considerable information in early January, along with the text of the agreement. Congress passed uniform customs levies on imports entering American and British colonial ports, and waived fees for American carriers entering lake or river ports along the frontiers. In addition, vessels had to carry specific licenses. With this foundation, the United States could appoint consuls in provincial ports. John Morrow became the first, in Halifax, 15 December 1830. American consuls had to be entrepreneurs themselves. They lived solely on commissions from trade promoted with their home country.[13]

While the diplomats moved closer to the eventual Anglo-American accord, the people living on both sides of the border continued to develop their own economy. Americans exploited opportunities in the provinces as well as in their own country. And they had provincial counterparts. Shifting laws and diplomatic understandings had only slight meaning for borderlanders who already saw the boundary as an illusion.

At the eastern end of the frontier in Maine the Penobscot customs collector operated along the St. Croix Valley. The American-provincial integration here stemmed from custom, family ties, history, proximity, and isolation from the economic centers of either country. Joshua Carpenter, the collector from 1828 to 1833, reported that spreading settlement stimulated local trade, especially winter smuggling when snow and ice made travel by sleigh over lakes and through woods easy. Roads to interior lumber camps on the Schoodac Lakes became small-scale commercial highways. Eastport remained a contraband center in the Bay of Fundy after the British withdrawal in 1819. Fishermen routinely smuggled as a sideline. Even United States infantry stationed at Houlton carted goods from New Brunswick in army wagons to augment army pay and supply services.

When Britain and the United States signed their agreement in 1830, the traffic swamped the available inspectors. Collector Ripley at Eastport complained that he could not control the many small vessels involved. No other frontier area, he ventured, had such "systematic & successful smuggling, as the port of Passamaquoddy." The presence or absence of tariffs and laws made no difference. Violations increased with the spread of population up the St. Croix River.[14]

The Champlain Valley and western New York duplicated the Maritime experience. As they had for decades, Vermont sheep farmers secretly marched their flocks into Lower Canada, sold the carcasses, and brought the skins back for American markets. At Ogdensburg, on the New York side of the St. Lawrence, cross-border trade persisted through the War of 1812. David Parish, a wealthy local businessman and smuggler, built a mansion on the river and facing the province that contributed so much to his fortune. The local ferryman was a well-known smuggler. Agents for Upper and Lower Canadian merchants traveled freely, taking large consignments of goods to Montreal and York.

The local American collector, Baron Doty, mixed rumor and fact in his reports. English businessmen advertised in the local papers and took up temporary residence in Ogdensburg. He had heard of caches of English merchandise on the provincial side. "From these indications as well as from the fact that many foreigners and other adventurers are visiting this region within the last month," he wrote in September of 1830, "there can be but little doubt that the business of smuggling is intended to be carried on extensively on this frontier this fall and Winter."

In the well-populated Niagara River Valley, smugglers crossed at will, running goods to and from the Erie Canal by 1830. The locals knew all the revenue agents and watched them closely. Even when seizures occurred, witnesses refused to testify. Merchants mobbed suspected informers at night. The Lewiston firm of John Young & Company apparently had an extensive contraband trade. But Seymour Scovell, the Niagara collector in 1831, could prove nothing. Collectors who brought charges risked nuisance countercharges of taking bribes or misusing government funds.

A borderland conspiracy of silence subverted the revenue laws. Local opinion simply did not view smuggling as a crime. Many Upper Canadians, who came originally from the United States, treated the border as they would the boundary between New York and Vermont. "Travellers cannot, therefore, understand why they should not be allowed to visit their friends in the United States, without being subjected to the payment of duties on their harness, waggons, etc., nothing of the kind being required by the existing regulations of the Canadian government."[15]

Everywhere along the frontier, customs collectors told the same story. At Buffalo, Pierre Barker complained of provincial merchants who seduced Americans into smuggling by offering high prices. Of course, American borderland entrepreneurs needed no British agents to tempt them. British goods were cheap and openly advertised. Americans crossed the border and bought new suits because tailored clothing was not dutiable, whereas cloth was. In Detroit, Andrew Mack vented his frustration. Americans and provincials were so similar in appearance, language, produce, taste, and wants they were indistinguishable on either side of the border.[16]

Through the 1830s, American and British officials smoothed over commercial misunderstandings and accepted the thriving continental economy. Americans anticipated that their free enterprise system would draw the provinces into their own national economy. This would boost American wealth. In 1837, a Massachusetts land agent expected increased traffic on the road north from the Aroostook region to inflate local real estate values over the next few years. Merchants in Maine and Newburyport, Massachusetts, wanted all British North American ports declared open for trade. By 1840, they moved freely into most New Brunswick and Nova Scotia towns, as well as Charlottetown, on tiny Prince Edward Island. Momentary troubles and bad feelings in Maine over the northeastern boundary had no impact on these entrepreneurial ambitions.[17]

The effect of the increased border trade was to mark American consuls in provincial ports important local figures and valuable sources of information for the State Department. These men reflected Jacksonian entrepreneurship both officially and personally. They enhanced their usefulness by collecting political as well as economic information and receiving fees for services rendered. They sent down to Washington the proceedings of the provincial assemblies, newspapers, and publications on trade regulations.

John Morrow in Halifax, Nova Scotia, reported on American vessels calling at Pictou, Yarmouth, Sydney, and Bridgport to load coal for New England. He eventually appointed agents at several of these small outports. Provincial papers in Morrow's dispatches portrayed local bustle and opportunity. Traffic dwindled over the winter months, but from 1835 to 1837 the tonnage of vessels in trade with the United States doubled. The Maritime–New England commerce employed over 300 vessels and about 2,000 Americans by 1838. The balance in 1838–39 favored the United States by $171,287.[18] This sum was tiny in the context of America's overall foreign trade, but it spurred the consuls to forecast a prosperous American-provincial commercial future.

One of the most politically adroit consuls, Israel Andrews, arrived in St. John, New Brunswick, in 1843. Born in Campobello, New Brunswick, he came to Eastport with his family at the age of four and became a naturalized American. Once appointed consul, a post he had pursued with some vigor, he deluged the State Department with information about the provinces. By 1846, many Americans had entered New Brunswick's lumber business, building steam sawmills. Andrews anticipated the political ramifications of the growing trade he saw would develop. The provincials wanted new markets, and if the United States lowered its duties, trade would grow "to be soon followed by a closer political union between the British North American Colonies and the United States of America."[19]

The American government appointed other consuls at Sydney, Cape Breton, in 1837 and Pictou, Nova Scotia, in 1838. Between 1833 and 1850, they shipped home an avalanche of economic, social, and political information as well as personal advice on future American policy toward the provinces. They all concluded that trade would grow and that the provincials had similar ambitions, ideas, interests, tastes, and values as Americans. The provinces and the states did indeed seem to be converging. Consuls encouraged American entrepreneurs, as well as United States policymakers, to appreciate the opportunities offered by the provinces. They continually pressured the State Department for the authority to appoint agents in smaller ports near their stations to stimulate further development. In the process, many consuls built tiny bureaucratic fiefdoms. In 1846, Luther Brackett, from his base in Pictou, controlled five such commercial vassals at Charlottetown, Prince Edward Island, and St. John's, Newfoundland, and three other ports. And after 1853, the completed telegraph between Halifax and Washington, D.C. enabled consuls to make their views heard with more immediacy.

B. Hammatt Norton, long a consul at Pictou, was enthralled with prospects for the future. In his view, once the British relaxed control over local coal and iron reserves, a large manufacturing establishment would emerge to supply the projected Pacific railroad. "*American Capital* and *American Enterprise*," would overcome all obstacles. "Believing as I do, that the whole continent of America, is destined at no distant day to come under the rule of the Anglo-American, I am of opinion, that facilities for frequent intercourse should be fostered by our Government, as far as is practicable." Commerce had political ramifications. Maritimers would be Americanized and a continental union could well result.[20] Norton's vision of an Anglo-Saxon continentalism inspired many on both sides of the frontier.

Consuls did not appear in Lower and Upper Canada until the 1850s. But information from businessmen and newspapers as well as trade statistics confirmed the impressions the Maritime consuls created. Speaking before the American Institute in 1841, James Tallmadge of New York noted the growth of the borderland trade and emphasized its value for the United States. He and others pointed to Oswego as an example of a lake port flourishing because of provincial markets. Oswego flour mills ground Canadian wheat for shipment to Kingston and down the St. Lawrence River. One-half of the sugar received at Oswego (nearly 4.5 million pounds) and 27 percent of the city's merchandise by weight went to the provinces in 1846. Railroad interests in Boston sought to compete with New York in part by tapping provincial trade. Boston's agricultural imports from the central provinces climbed from $5,204 in 1840 to $1,848,797 in 1849.[21]

After 1815 provincial news in American newspapers consisted mostly of reprints from provincial presses. The *Montreal Herald* and the *Quebec Gazette* were favorite sources, but American editors also created composite stories with commentary about American-provincial relations. General news items and economic issues appeared most often, suggesting the image of the provinces as sources of financial opportunities. New Englanders were concerned about access to the Maritime ports, the fisheries, and the plaster trade. New Yorkers looked to business conditions in Montreal. All reported changes in British or provincial regulations that would affect merchants.

Various periodicals covered a range of provincial affairs. *Niles' Register* published duties currently in force at provincial ports. The periodicals applauded when Halifax and St. John became free ports in 1818. They reported the provincial slump that occurred immediately after 1815, but noted that American pot and pearl ashes and lumber that floated down the St. Lawrence from northern New York still found a ready market in Montreal. In 1817, articles appeared on the discovery by New York merchants that Lower Canada had become a good wheat market due to British government contracts. Statistics seemed to dazzle Americans. Niles noted that the number of American vessels trading into all the provinces had risen from 250 in 1800 to 846 in 1815. Niles also reported on the growing provincial–British West Indies trade. Niles doubted that the provinces profited Britain, but they competed with the United States and sought unfair advantages. In another area of interest, the *National Intelligencer* noted that Nova Scotia authorities banned American vessels, thus monopolizing the plaster carrying trade to American markets and discriminating against the United States.[22]

Periodicals after 1815 advertised opportunities in the provinces for American entrepreneurs. Settlers arrived in small clusters in Quebec and other ports. Most such immigrants moved on to Upper Canada and often entered the United States. The provincial population grew, albeit slowly. American commentary often reflected national ideology. British institutions and methods were socially and economically stifling, and despite British liberalism, the provinces would eventually seek independence. The St. Lawrence River, as Niles noted, was important for Americans.

American interests soon realized that competition and cooperation for mutual profit were only a step apart. The Welland Canal, when completed, sent trade to Oswego as well as to Kingston and Montreal. New York City merchants were ardent free traders, and when they saw the growing exchange between the United States and the provinces, they argued for reciprocal trade as a path to eventual political union. The *Evening Star* stated in 1835 that "geographic position, kindred interests, language and laws, sympathy of origin and destiny, to say nothing of the oppressions of a hard-hearted stepmother, must ultimately, sooner or later, place the Canadas under the *Aegis* of this empire." At the same time, however, New York's canal champions viewed the provincial canal system as a competitor. Governor William L. Marcy noted that Canadian improvements would draw business to Montreal and away from American cities. Once through the Welland and into Lake Ontario American produce in provincial bottoms would float east, away from American centers. Enlarging the Erie, or building an American ship canal around Niagara Falls, would offset provincial competition.[23]

Ambitious Americans saw a connection between economic opportunities and national expansion. This idea received fuller expression during the reciprocity era of the 1850s, the next phase in the development of American-provincial economic relations. But in the 1820s, the idea of trade as a prelude to political union rarely surfaced. Instead, American entrepreneurs dwelled almost exclusively on expanding opportunities in the provinces. Newspaper and periodical items on provincial economic affairs sustained the theme of opportunity. Merchants were kept regularly informed about provincial prices and duties. Quebec's foreign trade data appeared frequently. In 1800, eighty or ninety vessels a season had entered and cleared; by 1829, the figure was over 800. Halifax trade also expanded. The provincial population grew. Montreal had 30,000 people by 1821. Nova Scotia's population rose from 82,000 to 128,000 from 1817 to 1827. In 1823 Pictou, Nova Scotia, had a flour mill where two years before, all flour had to be imported. Although provincial finances usually seemed rickety, and cycles of expansion and contraction generated uncertainty, the overall impression was of progress.

As it might be expected, Niles took a great interest in provincial growth. By the fall of 1825, more settlers were arriving, increased acreage came under cultivation, and future prospects seemed highly favorable. Between 1820 and 1826, Upper Canada's population reportedly grew from 50,000 to 200,000. British and provincial governments, as well as New York capitalists, made heavy investments in steamboats, banks, and canals. The Chambly, Lachine, Rideau, and Welland canals showed that the provinces could follow America's entrepreneurial example. Both American and provincial vessels used the Welland when it opened in 1829. Horatio Gates, an emigrant American entrepreneur, became a successful provincial businessman and one of the founders of the Bank of Montreal. He regularly reported to Albany papers on the Montreal market as though it were part of the American economic system, a natural center for producers and purchasers on both sides of the border. Gates detected a "great spirit" about these enterprises, and Upper Canada's growth seemed to equal "any of our new states." Specie moved back and forth across the border, often smuggled, and provincial notes traded in New York money markets.[24]

These developments encouraged commentators to forecast eventual provincial independence and ultimately, union with the United States. They perceived in the provinces a progressive, entrepreneurial society like their own entirely compatible in spirit, if not in institutions, with the United States.

Americans, however, distinguished between the Anglo-Saxon settlers and merchants and the French. Lower Canada, apart from Montreal, did not seem progressive. Most observers found the French naturally indolent, uneducated, and lacking the financial ambition of Anglo-Saxons. In addition, the Catholic religion, especially the Church's control over vast tracts of the best land, seemed to dampen the material aspirations of the French. A contributor to the *North American Review* blamed the lack of development on a combination of climate, poor soils, the absence of roads and bridges, the "primitive" state of society, and Catholicism, which was "essentially inimical to the lust of wealth." Another writer sneered at Lower Canada's legislators as "illiterate and bigotted members, as would naturally be expected from a people, who, like the generality of the Canadian peasants, are ignorant and suspicious." For Niles, Lower Canada was "rapidly improving, but its growth has been slow compared with that of the western part of New York, the state of Ohio, & c." In the United States, material growth by contrast was "civilization personified and embodied," as Edward Everett suggested in a speech at Yellow Springs, Ohio, in 1829.[25]

Admirers of material progress, Americans saw through the 1830s and 1840s an increasingly prosperous borderland economy. As steamships began to supplant sailing vessels in transatlantic commerce, Samuel Cunard, a Nova Scotian, built the first regular line between England and North America. One of Cunard's American acquaintances, Hamilton Hill of Boston, followed his friend's activity with keen interest, aware that his city would become part of a valuable North Atlantic communications network. Hill and other Boston merchants fought to have their city as Cunard's North American terminus. As provincial canals and railroads came into service, American papers were as pleased as if comparable projects had succeeded in Ohio.

American railroad promoters worked to include provincial lines as part of their networks. Boston speculators, who had first exploited provincial opportunities in the Maritimes by sea, later promoted a railroad to Montreal. In 1845, the British and Americans augmented the transit of goods in bond between the provinces and the United States to accommodate rail traffic. By the 1850s, water and rail links created an extended borderland network.

The provinces had resources as well as markets. The American forest frontier moved northward on two broad fronts—northern New England and the Great Lakes. In 1809, Americans poked into New Brunswick woods to cut timber, and spurned regulations to keep them out. The Maritime lumber industry became part of the borderland economy by 1812. In 1822, Americans and provincials rioted over control of timber reserves in the Miramichi Valley. Provincial woodsmen often lived on imported American supplies, and Maine shipwrights and millwrights, as well as seasonal woodworkers, found employment in New Brunswick. Maine lumber companies hired provincial shantymen. After 1833, American investors sparked a minor lumber boom in New Brunswick that the panic of 1837 abruptly halted. Along the St. Croix River lumber firms were international concerns.

In the Great Lakes Basin, Americans who had logged off much of their own best timber by the 1820s, turned to Lower and Upper Canada for new reserves. New York's canal network made southward transportation of bulky cargoes cheap and supplies flowed north to maintain the crews. St. Johns, on the Richelieu River, was the main lumber port, but after 1835, Americans moved directly into provincial woods. New York and Boston invested in railways to compete for this provincial resource. The New York Central system provided access to the provincial hinterland when it reached Buffalo in 1853. Boston capitalists had sought support from Vermont for their efforts as early as 1830 in a convention at the Pavilion Hotel in Montpelier. The Vermont Central eventually joined Boston with northern New York and Ogdensburg through Rouses Point in 1851. Then, Boston hosted a massive celebration, complete with a regatta in the harbor. Lord Elgin, British North America's Governor General, and President Millard Fillmore attended. In 1854, American money built a line north from Prescott to tap Ottawa Valley timber, first exploited by Americans who settled in Bytown in 1851. Other lines opened to the provinces in the 1850s, more than the traffic would support. But promoters, engineers, and directors were always optimistic about the value of the provinces in America's expanding economic system.[26]

Partly because it offered high prices for timber, advantageous locations, and access to the Erie Canal, New York finally eclipsed Boston in the American commercial struggle for the provincial hinterland.[27] But both these growing American cities had reached out by investing in transportation systems to control a hinterland that would sustain their growth and prosperity.

Signs of converging economic systems could be seen in other areas as well. The *American Almanac*, an annual publication after 1831, contained a regular section on the provinces. This usually listed vital statistics, but also the names of newspapers, the capitalization of banks, the names of consuls in provincial ports of entry, and notes on politics. Another instance of borderland integration occurred in the depression of 1837 as provincial and American banks sought to assist one another by transfering specie. At the same time, Rochester, New York, wanted federal government drawbacks from the duties on goods bound for the provinces to attract more provincial business on the state canal system. This would benefit both New Yorkers and provincials. Far to the east, in the St. Croix Valley, the *Calais Gazette* summarized the borderland economic spirit.

The trade on this river has been conducted for thirty years on terms of perfect reciprocity. Owing to our peculiar situation there is no such thing as enforcing the letter of our revenue laws. The lumber which floats on the bosom of our river cannot be characterized as either English or American. It is as impossible to discriminate between the growth and manufacture of the two sides of the river as it is to tell whether the water which washes the sides of our wharves on its way to the ocean came from an American or an English valley. And up to this time, by the universal consent of our citizens and the tacit agreement of both governments, our trade has been wisely suffered to take its own course without interruption. Indeed it must ever be so, or *it must cease to exist.*[28]

Although the provinces were clearly British possessions, the provincials were a people much like Americans, with comparable and compatible ambitions, interests, and values. Few Americans who discussed their relations with the provinces failed to speculate about the political implications of these similarities.

Trade periodicals mused about a continental future. Hunt's *Merchants Magazine*, America's preeminent antebellum free trade journal, covered provincial affairs from its first volumes. It noted that winter affected provincial business far more than in the United States. Severe weather shut down the lake trade. But Quebec had become a center of considerable activity by 1841, with many steamers under construction and over 1,300 vessels clearing more than fifteen mercantile houses. "The inland trade with the United States is considerable. A portion of the ashes, flour, and other provision consumed in Canada, are derived from thence. In early spring, teas, coffees, fruits, tobacco, and various groceries are imported from New York by the way of Lake Champlain." An extensive credit system had developed, so "the transmission of a bill of exchange on New York easily closes the transaction." Hunt's *Merchants Magazine* also observed that between 1830 and 1840, American-provincial trade had nearly doubled to over $8 million, although this was still only a small portion of America's overall foreign commerce. And American vessels carried much of this trade. By 1843, 29 percent of Detroit's exports went across the river to Upper Canada. As in this case, Hunt's articles usually stressed the provinces as consumers of American products and the potential of the borderland trade.[29]

Commercial news about the provinces appeared as far away as J. B. De Bow's *Review* in New Orleans. But Northern writers close to the borderland were most likely to emphasize provincial growth and potential. Albany keenly appreciated its northern commercial flank and generalized from its own trade to suggest a bountiful future for American-provincial commerce tied into the transport system of the United States.[30]

Expanding American commercial interests had come to view the provinces as a great collective entrepreneurial opportunity. A report from the House Committee on Commerce in 1848 noted that legislative restraints on trade had been gradually removed. Provincial business had increased since 1845, and Americans were drawing provincial produce because of New York's canals and ice-free ports. "There can be no doubt that our commerce with Canada may be greatly augmented by a farther relaxation of legislative restrictions." Reciprocal trade, the report concluded, would profit both countries. For the moment, the commerce committee had prepared only a bill on the free exchange of wheat, but clearly wanted much more.[31]

Britain's abolition of imperial protection in 1846 made American commercial expansion into the provinces easier. The steady, piecemeal development of American-provincial commerce, the growth of the northern borderland, a steady stream of petitions into Congress, the Anglo-American accord on trade, and the interests of national politicians combined with changes in the provincial economic situation after 1846 to promote what became the Reciprocity Treaty of 1854. The movement for an agreement began with American entrepreneurs, developed with expanding large-scale American business interests, especially on the borderland, and was buttressed by diplomatic agreements and federal support. This development led some Americans to believe in a continental economic system that had ideological and political overtones. Americans saw investment opportunities, jobs, markets, and resources in all the provinces. British North America promised to be as much a field of opportunity for American entrepreneurs as the newly emerging Midwestern states.

America's own economic expansion from 1820 to 1850 had been erratic. But it had produced a generally prosperous agriculture, flourishing domestic and international trade, and an extensive transportation system of canals, railroads, steamboat companies, and stage lines. Pools of investment capital accumulated locally throughout the states, but especially in New York, Boston, and Baltimore. Advantages of carrying costs, location, lower insurance rates, larger markets and better prices, as well as well-developed, year-round transportation systems contributed to America's successful bid to include the provinces in its economic life.[32]

Chapter 6.

The Provincial

Rebellions

Year after year British aggressions upon their rights, and indifference to their wrongs and oft-repeated remonstrances against grievances, had increased until all hopes of redress had passed away. In their distress they had turned their eyes to these United States, studied our glorious and peaceful institutions, until they imbibed the spirit of the heroes of the American Revolution, and felt the God-like divinity of liberty stirring within their souls, and rousing their slumbering energy to action.
—Linus Miller,
Notes of an Exile, *1846*

General Winfield Scott sat chatting with leading Whig politicians in the White House one winter evening in 1837, waiting to dine with President Martin Van Buren. Van Buren, a Democrat, was working the other side of the floor in Congress as wise presidents are wont to do. But Scott admired and felt close to the little wizard of the Albany Regency, the master American politician of his age. Van Buren's son had served as Scott's personal secretary for a time. Tonight, the President was late, in conference with his cabinet. When he at last came in, concern furrowed his face. British or provincial troops, Van Buren did not know which, he told Scott, had crossed to American soil at night and attacked a motley collection of provincial rebel refugees and American sympathizers on Navy Island in the Niagara River. The raiders also set fire to the rebel supply vessel, the *Caroline*, which was docked on American territory.

The first reports told of a massacre. Borderlanders in Buffalo and vicinity were in an uproar, beyond the control of local law officers. Who knew what would happen next, perhaps even an Anglo-American war, if calm were not restored. The general must head north immediately and restore order. Secretary of War Joel R. Poinsett would write out instructions. Van Buren was depending upon Scott.[1]

Scott was one of America's best antebellum soldiers, notwith-standing his reputation as "old fuss and feathers," his growing cor-pulence, and his curious mixture of political naïveté and ambition. Only a few days before his dinner engagement with President Van Buren, Scott had written to fellow officer William Worth, who would help control the border during 1838. "The news has just reached me that the Patriots of Upper Canada are in the possession of Toronto. God grant them success! My heart is with the oppressed of both Canadas." Despite such sentiments and his outrage at the British incursion, Scott pursued his mission with energy and zeal. Traveling almost alone by sleigh over snow-covered roads and trails along the northern frontier, often at night, he reminded sometimes angry crowds that the United States was neutral. Citizens must not usurp the national law. The president pursued redress through dip-lomatic channels and would defend American soil against further British invasions.

General Scott had little more than his own imposing appearance, reputation, and personality to maintain local order. Resplendent in his dress uniform, Scott draped himself in the national colors and appealed for calm. His patriotism could not be challenged. Had he not himself led American troops against the British in the prov-inces during the War of 1812?[2]

Scott triumphed, especially as he recalled the scene in his ego-centric memoirs. But others have agreed that he bought time for local tempers to cool and diplomacy to work what magic it could. He also reassured the genuinely frightened (as distinct from the Anglophobic rabble) that Van Buren would not cower before British aggression. Scott's reputation and emphasis on duty told. So did his ploy of hiring vessels out from under the rebel sympathizers to frustrate their schemes to "liberate" the provinces from the British yoke. Winter's blast also cooled local tempers, and the British made no further moves against the United States. In time, Scott built a network that controlled the border by gathering intelligence, com-municating with provincial authorities, and arresting filibusterers who invaded the provinces. This was an impressive accomplish-ment.

Several able officers eventually assisted General Scott. Hugh Brady worked in Michigan, at Detroit; William Worth prowled the Niagara and St. Lawrence regions; and John Wool and William Eus-tis guarded the New York and Vermont frontiers. These men may well have kept the United States out of a war with Great Britain in 1838. And success as a peacemaker earned Scott other such assignments. In 1839, when a crisis flared in northern Maine's Aroostook Valley, and in 1859, when the San Juan "Pig War" threatened an Anglo-American clash in the Strait of Juan de Fuca between Vancouver Island and the mainland, presidents sent Scott to soothe local tempers. He contributed handsomely to Anglo-American harmony in North America in each instance.[3]

When the provincial rebellions erupted in the fall of 1837, first in Lower, then in Upper Canada, many Americans believed that republicanism in the provinces had at last emerged. Americans, in the midst of the territorial expansion prompted by Manifest Destiny, had carried their national ideas and institutions into Texas in the 1820s. By 1836, out of a mixture of genuine fears and cultural arrogance, they rejected Mexican rule to establish an independent republic. Domestic American politics prevented immediate annexation, but a powerful Southern lobby worked toward eventual success in 1845. In the 1840s, Mormons streamed to Utah in search of a wilderness Zion. At the same time, migrants bound for another kind of Zion crossed the plains from Missouri to Oregon, to settle in the area south of the Columbia River jointly occupied by the United States and Great Britain since 1818. American ideas and institutions seemed on an historic march.

Americans had a sense of themselves as a vigorous people, expanding not simply physically and economically, but ideologically as well. When the provincial rebels rose up against the British monarchy and colonial rule in favor of democracy, independence, and even republicanism, the event fitted not only the apparent logic of the times, but also America's national myths. As the fiercely partisan editor of the *Democratic Review*, John L. O'Sullivan, stated:

> If freedom is the best of national blessings, if self-government is the first of national rights, and if the "fostering protection" of "paternal government" is in reality the worst of national evils—in a word, if all our American ideas and feelings, so ardently cherished and proudly maintained, are not worse than a delusion and a mockery—then we are bound to sympathise with the cause of the Canadian rebellion.[4]

Americans along the southern side of the provincial frontier sympathized even more ardently with the rebels. Popular opinion in the fall and winter of 1837 echoed O'Sullivan's sentiments. Vermont papers covered Lower Canadian politics extensively. Correspondents and editors eagerly pounced on signals that the provincials were about to seek an overdue independence from Britain. When Louis Joseph Papineau's rebellion collapsed, pathetic refugees with tales of woe and horror flocked across the border. They confirmed American suspicions of British tyranny and generated a sporadic call for the military liberation of Lower Canada.

In Vermont, Swanton and Alburg became sanctuaries and bases. Local presses supported the provincial rebels. Citizens' meetings in many towns were openly militant. Rebel leaders often had degrees from New England universities and enjoyed family ties with French settlers who had moved to the United States. Physicians, who had practiced on both sides of the border in the upper Champlain Valley, joined the would-be filibusterers. Papineau's *patriotes*, veterans of the fight at St. Denis, were pictured in the rhetoric of the day as the reincarnation of the revolutionaries of 1776. The ideological and human empathy were undeniably genuine. St. Albans residents declared "sympathy when we behold an oppressed and heroic people unfurl the banner of freedom." Independent Americans had a duty to support rebels "against the tyranny, oppression, and misrule of a despotic government."[5]

Some prominent Vermonters denounced such reckless theatrical declarations and supported the governor's proclamation of neutrality. Federal authorities under General John Wool's command of loyal militia frustrated the planned expeditions of liberation. A few pinprick raids achieved little more than vandalism. At first the *patriotes* had the best publicists. But local enthusiasm faded by the summer of 1838. The overall population, especially Vermont's sober and established citizens, never favored filibustering.

In New York, both Papineau's stand at St. Denis on 22 November 1837 and William Lyon Mackenzie's march on Toronto absorbed attention. Papers in Buffalo and Albany had followed provincial politics closely for some time. New Yorkers responded with variations on the Vermont theme, but their views were more complex and more dangerous to Anglo-American relations for several reasons. First, New York had a longer border with the provinces. Second, much of the excitement centered in Buffalo, flooded with refugees after Mackenzie's Toronto rebellion failed. Third, when local enthusiasm declined in the Niagara region, it shifted to other New York border points. Oswego and Ogdensburg became staging areas for later filibustering to "liberate" the provincials. Finally, New York enjoyed prominence and influence in national politics.[6]

The Albany papers provided a typical running commentary. In the late summer and fall of 1837, they reported the partisan clashes in the provincial legislatures and expressed disgust at the government's use of arbitrary authority. British tyranny would backfire, they asserted, and produce revolution, not obedience. By 24 November confused reports appeared in print, usually accompanied by sensational headlines. Four days later: "the ball of revolution in Canada is in motion." On 4 December, the "royalists" fled. "The slip from St. Albans comes to us with this endorsement on the envelope: 'Hurra for Papineau and Liberty.'" On 12 December, a correspondent in Upper Canada doubted that the authorities would "be able long to contend against a people who are determined to be free." Mackenzie had triumphed at Toronto!

But then Mackenzie fled to Buffalo to recruit an army that entrenched itself on Navy Island. The provincial refugees attracted local sympathy, a ragtag stream of volunteers, and a trickle of money. At the same time, most Americans who had any contact with Mackenzie soon saw that he was no Washington or Jefferson, to say the least. And Buffaloans were not all part-time provincial patriots. On 16 December, forty-two prominent citizens attested that both American law and the law of nations forbade arming against a friendly country. Peter Porter, a venerable local figure and a War of 1812 hero, denied that there was any tyranny to rebel against in the provinces. Such people, many with cross-border business, added that if offended, Great Britain might cut off markets for American produce. But then the provincial militia raided Navy Island and left a corpse, a wrecked steamboat, and bruised feelings behind them.[7]

The drama and emotion of the moment elevated one death into a slaughter and a raid into an invasion. The hyperbole rivaled the reports of the Boston Massacre of 1770. The British-provincial foray was symbolically ominous. Even so, Winfield Scott persuaded the Navy Island army to disperse. And he arrested their leader, down-at-the-heels former War of 1812 general Rensselaer Van Rensselaer.

New York governor William Marcy arrived in Buffalo too, not interested himself in provincial independence, but mindful of the political consequences of acting hastily against a cause that aroused America's Anglophobia. An ambitious Democrat, he supported Van Buren and was duty bound to uphold neutrality. Marcy had issued his own proclamation of neutrality, but was nevertheless friendly to some of the patriot leaders. Some were disgusted at Marcy's pandering to local feelings, but the governor successfully worked both sides of the fence.

Local feelings ran their course. Gradually, because of Scott's skill and the chemistry of time, the refugees and American volunteers drifted away from Buffalo. They collected in other border towns and formed a series of secret societies, generally known as Hunters' Lodges, to liberate British North America.[8] The potential for a forcible expansion of American ideology and political structure remained.

Elsewhere along the border in that depression winter following the Panic of 1837, many idle men attended meetings for fellowship in a cause that evoked patriotic impulses and for something to do. Cleveland and other Ohio towns issued hyperbolic statements about "gushings of sympathy for those who, like our forefathers, oppressed, and who, like them a handful, are determined to meet the innumerable horde of foreign mercenary soldiers, and to obtain . . . Victory or Death." Irish-Americans were abusively anti-British. In Michigan, Governor Stephens Mason duly declared neutrality, but many ignored him. An 1837 Christmas day meeting at Detroit's City Theatre collected $134 and ten rifles. A self-styled "General" Thomas Jefferson Sutherland, who may have taken his name too seriously, issued a pompous proclamation to the provincials to "rally then around the Standard of Liberty, and Victory and a glorious future, of independence and prosperity will be yours."[9]

The rebellions in both Upper and Lower Canada in 1837 arose from a complex of factors. Reform politicians in Upper Canada grieved over their electoral defeat in 1836. But they gasped and fell back when Mackenzie called for a republic. They opposed the government and the Family Compact that ruled Upper Canadian politics and society, but were both loyal and antirepublican. In Lower Canada, ethnic and religious differences reinforced political divisions. Impatient, Louis Joseph Papineau and his *patriote* radicals abandoned moderation and mobilized against the English. Riots led to armed clashes and rebellion. Defeat followed a brief victory against British troops.

Most Americans little appreciated provincial social, political, economic, and ethnic complexities. They tended to see in the rebellions in Lower and Upper Canada in the fall and winter of 1837 a reprise of their glorious republican revolution of 1776. The protagonists seemed the same—British overlords, royal minions, patriots protesting arbitrary power in the name of the people. America's republicanism had spread into Texas; why not to the provinces as well? Few rushed to liberate the provincials, however, partly because the rebellions were over before sympathizers even had a chance to organize, let alone march. More importantly, Americans were still conservative about foreign interventions, and both British power and a variety of interests deterred them from dashing north in a republican crusade.

All the state governors declared neutrality when news of the rebellions arrived, albeit with the silent, rather than vocal support of prominent local citizens. As a result, rhetorical enthusiasm for the provincial rebels was deceptive. Responsible editors were cautious, not inflammatory, unlike their excitable correspondents. The *Detroit Advertiser* cautioned Americans to "*examine* before they act, and even remember that Upper Canada is not Texas; that Canadians are not Texans; and that Great Britain is not Mexico." Most Americans expected that the British authorities would easily subdue the rebels, and those with provincial business interests were far more concerned about a disruption of their affairs than repeating the revolution of 1776. Ideological and financial sympathies remained in separate ledgers.[10]

National policymakers had been conservative about foreign revolutions, even republican ones, since the 1790s. Administrations in the Early National period extended only moral support to Latin American rebels seeking independence from Spain's rule. The Greek rebellion against Turkey in 1824 got little more. True, private citizens subscribed money and arms. Some even went to help and individual self-interest often mingled with political and ideological sympathies in the form of privateering. But all of this was political free enterprise. Officially, the United States let rebellions run their course and recognized whatever party emerged in power when the smoke and dust of battle had cleared.

Martin Van Buren's government at first paid the provincial rebellions little heed. The president invoked the Neutrality Act of 1818, designed to prevent flagrant filibustering in the Spanish-American rebellions. But the ideological, political, and geographic circumstances along the American-provincial border in 1837–38 were entirely different from those south of the United States when the Latin American revolutions raged. So Van Buren went further and sought greater authority to prevent American citizens from interfering in provincial affairs. Until Congress responded with legislation, he had to rely upon the state governments. The British accepted Van Buren's good intentions, and American and provincial officials cooperated closely throughout 1838 to forestall or defeat the plans of radical American sympathizers, especially the vest-pocket invasions that the Hunters' Lodges later organized.

By sending Scott to the border immediately after the *Caroline* incident, Van Buren stood in contrast to Andrew Jackson's passive response to the Texan rebellion of 1836. Southern political power and sympathy for expatriate countrymen rebelling against ostensibly despotic, Catholic Mexicans, compelled Jackson to ignore Southern filibusterers flocking to Texas. Besides, what was there to fear from Mexico? The provincial rebels, on the other hand, were few, only Americans by descent, and swiftly decamped British soil. No political bloc collected to support Northern filibustering, and both editorial and political spokesmen stood firmly against a conflict with Great Britain.[11]

Van Buren's policy emerged in a series of proclamations and statements to Congress. No congressman or senator contradicted the president's recommendations. Van Buren also sent his son as a courier to Lord Palmerston to show his personal good faith, despite his obligation to seek reparations after the *Caroline* affair. Both governments decided to downplay the incident, even though the British upheld the commander of the invading force. The correspondence between Secretary of State John Forsyth and Henry S. Fox, the British minister in the United States, was amicable throughout. On 5 January 1838, Van Buren warned Americans contemplating interference not to expect aid from their government if they fell into difficulties while violating neutrality "and the territory of a neighboring and friendly nation." American rebel sympathizers sneered at Van Buren's surrender of national principles, and federal officers had their hands full during the height of the commotion along the border. County sheriffs had called out the militia to guard the frontier after the *Caroline* attack, but as much to keep Americans in as to keep the British out.[12]

Congress was also distracted in the session of 1837–38. It was not even organized for regular business when the rebellions broke out. The continuing Seminole war in Florida, the Texas rebellion, and the economic depression all demanded attention. When Van Buren's message was read before the Senate, Henry Clay of Kentucky, a state that had been eager to march on Upper Canada in the War of 1812, and John C. Calhoun, another old militant, leaped to support the president. Americans might sympathize as they chose in foreign political affairs, but they must not interfere with another government. John Nornell of Michigan noted that "our own rights and liberties were too precious to be jeoparded in those premature and badly digested civil broils between different portions of the same foreign people." The rebels' swift collapse likely confirmed the congressional policy of inaction. And Robert Barnwell Rhett of South Carolina, a fire-eating secessionist in 1860–61, denounced William Lyon Mackenzie as an inflammatory influence who encouraged Americans to "assist in a rebellion of the subjects of a friendly power, who was rightfully endeavoring to maintain her institutions."[13]

The spread of America's glorious institutions, the natural right of revolution, British tyranny, the need for colonies to be free from Old World rule, all these well-used themes were conspicuously absent in congressional speeches. Others simply noted that social and neighborly relations united the people along the frontier. As far as the rebellions in the provinces were concerned, America's leading political spokesmen were steadfastly conservative.

Congress was also alarmed at the prospect of an Anglo-American crisis erupting from a border incident. The revised neutrality legislation passed after minimal debate and no opposition. As Thomas Hart Benton observed later, the national interest lay in good relations with Great Britain. For its part, Congress was content only to occupy itself with the increased costs of border defenses and neutrality operations.[14]

The furor over the *Caroline* incident faded, although it haunted Anglo-American relations down to 1842. A provincial, Alexander McLeod, was later arrested in New York for murder of the raid's only victim. A New York court acquitted McLeod after some anxious moments on the part of John Tyler's secretary of state, Daniel Webster. The Hunters' Lodges formed in 1838 to support the provincial rebellion posed a more serious running threat to American-provincial and Anglo-American relations when they became sufficiently organized to launch cross-border forays. Like the Fenians who would try to achieve Irish independence by attacking the British in Canada after the Civil War, these filibusterers were willing to see an Anglo-American war erupt to achieve their goals.

Men along the American-provincial frontier in the winter of 1837–38 had drifted into the meetings held to support the provincial rebels. Human sympathy, ideological convictions, reflex Anglophobia, idleness, greed for loot or power, the inflammatory rhetoric of refugees or editors, memories of the Revolution or the War of 1812, even simple curiosity or the urging of friends and neighbors had inspired the would-be liberators of British North America. The Hunters contributed to the growing Anglo-American tension after 1837, which was built upon the Maine–New Brunswick boundary difficulty, the Aroostook "War," disagreement over the future of Oregon, and rumors of growing British influence in Texas, Mexico, California, and the Pacific islands.

The Hunters determined upon an underground war to eject the British from North America. The Hunters, a mixed group of altruists, idlers, ruffians, and opportunists, knew little about provincial conditions or politics, apart from what they read in the more sensational newspaper reports, or heard in the hysterical accounts of routed refugees. Some were true borderlanders who saw no real distinction between provincials and Americans. Refugees and their American sympathizers launched several short-lived newspapers that were, in essence, serialized propaganda pamphlets. These papers, such as the Derby, Vermont, *Canadian Patriot*, Samuel P. Hart's *Lewiston Telegraph*, *The Oswego Patriot*, and the *Buffalonian*, promoted the provincial republican cause.[15]

The Hunters' Lodges were organized along Masonic lines and were equally secretive to prevent penetration by British or American government spies. Chapters appeared along the borderland and in Upper Canada. In Detroit, Henry Handy organized the "Secret Order of the Sons of Liberty." The general headquarters was in Cleveland, Ohio, where Dr. Charles Duncombe, a provincial republican and one of the leaders of the failed rebellion, gathered recruits and funds. Orrin Scott, General Winfield Scott's nephew, was a leading Hunter propagandist. Chapters on both sides of the frontier laid grandiose plans for coordinated uprisings and an invasion "to emancipate the British Colonies from British thralldom." They formed a republic in exile and promised land grants to volunteers, copying the Texan practice of attracting recruits.

Many Hunters later published narratives explaining their motives. The egocentric Irishman Edward A. Theller, for example, was strongly anti-British. The British captured him during one of the invasions, then tried and sentenced him to exile in Tasmania. Theller's cause was as much against England as in favor of provincial independence. Theller later made his way back to the United States, where he wrote to vindicate himself and the Hunters. The American part in the Battle of Prescott, where provincial militia and British troops pinned down and captured a ragtag invasion force, showed "the inseparable feelings and interests of the Canadians and the people of the frontier states of the American Union."[16] This was wishful thinking at best, but Theller was one of many who published narratives to make money, defend their filibustering, and excoriate the British.

For many American volunteers, filibustering became a great event in their lives, testimony to their faith in republicanism as a continental ideology. Whatever their motives, these former filibusterers wrote in language that they believed their readers would understand and accept. They employed a melodramatic style, in both memoir and fictional forms. They recalled the American Revolution and equated themselves with the Whigs of 1776. Thomas Jefferson Sutherland sounds merely pompous, but the Reverend Marcus Smith, of Watertown, New York, insisted that "Republican patriotism is not a phantom of the brain, but a deep principle of the heart." Those who marched to Prescott went "to liberate the oppressed" from military rule. Linus Miller toured Upper Canada after the rebellions began to satisfy himself that the rebels were justified. Because he had prejudged the situation, Miller had no regrets, despite failure. Perhaps, coming from a district "burned over" by the fires of religious revivals in the 1820s, Miller sought a crusade and martyrdom. If so, it was in a cause closely linked with his national ideology, which resembled in form and rhetoric a civil religion.[17]

Eventually, some 2,000 American soldiers patrolled the border from Vermont to Detroit. British troops and provincial militia watched the other side of the frontier. American and provincial authorities collaborated closely to spy on the Hunters and quash their planned invasions. Messages moved across the frontier between American and British officers, circulating information and offering suggestions. As a result, a cat-and-mouse game evolved through 1838.

The Hunters boasted of friends in high places in the United States, including President Martin Van Buren, Vice-President Richard M. Johnson of Kentucky, and Governor William Marcy of New York. But such claims were hyperbole at best. The Hunters invented sympathizers to sanctify their largely imaginary cause. Many of their members were nominal—and certainly included numerous American and provincial agents. People in the border region and officials both in the United States and the provinces were well aware of the Hunters' plans and activities.

From 16 to 22 September 1838, a grand convention met at Cleveland, Ohio. Although the delegates established a Canadian republic-in-exile, it remained a paper state. Most Hunter expeditions collapsed before they could be set in motion. If raids did cross the frontier, they faced swiftly mobilized royal troops and provincial militia. The Battle of the Windmill near Prescott, across the St. Lawrence River from Ogdensburg, showed that provincials were far from eager recruits for republicanism. In fact, they readily risked death to capture their liberators. Engagements, such as the Windmill fight, were a disaster for the Hunters and a tragedy for those who had lent their lives and liberty to an illusory cause. The last invasion, on 4 December 1838, came from Detroit. American officers forewarned the provincial authorities, who sent the Hunters packing. By 1839, the Hunters' efforts were indistinguishable from piracy and vandalism. They had become romanticized outlaws, and their meetings degenerated into drinking parties.

Martin Van Buren enforced neutrality, but his assault on rebel sympathizers added to the Whig vote in New York during the election of 1840. But William Henry Harrison and John Tyler, when Harrison died of pneumonia after a month in office, sustained Van Buren's policies. The Hunters' Lodges revived briefly during Alexander McLeod's trial, but their actions resembled reunions more than revolutionary cells. Hunters gangs did fire on British steamships in the St. Lawrence River and tried to blow up the Welland Canal in the summer of 1841. In July, Daniel Webster wrote to Tyler that the Hunters would create a war if they could. But they could not disrupt the processes that led to the emerging Anglo-American accord of 1842. Lord Durham's report and the arrival of responsible government in the united Canadas further frustrated and demolished the Hunters' pretensions. The only surviving issue was the detention of a few Americans in Van Dieman's Land (Tasmania) as punishment for their part in the provincial invasions of 1838. But by 1846, the British had released all the captives.[18] Guidebooks for tourists along the St. Lawrence River would list the Windmill as the site of a romantic historical episode, but not as a symbol of British tyranny or republican martyrdom.

Americans removed from the border region and its enthusiasts doubted that the provincial rebellions signified the evolution of republicanism in British North America. Certainly, the Hunters participating in the invasions through 1838 cleared up any doubts that the vast majority of provincials were loyal to Britain and utterly unwilling to fight for independence. The Van Buren administration worked from a national consensus that the provincial rebellions were entirely a British concern. Only the *Caroline* assault threatened to create an Anglo-American crisis, and federal authorities moved swiftly to defuse it while congressmen and editors urged caution.

Newspaper and periodical coverage of the rebellions was consistent with the increasingly milder sentiments expressed in the press toward the provinces from the War of 1812 down to Canadian Confederation in 1867. American periodicals and newspapers took a lively and sustained interest in provincial politics, society, and economics that betrays, if anything, a sense that the country emerging to the north existed on parallel, but separate lines. American editors saw their republican-democratic system radiating from the United States or perhaps from the very atmosphere of North America, but did not see it spreading as a result of direct occupation of provincial territory.

Most of American newspaper and periodical stories about the provinces consisted of the crimes, business items, fires, personal tragedies, petty political squabbles, scandals, and trivial gossip that masquerade for news even in our time. Upper Canadian politics seemed tempestuous, but rarely revolutionary. The anti-British tone of American papers softened gradually as the War of 1812 receded and diplomacy resolved Anglo-American difficulties. The provincial governors' throne speeches occasionally appeared verbatim as American editors strove to fill their columns. Usually, the political articles were simply reprinted from a provincial press.

Shortly after the war, in 1818, some papers did pick up the excitement in Upper Canada connected with Robert Gourlay. Gourlay was an immigrant Scottish author and agitator who clashed with Upper Canada's autocratic ruling circles, known as the Family Compact, over land sales. Arrested and tried for sedition, he was deported to Scotland. He came to the United States in 1836, but made no effort to establish himself as a revolutionary-in-exile, as William Lyon Mackenzie would do in 1838. Gourlay even advised Americans who would listen in 1837 not to support Mackenzie. Gourlay eventually returned to Canada in 1856, shortly before his death.

In 1818 and 1819, however, the *National Advocate* saw Gourlay as someone who had "sowed the seed of discontent too deeply to be readily destroyed." They argued that because the British conceded more liberties to provincials, and because of their innate Anglo-Saxon qualities and fear of contagion from the nearby American example, the provincials would inevitably seek independence. But Gourlay was a meteorite in provincial affairs, and American papers lost interest once he had left Canada. Other writers advanced the view that the provincials would never progress politically. The *National Intelligencer* stated that "you might as well manufacture the Devil into a christian as to make a republican of a Canadian Frenchman or an imported Scotchman, the one from ignorance, the other from obstinacy." The provincials lacked the imagination to become Americans, as Europeans who traveled through the provinces to the United States testified.[19]

News items on the provinces increased from 1820 through 1836. The stories focused on Lower and Upper Canada, drawing on Quebec, Montreal, and various Upper Canadian papers. The provinces seemed to be developing politically by the mid-1820s. Legislators increasingly challenged the provincial governors, and American editors sometimes embroidered these legislative-executive disputes over control of the purse into signs of imminent revolution. Editors reprinted debates from Upper Canada's House of Assembly, and one argued that government restraints could not conceal the fundamental republicanism of those arguing for the repeal of a sedition law.[20]

In 1827, provincial disturbances again attracted attention. A Buffalo paper noted scuffles over liberty poles being raised, taken down, and raised again. For Hezekiah Niles, the relentless Anglophobe, this illustrated "the miseries of colonial subjugation; and the necessity in any but a popular government, of flying from petty tyrants to the throne when seeking relief from arbitrary power." Disputes with the governor in Montreal had produced a stalemate. "Like proceedings lost thirteen colonies to Great Britain—and like causes may produce like effects, to bring about the loss of several more." Niles was eager to see revolution in the provinces and British embarrassment. But provincial politics remained more turbulent than revolutionary until the rebellions of 1837. American editors fully expected a reaction when a Nova Scotia editor was arrested, expelled from the provincial legislature, and imprisoned, despite a temporary freedom supplied when a mob rescued him.[21] On this, as on other occasions, American editors revealed more about their own ideological preconceptions than they did about provincial affairs.

Lower Canadian politics seemed different from those in Upper Canada because of the French and the power of the Catholic Church. Indeed, when Americans said "Canada," they really meant Lower Canada, and when they said "Canadians," they meant the French of Lower Canada. The British had won French loyalty, but still grappled with the "racial" division. French–Anglo-Saxon antagonism would not die. Antebellum Americans were quite conscious of ethnic categories and held the Anglo-Saxon "race" superior to all others.[22] Americans also disliked the quasi-feudal land system in

Lower Canada. It seemed a major impediment to settlement and generated political disputes because of the need to provide land reserves for the Protestant clergy to offset the power of the Catholic priests. And Americans saw Catholicism itself as a major problem for Lower Canada.

Americans in the antebellum period were strongly anti-Catholic. For many Americans, racial and religious differences meant inferiority. Americans overlooked Lower Canada's obvious disadvantages of climate and poor internal communications and attributed its poor development to "the natural indolence of the French inhabitants, arising, perhaps, from a disregard to what we call comforts, from education and habits, and from religious tenets." Many Americans agreed that "the state of society in Canada, it must not be forgotten, is a very primitive, we had almost said a patriarchal one." The French dread of union with Upper Canada, the power of the priests, the land question, all generated, from an American perspective, a unique political environment. In Montreal and Quebec, the French were better educated and took more interest in politics. There, the situation resembled the tyranny-versus-the-people image that delighted Hezekiah Niles.[23] Even so, this French element and the power of the Catholic Church, when added to British colonial rule, made many Americans skeptical that democracy would blossom in Lower Canada in the near future. The French seemed unlikely recruits for republicanism.

Upper Canada, where the provincials had an English, Scottish, or even American heritage to draw upon, was different. By 1837, Americans had often read of clashes between the legislatures and the royal governors in Upper Canada. At a quick glance, such conflict echoed American revolutionary legends of casting off arbitrary power. All the elements were there: popular struggle to control the public purse, the patronage of officials appointed from across the sea, the government efforts to muzzle critical editors or elected representatives. Provincial legislatures passed resolutions that resembled declarations of rights. Hezekiah Niles noted in 1834 that "Canada remains in a very agitated state—the representatives of the people resisting and protesting against the acts of the governor-general, against whom they were also preparing articles of impeachment." Popular leaders came forward, such as Papineau and Mackenzie. A conservative majority in the legislature often expelled

Mackenzie, but he was "as often and triumphantly returned by his constituents" of Toronto. Rumors also floated about a possible separation from Britain and union with the United States. Surely, writers and politicians intoned from time to time, Britain would stop her futile efforts to stay the course of history.[24]

Seen in this context, John O'Sullivan's ringing declaration for "the cause of the Canadian rebellion" was logical, even inevitable, especially to Americans predisposed to see a struggle between liberty and tyranny afoot in the provinces. Yet, as the editors reported events, plagiarizing one another with abandon in the process, they were more detached than involved. The *National Intelligencer*, admittedly a mouthpiece of the administration, wanted troops on the border to restore calm and keep order. President Van Buren's neutrality proclamation may not have brought the Navy Island patriots to their senses, but it showed that "criminal enterprises could no longer be carried on with impunity against the territory of a nation with whom the United States are on terms of perfect amity." The New York *Courier and Inquirer* quoted Madame Roland on her way to the guillotine during the French Revolution. "Ah! Liberty! Liberty! What crimes are there not perpetrated in thy name." A Boston paper sneered at the Lower Canadian rebels: "not being distinguished as an energetic people they have no cause which can inspire energy . . . and have no real grievance to complain of."[25] American editors and correspondents, despite occasional flourishes, saw the rebellions as an internal British problem, and not as an opportunity to expand America's political system.

Most Americans were content to await the development of time as far as the northward expansion of their republican ideology was concerned. After collecting an extensive file of clippings on the provincial political situation, including many of Mackenzie's writings, New England diplomat, merchant, and politician Caleb Cushing concluded that the right of revolution was sacred, but "not to be rashly called in for every petty occasion." The fiery O'Sullivan traced what he saw as inevitable provincial independence in detail. But even he did not insist on annexation. The Canadas might become part of the United States, or "maintain a friendly independence. We have no material objection to the English neighbourhood." If the provincials wanted freedom, then it was up to them, and if unable to do the job themselves, then the time was not ripe.[26] If these Americans believed that the passage of time would yield a republican nation to their north, they were ill inclined to hurry it along.

The persistent efforts of the Hunters and others to hasten provincial liberty through 1838 did nothing to alter this view. As Americans got a closer look at Mackenzie, he seemed "selfish, heartless, unprincipled, and cowardly," and at best simply ineffectual. New York papers generally portrayed him as a foreign agitator trying to antagonize Britain and the United States contrary to the best interests of both. A St. Lawrence River pirate, William Johnson, seemed far more exciting. In late May of 1838, he attacked a provincial steamer, the *Sir Robert Peel*. Johnson styled himself a Canadian patriot. No American borderland jury would convict any of Johnson's men, but the two governments launched a cooperative campaign to clean out the border brigands as a result.[27]

Although Johnson became a local hero, the Hunters were considered "deluded countrymen" and predators. Self-styled patriots or not, they were either fools or knaves. The *Ogdensburg Times* rejoiced that local citizens had not joined the invasion of Prescott that led to the Windmill fight. The *Albany Argus* dismissed the filibusterers as deluded or criminals. Talk of revolutionizing the provincials was absurd and American papers went back to reporting more mundane provincial political events, printing major documents such as Lord Durham's proclamation of general amnesty.[28]

Writers and politicians removed from the Hunters' ranks could not even make a case for British tyranny. Colonial rule in the provinces was benign, far different from that practiced before 1775 because the British had responded to change and provincial demands. The revolutionary image of tyrannical Britain had become a historical reflex, a memory rather than fuel for contemporary action. These incidents combined into an ill-advised "Patriot War" that embraced all filibustering in borderland folklore. But it was a folklore that excluded any sense of a missed opportunity to liberate the provincials from the British yoke.[29]

Thoughtful Americans examined Lord Durham's recommendations for the future political organization of Upper and Lower Canada carefully. Provincial union appeared to be a step toward the independence that many believed would eventually befall the provinces. Durham himself enjoyed a positive image in the American press, even in *Niles' Register*. O'Sullivan saw Durham as liberal and able, and French-English hostility as unimportant. Louisiana demonstrated that such differences need not contaminate politics forever. Foreign domination, of course, had driven the provincials to rebel, but independence would solve that. Durham's report confirmed O'Sullivan's view that the provincials wanted to separate from Britain. Union of the Canadas was a logical and positive step toward true independence.[30]

Christopher Dunkin, a provincial writing for the *North American Review*, knew local politics well and interpreted events from a conservative, but balanced perspective. He argued that some Americans had a biased view of the rebellions. The British had not been oppressive but had tried to redress provincial grievances. Ambitious colonials could move ahead in their system and hold high office on merit. Problems arose not from oppression, but from a defective constitution that tried to separate the English and French "races," from English politics, Britain's ignorance of colonial affairs, and the lack of a proper party system. Dunkin approved Durham's plan of union. The English should have followed the American example of Louisiana. No special barriers had protected the minority culture, and the French had been assimilated. Racial politics had never emerged. A unified Canada would therefore remove that source of contention within and between the provinces. Local oligarchies and French resistance to commercial development would evaporate to clear the way for a more progressive and democratic political and economic system.[31]

Dunkin's analysis was impressive and systematic, based on considerable information, a positive spirit, clear reflection, and embraced American cultural values. Had the British created a free American state, no trouble would have erupted. There was, in short, an American solution to the provincial problem. In his own gentle way, Dunkin was as much of a continentalist as O'Sullivan. But they were continentalists in the mind only. Both men believed that American political institutions, buttressed by democratic and republican values, would prevail in Anglo–North America. Yet both were willing to let the provincials make their own political decisions. They must be volunteers, not pressed recruits for republicanism. Continentalism and self-determination were compatible, not contradictory, components of America's expansionist ideology as it related to the British North American provinces in the 1830s.

Other writers operated from the same assumptions about provincial political development. An essential continuity characterized American ideas before and after the rebellions about the provincial future. Van Buren's policy of neutrality and the general reaction against active interference in British affairs were consistent with the national outlook, whatever momentary hysteria reigned along the border.

Lorenzo Sabine, the nineteenth-century American historian, made his reputation by his work on the loyalists in the American Revolution. He also wrote in the more cerebral periodicals of his day. For him, the rebellions arose from disputes over the land question, Sir Francis Bond Head's political ineptitude, and the general clumsiness of colonial administration. But the British had not been tyrants, and their rule scarcely justified violent rebellion. The provincial liberals were not modern versions of the American revolutionaries of 1776. In his view, Lord Durham's report had unfortunately spawned a structure of government that caught provincial governors between two contending masters—their constituents and their sovereign. The system had therefore failed from Nova Scotia to Canada West. Judges' salaries, inequality of representation in local assemblies, clergy reserves, a frustrated Anglo-Saxon commercial dynamism, and English colonial control would clash until Canada became independent. Reflecting his American values, Sabine argued that the British had no reason to retain the provinces, which "must become a nation by themselves, or form a part of ours. Laws which man cannot alter have fixed a limit to colonial dependence." Sabine preferred a "second confederacy of American States" to annexation. But either way, independence would come.[32]

Sabine accepted the ripe fruit, or convergence theory, of eventual American-provincial merger. Ironically, the children of the loyalists of 1776 were now acting upon the principles of Benjamin Franklin, James Otis, and other revolutionary spokesmen. Any workable scheme of provincial union must resemble the American model.

Sabine's articles were heavy going and reached a small readership. Yet other writers on provincial political development argued a similar thesis. Even the southern and commercial *De Bow's Review* in New Orleans argued that the environment was responsible for recent provincial gains. De Bow was willing to see the provinces eventually form part of a united North America, but that was for the provincials themselves or history, not aggression, to produce.

Niles' Register, ever interested in British affairs, saw English-French hostility a continual difficulty. But "all we have to do is remain quiet spectators. Canada will, beyond all doubt, become independent ere long, and if unwise counsels do not prevail, and matters are not unduly precipitated, will become so without violence or bloodshed."[33]

Newspapers, when not covering sensational events, also argued that political and ideological evolution would persuade the British government to agree to eventual provincial independence. After the death of Hezekiah Niles, the *Register* lost much of its old Anglophobia. The new editor saw peaceful political revolutions ahead and liberal principles taking hold in the provinces. The elections were freer and commerce progressing. Louis-Hippolyte La Fontaine, a leading Lower Canadian politician, on the other hand, appeared to be an "overrated demagogue" in April of 1843. Sir Charles Bagot was right not to be bullied into removing the government to Montreal. Lord Durham's wise groundwork was bearing fruit. "A more just, and therefore a more amicable and liberal spirit pervades the administration of affairs in Canada, and its effects have been as happy on our side of the line as on the other." In the 1840s, prosperity seemed to keep pace with political and social improvements. Americans remained confident that British control of the provinces would never last.[34]

Americans continued to assume that their republican-democratic values would expand. After the provincial rebellions failed, Americans expected that time alone would work a conversion experience on provincials. Beyond that, however, the American interest in provincial development assumed primarily an economic turn. As interest slowly stirred in the later 1840s for reciprocal trade with the provinces, some Americans argued that closer economic ties would encourage eventual political union. All along, Americans saw their form of economic organization as the wave of the future, and because they did not separate economic and political ideology, they assumed that economic exchange would have ideological and political ramifications. Here too, they believed that, the French aside, the provincials were really just Americans living under foreign rule.[35]

Once the anger arising from the raid on the *Caroline* had subsided and retrospective accounts were considered, reflective Americans saw the outlines of a distinct North American society in the north. Eventually, the provinces would achieve political and commercial independence because of the logic of history, the geographic separation from Britain, the inherent contradiction of attempting to juggle local interests in a democratic system with the wishes of distant imperial overlords, the temptations of sharing in American prosperity, and the infection of American republicanism.

Americans disagreed about whether this historical evolution would produce an American-provincial union. Most commentators, whether journalists or politicians, were prepared to let the provincials decide what they wanted to do themselves. These Americans accepted, in short, their own principle of self-determination. To be sure, they knew that Britain would never surrender the provinces to direct American control. Americans were also shedding their sense of an immediate British menace to the north. In addition, their awareness of political developments in the provinces, evident in newspaper coverage after 1815 and in their reaction to the provincial rebellions, produced a greater appreciation of provincial dislike of the United States.

Many responded hopefully to the provincial annexation movement that crystalized in Montreal in 1849. But this movement had economic rather than political origins, emerging from the provincial depression that ensued after Great Britain abolished the Corn Laws and threw the provincials onto a world market. Americans awaited a provincial request and did not exploit the situation to subvert British rule. And because the provincial interest in annexation was based on a fear of ruin, not on an ideological identification with the republic to the south, it proved short-lived. The return of prosperity and the advent of the Reciprocity Treaty of 1854 killed provincial support for annexation, except among a few fanatics who were as zealous and as deluded in their way as the Hunters had been before them.

Chapter 7.

The Northern

Tour

*I fear I have not got much to say
about Canada, not having seen
much; what I got by going to Canada
was a cold.*
—Henry David Thoreau, 1866

Ideas about America's future varied during the era of Manifest
Destiny. Americans were not always satisfied about their
country's progress. Many identified and tackled social evils,
such as war, slavery, or drunkenness. Others, such as the Mormons, fled the United States to create their own life. Complacent
or critical, all contributed to national expansion because they carried a core of common assumptions, ideals, and values wherever
they went.

Travelers in the antebellum period were usually temporary "comeouters" who took the dominant national ideology for granted. In
their curiosity about foreign or neighboring societies, they betrayed
a sense of America's destiny. They judged their hosts in American
terms and trumpeted the American way. Once home, they often
shared impressions and conclusions through publication.

British North America was a favorite destination for American
travelers throughout the nineteenth century. Initially, travelers
saw the provinces as British bases, but by the 1820s, they more
often compared provincial development with progress in the United
States. By the 1840s, many prophesied a future American-provincial convergence, but some perceived the evolution of a distinct
British American society.

Philip Stansbury embodied many of these responses. In October
of 1822 he walked from New York to Montreal via Niagara Falls
taking the time to enjoy the northern frontier's history and natural
beauty. Walking freed him from timetables and the petty tyranny of
coach drivers or ship captains. He hiked up the Hudson Valley to
West Point and Albany, along the Mohawk River by the nearly completed Erie Canal, through the growing western New York towns
of Utica, Ithaca, and Genessee, until he reached Niagara Falls, already a tourist mecca. Next he sailed to the point where Lake Ontario narrowed into the St. Lawrence River at Kingston and walked
downstream to Montreal and Quebec City. He found the French

strange, almost European in their habits. Stansbury finally returned to the United States via Chambly and Vermont.

Stansbury was a committed patriot on vacation. He carried his ideology in his knapsack and his prejudices as the lens through which he judged this foreign society. The provincials were a curiosity. He also wanted to learn how the English and French Canadians viewed the United States and "contrast the defects of that subjected nation, with the excellencies of our republican form of government."[1]

Stansbury found what he sought. The provincial settlements seemed very English, with a military appearance "that casts over it an aspect of stern grandeur, which we will look for in vain, in a town of the United States." Provincials of American origin seemed more egalitarian than British settlers, however loyal to the Crown and antirepublican they all might be. In Lower Canada, he asserted that "despotism seems to have stamped a feature of low submission upon the plodding, unambitious peasantry, whose minds are, moreover, awed into superstition, by the displayed crucifix of their Catholic priests;—and as the American journies onward, he cannot refrain from exclaiming, when he recollects the freedom and joyous enterprize of his own country."[2]

He also betrayed a romantic's admiration of nature. Stansbury waxed rhapsodic about provincial waterfalls—Niagara, Chaudière, and Montmorency. Old battlefields evoked past triumphs and tragedies. In Lower Canada the French peasants might be dim and dominated, but the costumes and manners of the people in Quebec City charmed him. He apparently understood French, so he remarked on the "gay spirit" of old France. But, although the habitants were hardworking, generous, polite, and open, they still seemed short, misshaped, swarthy, even vaguely savage. And they overcharged. Consequently, at Chambly, on his way home, he rejoiced to see America's stars and stripes flying on a Lake Champlain steamer.

Stansbury was happy to leave Canada and contrasted the French habitants with America's "plain, open-hearted, merry-making farmers," and its poor and unproductive economy with American abundance and growth. Canada's life suggested a timeless monotony in stark contrast to America's enterprise and "public spirit." Americans were free, "the landscape bright and beautiful; and nature herself smiled." In keeping with Voltaire's remark that Canada was a few acres of snow, Stansbury shuddered at a "climate chained by eight months of winter." The United States had decently balanced seasons. "Clouds, cold and storms, had been left with Canada, whose horrible hemlock swamps spread its wide prospect to the north." His steps quickened, his stride lengthened. He was an American glad to be home.[3]

Stansbury was both typical and atypical of American travelers visiting the provinces between 1815 and 1871. An unusually fierce anti-British prejudice, fed by memories of the War of 1812, warped Stansbury's judgment as he walked provincial soil. For most Americans, the provinces ceased to be an enemy base. Visitors would gaze at battlefields such as Queenston Heights with dispassionate curiosity, reflecting on the fallen heroes of both sides in the War of 1812. Further, few tourists followed Stansbury's example and walked. Henry David Thoreau and his companion Ellery Channing would in 1850. But most travelers preferred the greater ease and speed, if not always greater comfort, of canal barges, stagecoaches, sailing vessels and steamers on the lakes and rivers, and railroads. Stansbury's choice of season—fall—was also unusual, although the foliage would have been magnificent. Yankee tourists usually traveled in the summer. Guidebooks recommended July and August to avoid chills. Even so, most travelers shivered involuntarily at the thought of frozen waterways and all the winter snow.

But Stansbury was like many American travelers in that the ideology and patriotism of antebellum America often predetermined his reactions to the provinces and the provincials. The Jacksonian American was brash, bustling, eager to succeed, and willing to take risks. But he also had a tendency toward religious bigotry, xenophobia, racism, and a puzzled arrogance over how any people could reject America's republican political system. And materialism approached fanatical levels. Considered as a group, travelers to the provinces were neither the best nor the worst of Americans; they simply reflected the perceptions and concerns of a young nation expanding on many fronts.

The rise of the American tourist industry to the British North American provinces and its steady growth during the era of Manifest Destiny reflected America's coming of age. Transportation was primitive, but President James Monroe's postwar Northwestern tour highlighted new plans to construct a road network into the region. The Erie Canal, begun in 1817, was completed in 1825, and the road and canal systems spread. The application of technology to transportation accelerated both the volume and pace of travel. Rail networks penetrated the northern wilderness and reached along river and lake fronts by the 1850s. In 1854, the first through system between Boston and Montreal opened, with other American-provincial lines opening shortly thereafter. Service industries—hostelries, hotels, restaurants—appeared along these routes. Americans traveling for pleasure or business discovered declining costs, greater speed and comfort, and a greater variety of destinations.[4]

As the Jacksonian middle class grew in numbers and wealth, the possibility of travel for relaxation, recreation, and enlightenment increased. Only the rich could afford a European tour. But North America itself had natural wonders to behold and even a touch of Europe in the British province of Lower Canada. Travelers on what came to be called the northern tour generally lived in New York or New England, although some came from farther south. Americans closest to the boundary naturally knew the most about the provinces. And because geography encouraged north-south travel, many Americans embarked on a brief visit to British North America.[5]

The volume of travel and traffic increased substantially between 1815 and 1871. And travelers began to view British North America as a curiosity, rather than as a menace. In 1826, the band of the Seventy-Sixth regiment played "Yankee Doodle," "Rule Britannia," and other tunes for the amusement of twenty-nine Americans visiting Montreal. By 1834, provincial steamship lines advertised regularly in New York newspapers to attract both passengers and freight. By then, steamers crossed the Great Lakes as far as Sault Ste. Marie.[6]

Before the War of 1812, a one-way trip between New York City and Montreal consumed a week. By 1853, coordinated steamers on Lake George, Lake Champlain, and the Hudson River, along with train portages, reduced the time to just over one day. By the 1850s, northern New York, especially the Adirondacks and the Thousand Islands region of the St. Lawrence River, were becoming major resort attractions.[7] This traffic spilled over into the provinces. Once as far as the New York shore of the St. Lawrence River, foreign soil lay just across the water. Local ferries had linked the provinces with New York State even before the War of 1812, and each town had its landings and ferries to facilitate travel to the British dominions.

The provinces drew tourists for several reasons. To begin with, they were close, "just upstairs," as author Horace Sutton has put it in modern times. Next, the provinces had a touch of the exotic with their colorful British garrisons and French people, architecture, and institutions. Americans, too, were curious about neighbors who so closely resembled themselves. The British provincials seemed a variation on the American theme, industrious, democratic, albeit not republicans, eager for economic and political freedom. The 1837 Canadian rebellions and the filibustering of the Hunters' Lodges rendered Americans temporarily unwelcome in some parts of the provinces, but this was a brief hiatus in a continuously growing interchange.

Tourists from 1800 to the 1860s followed one of a limited number of routes. The primary one was from New York City up the Hudson River to Albany, across to Buffalo and Niagara Falls, either by the Erie Canal or later by railroad. After lingering at Niagara, tourists sailed down Lake Ontario, in a British or American vessel, depending on minor stops desired, and landed either in Kingston or Ogdensburg. Before canals bypassed the Long Sault rapids on the way to Montreal, travelers floated downstream in barges or on rafts with French-Canadian rivermen. On shore, bone-jarring rides on unsprung coaches provided the only alternative to walking. Shallow-draught steamers smoothened the trip, as did the canals that bypassed the roughest waters. Eventually, the provincial Grand Trunk Railway linked York (Toronto) with Montreal.

Alternatively, after Albany, travelers could sail up Lake George and Lake Champlain to Rouses Point and enter the provinces via Chambly. Then coaches or railroads connected to La Prairie where ferries crossed to Montreal. By 1859, the Victoria Bridge was under construction to connect the Grand Trunk Railroad with American railways and provide continuous service from the United States to the provinces. Travelers then turned east for Quebec City or west up the St. Lawrence to Kingston and the lakes. Less common routes were Albany to Oswego and along the lakes, or a complete transit of the provinces to Nova Scotia.

Travelers sought nature as well as society. Under the influence of

American romanticism, travelers dwelt upon natural themes and settings. Moreover, the wilderness was already important for the American sense of its identity from Europe. William Cullen Bryant celebrated nature in his poetry as Thomas Cole did in his landscapes. The entire Hudson River School exemplified the new romantic conception of the beauty and tranquility of nature in America. Albert Bierstadt's huge canvasses, on the other hand, portrayed the immensity of the unsettled American wilderness. Americans painted Niagara Falls to capture their grandeur and unharnessed power. Henry David Thoreau went to Canada partly to find more wilderness than seemed available around his native Concord.

Furthermore, Americans were agrarians. The Jeffersonian ideal of the farmer as a chosen man of God had sunk into the American national soul. So American travelers admired land for what could be grown upon it, as well as for its aesthetic qualities. And as an ideological corollary, American travelers judged a people on how agriculturally productive they seemed in comparison with the United States.[8] All these themes tied in with American continental expansion and came through clearly in travel commentary on the provinces.

Guidebooks, available in the United States as early as 1825, dwelt upon the natural attractions of the northern tour, lumping the provinces in with northern New York and New England. Waterfalls invariably received attention. Writers wooed their readers with delicious descriptions of the awaiting magnificence. Henry Gilpin alerted coach passengers to the beautiful and well-cultivated provincial countryside through which they would pass between Niagara and Montreal. Guides recommended such vistas as the St. Lawrence from Mont Royal or from Cape Diamond at Quebec City. Gardens and the scenic pleasures of boat trips down the St. Lawrence River, or down Lake Champlain to Rouses Point, were other popular attractions.[9] The preoccupation with nature not only helped to draw antebellum Americans west to the Great Plains and the Rockies, but also north to the British provinces.

Niagara Falls was the great northern magnet. Timothy Bigelow set out with four companions in July of 1805, and later published the first narrative of the northern tour. Frontier travel was then an uncomfortable adventure, but all endured for the pleasures of the journey. The American side of Niagara was unsettled, so Bigelow's party ferried across to lodge with the British. Packing picnic lunches, they walked along the river and descended a perilous ladder to view the cataract from below. At the falls and on lake vessels, they met other travelers from Baltimore and Philadelphia. All shipped for Kingston, Montreal, and later home.[10]

The Niagara Falls area became a circus in the 1830s, with publicity stunts, tea gardens, pagodas, and souvenir shops alongside the hotels. In 1837, the Lockport and Niagara Falls Railroad opened and took 1,300 passengers to see the sights. By the 1840s, tourism had become a major industry that stimulated the development of the Niagara borderland. American entrepreneurs had scrambled to match the provincials, who monopolized Niagara tourism in the 1820s.

In time, travel became more comfortable and frequent, and guidebooks devoted exclusively to the falls laid out safe, romantic, and leisurely walks along the river with vantage points, recommended accommodations, recounted myths and legends, and usually included maps and engravings. The first "Maid of the Mist" took thrill seekers close under the falls for a shower in 1846. In 1847, the International Suspension Bridge Company, with an American-provincial board of directors, erected a cable car to carry the daring across the Niagara gorge in a basket. The famous engineer John Roebling began his suspension bridge in 1852, and the first locomotive crossed three years later. By then, travelers could choose from several reportedly excellent hotels on the American, as well as on the provincial side. For travel east, the Ontario and St. Lawrence Steamboat Company, another American-provincial operation, competed with established lake packets. The company, which began business in 1848, ran eleven steamers that touched at provincial and American ports as far as Ogdensburg and Lewiston, New York.

John Vanderlyn, of Kingston, New York, was the first American painter to visit the falls in 1802–4. Artists used small canvasses, camera obcsura, and even dioramas to bring Niagara's glories to those who could not afford the journey. Godfrey Frankenstein of Germany was the best known artistic entrepreneur. In 1853, his drawings appeared in *Harper's New Monthly Magazine*. Frankenstein spent nine years painting over 200 pictures from both sides of the Niagara River. His moving panorama show, on its grand tour in

1853–54, lasted well over an hour while large canvasses unrolled on either side of an audience to simulate a Niagara boat ride.

All this stimulated further travel to the falls, and therefore to the provinces. 45,000 tourists came in 1847, but 50,000 arrived annually during the 1850s. Hotels proliferated and guides appeared annually. Some authors connected nature and their national ideology. A *Knickerbocker* contributor, for example, felt obliged to remark that although the provincial falls were larger, America was still the more impressive nation because of its "free-born genius," energy, and republican institutions. In 1853, *Harper's* lampooned this parochial viewpoint: "Our rather slow neighbors across the river have been wont to plume themselves upon the possession of the more magnificent part of Niagara; while young America has been heard to mutter between his teeth something about 'annexation,' on the ground that the lesser nation has no fair claim to the possession of the major part of the crowning wonder of the Continent."[11]

Guidebooks conveyed complex images of the provinces, using both natural and human wonders to promote tourism. They described scenery, cultivation, commerce, towns, cities, the conditions of farms, cultural attractions, the natives, British garrisons, historic sites, and engineering advances. The guides listed competing railroads and steamship lines with all stops along the way. They stressed the ease and comfort of modern travel and suggested how extensive lake and river traffic in the Great Lakes borderland had become by the 1850s. The Ontario and St. Lawrence Steamboat Company's guide, for example, listed two daily runs between Montreal and Lewiston, New York, the railhead for New York City. This guide embroidered its pages with engravings of natural and historical sites.

John Disturnell's guides had specific readers in mind, such as Europeans landing in New York taking the northern tour, or Americans on the western Great Lakes, or travelers on the more conventional routes. Hunter's *Panoramic Guide* was short on narrative, but its lengthy folding pictorial map covered the ground from Niagara Falls to Quebec City. This thirty-six-page monster must have cascaded onto many railroad car aisles, steamer decks, and feet as eager tourists poured over its engravings of falls, forts and Martello Towers, lighthouses, suspension bridges, engine houses, trestles, canals, cities, and French Canadian villages complete with miniature habitants, Indians, nuns by their convents, and priests by their churches.[12]

American tourists went to the provinces on business, to see relatives, or to gather material for writing, as Thoreau and Richard Henry Dana did. American notables also took holidays there. General Alexander Macomb, who had once invaded Lower Canada at the head of a hostile army, received a hospitable welcome at Quebec in December of 1835. The following summer, Governor William L. Marcy of New York took a tour. In 1851, an obscure army officer, Ulysses S. Grant, traveled to Montreal, attracted by reports on the scenery.

William Henry Seward was one of the most famous American visitors. Seward, along with his son Frederick, Francis P. Blair, and Preston King, toured from Niagara Falls through Hamilton, Toronto, Kingston, the Thousand Islands, and Montreal in 1857. The party then broke up, but Seward proceeded to Quebec City, where he hired a schooner to descend to the Gulf of St. Lawrence for fishing and relaxation.

Americans rarely journeyed so far east, although anglers often went to New Brunswick in search of fresh-water salmon. Frederic Cozzens, diverted to Halifax on his way to Bermuda, was a rare reporter on the Maritimes. Although unimpressed by the settlements, he was awed by vistas of Cape Breton's Bras d'Or. Because rich resources lay unexploited and apparently ignored, he concluded that Maritimers lacked *"enterprise."* A frivolous vacationer to the Bay of Fundy in 1870 remarked that "Americans would hardly be content with this nature unadorned. Stately summer residences would perch upon every bluff or look out from every glade."[13] Americans believed that nature existed to be used as well as admired. In time, Americans would build summer residences, stately and otherwise, in all the provinces. After 1867, Canada became a refuge for Americans, a place to rest while on vacation.

If Niagara Falls was the principal natural attraction, Lower Canada, especially Montreal and Quebec City, provided the main cultural attractions in the provinces. Their monuments and buildings only partly explained this interest. Most visitors and writers found the French exotic. They spoke another language, had antiquated customs, different values, and were Roman Catholic. In 1851, *The*

Knickerbocker contrasted Quebec City unfavorably with American towns. But to a *Harper's* writer, "the unfamiliar ideas of the internal mysteries of the nunneries, and cloisters, and monastic life, wedded to the most stirring historical associations and natural scenery extremely beautiful and picturesque, render Quebec the most attractive city on the continent for the curious, pleasure-seeking appetite of the traveler."[14] This was invaluable publicity for the burgeoning provincial tourist industry.

The *Harper's* correspondent of 1859 captured the charm many Americans found in Quebec City, a "quaint old town . . . within solid walls built long ago by cautious Frenchmen." The locals spoke a "salmagundi, composed of all British tongues, largely mixed with the corrupted Gallic spoken by the habitans." He explored the town with two ladies and viewed Jacques Cartier's winter harbor, the ruins of the intendant's palace, and Montcalm's headquarters. A macadamized road led to Montmorency Falls and General Frederick Haldimand's nearby mansion. This article's many illustrations provided a vivid window on Quebec City.[15] Free of overt anti-Catholicism, the correspondent typified American fascination with the exotic and with romantic artifacts of antiquity.

American anti-Catholicism ebbed and flowed during the period of Manifest Destiny. Americans were steeped in anti-Catholic prejudice. Roman Catholics had been the historical enemies of Anglo-Saxon Protestants. Despite an ensuing interlude of tolerance, anti-Catholicism remained powerful on a popular level and flared again in the 1820s and 1830s, especially in New England and New York, the point of origin for most of the American travelers and tour guide authors who came to the provinces. The influx of Roman Catholic Irish alarmed New Englanders. The final links in the chain that produced a powerful anti-Catholic outburst in the 1830s were local controversies over church property and imported English tracts denouncing priestly corruption and "exposing" the secret horrors of convents and monastaries. The burning of the Ursuline Convent and school in Charlestown, Massachusetts, in 1834, sparked a wave of assaults on the Catholic Church in the United States.[16]

As Americans expanded beyond their borders, even as tourists, they carried such prejudices with them. Poet Moses Guest, in Lower Canada in 1796 on a trading expedition, was shocked at the "unnatural, unreasonable, and superstitious custom" of putting women in convents. In 1805, Timothy Bigelow found that "the mummery, frivolity, and silly ceremonies of the service, exceed what I had expected even from Papists." Joseph Sansom was not blatantly bigoted, yet Catholicism explained most of French Canadian "backwardness." Worse, priests exploited their parishioners and kept them in ignorance.[17]

Many Americans read about sensational events in the Montreal convent, the Hôtel-Dieu, in 1836 in Maria Monk's concocted "confessions." She claimed to have escaped from the convent, and, in several volumes, designed by the actual authors to produce profit from prejudice, told of priests and nuns living in sin, strangling and burying in cellars the babies they produced from their corrupt coupling. Her first book sold three hundred thousand copies between 1836 and 1860, rivaling *Uncle Tom's Cabin* as a national best-seller. Colonel William Stone, editor of the *New York Commercial Advertiser*, shredded this fraud in print, but Monk's outrageous claims confirmed preconceived ideas of American anti-Catholicism and so were widely believed.[18] In this curious and underhanded way, entrepreneurs found other opportunities in the provinces. Travelers rarely indulged in such sensationalism, but they usually betrayed the prejudices common to antebellum Americans.

A Virginian, J. C. Myers, explored the churches and seminaries with great interest, prepared to be appalled at what he saw. His remarks were mild compared to the kind of denunciations that appeared regularly in America's radical Protestant press. He believed that Roman Catholicism was a mindless religion that stifled curiosity and retarded public education. Lower Canada seemed to confirm this, "for the common class have very little or no education whatever." *The Protestant* probed for Catholic corruption in Canada. Even Henry David Thoreau found that the French Canadians had "fallen far behind the significance of their symbols." After looking into a local school, Thoreau concluded that "obfuscating the mind was going on, and the pupils received only so much light as could penetrate the shadow of the Catholic Church."[19]

Guidebooks echoed American anti-Catholicism, but usually stressed the cultural and physical attractions of Lower Canada that they thought would appeal to travelers. Along with cathedrals, churches, convents, these included the imposing public buildings, baths, monuments, and inns.

The populace, however, was the primary focus. The French remained figures from the past to Henry Gilpin, "and present a strange contrast to the inhabitants of the United States, and even of Upper Canada." John Disturnell warned tourists that Lower Canada was a "foreign country." The people were quaint, with "antique" fashions, albeit "frugal, honest, industrious, and hospitable," despite their ignorance and the clergy's "almost despotic influence over popular opinion and conduct in all public matters." Americans expected ethnic groups to be easily assimilated. They were surprised to discover that English rule had not altered the French significantly. Charles Lanman reported that the kind and polite, but dim and unenterprising "Habitans" professed a preference to be Americans rather than royal subjects. The haughty Lanman, however, doubted that republican rule would overcome their inherent inferiority. Richard Henry Dana summed up many American reactions. "How strange! How different from everything American is Quebec!"[20]

American travelers in the provinces betrayed what amounts to racial prejudices in comments on the French Canadians. Prejudice against non–Anglo-Saxon peoples pervaded antebellum society, as attitudes toward Indians, blacks, orientals, and Mexicans revealed. French Canadian racial inferiority invited the dead weight of the seigneurial system, Roman Catholicism and priestly domination and helped account for Lower Canada's stagnation. The people appeared unindustrious and "ignorant, superstitious, prejudiced, mean-spirited, and slovenly. They are hardly to be distinguished in their complexion from the Indians, and in many things they even affect the Indian manners," wrote Timothy Bigelow. Joseph Sansom found them lazy, low, simple, poor, unambitious, without national feeling, obedient, "ready to admit the superiority of the American character." The townspeople seemed more sophisticated and urbane, but no better educated. Sansom's remarks say much more about himself than about the French Canadians.[21]

Condescension and paternalism were merely a step above open prejudice. Benjamin Silliman saw the French Canadians as content to remain the same through many generations because they were essentially a peasantry, albeit "vastly superior to European peasantry in comforts and in privileges." Thoreau noted saw pits producing planks for paving in Quebec City and wondered why waterpower had not been harnessed for such work. This "reminded me that I was no longer in Yankee land." He thought that people around Montmorency were inferior intellectually and physically to New Englanders. The French seemed a millennium out of date, divorced from modern progress.[22]

Guidebooks occasionally echoed these private sentiments, warning tourists to expect backwardness in Lower Canada. Theodore Dwight noted the priests perpetuated ignorance and anti-Protestantism so that progressive American values had little chance to penetrate and improve the quality of life.[23]

Travelers' comments about the provincials provide a clear picture of the rising middle class in the United States that counted intellectuals, businessmen, politicians, clergy, and journalists in its ranks. This is equally true about their remarks on dominantly British Upper Canada. Here they saw Anglo-Saxon cousins with apparently similar interests who might be developing along American lines, and so the comparisons and contrasts with American ideas, systems, and practices were therefore sharply drawn. If the inferior, priest-ridden French were backward, the Protestant Anglo-Saxons should have been progressive.

Most American travelers, however, were disappointed at the lack of material development among British provincials and were distressed not to find more enterprise. Monarchical government was the culprit for some. But American ideology provided a handy explanation for the gap between provincial and Yankee progress. Loyalists and their descendants still occupied many provincial offices right through the era of Manifest Destiny, forming the powerful Family Compact in Upper Canada. Americans attributed this to the power of the Crown. Reflecting the republican view of the superiority of a citizens' militia over standing armies, many noted with disapproval the obvious military strength in such large provincial towns as Kingston, Montreal, and Quebec City. Travelers viewed these troops, not as a menace to the United States, but rather as evidence of arbitrary monarchical rule.

Recalling only their preconception about the British penchant for military force, Americans discounted the careful control the British government exerted over its military establishments. Benjamin Silliman noted that the traveler "perceives the British uniform and the German in British service, which remind him that the country has masters different from the mass of its population." The government was an alien force relying upon martial power, not consent, for its perpetuity. William Tappan Thompson, speaking through his fictitious "Major Jones," was still more emphatic. The British kept troops in Canada to subjugate the people, not protect them. Thoreau witnessed British military parades with tolerant amusement. "This universal exhibition in Canada of the tools and sinews of war reminded me of the keeper of a menagerie showing his animals' claws." Thoreau, a staunch Jeffersonian as well as a pacifist, concluded that the provinces simply had too much government.[24]

American comments on free enterprise put the United States on the cutting edge of nineteenth century civilization. William Darby, a member of the New York Historical Society, approved as the provincials transformed their wilderness into settled country. Because of this enterprise, Darby believed that a separate nation would emerge from the provinces in the future, a possible rival to the United States. "There now exists two English nations, who are, with all their moral resemblance, politically separate, and opposed to each other in views of commerce and national power." An 1834 guidebook noted that improvements in Upper Canada had overcome the climate and the wildness of the country. The Canada Company was importing settlers, funds and engineers, building the Welland Canal, and founding towns. Canadian cities along the St. Lawrence River were smaller than those on the American side, but Kingston flourished, Ottawa was opening, and trade growing. By 1841, Toronto seemed commercially progressive, and around Niagara "the state of improvement is very respectable; the whole tract is only equalled by Western New-York, whose inhabitants in enterprise are yet considerably in advance of those in Canada."[25]

"Major Jones" satirized American anti-British prejudice instead of making careful observations when he wrote that "None of these towns along here on the Canady side ain't no grate shakes, and all of 'em makes a monstrous bad contrast with the smart bisness-lookin towns on the American side, showin plain enuff that our institutions is best calculated to promote the prosperity of the peeple."[26] Yet American travelers clearly expected Anglo-Saxons to be doing better than the provincials were. True progress had an ideological base—republicanism.

By 1850, other Americans reported considerable material progress in the provinces and suggested that the two societies might be converging. Provincial society increasingly resembled that of the United States. The suspension bridge under construction at Lewiston over the Niagara River was one example. Toronto and Montreal suggested potential greatness because English and Scottish capitalists had built up a prosperous and growing trade. New Brunswick had both wealth and potential because of its fishing, lumbering, and shipbuilding. Guidebooks placed natural, historical, and material attractions on the same moral plane, as it were. Suspension bridges rivaled Isaac Brock's monument or Montmorency Falls as tourist attractions.

Indeed, John Roebling's suspension bridge at Lewiston, the Victoria railway span across the St. Lawrence at Montreal, submarine cables, and other manifestations of progressive engineering counted among the wonders of the age to people of the mid-nineteenth century. These developments proclaimed the worth and dynamism of modern civilization. Hunter's guide waxed rhapsodic about the Grand Trunk Railroad, Montreal's water works, its banks and wharves. "What a pigmy would not the Colossus of Rhodes be . . . were he placed beneath the centre arch of Stephenson's much more colossal road, the Victoria Bridge!" John Disturnell noted the commercial potential in oil wells around Sarnia and treated the Canadian and American sides of the Great Lakes Basin as a single economic unit. The provinces would blossom as part of American material expansion. Sleepy towns would burst into bustling centers. One author boldly projected tiny Island Pond as "the great inland center of a most magnificent net work of Railroads, and in time will probably be the principal port of entry on the Canadian frontier."[27]

For Americans, provincials were slightly behind the times as they sought to reap the social and material bounty of the age. William Henry Seward connected this judgment with musings about future American-provincial political changes. British North America had enough land to form a "great empire." The people were "vigorous, hardy, energetic, perfected by the Protestant religion and British constitutional liberty." He noted, however, that they were also wary of both the United States and Great Britain. "I know they will neither be conquered by the former nor permanently held by the latter. They will be independent, as they are already self-maintaining."[28]

Seward saw British North America and the United States as two variations on the theme of modernization. Would the two societies converge or would an independent British America form? Seward did not know, but saw both possibilities. He was not an annexationist. Emphasis on a common North American destiny emerged in the Anglo-Saxon union movement of the late nineteenth century. Annexation of the provinces, or Canada after Confederation in 1867, however, had little popular appeal in the United States.[29]

Many American travelers before the Civil War believed that the provinces would unite with the United States to form a single political unit at some future time. Their faith grew from perceptions of a common cultural, religious, and political heritage, from personal ties, from commercial interchange, and from geographic proximity. Before 1812, some argued that the mere influx of American settlers would produce eventual merger. In 1807, Christian Schultz spoke with settlers around Queenston who were partial toward the United States and "almost avowed hostility to the British government." Schultz and other Americans of the time expected these settlers to rise up against Britain in the event of an Anglo-American war. They would then fuse Upper Canada with their native country.[30]

After 1815, the traveler's vision of the provincials changed. William Darby, the New York booster and commercial dreamer, saw two "English nations" emerging by 1818. These were "two fragments of a congenerous people," parts of a common civilization with a mutual interest in economic development around the Great Lakes–St. Lawrence River basin. Benjamin Silliman believed that Lower Canada would progress "as the British and Anglo-American population shall flow in more extensively, and impart more vigour and activity to the community." An 1841 guidebook stated: "The proximity of the two countries, the same language, and similarity of pursuits, have so assimilated the inhabitants that a stranger, not knowing the political division, in passing from one to the other, would still think himself among the same people." Superior Anglo-Saxon energy and ambition made Montreal a bustling commercial city, despite its French population.[31]

Tourists and guide writers occasionally implied a common history. Few American visitors to Quebec City failed to view the Plains of Abraham, to "stand on the place where Wolfe expired." They admired General James Wolfe as though he were an American, rather than a British national hero. As time passed, memories of the War of 1812 faded and guidebooks described the battlefields and monuments as a common heritage, offering General Isaac Brock as a man esteemed by both sides. Military installations became tourist attractions rather than enemy bases. Guidebooks to Niagara Falls implied that a single borderlands' lore had emerged from the common war experience. *Hunter's Panoramic Guide* described the Battle of Lundy's Lane from the War of 1812 as between the "English and the Americans," leaving the provincials out entirely.[32] This sense of a common history was a contrived cultural memory on the American side. Few provincials felt that way. But Americans in the borderland did not see the international boundary as a sharp division between the two peoples.

American travelers were convinced that an economic convergence, at least, was underway between the provinces and the United States by the middle decades of the nineteenth century. For some, this implied eventual union. Even though the provinces usually came off unfavorably in economic comparisons with the United States, Americans saw economic growth as the basis for future historical change. Despite a different system of government, human energy and abundant resources would produce the same results in a North American setting—material progress and democratic independence. In 1818, Detroit's trade went into a "foreign state," but this would not last long, according to William Darby. In fact, time would reverse the trend. The completed Erie Canal would tie the entire Northwest to New York City. The provinces would become part of New York's hinterland, and profit-seeking provincials and Americans would dismantle political barriers. Geography would not master, but serve commerce.[33]

This happened to a limited degree. A noticeable provincial-American convergence in economic spheres developed by the 1850s, as the Reciprocity Treaty would confirm. While in the provinces, Joseph Sansom noted that "the relations of trade increase daily between this place and the United States; and such is the course of exchange that the notes of our principal banks circulate freely in all the towns of Canada." Some spoke of building a connecting road to Canadian settlements from the border, and Benjamin Silliman believed that Montreal would become a great North American, not simply provincial, metropolis. The cultural similarities travelers identified between the two societies did not, however, overcome ideological and political differences. Economics did not conquer all.[34]

American tourists to the Maritime provinces came to a similar series of conclusions. J. C. Myers was unimpressed with the Maritimes in general, but noted the extensive exports of potatoes, gypsum, coal, and lumber to the United States. Frederic Cozzens commented that it took a mere thirty-six hours to travel to Nova Scotia from New England ports on a Cunard vessel. As a result, many young men left the province to seek advancement in the United States.[35]

The increasing ease of travel alone testified to the converging American-provincial transportation network. For some time, Americans found it easier to reach Detroit through Upper Canada than by an all-American route, and George Thayer was one of many lake passengers who traveled from Buffalo to Detroit on a Canadian steamer. Many steamboats plied the Great Lakes and St. Lawrence River and they had become vital to the borderland trade and commerce.[36]

As American tourism to the provinces expanded after 1850, the tour guides disclosed the increasingly complex borderland transportation net. John Disturnell's several books were the most thorough in this respect. The many railroads from Boston and Portland, Maine, to Montreal convinced him that the St. Lawrence River would become "one of the great outlets for the immense products of the upper valley of the Mississippi" and would eventually compete with east-west links wholly in the United States. He detailed the interlocking rail routes and schedules as well as steamer runs on the Great Lakes. He also described American-provincial telegraph lines and hotels in Montreal and Quebec City that supported this network. His advertisers included several New York freight and passenger companies boasting of frequent departures, easy connections, swift haulage, bills of credit and exchange, and provincial offices to service Americans having business in the provinces.

A separate Disturnell publication in 1863 covered the western

Great Lakes. And Disturnell argued that even distant Pembina on the Red River north of Minnesota had great economic potential. Americans would carry the produce of this region to points of embarkation for lake steamers that would carry them to eastern markets. The Niagara Railway Suspension Bridge united "the territories of two different Governments" and insured continuous American-provincial exchange.[37]

Other guides were sketchier than Disturnell's. Most presented brief lists and descriptions of provincial attractions. But all conveyed a similar impression. Crossing between the states and the provinces was easy and comfortable, especially from major centers such as Boston or New York City. The *New York Times* correspondent moved easily on his August 1853 tour, noting the Canadians on Ogdensburg streets and the regular ferry service. The *Harper's* correspondent passed to Canada over a "Symbol of union," the suspension bridge at Lewiston, New York. Only a small boy stood guard to collect a shilling toll. Another *Harper's* correspondent covered the laying of the submarine cable off the Newfoundland coast in 1855. American tourists flocked ashore in Halifax while he awaited passage on the cable ship. The expansion of tourism alone suggested an accelerating convergence between the two peoples in the 1850s.[38]

Travelers on the Northern Tour constituted one aspect of American cultural expansion in the era of Manifest Destiny. They judged the provinces by American political, economic, religious, and ideological values. After all, they were Americans—sturdy patriots convinced of democratic-republican superiority, typically only mildly anti-British, materialistic, entrepreneurial, anti-Catholic, and racist. They were also curious about their British and French neighbors and aware of the growing economic interlinking of the provinces with the United States. Many believed that the provinces would eventually form an entirely separate country and all recognized that to the north lay a different people, neither wholly British nor wholly American in character.

Travelers on the northern tour also proved eloquent witnesses to the American faith in converging societies that became a staple for understanding the developing relationship between the United States and British North America and tempered urgings of Manifest Destiny in American-provincial relations.

Chapter 8.

A Northern

Refuge for

Slaves and

Rebels

Farewell, old master,
Don't come after me.
I'm on my way to Canada
Where colored men are free.
—American slave song

Nothing so irritating has ever oc-
curred across the border, as the open-
armed reception given to the traitors
who sought refuge there; and if the
abrogation of [Reciprocity] . . .
pinches the Provincials, no one on
this side [of] the line will regret that
the pinching comes when it is so well
deserved.
—Albany Evening Journal,
July 1865

*T*he slavery issue in America exacerbated sectional conflict and eventually led to the Civil War. The political and
military imperatives of the war affected American views of
the provinces in two principal ways. To begin with, the
provinces had eradicated involuntary servitude even before imperial abolition in 1833, and this impressed all parties in the debate
on slavery in the United States. American abolitionists gleaned
moral support from their British counterparts before 1833 and after-
wards displayed Great Britain as an example of enlightenment. Pro-
slavery spokesmen fumed because the provinces provided a refuge
for their slaves escaping north via the Underground Railroad. Both
slaves and free blacks considered Canada a Canaan, a sanctuary
from racial oppression.

British North America also became a factor in the Civil War that
erupted following Southern secession and the creation of the Confederacy in 1861. The provinces were, after all, neutral territory.
Neither the British nor the Union government stood guard at the
open frontier that had developed by the 1860s. But now a trickle of
Union deserters and escaping Confederate prisoners mingled among
the usual travelers north to the provinces. And Confederate agents

used the provinces as bases for planning operations against the Union. The resulting stabs across the frontier were gaudy gestures, fantasies realized rather than effective military operations. Borderland Northerners were nevertheless disturbed, and President Abraham Lincoln's administration watched the frontier closely, eventually applying a temporary passport system.

The slavery issue interwove with American views of the provinces in the years before 1861. The provinces were neither as free from prejudice nor as filled with opportunity for Negroes as abolitionists, Southerners, or blacks imagined. The Canadian Canaan was a myth. Many blacks evacuated New York as freemen and with loyalist masters in 1783 as part of the British-loyalist exodus from the new United States. Those blacks did not find social, economic, or legal conditions in the barely converted provincial wilderness much better than they had in the older colonies. Runaway slaves and free blacks escaping racial discrimination in the northern states after 1800 nevertheless found in the provinces equality before the law and a general freedom from persecution. Upper Canada was the most frequently mentioned terminus of the Underground Railroad, even though far fewer slaves escaped there than either Southerners or abolitionists maintained. In fact, most black migrants to Canada were free, not slaves.

After the loyalist exodus, the first large group of free blacks departing the United States for the provinces left in 1829. Black leaders in Cincinnati, Ohio, were deeply disturbed by an upswelling of racial prejudice, backed by local political pressure. As a result, the city had ordered free blacks to post a bond of $500 or leave the city. Since few blacks had or could raise such a sum, this amounted to an eviction notice based on race. After a lengthy meeting and discussion, the Cincinnati blacks sent Israel Lewis and Thomas Cressup north to Upper Canada to seek from the provincial government permission to emigrate and a grant of land for resettlement. British authorities were both sympathetic and receptive. Lewis and Cressup returned to Cincinnati to organize the 1,000 free blacks willing to make the move.

It did not matter that Cincinnati's mayor, responding to a potential labor shortage if free blacks left the city, had the bond ordinance withdrawn. The Lewis and Cressup group left as planned. Resettled, they formed the nucleus of what became known as the

Wilberforce Colony, near London in Upper Canada, named after the noted British abolitionist. Benjamin Lundy, the American abolitionist and editor, later visited Wilberforce to see how the refugees had prospered. He also wanted to investigate Upper Canada in general as a potential refuge for other American blacks.[1]

Lundy was favorably impressed, as he reported in his paper, "The Genius of Universal Emancipation." The soil struck him as potentially productive, and water was abundant. London was growing and seemed much like similar sized towns in the United States. Whites in the vicinity were "mostly Europeans and their immediate descendants born in Canada," but Americans were moving in as well. Black refugees, like any immigrants, would have to be realistic about managing their affairs. But this was a minor caveat. Immigrant Americans coming to live among the "monarchists . . . would act wisely to assume fewer airs, and submit cheerfully, like good 'liege subjects,'" to a British law that protected blacks as well as whites. Lundy pronounced Upper Canada a decent refuge for blacks seeking asylum from persecution.[2]

Americans who were in the habit of denouncing British tyranny over their colonial forefathers overlooked American tyranny over the blacks, whether free or slave. That irony did not escape Lundy or other American abolitionists in the antebellum period. By the 1830s, monarchism was freer than republicanism. Provincial authorities decreed gradual emancipation in Upper Canada 11 on July 1793. The first few black refugees arrived from the United States nearly twenty years later, just after the War of 1812. Their mere existence lent the provinces their collective image as a sanctuary that blacks expressed in biblical terms. When blacks talked about Canaan, the Promised Land, or the New Jerusalem, they usually meant Upper Canada, although they occasionally referred as well to Africa. The Detroit River therefore became a symbolic River Jordan, although the St. Lawrence played the same role for blacks escaping up through New York.

Abolitionists and free blacks formed several refugee settlements in Upper Canada as they helped blacks on the run from slavery. Few of the "colonies" proved successful. Funding was scanty, and some American abolitionists wanted their monies used to end slavery in the United States, not to subsidize foreign sanctuaries. The black provincial centers were nevertheless a part of the colonization phase of American abolitionism that also sent refugees to Liberia and Sierra Leone. The provincial ventures could also be seen as black versions of the utopian come-outers, such as the Mormons, who fled conventional society in the northern United States.

Blacks encountered severe racial discrimination in Pennsylvania and Ohio. Reverend Richard Allen of Philadelphia, founder of the Bethel Church, favored black emigration from the United States only if Canada were the goal. In September of 1830, a national convention of free blacks met in Philadelphia and recommended that their brothers and sisters flee to Upper Canada to escape racial oppression in the United States. Perhaps 800 to 1,000 reached all the provinces between 1830 and 1840. Wilberforce especially drew black attention because it was the first effort by free blacks to form their own community.

In 1842, American and British abolitionists formed Dawn, what might be called a borderland colony at London. Both Wilberforce and Dawn had leadership and financial difficulties. As a result they limped, rather than strode along as experiments in black communal living. Only Elgin, founded by an Irish minister who had settled in Louisiana and then led the slaves he had inherited to freedom, survived economically.[3] But these difficulties did nothing to spoil the image of the provinces as a refuge for persecuted blacks. The myth of the Canadian Canaan persisted.

Provincials shared the racial prejudice of many Anglo-Saxon Americans. Blacks were nevertheless reasonably secure once in British North America. Southerners who had lost slaves to the provinces occasionally tried judicial pursuit. In 1829, Paul Vallard escaped with an Illinois mulatto slave to Upper Canada. Acting on behalf of the owner, Secretary of State Henry Clay demanded that British authorities prosecute Vallard as a thief. Clay requested Vallard's extradition from Sir James Kempt, the provincial governor. Kempt refused and cited his council's ruling that fugitives could be returned only if they were accused of a crime that was also a crime in Upper Canada. Provincial law would not recognize slavery, so any slave who entered British North America became free. After 1833 and British abolition of slavery within the empire, refugee blacks became even more legally secure. In the Blackburn case, provincial judges refused to extradite a black couple who had fled the United States entirely because of the fugitive slave law.[4]

Despite Southern protests and claims, not many refugees fled to the provinces. As few as 6,000 slaves escaped to Canada during the entire antebellum period. By 1860, just before the Civil War began, the Canadian census showed only 11,000 blacks, although abolitionists suggested that as many as 25,000 to 30,000 blacks lived in the provinces by that time. Abolitionists were determined to prove how odious slavery was and may have exaggerated the numbers of escapees. The exact routes and dates of black migration remain unclear. Southerners also exaggerated the number of escaped slaves. The abolition of slavery in the provinces was an affront to Southern slaveholders. The most stringent fugitive slave laws could not operate in a foreign country. The South won a tough law in the Compromise of 1850, but hundreds of blacks living in Northern states simply uprooted to march across the frontier to Upper Canada.

American abolitionists visited, studied, and talked about the provinces throughout the antebellum period. Levi Coffin, a principal organizer of the Underground Railroad, scouted Upper Canada for locations for his personal refugees. A Canadian abolitionist, Dr. Alexander Ross, came to the Southern states to help blacks escape north. After her own escape, Harriet Tubman did the same, sending many of those she helped on to the provinces.

Something of a borderland abolitionist movement developed over time. The American Missionary Society, organized at Albany, New York, in 1846, made grants to its "Canada Mission" until 1864, when it suspended operations. Michigan and Upper Canadian abolitionists cooperated to form the Refugees Home Society. The Society placed fugitives on land in Upper Canada. The Anti-Slavery Society of Canada was formed in Toronto in 1851 specifically to help the American Negroes. Frederick Douglass and Elihu Burritt both spoke in Toronto, and Harriet Beecher Stowe's *Uncle Tom's Cabin* sold well in the city. In 1858, John Brown attended an abolitionist convention at Chatham, Upper Canada, where he formed the plans that led to his Harpers Ferry raid the following year.[5]

By 1852, black settlements stood at Buxton, Colchester, Dawn, New Canaan, and across the river from Detroit at Sandwich. The distance between the slave South and the provinces was both attractive and a deterrent. Some slaves, although ignorant of the legal protection Canada afforded them, simply decided on the provinces as a goal because they were too far away for their masters to reach them. To discourage runaways, slaveholders told of northern cold, but the myth of Canada as Canaan and the prospect of freedom easily outweighed such descriptions. At the same time, only the boldest, hardiest, and most determined slaves were willing to press the frightening and exhausting trek to its conclusion.

Potential runaways focused on Upper Canada because the Maritimes were too distant and difficult to reach. And both abolitionists and blacks understood that Lower Canada was Francophone and Roman Catholic and therefore alien. Perhaps most important, Upper Canada lay alongside a northern tier of states where runaways could find assistance. Although many who landed in Upper Canada found local whites racially prejudiced, at least the law protected them. As Thomas Likers told an American Freedman's Inquiry Commission interviewer in 1863, "the law makes no difference between black & white. If it had not been for that, I would not have gone to Canada."[6]

Mary Ann Shadd ran a school at Windsor, Upper Canada. In 1852, to clear up what she knew of black ignorance and apprehension about the provinces, she prepared an extensive report. The climate, especially in Upper Canada, was not as severe as rumor suggested. The soils were rich and productive, fruits grew well, and in the Michigan State Fair of 1851, provincial farmers had walked away with prizes for their fruit, cattle, and fowl. Jobs seemed readily available (the depression after Britain abolished the Corn Laws in 1846 had passed by then), and provincials judged work on merit, not skin color.

Shadd found that the provinces extended blacks rights they did not have in the United States. Equality of access existed in education, politics, and religion. Blacks could vote, although like any immigrant from outside the British Empire, refugees had to take an oath to the Queen and qualify under the property requirements. Shadd reported little poverty among black people in Upper Canada. The French were kind, although ignorant and crude. And even if blacks encountered prejudice, they could sue in the courts. "Persons emigrating to Canada, need not hope to find the general state of society as it is in the States. There is as in the old country, a strong class feeling—lines are as completely drawn between the different classes, and aristocracy in the Canadas is the same in its manifestation as aristocracy in England, Scotland and elsewhere."

But for Shadd the "aristocracy of birth, not of skin, as with the Americans" made British-ruled provinces far preferable to the racial and legal oppression of the more democratic United States.[7]

The provincial borderland on the Pacific also offered a refuge. By the 1850s, a multiethnic society that included blacks had collected in California in the wake of the gold rush of 1849. Racial prejudice in California was directed primarily against Mexicans. British Columbia was a frontier province, shaped by superannuated Hudson's Bay Company employees and colonial officials. The Pacific borderland was barely developed, but even so, British territory swiftly acquired the image of a refuge.

Between 1850 and 1852, California passed discriminatory ordinances and a fugitive slave law. The San Francisco school board insisted that blacks be educated in segregated facilities. California blacks met and debated whether to migrate to Vancouver Island or Sonora, Mexico. They decided to send an advance party north to see if the British would receive them. Eager for settlers, the British welcomed the prospective immigrants. The Californians "determined to seek an asylum in the land of strangers from the oppression, prejudice and relentless persecution that have pursued us for more than two centuries in this, our mother country." Their delegation to Vancouver Island had found a sanctuary and presented, "in our darkest hour, the prospect of a bright future." Perhaps 400 blacks went north to live "under the genial laws of the Queen of the Christian Isles" on Vancouver Island.[8]

The Fraser River gold rush combined with a labor shortage in Victoria, on Vancouver Island, to pull more blacks into British Columbia. Although she did not travel there, Mary Ann Shadd included Victoria in her commentary on the provinces as refuges. Here, as in the eastern provinces, if blacks found racial prejudice, it was because of the many white Americans. Many of the white settlers in British Columbia came because of the 1857 gold rush. But most of them soon left when the gold fields failed to produce the anticipated bonanzas. Besides, Americans bristled under British efforts to control the immigration into their tiny Pacific colony. Most of the blacks who settled on Vancouver Island, like so many from Upper Canada, eventually returned to the United States during and immediately after the Civil War.

Abolitionists thought highly of British North America, its officials, and its people because all seemed to welcome blacks and to sympathize with the antislavery movement in the United States. Hiram Wilson, a Lane Seminary rebel who in 1842 founded the British-American Manual Labor Institute in St. Catherines, Upper Canada, remained for many years as a station master for the Underground Railroad. Wilson even persuaded provincial authorities to exempt supplies for the fugitives from usual customs duties. William Lloyd Garrison wrote to Wendell Phillips in 1839 that many slaves "are safely landed in Canada, to receive liberty and protection under the flag of Victoria. May their numbers increase." In Canada, blacks found "recognition of their common humanity" despite the exchange of flags and allegiance. Garrison, however, was disappointed in 1853 over the conditions he found at Windsor and Sandwich and seemed prejudiced toward the French Canadians, whatever his feelings about black equality.[9]

If abolitionists praised provincials for providing a refuge for blacks, Southerners fumed. In the 1820s, some argued for closing what was scarcely more than a symbolic escape valve. On 24 January 1821, Congress heard a resolution from the General Assembly of Kentucky protesting the refuge fugitive slaves found in the provinces. Kentucky wanted to negotiate extradition with the British, by which it meant that the British should surrender any refugees forthwith. In 1826, Henry Clay instructed Albert Gallatin to raise the issue in the context of discussions about the joint occupation of Oregon. Congress accommodated Southern interests by formal resolution in June of 1828. Clay professed that the "evil" of refuge was growing. In the future, the issue of fugitives "might disturb the good neighbourhood which we are desireous of cultivating with the adjacent British Provinces." If slaveholders pursued their property, and the fugitives defended themselves, an Anglo-American crisis could well result.[10]

The British refusal to return refugees infuriated Southerners. They echoed their demand that the fugitive slaves in British North America be extradited. In 1841, the Senate resolved that the Foreign Relations Committee urge such discussions with Great Britain. Deep in talks with Lord Ashburton on far more important matters, Daniel Webster ignored the Southern interest. In 1842, the British refused again to negotiate extradition. But when provincial authorities decided to send back Nelson Hacket, the Canadian refuge came into immediate jeopardy and almost collapsed.

When Hacket escaped, he stole several items from his Arkansas merchant master, Alfred Wallace. Wallace tracked Hacket to Chatham in Upper Canada and had him arrested for theft. Next, he indicted Hacket in Arkansas and petitioned Governor Archibald Yell for extradition under Article Ten of the recent Webster-Ashburton Treaty. That article covered criminal matters, but not the extradition of runaway slaves. The provincial authorities agreed to return Hacket as a criminal. But abolitionists organized protests in both the provinces and the United States and demanded an investigation of Hacket's case. Wallace and Yell lost. The British and provincial authorities placed the protection of refugee blacks above the terms of the Webster-Ashburton Treaty. Furthermore, the British promised that they would guard against future abuses of criminal extradition. The British kept their promise. In 1861, even an attempt at extradition for murder failed.[11]

In the meantime, because of the Fugitive Slave Law of 1850, the movement of black refugees to the provinces quickened. Free blacks in borderland states fled to avoid capture and transportation south. Perhaps two-thirds of all black refugees to the provinces arrived during the last decade before the Civil War, the truly active period for the Underground Railroad.

Journalists recognized the potential political ramifications of this expansion of the nation's domestic discord. The *New York Times* noted that although Southern spokesmen had always opposed annexing the provinces, Canada's role as a refuge after 1850 had changed things. The *Times* mocked Southerners who would now demand annexation "as a Constitutional right they have, to regain their property." Southerners now defined continentalism as the right to chase runaway slaves anywhere and everywhere. But the *Times* was also genuinely concerned about the fate of fugitive slaves in the provinces. Its editors applauded the Underground Railroad's apparently successful defiance of the new Fugitive Slave Law.[12]

Blacks themselves cherished their provincial refuge, although time spent there stripped them of any illusions about the Canadian Canaan. The Cincinnati refugees were deeply grateful, even if Wilberforce did ultimately fail. Samuel Ringgold Ward, who bolted north in 1851, recalled an immediate sense of "fellow feeling" with the provincials. Blacks had free access to schools and the courts even though they usually occupied the lowest economic levels. The provincials were prejudiced and viewed the blacks as refugees rather than social equals. Samuel Gridley Howe found similar conditions during his Civil War visit to the refugee communities. Howe had fled to the provinces himself as a member of the "Secret Six" supporting John Brown's raid of 1859, so he knew how it felt to be a refugee. In 1863, he gathered information for Congress on the implications of black freedom in the postwar years. The provincial experience suggested that the blacks would form stable families and communities. He also noted that once slavery ended, most of the refugees would likely return as they had fled oppression, not American ideals.[13]

Howe's judgment was sound on all points. Once emancipation became a war aim in 1863, blacks in the provinces drifted back to the United States. They virtually deserted Vancouver Island in the Pacific Northwest. Many migrated to the South after the Confederacy collapsed in 1865. The loyalists and others had seen the provinces as a permanent refuge. By contrast, slaves and free blacks living in northern states in the antebellum period for the most part sought only a temporary shelter until conditions in the United States improved.

This image of the provincial refuge led many Northerners to expect open sympathy and assistance against the Confederacy. But British and provincial antislavery sentiment did not translate automatically into support for the Union. So many unionists soured on the provinces. When Britain's government, at Lord Palmerston's direction, recognized Confederate belligerency in 1861, it only intensified Northern disappointment with all things British. Anglo-American relations deteriorated during the Civil War, and American-provincial relations tended to sink along with them.

After the war began, the provinces became a different kind of refuge as neutral soil. Draft dodgers in the Northern states and bounty jumpers living close to the border could hustle into the provinces, either to sit out the war or return and enlist under another name for another bounty. Opponents of Lincoln's Republican administration who found themselves in legal difficulties, such as the vilified "Copperheads" and fringe elements plotting with Confederates, also found the provinces a convenient sanctuary. The Confederate government under Jefferson Davis saw after a time that the provinces might be useful bases for raids on northern territory. The romantic zealots who clustered in rebel rendezvous in Toronto and Montreal plotted and attempted to effect uprisings in the North that would defeat Lincoln and the Republicans.

Resentment against Great Britain over her policies erupted in periodic antiprovincial statements in the Northern states. The strident editor James Gordon Bennett made his *New York Herald* almost synonymous with annexationism, for example, partly because of his sense of America's destiny and partly out of anger against Great Britain. The *Herald* argued in February of 1861 that the free areas should unite to repair the loss of secession. "Now that the South is wrest from us, our destined expansion is northward, and nothing can arrest our progress." Bennett gave the American convergence thesis an aggressive edge it had not had for years. The provincials were "hardy and thrifty, and homogeneous with our own Anglo-Saxon and Anglo-Celtic population—the very flower of the Caucasian race." The *Charlestown Advertiser*, recycling the common American conceit in the era of Manifest Destiny, declared that the provincials would welcome annexation. "In the homogeneous character and common origin of the two peoples also would be found powerful means for affiliation and unity."[14]

Northern editorial vulcanism alarmed provincials and their British protectors. Both feared a possible invasion because of bruised American feelings. The British bolstered their provincial garrisons by sending troops in *The Great Eastern*, the largest ship afloat at the time. The *Trent* affair of November, 1861 posed the greatest potential danger, but cool counsel prevailed in both Washington and London. No clash flowed from the crisis, despite Secretary of State William H. Seward's widely known penchant for stridency when dealing with the British. One war at a time was enough for Lincoln and Seward. But there can be little doubt that American troops would have marched toward the provinces if a conflict had erupted.

Seward was far less erratic than he seemed to foreigners, and unlike the fulminating Bennett, he did not see the provinces as a potential partner in a free-republican North. Seward was also well acquainted with the borderland and the provinces, and although he respected British power, he never expected trouble to come from either the British or the provincials. Lincoln's government knew about the Confederate agents in the provinces, as Seward had in 1861 established special operatives to watch the border. Paying them out of Secret Service funds, he formed an intelligence network that supported the American consuls in provincial ports.[15]

Lincoln and Seward, along with many Union officials in and out of the military, knew that the Confederates could launch raids from provincial bases against Union territory. At the very least, these Confederates could work with Northerners opposed to Lincoln's prosecution of the war. But the provinces were far from Confederate lines, and a hostile North made movement and communications difficult. War exerted enormous pressure on the South. Confederate President Jefferson Davis and his secretary of war, James Seddon, were therefore slow to consider using the provinces in this way. Lincoln's administration nevertheless took early precautions. The president prohibited exporting any war materials in November of 1862, citing arms "bound for Canada" seized at Rouses Point, at the northern end of Lake Champlain in New York, as an example of a potential danger to the Union war effort.[16] British authorities and American watchers in the provinces maintained a constant stream of intelligence about suspected or known Confederates in the major provincial centers.

After 1863, however, the Confederates found their position becoming untenable and these agents became more active. Seddon sent Captain Thomas Hines, one of John Hunt Morgan's cavalrymen, to Upper Canada to collect escaped Confederate prisoners and return them via blockade runners to the South. In April 1864, Davis sent a commission consisting of Jacob Thompson, Clement C. Clay, and J. P. Holcomb to Upper Canada. They were to meet with prominent opponents of the war, such as Republican Horace Greeley and Copperhead leaders such as Clement Vallandigham of Ohio, who spent several months in Upper Canada. Davis also expected them to propagandize for the South in sympathetic Northern newspapers, entering the United States across the neutral frontier.

Jacob Thompson was the main Confederate agent in Canada, and he chose Toronto as his base of operations. The provinces seemed to Thompson and his coconspirators ideal for plotting against the Union, especially in the Northwest, the center of Democratic opposition to Lincoln's war. Thompson also hoped to free Confederate prisoners held far from the battle lines in such locations as Camp Douglas, Illinois, near Chicago. In 1864, Thompson and his colleagues hatched a plot to seize Union lake steamers and free prisoners. They also imagined setting Cincinnati and New York ablaze. Few of these schemes came to more than a series of midnight rendezvous. The *Philo Parsons* plot was an exception.[17] Thompson intended to seize the only armed American vessel on Lake Erie, the USS *Michigan*. They would then turn the *Michigan*'s guns on nearby Johnson Island to free captive Confederates.

After much discussion, the operation lurched into motion in September of 1864. The Confederate agents gathered at Windsor, across from Detroit, and boarded a provincial steamer, the *Philo Parsons*. Then they unloaded a trunk of revolvers and cutlasses and seized the vessel. They next intended to storm the *Michigan*. But provincial authorities helped to thwart this plan once the Confederates had taken the *Philo Parsons*. This opera bouffe raid nevertheless threw the American side of the border into a momentary panic. In Lincoln's cabinet, however, only Secretary of the Navy Gideon Welles was actually alarmed. Seward maintained that "the Canadian authorities seem to have acted in a friendly and honorable manner" throughout.[18]

The Confederate forays from the provinces were pinpricks, of greater psychological than military importance. Southern agents in the provinces nevertheless manipulated a minor propaganda victory in early 1864. Joshua Giddings, the American consul general in Montreal, was a fierce antislavery unionist. Disguised Confederate agents maintained to Giddings that one William L. Redpath was a dangerous Southern spy. The only way to deal with Redpath, they persuaded the consul general, was to kidnap him and spirit him out of Lower Canada for incarceration in the United States. Utterly duped, Giddings agreed and set the kidnapping plan afoot. The Confederates then tipped off British authorities in Lower Canada what Giddings was up to. Giddings found himself swiftly arrested for violating British law.

Members of Congress were outraged. American consuls were primarily commercial agents, but because Giddings was consul general, he had a quasi-diplomatic status in addition to his commercial duties. Congressmen argued that Giddings should have freedom from arrest as part of the "privileges and immunities of an ambassador." Secretary of State Seward, however, denied that Giddings had any diplomatic status whatever. Even if he did, no American could be immune from arrest if he broke provincial laws. Seward handled the entire affair with an eye to overall Anglo-American relations. Both Giddings and Seward understood that they were victims of Confederate trickery aimed at eliminating a strong Union supporter from action in Montreal. But Giddings never forgave Seward's apparent betrayal.[19]

The hundreds of escaped Confederate prisoners and agents in the provinces by 1864 made other officers feel insecure. In August of 1864, a Union officer traveled from Pittsburgh to Erie, Pennsylvania, to investigate "disturbances on the Canadian line." The officer dispatched a subordinate to Cleveland, and another to Clifton House, in Canada. He himself went to Buffalo. The Confederates in the provinces met and schemed, but the Buffalo Provost Marshall believed that "the Canadians would not permit any open act of hostile organization."[20] Major General John A. Dix insisted to Secretary of War Edwin M. Stanton that the British had to prevent marauders from even organizing. The boundary was far too long to police effectively, despite the concentrated use of some border crossings, such as over the Niagara gorge. Raids across the line "will lead to a border war in spite of any precautions we can do." Reports on the assemblies of Confederates in Montreal streamed to Washington through the summer of 1864. In October, a small band of these refugees created a borderland cause célèbre—the St. Albans Raid.[21]

Confederate lieutenant Bennett Young led the St. Albans marauders. Their aim was little beyond arson, bank robbery, plunder, and terror. At best, Young led a romantic gesture, not a military expedition with political objectives. On 10 October, Young's band, fortified with alcohol, rode south from Montreal to the American border. St. Albans lay only a few miles beyond, on the Vermont shore of Lake Champlain. The Confederates shot up the town, snatched what loot they could, and set some fires before fleeing back to their provincial refuge, hotly pursued across the line by a makeshift posse. British authorities promptly arrested Young and his men. Seward applied for criminal extradition, and United States attorneys appeared before British Judge Coursol to plead the case. But

Judge Coursol dismissed the raiders on a legal technicality and even returned their loot, much to Confederate delight and Union indignation.[22]

The threat of retaliation against the provinces arising from popular American outrage was real. The fiery Zachariah Chandler warned that revenge would surely follow if the provincials let Confederates raid his native Michigan. Members of the House of Representatives demanded immediate cancellation of the Reciprocity Treaty. Seward was also outraged. He ordered federal troops to pursue and capture any such bandits in the future, even across the line into the provinces. Further, they would refuse to surrender any captives they took if provincial troops or police came on the scene. Lincoln told Congress on 6 December 1864 that the United States had given Britain six months' notice of the intent to increase Union naval forces on the Great Lakes, and might restrict the free movement of goods on the border as well. On 17 December, Seward imposed a passport system for the first time during the war. He also suggested suspending the Rush-Bagot agreement. Alarmed, the British placated the Union government. To begin with, John A. Macdonald created a special provincial police force to patrol the borders.[23]

The Lincoln government moved to solve a military problem that had arisen because the Confederacy had exploited neutral territory along the lengthy northern frontier. The anger in Congress was genuine. But Seward knew that the passport system could never be enforced and if sustained would damage American interests in the borderland trade. Lincoln removed the passport edict when Canada voted and paid $50,000 to the grieving St. Albans's banks. Seward dropped his threats about abrogating the Rush-Bagot agreement when the provincials passed more stringent neutrality laws to preempt Confederate activities. Many Americans were satisfied. They respected the actions of a foreign neighbor to preserve its neutrality under difficult circumstances. Lincoln's December message noted that the provincials had not been "intentionally unjust or unfriendly," and that provincial and imperial authorities would stop future assaults. Seward agreed because he was largely responsible for this statement. He wrote privately in March 1865, "It is reasonable to hope that the energy with which justice is being administered will bring to an end the war we have so long suffered from the British colonies on our border."[24]

By the fall of 1864, the Confederacy approached collapse. Davis's government had focused on defense of the homeland against Union invasion and on pleading for foreign recognition and intervention, especially from Great Britain. The provinces were a sideshow, a refuge, but potentially dangerous only if the Union and British governments had not cooperated to resolve difficulties that arose from Confederate plots hatched on provincial soil. Impending defeat did not, however, discourage Southern fantasies of revenge.

Perhaps the most notorious schemer to find a temporary refuge in the provinces was John Wilkes Booth, Lincoln's assassin. In October of 1864, Booth registered at the St. Lawrence Hotel in Montreal. He gave some readings, met furtively with local Confederate agents, and left cash in the Ontario Bank. Then he decamped for the United States, shipping his theatrical wardrobe for New York on the *Marie Victoria*. When the vessel foundered, Booth's clothing was auctioned in Quebec City, prized by then because of Booth's new notoriety.[25]

Only a few of the estimated 15,000 Confederate refugees in the provinces were party to such plots as the *Philo Parsons* affair or the St. Albans bank robberies. Most simply found a temporary haven and either worked to travel to Nassau or Bermuda, where they could return to the South on blockade runners, or settled down quietly to await the end of hostilities. John Hunt Morgan's cavalry raiders, after a rampage through Ohio, rested briefly in Upper Canada before returning south to fight again.

Charles Coon, who in the fall of 1863 escaped from Camp Douglas, near Chicago, was a passive Confederate refugee. He wandered over Upper Canada, but found it cold and lonely. He pined to return to the South to fight the Yankees. Denied that, he linked up with other escapees and stayed at a private home in Toronto. Then his outlook brightened. He attended lectures at the University of Toronto and met pretty girls at skating parties. Later, he attended Toronto's medical school and roomed with the son of Kentucky governor Magoffin. But he never reconciled himself to life in the provinces. After returning to the United States, he was graduated from the University of Louisville in 1866, only to die three years later.[26]

One of the last Confederates to find a temporary refuge in the provinces was Jefferson Davis. Union authorities held Davis in Fortress Monroe following his capture after the Confederacy surrendered. Released 13 May 1867, Davis traveled to Montreal and then to Niagara. There he visited with James M. Mason, a former United States senator, and one of the men seized by the Union navy in the *Trent* affair. Mason and Jubal Early were two prominent former Confederates who had taken refuge in Upper Canada after Union authorities had released them. Davis returned to the provinces after his final liberation 25 December 1868, stayed until the summer of 1869 to work on his book about the war, and then journeyed to England.[27]

Northerners, as well as Confederates, found sanctuary in the provinces during the Civil War. Union recruiting officers accurately predicted that once the draft came into effect, some Northerners would flee to the provinces. Many in uniform had second thoughts about the war and deserted. Reports suggested that about half of the deserters from New York regiments were in Upper Canada by 1863. The provinces were indeed accessible, and bounty jumpers or military deserters could move across the border as easily as Vermont farmers could smuggle their produce. Some Union politicians, such as Senator Wilson from New York, estimated that 10,000 to 15,000 had fled. But the bounty jumpers moved back and forth as frequently as they dared. Northerners resented the provinces for providing such an easy refuge. Detroit papers, for example, insisted that provincial authorities catch the shirkers.[28]

Outspoken opponents of the Republican war effort also sought temporary refuge in the provinces. Lincoln's government banished Copperhead Clement L. Vallandigham of Ohio from the Union to the Confederacy in 1863. Vallandigham stopped at Windsor, Upper Canada, across from Detroit. In exile, he ran for governor of his state. Visitors flocked over after Vallandigham took up residence. Lincoln's cabinet knew that Confederate agents Jacob Thompson and his assistants, Clement C. Clay and W. W. Clearly, conferred with Vallandigham. Union authorities also knew of Horace Greeley's meeting with Confederates at Niagara Falls. The neutral provinces provided a convenient refuge for this "peace" conference. But Greeley had no authority, and the South wanted only independence, which Lincoln and the Republicans refused to grant. Peace Democrats also met in the provinces. William Jewett, for example, traveled north on a futile errand to urge the British authorities to mediate the conflict.[29]

If the provinces offered a refuge for Northerners unwilling to serve in Union regiments, they also provided recruits who somewhat offset those seeking sanctuary. In the Windsor-Detroit area, as elsewhere on the borderland, Union recruiters reached across the boundary. Lincoln's government frowned on the practice of "crimping"—illegal recruiting—in the provinces. But perhaps 40,000 provincials eventually joined to fight in Union armies.[30]

The pressures produced by the slavery issue and the Civil War helped to resurrect long-held American perspectives on the British North American provinces. Slavery renewed the American image of the provinces as a refuge, although only a handful of runaway slaves fled north across the border. Far more free blacks entered the provinces to escape racial prejudice in the North. Once the war broke out, the provinces also served as a refuge for Confederates who slipped out from northern prison camps. The provinces also provided a convenient refuge for deserters and bounty jumpers from Union armies. Finally, a handful of former Confederates found a postwar provincial refuge after the South's surrender.

Other established American images of the provinces received new emphasis. For example, American abolitionists saw potential converts to their cause among the provincials both because Britain had eradicated slavery and because provincial people and courts seemed color-blind. The provinces also supplied recruits for the Union and the war on slavery. The image of the provinces as an enemy base also took on new twists for Americans. Southerners saw a potential threat beyond what they believed already existed in the increasingly hostile North. If the provinces ever joined the United States, slavery would drown in a free soil sea. After the fighting erupted following the bombardment of Fort Sumter, the Union also saw the provinces as an enemy base. They no longer feared the British garrisons, but the Confederates exploited British neutrality and the long boundary to plot and conduct raids and aggravate disaffection in the North.

Although American suspicions were revived, a spirit of accommodation prevailed at the highest levels. Neither British nor American officials permitted public spasms of anger to undermine larger policy interests. And when the Confederates violated provincial neutrality by launching raids, the British cooperated to control further abuses. The forces behind the American Civil War had by a sort of centrifugal force pushed quarreling and warring Americans beyond their national boundaries, but American relations with the provinces evinced a steadily growing maturity.

PART 3

The Era of

the New American

Empire Dawns,

1850–1871

Commercial, ideological, defensive, territorial, and even cultural factors propelled American expansionism from the end of the War of Independence to the 1850s. But fears about security faded among high policymakers and scarcely seemed an issue by 1850. The British encirclement threat evaporated when the United States acquired Oregon and achieved victory in the Mexican War. Despite occasional alarms during the Civil War, few Americans saw the provinces as an enemy base after 1854. By 1871, when Great Britain continued dismantling her North American empire with a phased withdrawal of her troops from provincial garrisons following Canadian Confederation, the idea of the provinces as an enemy base had no currency at all in the United States.

Ideological and political developments by 1850 revealed that internal, rather than external, discord imperiled the nation's security. And territorial expansionism seemed by 1860, because of its association with the South and the spread of slavery, part of that danger. Antebellum Northerners came to believe that Democratic opposition to national economic policies also exposed the self-serving nature of Southern efforts to dominate the country's affairs.

Alexander Hamilton was the first to argue that the federal government should engineer national economic development. Henry Clay sustained this theme in his "American System," and the Whig Party made national economic development part of its platform in the 1830s. During the Jacksonian period the Democrats opposed such policies on several grounds, including strict constitutional construction and economy in government. Such thinking lay behind Andrew Jackson's veto of the Maysville Road Bill. In November 1845, a convention at Memphis, Tennessee, called for federal action to enhance internal transportation systems, but James K. Polk's veto of the 1846 Rivers and Harbors Bill echoed Jackson's earlier opposition to the Maysfield Bill. Later, Franklin Pierce and James Buchanan vetoed other legislation for internal improvements.

This opposition frustrated and alienated Western Democrats. Many of them in the Northwest eagerly anticipated a Pacific railroad, but that goal was set aside in the sectional squabbling that characterized the 1850s. The Gadsden Purchase in 1854 of a small strip of land along the Mexican border was the only tangible step forward in creating a transcontinental railroad, but was useless to northwesterners who wanted the line through their section. By opposing improvements that would bolster economic growth in the country's largest sections and calling for territorial acquisition to serve slavery, the South transformed its own worst fears of persecution into reality by consolidating an opposition that could outvote it.

By the 1850s, changes in America's economy and shifting views about the country's future meant that expansionist ideologues identified commercial rather than territorial or political goals outside national borders. These commercial goals changed even as the United States itself changed from an agrarian-mercantile to an agrarian-mercantile-industrial economy.

The United States economy diversified and grew steadily through the middle decades of the nineteenth century. Americans aggressively pursued the promises of material reward throughout the antebellum period. The Jacksonian cult of the self-made man testified to values that the family, the education system and its exhortatory texts such as the famous McGuffey readers, and the pulpits reinforced. Preachers such as Henry Ward Beecher, for example, extolled the virtues of material progress along with spiritual betterment.

Some parts of the country prospered more than others because the nature of economic growth varied from section to section. In the South, cotton was the great story, spreading across the Mississippi Valley well into Texas by 1860, and rising to about 50 percent of the nation's exports by value between 1840 and 1860. Agricultural output in New England declined, but industrial productivity rose as the factory system developed. Overall, the nonslaveholding sections of the country did better than the South, despite the existence of a truly national market by 1840. Private corporations in both primary and service sectors gained self-assurance, strength, and wealth.

Whether banks, manufacturers, or transportation companies, the corporations petitioned aid from municipal, state, and federal levels of government. The American faith that free enterprise was divorced from government was in large measure a rhetorical phenomenon. Henry Clay believed thoroughly in private enterprise, but maintained with equal vigor that government had a responsi-

bility to create conditions or grant assistance so that private entrepreneurs could operate successfully. By the 1850s, most Americans
involved in economic affairs believed that the national prosperity
rested upon free competition, representative government, and international harmony. Thus early proponents of the "New American
Empire" would weave internal and external policies to create an
apparently unified program to achieve national prosperity.

The early articulation of this phase in American economic-ideo-
logical evolution bridged the 1840s to the 1870s. The national
economy grew more complex as manufacturing and the processing
of foodstuffs were added to the production of raw materials such as
cotton for export. William Gilpin, Asa Whitney, Matthew Fontain
Maury, Perry McDonough Collins, and William Henry Seward also
portrayed the United States as the future emporium of exchange
between Asia and Europe. The Mississippi Valley would become a
global entrepôt. These men were merchants, not industrialists. But
as expansionists, they sought ports on the Pacific coast of North
America, transcontinental railroads and telegraphs, and an international free market system. They believed that the United States
would dominate the world because of national energy, drive, republicanism, and its laissez-faire economy.

Manufacturing interests initially sought protection for their in-
fant industries, but they also embraced a vision of national expansion and empire that cut across old party labels by the 1850s.
Manufacturers and merchants alike quickly recognized the advantages of access to foreign markets and raw materials. The Republican Party's economic policies reflected such views. As America's
economy became increasingly complex in the antebellum period
and as it diversified during and after the Civil War, those favoring
overseas commercial expansion enjoyed greater support and access
to Washington's chambers of power.

British North America fitted comfortably into this matrix of expansionism. Many Americans recognized the emergence of a borderland economy from Detroit to the Bay of Fundy as early as the
1820s. The provincials resembled Americans, with similar tastes
and a parallel, but less robust economy. An extensive cross-border
trade achieved the gradual blending of two economies that American journalists, officials, and politicians often noted.

Careful investigations during the reciprocity negotiations exposed the commercial crisscrossing of the American-provincial boundary by the 1850s. American wheat used provincial mills, and vice versa. Provincial lumber found New York and even Southern markets, coal from Pennsylvania and West Virginia sold in Upper Canada, and Nova Scotia coal supplied a New England market. Like the canals before them, the American rail networks gradually connected with provincial lines both at the border and by bridges spanning the Niagara and St. Lawrence rivers. American money flowed north to invest in Ottawa Valley timber or Sarnia oil. The provinces represented economic opportunity for Americans. A limited continental economy evolved because of American-provincial common business methods, cultural similarity, economic compatibility, geographic proximity, history, and personal ties that reached decades into the past.

Territorial ambitions for the provinces had never been strong or widespread in the United States. Most Americans after 1850 saw the provincials as neighbors or vaguely believed that at some point in the future the provinces and the states would merge peacefully of their own accord. Politicians eager to pull the British lion's tail and editors gleeful over any British embarrassment applauded the Fenian invasions of the provinces after the Civil War. So the Andrew Johnson and Ulysses S. Grant administrations enforced neutrality in a measured, rather than aggressive, way.

To the provincials, Canadians all after Confederation in 1867, the American neutrality seemed a pretext for shielding rampaging Irishmen or revenge against Britain for aiding the Confederacy in the Civil War. But Americans adhered to their policy. Minnesota's annexationists, grasping for the Red River colony, found no more than private sympathy in Washington. Their hopes collapsed when Manitoba entered Confederation in 1871. William Henry Seward may well have seen the purchase of Alaska as a step toward the acquisition of British Columbia to complete his geopolitical vision of an overland connection with Asia. But he and other spokesmen of the New American Empire were silent when British Columbia agreed in 1871 to enter Confederation.

After 1867, most Americans accepted what many had believed would happen all along. The two Anglo-Saxon nations, deceptively similar but undeniably distinct, would share North America. Confederation was a phase in the plan to grant independence to Great

Britain's continental North American empire, an effort that began with the Corn Laws of 1846. The American government tacitly recognized Canada's semiautonomy in 1871 by greeting Canadian prime minister John A. Macdonald as part of the British party negotiating the Treaty of Washington. And into the bargain the United States Reciprocity Treaty was officially the product of Anglo-American negotiations, but both were genuinely triangular. American expansion, as it applied to what was now Canada, would henceforward be limited to economic and cultural spheres. Canada was truly a neighbor.

This transition meant that Canadians no longer were serious prospects as recruits to republicanism. Even those Americans who still talked about an eventual American-provincial merger pushed the event far into the future. At the same time, with the end of the Civil War, Canada became only a potential sanctuary once again. Many black refugees from the antebellum period returned to the United States. Tourists, on the other hand, continued to seek a temporary haven in Canada in ever growing numbers.

In 1775, Americans perceived the British North American provinces primarily as an enemy base. By 1871, American views of the provinces were complex, sophisticated, and subtle, reflecting the evolution and early maturing of the United States and its people. The views of the provinces held by individuals and groups within the United States changed over time. A sense of the provinces as sources of opportunity, on the other hand, rose steadily to become the overwhelming image by 1871. The idea of provincials as potential republican recruits rose, fell, and ultimately blended into the convergence thesis, or fruit-drop theory of empire. Perhaps most important, Americans came to see provincials, and then Canadians, as neighbors. Given the aggressive style of American expansionism in the 1890s, this tendency to see friends, neighbors, and historical equals to the north was an important backdrop to the Anglo-Saxon union movement that spread through the United States, as well as Great Britain and Canada, as the modern age dawned upon North America.

Chapter 9.

The Reciprocity Treaty and North American Convergence

It seems to be taken for granted . . . that the Canadas and the other Provinces will ultimately be annexed to the American Union; and the question was whether that event would be hastened or retarded by the establishment of free trade between them and us.
—North American Review, *October 1854*

*I*srael Andrews was a man with a mission in 1854. For years, his consular reports from New Brunswick had begged successive secretaries of state to pursue reciprocity. He had traveled widely to solicit funds and support from the secretary of state, various American chambers of commerce, especially in Massachusetts and New York, and to corner virtually anyone who would listen about the benefits of reciprocal trade. Once Lord Elgin, the provincial governor general, and William L. Marcy, President Franklin Pierce's secretary of state, had negotiated terms, Andrews waged a one-man war to persuade members of the American Congress and the various provincial legislatures to support the treaty.

Andrews, a child of the American-provincial borderland, was born of Nova Scotian parents in New Brunswick. But his paternal grandfather had come from Massachusetts long before the American Revolution. As a youth, Andrews dabbled in smuggling around Eastport, Maine. Later, he became a naturalized American citizen.[1] He petitioned for a post as New Brunswick consul in 1848, and took the occasion to outline the potential benefits of reciprocity to Secretary of State John M. Clayton. Provincials were an ambitious and industrious people, although behind Americans because they lacked republican institutions. Andrews nevertheless believed that the forces of history and nature would eventually fuse the provinces with the United States.

In July of 1849, Clayton assigned Andrews to collect provincial economic intelligence, "especially in connection with their present and prospective relations with the United States." Andrews set to work and deluged Washington with reports as he darted among such provincial centers as St. John in New Brunswick, Halifax in Nova Scotia, and Montreal and Quebec in Lower Canada. He wrote that attitudes in the provinces would change slowly because "the education & prejudices of half a century cannot be eradicated in a day. The political hacks & the cliques are opposed to annexation or indeed any change if they are paid and can enjoy the patronage and emoluments of office." In Montreal, however, Andrews landed in the middle of the annexation movement spawned by Britain's 1846 abolition of the Corn Laws. Andrews equated provincial outrage against Britain with enthusiasm for joining the United States. "The annexation movement stands well and is moving ahead. If the newspapers state to the contrary you need not give them your confidence." If Southern opposition to reciprocity could be blunted, the provincials would move closer toward union.[2]

Eventually, Andrews wrote a massive report that became the principal source of information on the provinces for the Franklin Pierce administration and Congress. Andrews marshaled statistics to argue the potential benefits of reciprocal trade. Reciprocity would soften current provincial agitation and would "defer the question of annexation to a more distant day, while it would no less certainly ensure the ultimate accomplishment of this great measure, not by violent and dangerous disruption." Closer ties with the United States would gradually loosen the "chains which bind the colonies to the Mother Country." A "community of sympathies and interests between the two countries" would follow that would render annexation an "inevitable political necessity."[3]

Reciprocity was a step toward continental union for Andrews. As a borderlander, he tried to transform his heritage and personal vision into political reality. He believed that Americans neither recognized the provincial potential nor realized "how much the spirit of our institutions, together with the assimilating influence of a daily commerce, proximity, and the stronger bonds of sympathetic affinities have operated upon our Northern colonial brethren." Andrews believed in the American national mission. Republican values and institutions would convert other people by the sheer power of example. Americans should seek out their northern star and forget Southern ambitions. North Americans were a "kindred people," and the barriers between them had to be broken.[4]

After Congress, Britain's Parliament, and the provincial legislatures accepted the Reciprocity Treaty of 1854, Andrews went on to become for several years the American consul general to Canada, resident in Quebec. He continued his detailed reports on American-provincial trade, never doubting the ultimate convergence of the two societies. Suffering from ill health and in financial difficulties from 1856 until his death, he petitioned payment from provincial and American governments to offset what he claimed to have spent in the cause of reciprocity. His petitions went largely unheeded, although the Boston Board of Trade helped him out financially on several occasions. He became embittered, eventually lost his government post, and fell into debt. Hounded by creditors, he spent a term in prison and finally died of alcoholism in a Boston city hospital in February of 1871, a self-made martyr to his mission. Andrews was in large measure the architect of the Reciprocity Treaty of 1854, but at a personal cost far beyond his expectations.[5]

The Reciprocity Treaty of 1854 was a multilateral agreement among the United States, Great Britain, and all the British North American provinces except Newfoundland. It reflected the early gropings toward the new American empire as well as the American belief in the opportunities to be found in the provinces and the realities of borderland commerce. Reciprocity provided for limited free trade, American navigation of the St. Lawrence and St. John rivers, and American access to provincial fisheries.

The provincials made the first overtures. When Great Britain discarded the last of her old Navigation Acts in 1845 and abolished the Corn Laws in 1846, she in effect threw the provincials onto the world market. The provinces were granted virtual economic independence, but many provincial merchants saw ruin, rather than opportunity, in this new freedom. Some argued that only expanded trade with the United States could salvage the provincial future. A few even argued for political as well as economic union. The British-American League met at Kingston, 25 June 1849, but rejected annexation. The Annexation Manifesto issued in Montreal the following October had little support outside the metropolitan area. Provincial annexationism faded quickly once a measure of prosperity returned after 1850.[6] Andrews therefore found in the provinces in the years between 1848 and 1854, an atmosphere of commercial and to some extent political uncertainty, and it deeply impressed him. To some extent, he believed what he wanted to believe, but at the same time the possibility of union with the United States received wide circulation in the provinces.

The American government took no positive action on reciprocity until 1852. Andrews's barrage of reports nurtured the issue within successive administrations. So did petitions from special interest groups with provincial connections. In early 1849, the American minister in Great Britain, George Bancroft, urged elimination of all restrictions on navigation between the provinces and the United States. Bancroft thought he saw the beginning of a decolonization movement in England that would benefit his country. Canadian self-government would mollify provincial politicians and "connect their interests with those of the United States." Then Secretary of State John Clayton unleashed Andrews on his monumental diplomatic and commercial reconnaissance of the provinces. Clayton resigned when President Zachary Taylor died suddenly, and Daniel Webster donned diplomatic harness once more. He inherited both the reciprocity issue and Andrews.

Webster sustained the drive to avoid Anglo-American confrontations that had characterized United States foreign policy after 1815. Then a sudden crisis erupted in the North Atlantic fisheries. By itself, reciprocity could not have drawn the American government forward, but the fisheries rang economic and historic alarms. Webster combined the two issues.[7] The draft of a treaty emerged by the fall of 1853.

When William Marcy became Secretary of State, he saw the treaty as a panacea to settle a number of issues with the provinces. Its purpose was not only to increase "the commercial intercourse, mutually advantageous, but to stimulate and extend an increased regard and interest for this country [United States] and its institutions." Marcy was a cautious continentalist. The treaty soothed Anglo-American relations and settled important commercial questions. It also served as a second chapter to the Clayton-Bulwer Treaty of 1850. Combined, the two agreements showed that the United States and England were moving toward a broad understanding about sharing in the future development of North America. This diplomatic progress built also upon a close personal relationship that developed between Marcy and John Crampton, the British Minister. Finally, Marcy maneuvered behind closed doors in Washington. President Franklin Pierce's administration supported reciprocity and lobbied Congress. So did Lord Elgin on his convivial visit to Washington. Combined, they allayed fears about reciprocity and produced Senate ratification of the treaty.[8]

Washington officials had become increasingly aware of the growing borderland trade of the 1840s and 1850s. Andrews believed that formal reciprocity would only encourage such growth. Given economic conditions in mid-century, American-provincial commerce would have blossomed regardless of diplomatic arrangements. But because trade grew while the Treaty was in force, Washington officials concluded that diplomacy had produced economic dividends.[9]

The secretary of the treasury had recommended reciprocity in 1851, submitting Andrews's weighty study of provincial economic affairs as part of his report. Without reciprocity, coal producers in Pennsylvania and shippers in the Northwest, who sought free navigation of the St. Lawrence River during the ice-free season, would all apparently suffer. In 1853, the House Committee of Commerce reported on several private memorials seeking reciprocity with the provinces. Chairman D. L. Seymour noted the increasing cross-border trade, traced the history of economic relations with the provinces, and cited, among other documents, a favorable report on reciprocity by the Board of the Chamber of Commerce of New York City. Opportunity lay to the north. Railroads and canals would have more goods to carry. Americans would replace Great Britain as provincial suppliers. New timber reserves would become available. The St. Lawrence River would open to American vessels. The fisheries question could be settled. Finally, Anglo-American relations would improve. The House Foreign Affairs Committee agreed. Chairman Alexander Buell of Michigan concnetrated on inland navigation in response to petitions and memorials from his home state and her neighbor, Wisconsin. The few comments in Congress from 1848 to 1854 reflected the almost exclusive commercial expectations of both champions and critics of reciprocal trade.[10]

The contemporary press in the early 1850s also concentrated on the commercial issue. During the reciprocity negotiations, Hunt's *Merchant's Magazine*, a leading New York business journal, argued that freer provincial-American trade was inevitable. Geography "would infallibly insure to the United States almost the whole supply of the Canadian market." The *American Almanac* summarized the treaty and continued its practice of listing provincial economic statistics and accredited American consuls. The *North American Review* of Boston could scarcely "find words to express, or figures to measure, the infinite and ever-multiplying benefits that must ensue from releasing this vast tract of country from all legislative and international impediments."[11]

Because the Reciprocity Treaty coincided with the rise in American-provincial trade, contemporary observers confused cause and effect. Many factors produced growing American-provincial trade after 1850. To begin with, both population and transportation systems for domestic and foreign markets expanded at roughly the same time. The borderlands from the Bay of Fundy to Michigan had exchanged products and services across the frontier for decades. Their north-south links ignored customs barriers through smuggling. The railway era opened new markets for Canadian products and cheaper transport in the borderland region for bulky cargoes. Both English and American financiers saw opportunities for investment. Trade grew in unlisted commodites, such as lumber, and where transport lines in canals and railroads facilitated the movement of heavy goods. Economic factors were also at work. Nova Scotian coal undersold Pennsylvania's in New England. Provincial lumber was cheaper in New York than its competition from Michigan and Wisconsin. When prices rose in the United States, provincials could market more wheat, despite duties and extra freight charges. And later, the American Civil War generated new demands, such as for horses.

The data for the reciprocity years, nonetheless, are impressive. Both domestic and foreign exports to the central provinces from the United States had a value of $10.5 million in 1852. By 1856 this figure had climbed to $29 million, falling by 1860 to $22.7 million. Imports from the central provinces to the United States went from $6.1 million in value in 1852 to $21.3 million in 1856 and $23.8 million in 1860. The balance generally favored the United States down to 1860, when the impact of the Civil War distorted the nature of the exchange. In the Maritime provinces, the balance dramatically favored the Americans. The value of exports to the Maritimes in 1850 was $3.1 million. In both 1856 and 1860 the figure was $7.5 million, and it rose to $12.3 million in 1864. Imports, on the other hand, were $1.3 million in 1850, $2.9 million in 1856, $4.9 million in 1860, and $7.9 million in 1864. Between the American Pacific states and British Columbia, on the West Coast, the United States had the advantage by nearly $1 million. At the same time, the United States absorbed well over 50 percent of Canada's total exports between 1855 and 1860. This period presaged Canada's career as America's best customer and supplier in the twentieth century.[12]

American State and Treasury Department agents in the provinces believed that reciprocity had stimulated cross-border trade. B. Hammatt Norton watched coal flow out of Pictou, Nova Scotia, and a variety of American manufactures flow in. Israel Andrews attributed his posting to Montreal to "the rapidly increasing commercial intercourse between the United States and Canada." C. Dorwin believed that once the treaty took full effect it would knit American-provincial trade and especially benefit the New York canals and all northeastern seaport towns of the United States. By 1855, the treaty had increased the "value of farms and landed estate, on this side of the line" and had attracted American investments in provincial forestry. More business meant more cross-border travelers. And John Babson, a secret Treasury agent on the Great Lakes in 1858 and 1859, concluded that the treaty had "quadrupled" trade, but reduced the national revenue because of increased smuggling.[13] Americans viewed reciprocity differently, depending upon their interests and perspectives.

Aside from the immediate diplomatic and commercial context, the idea of reciprocity had a long history in American-provincial relations. In 1815, for example, Albert Gallatin negotiated a trade agreement with the British that was never consummated. But British trade policy became more liberal in the 1820s, and in 1830, Britain removed duties on American produce imported to the provinces to encourage indirect trade with her declining West Indies. No comprehensive agreements existed, however, when the House Committee on Commerce drew up the first reciprocity bill in 1848. Such important Democratic politicians as James Buchanan of Pennsylvania, Robert Walker, secretary of the treasury, and Joseph Grinnell, chairman of the House Committee on Commerce stood behind this bill. The House passed the bill with amendments, but the Senate tabled reciprocity. There were several reasons for Senate opposition, one of which was a belief that the president had exceeded his constitutional authority when negotiating the 1844 commercial treaty with the German Zollverein. This reason alone was enough to keep the Senate from proceeding with provincial reciprocity.

In 1850, a fresh legislative attempt incorporated the old bill plus free navigation of the St. Lawrence River. By this time, the free-trade–protectionism debate had become a major force in shaping national economic policy. Congressional protectionists opposed reciprocity. And congressmen and senators now hesitated between a treaty and concurrent legislation by all the governments concerned. President Zachary Taylor submitted all correspondence on reciprocity, as requested, to speed passage. But the Democratic free traders pressed ahead. Whigs and their Northern manufacturing supporters leaned toward protectionism, and the Republican Party inherited this outlook, along with a greater concern for national economic development. In the 1850s, however, protectionism was only strong enough to delay reciprocity.

Daniel Webster's death in office in October of 1852 created a new obstacle. But Franklin Pierce, the new Democratic president, and William L. Marcy, his secretary of state, both supported reciprocity and, like Taylor and Webster, also wanted to settle the fisheries conflict. Marcy diverted funds to Andrews for his provincial lobbying and assured Southern senators that reciprocity did not herald new free territory coming into the union. Marcy also accepted aid from the provincial governor general, Lord Elgin, who while in Washington entertained skeptical senators lavishly. Marcy's arguments, Lord Elgin's conviviality, party loyalty, and the need for legislative help to maneuver the Kansas-Nebraska bill through Congress created a coalition behind what became the Reciprocity Treaof 1854.[14]

Americans reacted variously to the advent of reciprocity. Special interests, political persuasion, and regional biases shaped overall responses. Proximity to the provinces did not mean automatic support for reciprocity. If Michigan and Wisconsin favored freer trade with the provinces, Vermont did not. Nor did Buffalo businessmen, despite their extensive provincial connections. They were more concerned about shielding their burgeoning local industries and steering the upper lakes traffic through the Erie Canal.[15]

The American response to reciprocity reflected both economic and cultural perspectives on the expansion of the United States. The defensive expansionism that arose from considerations of security had given way to a feeling of confidence that the United States, because of its liberal, democratic, and republican institutions, was an important agent in modern history. These impulses were aggressive only in a commercial sense. By the 1850s, American policy-makers sought liberal commercial arrangements to supplement the private enterprise expansionism of frontiersmen and entrepreneurs.

The Reciprocity Treaty of 1854 formalized the growing American exploitation of provincial business opportunities since 1815. Reciprocity summarized historical development as much as heralded future prospects. By 1819, American exports to the provinces surpassed those to the West Indies by a ratio of three to two. In 1850, dutiable imports to Canada from the United States were nearly $6 million; by 1853, this figure had risen to $10.6 million. The provinces fell into the orbit of America's expanding lumber industry in the 1830s and 1840s.[16] As early as 1825, the American transportation network snatched at provincial trade when the Erie Canal and its tributaries pushed into the Great Lakes Basin.

The expanding American railroad interest in the provinces drew its momentum from several sources: from urban boosters promoting their cities as emporiums for the West, from merchants seeking new markets and materials, from transportation magnates seeking the carrying trade to the west, and from capitalists seeking profitable new investments. The *Railroad Journal* regularly reported on provincial railroad developments as an extension of American railroad grids being established along the borderland. In 1851, Boston financiers sought $1 million to supplement the provincial Great Western Railway. Erastus Corning, the mastermind of the New York Central and a Great Western director, wanted a provincial link in his growing transportation system in the Northwest. Americans eventually bought 8,000 shares of Great Western stock, but most later sold out because of conflict with English investors. An East Coast promoter, John A. Poor, saw Portland, Maine, as a rival of Boston and New York for the Great Lakes trade because of its planned railway link with Montreal. The project, begun in 1844, did not open until 1871 and never met Poor's expectations. Yet it was one of several borderland railway systems built after 1840 over which goods freed by the Reciprocity Treaty would flow.[17]

Increases in smuggling inevitably followed the rise in legal trade along the American-provincial borderlands.[18] The continuous ap-

pointment of new American consuls in provincial ports also testified to the growth of the trade and to confidence in its future, as did
reports that came before Congress.[19] The Reciprocity Treaty, of itself, did little to stimulate American-provincial trade, despite its
champions' claims.

The advocates of reciprocity in the 1840s and 1850s saw commercial development as a hallmark of the progressive character of
American civilization. Israel Andrews associated free trade with
republican ideology and believed that inevitable provincial movement toward republican liberalism would "sweep away colonial
thralldom."[20] Hammatt Norton, stationed at Pictou, Nova Scotia,
misinterpreted overheard remarks to the effect that the economic
difficulties after 1849 had apparently eroded loyalty to the Crown
in the provincial Maritimes. C. Dorwin wrote from Montreal that
reciprocity was "the greatest measure that has ever been entered
into between the two Countries to strengthen the Bonds of Friendship and increase the Commercial Intercourse." Soon, he predicted,
Lower Canada would abolish "Feudal or seignorial tenure of lands,
which . . . when accomplished will have a tendency to American
emigration and Americanize the Colony."[21] Internal provincial
changes combined with reciprocity would promote eventual provincial-American convergence.

Several statesmen and writers to 1854 believed that reciprocity,
commercial annexation, and political union were causally connected. George Bancroft, for example, believed that reciprocity
would weaken Britain's old colonial system. And Secretary of State
Marcy told Andrews that a people's political sympathies sometimes
followed the routes of their trade and commerce.[22] The *Democratic
Review* regarded free trade as a fundamental American principle
identified with peaceful progress. In 1852, its editor called on Britain to abandon her North American colonies. British political and
social institutions ill suited the provincials, Americans, and the
world.[23]

The *American Railroad Journal* was less dogmatic, but relentlessly linked commercial interests to America's developing culture
and the idea of universal progress. Surely, the provincials would
see that for genuine advancement they "should have turned to the
United States of America, and mortgaged their whole value, Crown
revenues and all, to connect their interests with that country by

MAP 3. *Great Lakes Basin Commercial Borderlands, ca. 1860*

LOWER CANADA

Montreal

To Portland

Ottawa

To Boston

LAKE CHAMPLAIN

VT.

ngston

NEW YORK

NTARIO

Oswego

MASS.

Hudson River

CONN.

ENNSYLVANIA

New York City

railroad communication." Provincials were "hardy, frugal, industrious, patriotic to a fault, and honest." In short, they were just like Americans, would chafe under British misrule, and naturally emulate prosperous, liberal, and enlightened Americans. The *Philadelphia American and United States Gazette* noted that the Yankee spirit of enterprise had aroused provincials from "drowsy inactivity, and infused them with new life." There could never be too many railways, and American-provincial lines had an international significance. The *Railroad Journal* saw the Reciprocity Treaty as "gratifying evidence of the progress of liberal ideas in international intercourse." Commercial union was certain to follow.[24] Provincials and Americans already seemed one people, artificially separated only by different political systems.

Other editors saw the same implications in the Reciprocity Treaty and championed the free-trading ideas that dominated American commercial thinking by mid-century. For *De Bow's Review*, regulated trade rested upon a false principle. Why had provincials not copied Americans and freed up their commerce? (De Bow was ill informed. Repeal of the Corn Laws had done just that.) British monopolies on Nova Scotia's coal resources stifled development. "The exclusive rights enjoyed by the mining Association are represented to be the depressing influence which weighs like an incubus upon the prosperity of Nova Scotia." The *Merchant's Magazine* noted that the provincials had developed a liberal government that promoted fusion, not of laws, but interests, as Americans and provincials blended their trade and ideas. The American example of seeking freedom in the Revolution had infected the provincials. Liberalism had been slow in coming, but "why should we seek to keep asunder States which Time and Events, Nature, and Science thus unmistakably join together?"[25]

The *Merchant's Magazine's* lead article in March 1853 warned that the recent focus on Cuba must not blind Americans to the more commercially important British North American provinces. Anglo-American policy should encourage the "political gravitation of these dependencies of hers, which, as John Quincy Adams said of Cuba, would cause them, when disjoined by any means from their present unnatural connection, to fall into the bosom of the American Union." Not least, reciprocity would partly reunite "the old British colonial empire, enkindling a friendly feeling throughout the provinces. . . . It would undoubtedly be an initiatory step to . . . reincorporation of the provinces into our system, and their re-attachment to our destiny." After the Reciprocity Treaty passed, the *Merchant's Magazine* published more provincial news from local correspondents, such as Charles Seymour of Montreal. Seymour saw in the provinces a version of American society. Aristocracy had yielded to individual industry, intelligence, and character.[26] And the *North American Review* noted that the "social and moral effects of such a state of things as the treaty will bring about cannot but tend to make us one people, and absorbed irresistibly, although insensibly, into each other. A people so identified, it is argued, cannot long remain politically separated, but must be united by annexation."[27]

The political implications of economic change constituted a major refrain in commentary on reciprocity. The *National Intelligencer* praised a commercial agreement as true progress. Although it was a "mere accident of political history" that the provincials were not part of the American confederation, provincials had "assimilated with the people of the States in industry, enterprise, intelligence, and the love of liberty, while personal intercourse and political sympathy have established numerous grounds of common sentiment and interest." The border was almost a fiction. Provincials had the "Anglo-Saxon love of freedom and impatience of a foreign yoke, however legitimate and however light. They have taken many of the first steps which we took toward political emancipation." Provincials were, in short, Americans under an assumed name.[28]

The New York newspapers, as might be expected because of New York's extensive northern connections, printed much news of the provinces. The *Albany Argus* pronounced the 1846 Corn Laws abolition a "triumph of *liberalism* over *feudalism*, and a mighty victory of Right over Privilege." Federal Senator John Dix argued that the provincials could be dealt with as equals because they now had responsible government. The Montreal Annexation Manifesto proved provincial ambitions for liberty, despite the lack of political autonomy.[29]

Provincials and Americans seemed to have converging interests and destinies. Economic forces, in short, generated ideological sympathies. The provincials lacked American enterprise, but were, as one editor put it, "going ahead fast": "The Canadians are running a noble race. A pity they *carry weight!* We mean the control of the home Government." Despite this, Upper Canadian education and cultural institutions proliferated, and the provincials grappled with "all the questions of progress in a spirit of the highest intelligence."[30] These Americans applied their own values to provincials. Israel Andrews, despite his provincial origins, was no different. Reciprocity was "in harmony with the enlarged commercial ideas of the present age, and with that catholic spirit which modern mechanical science is extending by annihilating space, time, and prejudice, in the intercourse of distant and once hostile nations."[31]

This ideology pervaded American expansionism in the middle years of the nineteenth century. It combined remnants of Manifest Destiny with a more quietly assured commercial vision of America's future. In the Pacific and Asia, American merchants, diplomats, and missionaries were drummers for the American way of life. Americans overseas preached the virtues of their republican capitalist system, just as Andrews defined his mission as bringing the provinces within the pale of American progress. The American government supported these views. President Millard Fillmore had commerce more than castaway sailors in mind when dispatching Commodore Matthew Perry's famous expedition. For Perry, and for such lobbyists as New York commission agent Aaron H. Palmer, spreading commerce was synonymous with spreading American social and political ideals.[32]

Americans were not blindly insensitive to foreigners, but they approached all cultures from the same ideological perspective. Americans in the Mediterranean exported their maritime technology and hawked their manufactured wares on the basis of reciprocal trade with local potentates. They also applauded Europe's liberal revolutions of 1848, even as they welcomed what they imagined was republican progress in the provinces. The Young America movement believed that commercial development and republican freedom went hand in hand. A proper national policy should be based, therefore, on both foundations.[33]

Commentary on the provinces reflected this American faith that commerce and politics were ideologically symbiotic. Some even saw imminent annexation. The reasons for this varied. The *Democratic Review* observed that provincial growth accelerated imperial collapse. Annexation would follow. The provinces were "destined to swell the still accumulating momentum of our progress." The Chicago *Democrat* promoted annexation because it wanted to eliminate a refuge for runaway slaves. The *New York Times* and the *New York Daily Tribune* seemed equally aggressive.[34]

Despite this, when provincial annexation arose, officials reacted cautiously, and journalists on the whole reported provincial annexationism dispassionately. The sources of American interest were too widely scattered, and sectional rancor too strong, to permit a unified, positive response.[35] Consul Israel Andrews believed in American-provincial convergence. He concluded that "though under different governments we shall be one people, laboring hand in hand to accomplish the high destiny of the North American continent." Others argued that American prosperity would convince provincials to exchange monarchism for republicanism.[36] This fantasy acquired a certain theoretical dignity in the term "political gravitation."[37]

In the American mind, republican liberty, free enterprise, prosperity, and moral superiority constituted a magnetic force that would inevitably capture other people. Travelers to the provinces, such as Joseph Sansom, a veteran of the War of 1812, believed that Upper Canada, and even Montreal, were becoming Americanized. Most provincials were Anglo-Saxons, so a "racial" affinity existed in a time when Americans were highly conscious of ethnic distinctions.[38] Many believed that national ideology and the sense of mission dictated an ultimate American-provincial convergence.[39]

The Reciprocity Treaty appeared to be a step along this path. Israel Andrews and the Pierce government saw it that way, although the administration had dawdled on reciprocity initially. The government wanted the provincials to accept the treaty willingly. Consul Dorwin in Montreal believed that the treaty would simultaneously stimulate trade and friendship.[40] The *Railroad Journal* argued that freer trade would extend "so that *practically* the people of both will form one community, whatever may be the peculiarities of their local institutions." Other writers assumed the inevitability of political union once the treaty had been effected.[41]

Visions of commercial continentalism appeared everywhere. The *National Intelligencer* believed that the provincials were becoming fellow republicans seeking guidance from the United States. The treaty might have undercut the rationale for annexation, but not for American-provincial convergence. Travel articles in New York's popular *Frank Leslie's Illustrated Newspaper* portrayed Canada West, or Upper Canada, as progressive in the American sense—"vigorous, inventive, and ahead-going." Provincials and Americans, moreover, were commercially, ethnically, and geographically "one people," despite differing political structures. The Grand Trunk Railway was only one bond of union. A united North America would advance with unprecedented strides.[42]

As the 1850s unfolded, observers concluded that the Reciprocity Treaty was a success. It placed provincial-American trade in certain items on a regular footing, and the statistics revealed growth. In fish, for example, imports to the United States doubled by 1856. As proponents of the Reciprocity Treaty had shown, Nova Scotia coal was convenient for New England, and Pennsylvania coal was convenient for the Canadas. The Boston Board of Trade's annual reports not only favored the treaty, but devoted increasing space to American-provincial commerce. The timber trade along the Aroostook Valley became easier with free access to the St. John River and forest exports from New Brunswick to the United States increased. On the other hand, some commodities declined. But the Reciprocity Treaty was not as responsible for the gains and losses as its champions and opponents insisted.

Many factors shaped provincial-American trade patterns in the period of reciprocity: political and financial needs of the two governments, world market conditions, and later, the Civil War and the rise of protectionism in the northern states. The lumber trade, for example, increased because declining domestic American supplies coincided with increased demand from canal, railroad, and building industries. And provincial wheat and flour sales in the United States rose because of changes in price differentials.[43]

Critics of the treaty eventually coalesced into an opposition movement. Reciprocity was unsatisfactory to these observers, despite a trade balance in favor of the United States by over $15 million between 1854 and 1866. New York merchants wanted to eliminate the St. Lawrence River as a rival to the Erie Canal. Maine timber and shipbuilding interests grumbled over unfair competition. Changes in the provincial tariff structure on items not covered by the treaty angered American manufacturers who believed that they deserved open access to all provincial markets. Coal interests in Maryland and New Jersey disliked Nova Scotia's competition. Protectionists in the industrializing middle states of New York, Pennsylvania, and New Jersey saw in reciprocity a vestige of obsolete free-trade ideas. Some Republican politicians, bitter over Confederates using the provinces as a refuge and base during the Civil War, wanted to cancel reciprocity in revenge. Critics and Treasury Department officials pointed to reduced revenues along the northern border. Finally, a few political continentalists believed that canceling reciprocity would beggar the provincials into demanding union with the United States.[44]

Many specific arguments stemmed from changing American ideas about national expansion. Joshua Giddings, victim of Confederate plotters and the American consul general in Montreal from 1860 to his death in a local billiard parlor in 1864, was generally happy with reciprocity, although he told his son that the United States owed the provincials no favors for harboring Confederates. Consul C. Fields argued for cancellation: apart from provincial economic dependence on the United States "the *ill feeling* displayed toward us, in our distress, deserves some punishment." The *New York Times* ventured that trade would be much the same with or without the treaty, that American farmers confronted unfair competition, and that the provincials were cynics who had violated the spirit of the treaty by raising tariffs. The New York Chamber of Commerce generally supported reciprocity, but noted in 1862 that it had "mingled merits." The major benefit had been to create a "half-way house" pointing "toward a system of absolute and entire reciprocity, so that each people may enjoy the full legitimate advantage of neighborhood to the people, territory and possessions of the other."[45]

E. H. Derby reviewed the impact of the treaty on American trade and revenue for the Treasury Department in 1866. His closing plea for cooperation contradicted his many arguments for abrogation. Without directly stating it, for example, he implied that the provinces had done better than the United States in agreeing to reciprocity. In the Senate, Charles Sumner blasted St. Lawrence navigation as a paper concession. Shifting economic conditions, not the

treaty, had enlarged American-provincial trade. The national revenue had forfeited over $16 million. Only the fisheries had value for
the United States.[46]

The telling arguments against reciprocity were more emotional
and political than economic. The Treaty had a stipulated life of one
decade and either Great Britain or the United States could annul it
in the interim upon one year's notice. Once Secretary of State William H. Seward so notified Great Britain, a political momentum
developed that was impossible to stop in the postwar atmosphere.
Congress had expressed its views, Treasury Secretary Hugh McCulloch wrote to Seward. "It would be particularly inappropriate . . . to
negotiate any similar treaty respecting trade with the provinces in
the absence of a further expression of the views of that body."[47] The
Andrew Johnson administration, beset by multiple political trials
arising from the legacy of the Civil War, would not pursue reciprocity with British North America without strong congressional
support.

The treaty's defenders rallied in 1865 and 1866 to deflect what
seemed inevitable cancellation of reciprocity. But even the defenders mostly agreed that the treaty of 1854 had outlived its usefulness. Strong support for unqualified continuation existed only in
the Great Lakes borderland, especially in Detroit, and among New
York City free traders. Many others, in Baltimore, Chicago, Philadelphia, and Portland, for example, wanted revision rather than a
mere maintenance of the status quo.[48]

The old idea of an eventual Anglo-Saxon continental union had
not by any means evaporated, but it had developed a dominantly
commercial orientation consonant with the ideological shifts at the
dawn of the new American empire. Many in the United States believed that a single North American economy would inevitably develop, whatever the political future of the two sections. The chamber of commerce of St. Paul, Minnesota, wanted the Reciprocity
Treaty enlarged to include central British America and create a
"Zoll-verein or Customs Union." Free-trade periodicals argued
that the commercial ties with the provinces were strengthening
daily. "The success of the loyal States is the commercial success of
Canada, and so blended are our mutual interests, that the ruin of
the North would be the ruin of Canada." Despite momentary anger
at Britain or the provincials, Americans should still pursue the

"future freedom of commercial intercourse, not additional restrictions." The Boston Board of Trade, focusing on the fisheries as the first casualty of a canceled treaty, noted that American-provincial interests were so intertwined that smuggling would simply replace legitimate exchange.[49]

E. H. Derby's 1866 report summarized the arguments most acceptable to Congress. Derby emphasized that the treaty had stimulated friendship between "contiguous nations of the same origin." Revisions should "let the Provincials look forward to a union which will eventually remove" all duties, "increase their wealth, and contribute to their improvements." And a committee of New York's chamber of commerce asserted:

> Across, and far beyond a remarkable natural chain of lakes and rivers, which seems to be rather a bond than a barrier, there is a country to which we wish well, as our fathers did. Its institutions assimilate to ours, and, if not entirely so, it is its own business. In the largest degree, the population has with us a common ancestry, and such portions of it as have not, may find among us great numbers of their own language and creed, who have found here their preferred home.[50]

This ideological perception that American commercial expansion would produce a continental civilization was perhaps the most important element in the image Americans had of their future relationship with the British North American provinces. The presence or absence of treaties or other regulations made little difference to the course of history. J. D. Hayes, of Buffalo, argued that uniform tariffs, internal revenue systems, security of property rights, and common weights and measures, "might cover all our difficulties and unite us as one people, bringing together in harmony and good feeling, the flags of two nations, the most enlightened and powerful on earth, into one interest."[51]

Reciprocity's defenders met at Detroit in 1865 to publicize and gather support for their cause. The meeting developed into an American-provincial mutual admiration convention. Hamilton Hill, a Boston delegate and self-appointed historian of the convention, reported that most American delegates believed in an eventual merger with the provinces. But, as true republicans, they would leave this entirely up to the free will of both parties. At the same time, they believed in the power of mutual commercial interests to hurry history along.[52]

The Treaty's career reflected several facets of the evolution of United States expansionism with respect to the provinces. Reciprocity proved a convenient way of achieving common ground on the issues of free trade and the fisheries. After 1815, and especially beginning in the 1830s, increasing numbers of Americans traveled, invested, and did business in the provinces. Economic changes on both sides of the border encouraged a growth of commerce by the early 1850s to such a degree that reciprocity seemed a natural consequence. This was part of the development of a North American, rather than a strictly provincial or American, economy. The treaty was a product of the free trade ideas that Americans held in the mid-nineteenth century as well as American commercial liberalism.

Treaties are formal arrangements that reflect a coincidence of interests at a given moment. The Reciprocity Treaty recognized past developments, current views and conditions in the United States, Great Britain, and the British North American provinces, and future expectations as of 1854. By the middle 1860s, however, much had changed for all the original signatories. Those shaping policy were different men. The Civil War had pushed American-provincial affairs in unnatural directions while it lasted and deposited a residue of anger among northern Americans. Resentment reinforced Republican protectionism expressed in the Morrill Tariff Act of 1861 and the more candidly protectionist acts of 1864 and 1865. A continentalist ideology interwove with commercial ambitions and expectations to produce a doctrine of American-provincial convergence that did not need to depend upon reciprocity.

A variety of political and economic interests lined up against the treaty when Seward submitted notice of its cancellation. Senators, concerned about revenue to offset the war debt, provincial competition in basic industries, and provincial and British favoritism toward Confederates during the war, refused to protest the abrogation of the Reciprocity Treaty of 1854.[53] In many respects a phase in the history of American-Canadian trade, the Reciprocity Treaty more importantly reflected the interplay between American expansionism and the British North American provinces in the nineteenth century.

Chapter 10.

The Dawning

American Empire

and the Provinces

*It now appears that the social inter-
course which results from our railways, and the intimacies and business connections established and
increased thereby, will exert a very
potent influence upon the people, in
all the countries where they are
established.*

. . . .

*The silent influence of example, and
the potent arguments presented in
the rapid prosperity and advancement of our country, are exerting a
powerful effect upon the public mind
in Canada, which all the vain pomp
and splendor of provincial authority
cannot arrest.*
—The Boston Committee in
Canada, *1851*

America's industrial transformation quickened in the middle decades of the nineteenth century. Mechanical production methods augmented and then slowly began to replace hand labor in agriculture and manufacturing.
America's exports changed in character and complexity, and American business success accumulated capital that found external as
well as internal investment markets.

Demographic and political expansion proceeded to the Pacific
Coast. Minnesota and Oregon became states in 1858 and 1859.
Washington did not achieve statehood until 1889, but American
commercial interests appreciated the potential of the timber stands
and waterways of Puget Sound for the national economy and for the
Pacific Ocean trade. After 1849, California gold provided the financ-
ing for subsequent mineral exploitation in the Rocky Mountains.
New borderland regions formed by the 1860s, between the Red
River colony and Minnesota west of Lake Superior and in the Pacific Northwest. The American-provincial borderland reached from
sea to sea.

Few individuals epitomize such complex historical developments. Yet William Henry Seward came as close as anyone can to
personifying the times. A New Yorker who matured in the Jacksonian era, Seward rose through state politics to be governor by 1838.
From 1848 to 1861 his ambition and talents gave him national
prominence as a senator. A Whig, he joined the Republican Party
after 1854 to become one of its towering figures. But, frustrated in
his drive to gain the Republican presidential nomination in 1860,
he accepted the post of Abraham Lincoln's secretary of state. The
Whigs had generally opposed territorial acquisition in the 1840s,
but Seward embraced a complex expansionism based on a personal
vision of the nation's future.

Seward, like many other antebellum politicians, harnessed popular territorial and commercial ambitions. He believed that statesmen should guide such impulses, lend them orderly expression, and
not resist them. The United States had been historically designated
to carry the banner of political freedom in the world. National expansion meant global progress because it extended history's most
advanced civilization. Hence it was important to settle America's
western territories and develop a transcontinental railroad. Seward's vision, however, was more economic than territorial. He believed that the United States would eventually command a global
commercial empire in the Pacific Basin.[1]

Seward, who distinguished between monarchism and republicanism in moral terms, was unrealistic about the eagerness of other
peoples to accept American ideological and institutional superiority. Despite this, Seward developed a fairly rounded vision of his
country's future. He endorsed the Republican program for national
development; western land policy, the containment of slavery, federal sponsorship of internal improvements, the process of territorial
extension, and overseas commercial growth guided his Republican
partisanship and his national ideology. And the strength of his commitment allowed him to develop a consistent American foreign
policy between 1850 and 1869, the disruption of the Civil War
notwithstanding.

Seward often devoted at least a paragraph of his public speeches
to America's destiny. And having spent his early career in a borderland state during the 1830s, when the provinces enjoyed a high
profile in America because of the rebellions, Seward often remarked

on changes in British North America. Dedicating a university in Columbus, Ohio, in 1853, for example, Seward reflected that American telegraph, railroad, and steamship lines joining the provinces with the United States demonstrated the spirit of expansionism. Political results would flow from this economic growth. Provincial and American "principles, interests, and sympathies" converged as the former moved toward "separation from the parent country. Canada, although a province of Great Britain, is already half annexed to the United States. She will ultimately become a member of this confederacy, if we will consent—an ally, if we will not allow her to come nearer."[2]

Seward saw the provinces and the United States on converging historical tracks and even mused about the eventual unity of all of mankind around the principles of humanity and liberty. But there would be no American-provincial political union without the free consent of all parties—the United States, Great Britain, and the provinces themselves, Seward insisted. He favored extending national power and would maneuver to obtain portions of British North America if he could, but he never argued for or pursued an aggressive policy.

In a journal Seward kept as he descended the St. Lawrence in a schooner in 1857, he noted how thin settlement was behind the river banks. French Canada, he concluded, had not changed since 1760. Once in the Gulf of St. Lawrence, the Sewards fished and sailed among provincial and American fishermen. British America, he reflected in an entry written below decks one night, was better than the static French. It had a territory of continental proportions, "a region grand enough for the seat of a great empire" with mineral and agricultural resources. British provincials were vigorous, independent, and Protestant. They would certainly reject the "curse of slavery." The United States should "secure the alliance of Canada, while it is yet young, and incurious of its future. But on the other hand, the policy which the United States actually pursues is spurning vigorous, perennial, and ever-growing Canada, while seeking to establish feeble states out of decaying Spanish provinces."[3] Immersion in America's sectional schism warped Seward's perception of British North America. He also overestimated the power of republican ideas in a British setting. But most Americans would have committed the same error.

A republican-capitalistic ideology shaped Seward's thinking on the provinces as well as the emerging American empire. Seward also built upon a personal vision of his own country's future. Given to hyperbole in his public remarks, he often seemed more aggressive than he was. Campaigning at St. Paul, Minnesota in 1860, for example, he gestured north, toward "Rupert's land and Canada." There worked "an ingenious, enterprising and ambitious people, occupied with bridging rivers and constructing canals, railroads and telegraphs," making "excellent states to be hereafter admitted into the American Union." Seward meant eventually and by free consent, but listeners could read his remarks as anti-British and as flattering their own ambitions to control the Red River colony. Because republicanism was universally applicable, history would ultimately unify society in North America.[4]

Then the Civil War came, and the provinces became a refuge for Union draft evaders, escaped prisoners, and Confederate raiders. The border posed a nuisance, even a danger, to officials in the borderland states. Seward imposed a temporary passport system. This was not an expansionist pressure tactic, but a war measure to force the British and provincial authorities to guard the borders against Confederate violations of imperial neutrality. In 1865, expressing Republican protectionism and anger that the provincials had violated the spirit, if not the letter of the Reciprocity Treaty, Seward notified Great Britain that the United States would cancel the 1854 agreement.

After 1865, Seward retired from active politics, although he remained secretary of state until 1869. He seemed at last to turn toward aggressive expansionism. Was the Alaska Purchase in 1866 and 1867 a move in a larger geopolitical game? Seeing North America as a global commercial nexus, Seward speculated that the United States might shortly acquire the entire Pacific Northwest. His vision of America's republican-commercial greatness, however vague at times, still directed his policies. After the abrogation of reciprocity with the provinces, he favored a customs union, or "zollverein," with British North America. He did not share the view expressed by the American consul in Montreal that cancellation of reciprocal trade would force the provinces into the Union. Seward was consistent. Any American-provincial merger would have to be by mutual consent.

In the east, the Maritime provinces had become a link in American communications with Europe. Cunard steamers called at Halifax on the way from Liverpool to Boston and New York. The transatlantic cable reached Newfoundland in the summer of 1866. And by 1867 several borderland railroads wove the provinces into America's northern transportation network. Seward and others, such as Perry McDonough Collins, forecast a comparable communications chain around the North Pacific to China. Alaska seemed a stepping stone, a way station to a Pacific Basin trading empire. This was the logic Seward and the Johnson administration used to persuade Congress to accept the Alaska purchase.

The reality of American relations with the Pacific never fulfilled the hopes of American visionaries. Seward likely wanted British Columbia as part of a future American commercial empire. Control of the entire Pacific Coast from Mexico north seemed logical to those with geopolitical imaginations. In 1864, Seward issued a public reply to Senate Foreign Relations Committee Chairman Zachariah Chandler's support for a Pacific rim telegraph. How could Americans "assign limits to the increase of national influence, which must necessarily result from new facilities we should acquire in that manner for extending throughout the world American ideas and principles of public and private economy, politics, morals, philosophy, and religion?" British North America represented only a small prize for someone with such global ambitions.[5]

Americans usually exaggerated provincial interest in joining the United States, so the rise of an annexationist movement in Victoria, British Columbia, received more credence than it should have. Provincial annexationists encouraged Seward to think that Alaska might indeed be the first step in America's Pacific empire. As a result, he attempted to maneuver Britain into offering British Columbia to satisfy American claims for damages arising from the depredations of the Confederate raider *Alabama*. But the annexation movement in Britain's Pacific Coast colony was not as strong as it appeared to those in Washington, D.C. Seward never appreciated provincial fear of absorption by the United States. Furthermore, the British refused to even consider trading colonies for claims. Shortly, British Columbia agreed to join the new Dominion of Canada, foreclosing lingering American territorial ambitions.

Seward did not seem disappointed by this apparent setback. He left office in 1869, still favoring the global expansion of American commerce. On a tour of the Northwest after retirement, he stopped in Victoria, British Columbia, and Sitka, Alaska. The whole area struck him as one unit. The elements of his ideology—geopolitics built on a foundation of global commerce, common interests, ambitions, institutions, and the inevitable historical triumph of republicanism—sustained his faith in an eventual American-provincial merger.[6]

National expansion was not popular during Reconstruction. Internal difficulties pressed on every hand. The national debt stood at $2.5 billion, linked with the circulation of greenbacks that many wanted to retire as quickly as possible. Assistance for the freedman and the status of the Confederate states evoked a furious controversy. President Andrew Johnson's policies after Lincoln's assassination antagonized Republicans in Congress. The South experienced economic, political, and social turmoil. And national projects such as the Pacific Railroad and the Plains Indian Wars drew attention to the sparsely populated western United States.

Given the problems the United States had governing existing territory, many editors argued that the country had land enough. Further additions might create dangerous, expensive, and unprofitable foreign entanglements. As the example of Seward shows, the dominant Republican Party had inherited the Whig antiexpansionism of the antebellum period. Conquest contradicted America's national spirit. Republicanism would spread by its accomplishments and example, not through territorial acquisitions. The Alaska Purchase had disturbed some politicians and editors, and Seward's drive for the Danish West Indies distressed Gideon Welles, his cabinet colleague. After the Alaska Purchase, congressmen ridiculed and denounced expansionist schemes. And Seward got little further with a Hawaiian reciprocity treaty that implied eventual American annexation. Neither treaty passed the Senate.[7]

Those few congressmen who called for annexation of the provinces in 1866, therefore, did not find much sympathy. They spoke as individuals, without political and popular support, despite the excitement they created in congressional debates. Senator and former Union general Nathaniel Banks, for example, proposed that the United States underwrite provincial debts and take control of the provincial canals, customs system, navigable waterways, and post offices. Banks also suggested that the United States grant the provinces $85 million, and thereafter $1.5 million in annual subsidies. In return, the provinces would send representatives to Congress. Zachariah Chandler, Charles Sumner, and Benjamin Butler, among other prominent Republicans, supported Banks.

These men, however, had only a superficial, even ephemeral, interest in annexation. When Butler visited Charlottetown, Prince Edward Island, in 1868, he spoke of renewed reciprocity, which, he confided to E. H. Derby, the Treasury Department official preparing reports on American-provincial trade, would promote annexation. But Butler wanted reelection in the fall of 1868, not Prince Edward Island or any other province. Once victorious at the Massachusetts' polls, Butler promptly dropped "reciprocity" and acquired other interests. His interest in annexation was merely a ploy to garner votes from Anglophobic Irishmen in Massachusetts. Banks also eyed the Irish vote. Politics, not territorial ambition, lay behind Republican annexationism in 1866.[8]

Editor Joseph Medill of the Chicago *Tribune* favored an American-provincial union, but ignored the political rationale for Banks's bill. Medill contrasted the violent empires of the past with a beneficent United States that offered provincials money for their debts, new markets, stable government, on the basis of "come in now if you choose, if not, wait until you are ready." Few provincials would have shared Medill's faith in American generosity.[9]

The ambitions of James W. Taylor of Minnesota and E. H. Derby seemed more serious. Taylor, who prepared a massive 1866 report on American-provincial commercial relations, subscribed to the thesis of inevitable American-provincial union. But he was also prepared to be more aggressive. Crossborder trade had expanded during the past decade, he noted, although the war had distorted the normal traffic by emphasizing provincial exports that supplied Union armies. Derby also stressed provincial economic growth, especially in Upper Canada. He noted that the Great Lakes Basin borderland economy had a shared interest in open navigation from the tip of Lake Superior to the Atlantic Ocean. Derby, like Taylor, considered the newer British colonies to the west—"Central British America" —as well as the established provinces in his evaluation. He and Taylor believed that genuine Americanization was at work from the Red River settlement west. They asserted that strong connections existed between central British America and the northern plains states, and the unity of the Pacific Northwest suggested a common interest in building an "international railroad from Halifax to the North Pacific coast." Both men reflected the assumptions of the new American imperials that economic interests would ultimately forge ideological and political bonds.[10]

Americans who subscribed to the convergence theory believed in a common Anglo-North American destiny. One writer argued that mankind had moved from chaos through development to unity and "unitization" was inevitable, with irresistible global implications. If "commercial, industrial, and social dependence" developed on a continental scale, "political jurisdiction" should embrace it all. Horace Greeley was more explicit. "We, too, believe in the 'Manifest Destiny' of all the English-speaking people of the continent to form at last one great, free nation." Industrial development and domestic reform would accomplish the task "by the simple force of political gravitation." Charles Francis Adams, the American minister in Great Britain, was perpetually uneasy about Seward's expansionist maneuvering. Adams had "taken some pains to ridicule the notion that we have the smallest desire to appropriate Canada by conquest," as much to discourage Seward as to explain American policy. But despite Adams's efforts, British officials doubted that Americans followed a path of "patience, conciliation and the establishment of a harmony of interests that would bring on [annexation] as a perfectly natural result."[11] Provincials as well remained dubious about American innocence.

The efforts to trade parts of Canada for the *Alabama* claims revolved around these themes.[12] Charles Sumner often spoke of such an exchange, and Seward tried to promote the idea as well. Although a continentalist, Sumner opposed territorial expansion prior to the Civil War because of his abhorrence of slavery. Although he briefly considered annexing the provinces in 1861 as compensation for the seceded slave states, he disliked the Alaska Purchase, "a visible step in the occupation of the whole North American continent." Nevertheless, his vision of America's future suggested a "time when the whole continent, with all its various states, shall be a Plural Unit, with one Constitution, one Liberty, and one Destiny."[13]

In Sumner's mind, treaties and purchases could transfer only sovereignty over territory, not a people. Sumner insisted that the invitation to union first broached by the Continental Congress still stood, but he was a passive expansionist. Despite rumors about his designs on the provinces, Sumner believed that shifting economic interests, social reform, and mutual consent would produce American-provincial convergence.

Seward's efforts to gain added territory and occasional calls for annexation generated a minor debate about the future of national expansionism. Orestes Brownson believed that the provinces, along with Central and South American countries, "might be absorbed in the United States without being missed by the civilized world" because they did not represent any compelling principles. In addition, for him the very term "America" implied a continental destiny. But he insisted that "subjugation and liberty do not go together. Annexation, when it takes place, must be on terms of perfect equality, and by the free act of the state annexed." E. L. Godkin opposed territorial expansionism beyond existing borders on grounds of racial incompatibility between Americans and other peoples. But Canada seemed a special case. To the north lay "several millions of a hardy and industrious population, of the same origin as our own, speaking the same language, and imbued with the same social and political ideas, and already used to self-government." Godkin echoed Brownson's caveat that annexation must never occur except by mutual consent. J. B. Austin expected Canada to collapse, and once this occurred, the logic of the convergence thesis would apply. "Manifest Destiny can be so attained that its processes will be entirely peaceable and harmonious while accompanied by the enthusiastic support of whole populations."[14]

The Civil War behind them, American writers expressed a new wave of nationalism based on the successful struggle to maintain the Union. Faith in this ideology sustained the convergence thesis, and the knowledge that Britain would never yield the provinces to pressure along with the increase in provincial political difficulties provided pragmatic support for this position. Even so, James Gordon Bennett, expansionist editor of the *New York Herald*, noted that the "revolution in Cuba, the insurrection in the Winnipeg country, the application of the people in British Columbia for annexation, the chronic disorders in Mexico, the growing dispositions of the Canadians and other British American colonists to be united with us, and the condition of the West Indies generally show that our republican empire must become continental."[15]

Such views, however, had scant impact on policy making after 1865. Furthermore, ideological elements tugged in different directions. On the one hand, a belief in republican destiny led writers and politicians to forecast a unified North America. On the other, future political mergers must come by mutual, free consent. Because republicanism and conquest were contradictory and antithetical in the American mind, no consensus emerged among those who talked about an immediate or distant American-provincial union. And the lack of political or popular support for expansionism during the Reconstruction era produced an essentially passive policy, as Seward's experience demonstrated.

In the meantime, American-provincial connections encouraged patience to allow convergence to develop. The fact that the provincials were migrating westward, and had established themselves on the Pacific Coast, reinforced continentalism. After Canadian Confederation in 1867, the convergence thesis may well have become a rationalization, but many Americans nevertheless doggedly insisted that Anglo-Saxon unity would be ultimately achieved in North America.

Treasury Department officials, for instance, incorporated the convergence thesis in their reports on American-provincial commerce. Emphasizing continued interdependence, James Taylor noted that in 1865, trade with the provinces was second to that with Great Britain herself, America's largest economic partner. The value of American-provincial exchange exceeded 10 percent of America's aggregate foreign commerce. This was heaviest along the Atlantic Coast and in the Great Lakes Basin, but now included the Great Plains and the Pacific Coast.

In 1869, Israel Hatch argued that the end of reciprocity had not disturbed the unity of American-provincial trade. Geography and climate meant "the supremacy of our markets and our carrying systems for the inland commerce of North America." Canadians competed for the interior carrying trade, but their canals and railways were inferior. Hatch recommended improving the transport system as a national enterprise because "the trade and commerce of the border nation would in the future, as in the past, contribute to our public welfare, yielding to the supremacy of our national advantages."

Finally, Josephus Larned noted that in the Maritimes and the Great Lakes Basin borderlands, geographic and economic forces pushed aside international boundaries. Larned even argued that "the political institutions of the ill-named Dominion of Canada are scarcely less republican, either in operation or in principle, than our own." Provincials would have been astonished at such a remark. Free trade with the provinces would end the "commercial belligerency" between Americans and their "quasi-foreign neighbors." Continental industrialization would likely follow. The provinces should form a "zollverein, or a customs union" with the United States. America had no ambition for annexation, Larned insisted, but the provinces could join the union of their own free choosing.[16]

American businessmen, as well as officials, politicians, and editors, sensed that the United States would be sharing North America with the provinces into the indefinite future. Transportation spokesmen in northern states, as Larned implied, understood borderland unity. In 1865, the Boston Board of Trade promoted a northern Pacific railroad from Minnesota to Puget Sound to link New England with Pacific and Asian commerce on the one hand and with the Grand Trunk Railroad in Canada on the other. "The roads on both sides of the national boundaries are now embraced in one system; they receipt for freight, and they book passengers interchangeably; they make joint tariffs." The *American Railroad Journal* condemned Civil War disruptions in cross-border rail service, but still boasted of the overnight travel between Boston and Montreal because of the new Victoria Bridge across the St. Lawrence River. Planned railway projects would accelerate the already close American-provincial relations along the entire borderland.[17]

John Poor, who promoted railroads from Portland, Maine, embraced the vision of a new American empire. His European and North American Railroad was part of a projected global economic system with the United States as a nexus and Portland as a metropolis. The Portland-Montreal line would stimulate the "social, political, and commercial notions and relations of the two countries. The beginning of that new order of things developed by our international lines of railway and steamer, is making the English-speaking people of this continent one in sentiment and in commercial undertakings." Commerce embodied the genius of the age and would sweep across political boundaries as it had swept throughout the United States. Poor forecast an American-provincial customs union, but annexation had no place in his vision.[18]

American capital moved into the provinces as part of America's international industrial and commercial expansion. Speculators took up residence in Hamilton, Canada West, to develop provincial oil reserves because Pennsylvania's production could not satisfy the rising demand in the United States. Money, contractors, and civil engineers built provincial railroads in the 1860s, encouraged by provincial and Canadian policies favoring foreign investment.

Provincials therefore competed with Americans for jobs and suffered from some of the same shoddy work and corporate manipulations that plagued railroads in the United States. On the other hand, Americans were not always happy with business conditions in the provinces. Erastus Corning, the mastermind of the New York Central conglomerate, and his partner, Robert Forbes of the Michigan Central, sat on the provincial Great Western Railway's directorate. They withdrew in 1854, frustrated over their inability to control the company, even though 40 to 60 percent of the Great Western's traffic came from American sources. The United States was crucial to provincial railroad survival. In cities such as Detroit, however, dependence became reciprocal. That city relied heavily on transportation through Upper Canada, and Detroit business leaders lobbied in Washington for harmonious American-provincial relations.[19]

American consuls in provincial cities reflected both their borderland connections and the spirit of the new empire that shaped America's policies after the 1860s. David Thurston, the American consul in Toronto, sending his dispatches to Washington on the Montreal and United States Telegraph lines, reported on the flow of capital from Northern states into his jurisdiction and the revival of provincial business after the Civil War. The failure to renew the Reciprocity Treaty had no apparent impact on provincial preparations for business with the United States. Lumber buyers sought supplies, and merchants collected foodstuffs. Both anticipated good markets. E. S. Winus, Thurston's agent in Cobourg, noted that a new railroad had opened up local iron mines and expanded exports by late 1867. Toronto solicitors had many American clients as well as American Express Company offices. Canada's attempts to foster trade with the Maritime provinces seemed a failure, he told Seward in early 1868, because the provincials still thought of the United States as their natural economic partner.[20]

The consuls in Canada during the Reconstruction period all noted the steady flow of business, whatever their views on changing provincial political arrangements. James Weldon in Prescott, Ontario, for example, reported that Ottawa Valley lumber exports to the United States had climbed so dramatically that he could not keep track of the inflow. Prescott became a minor entrepôt for several other provincial towns because steamer and ferry traffic connected it with Ogdensburg and Morristown, across the St. Lawrence River in New York. American development of Canadian forestry went beyond mere extraction. Another consul boasted that "American capital, guided by enterprise, determination, and integrity, has erected at Ottawa the finest lumber mills in the world."[21]

Americans were also aware that new provinces were developing farther west. Journalists had visited New Caledonia, later British Columbia, in the Pacific Northwest, and the Red River colony, later Manitoba, even before the Civil War. The Reverend Burdett Hart insisted that these settlements were in reality a British project to block American expansion.[22] Americans in the later 1860s focused principally on the Manitoba-Minnesota borderland. The rugged Canadian shield cut settlers in the Red River colony off from easy communications with eastern British provinces. As Indian resistance waned in the northern Great Plains and railroads pushed west of the Mississippi River, St. Paul became an entrepôt for the Métis and other British North Americans who founded Winnipeg. St. Paul politicians saw the Red River colony as an extension of their own commercial frontier. So did Michigan politicians, such as Zachariah Chandler and Jacob Brown. New York financier Jay Cooke foresaw profit in a railroad branch line to Winnipeg. St. Paul land speculators and businessmen had willing accomplices in their provincial ambitions in the St. Paul press, and in James Wicks Taylor, an intimate of Ohio Republican circles.[23]

Taylor, the Israel Andrews of his day, turned his interest in Manitoba into a cause. After a stay in Salmon P. Chase's law office in Ohio, Taylor migrated to St. Paul on the Minnesota frontier as state librarian in 1856. Although not yet an expansionist, Taylor concluded that central British America would become productive in the future. When Taylor reached St. Paul, the Red River Métis settlement had close links with Minnesota, but none with Upper Canada. Taylor argued for American expansion north. If the Red River area became economically dependent upon Minnesota, the United States would acquire the region virtually by default.

Adopting the ideology of the new American empire, Taylor joined Minnesota railroad promoters in 1857 and worked for a north-south line that would help realize his dream. As a special Treasury agent, he investigated American-provincial trade, attended the Detroit convention of 1865 that protested the abrogation of the Reciprocity Treaty, and urged provincial annexation upon his Republican contacts. Taylor drafted Nathaniel Banks's 1866 bill and lobbied to create a political bloc behind a drive north. His ideas were narrow, focused only on the prairies and Minnesota interests. Persistence was his greatest virtue. American politicians held Taylor in high regard as a provincial specialist, but he remained more a consultant than a policymaker. Annexationism stirred only limited interest outside Minnesota.[24]

Even this acolyte expansionist only seemed aggressive. In a paper prepared for Senator Alexander Ramsey to deliver to the Minnesota legislature in 1860, Taylor stressed the ease of navigation on the Red River and the fertile lands along the Saskatchewan River. He projected a customs union with the provinces or perhaps extending the Reciprocity Treaty to the Pacific Ocean as a way of promoting trade. Free trade and navigation with the provinces "would give to the United States, and especially to the Western States, all the commercial advantages, without the political embarrassments, of annexation." He did, however, suggest that if war erupted over the *Trent* affair, Minnesota would "claim the distinction of a winter campaign for the conquest of central British America."[25]

Such hyperbolic spasms passed quickly. Underneath lay Taylor's conviction that the geographic and economic unity to the Great Plains implied a common destiny. He cited the Great Lakes and the St. Lawrence River basins as examples of similar situations. "Reciprocity of action has led to unity of interests and sentiments on the opposite coasts of the St. Lawrence and the great lakes, itself an effective bond of peace. Why not disarm the whole frontier of the north by constant multiplication of such ties and guarantees of international concord?" Taylor also authored a memorial from Minnesota asking for a larger federal presence in the state, hinting that annexation of the Red River area lay just ahead.[26] Although he subscribed to the convergence thesis, Taylor was impatient. The inevitable might be too slow in coming.

Taylor solicited support from government officials, such as William Henry Seward and Edward Cooper, assistant secretary of the treasury, for promoting borderland economic links on the Great Plains that would produce an eventual union with Canada. He urged Minnesota Senator Ramsey to present resolutions in the Senate on free American-Canadian trade that embraced elements of the defunct Reciprocity Treaty, common copyrights, patents, postal rates, and the cession of British territory from Manitoba to the Pacific Ocean.[27]

The Red River Rebellion in 1869 provided what Minnesotans and the American continentalists saw as a political opportunity. The American consul in Winnipeg, General Oscar Malmros, tried to help the rebels and tie them to the United States. Most members of Congress were indifferent, however, and the new president, Ulysses S. Grant, refused Malmros's request for American funds to sustain the rebellion. His secretary of state, Hamilton Fish, appointed Taylor as a special agent for six months to report on the Red River colony's society, politics, economy, and communications with both Canada and the United States. Predictably, Taylor exaggerated the settlers' eagerness for annexation. Fish, who was willing to see Canada merge with the United States, but only after favorable popular referenda and formal Anglo-American diplomatic agreements, had a larger vision than Taylor. The secretary of state refused to jeopardize settlement of the *Alabama* claims and other differences with England to satisfy local ambitions, and Minnesota speculators and politicians lacked the power to shape policy, Taylor's energy notwithstanding. Besides, Canada's Prime Minister, John A. Macdonald, compromised and made a good offer to Louis Riel, the Métis leader in Red River. The rebellion disintegrated, and Manitoba entered Confederation, lost forever to Taylor and his expansionist cadre.[28]

Special Minnesota interests aside, the scheme to manipulate the Red River Rebellion and add central British America to the United States collapsed for want of any but local support south of Winnipeg. Furthermore, entrepreneurs in Minnesota discovered the principal themes of the new American empire. They could establish their railroad lines and expand their commerce without the entanglements of political action.[29] This very conclusion rendered American policies toward Canada largely passive. National influence was dependent on productivity, profits, and control of trade and transportation routes, and territorial additions were largely irrelevant to such progress in most American minds after 1865.

The same issues emerged prior to 1871 in the final segment of the American-provincial borderland, the Pacific Northwest. Like its counterparts east to the Bay of Fundy, the Pacific Northwest borderland resulted as the natural north-south lines of communication in North America gained economic precedence over east-west linkages that were largely political in nature. In the United States, of course, a hospitable climate from the northern border south and a large land area have meant that the north-south and east-west tensions have been roughly balanced. People in any sector along the northern tier of states could orient themselves along either axis.

The Pacific Northwest was isolated, largely unresponsive to eastward tugs until the completion of northern transcontinental railroads in the later nineteenth century.[30] American territorial expansionists considered adding British Columbia to the United States before the British colony joined Canadian Confederation in 1871. But as the Minnesota expansionists discovered, such projects did not elicit much support. At the same time, champions of the new American empire saw the Northwest Coast, especially Puget Sound, as vital to the national future.

In the early 1850s, few Americans knew of British Columbia as more than a distant, mysterious, and undesirable land perched between rugged mountains and the stormy north Pacific Ocean. In 1854, President Franklin Pierce requested Congress to settle disputes over land in the Pacific Northwest. The Hudson's Bay Company subsidiary, the Puget Sound Agricultural Company, had retained titles by the terms of the Oregon Treaty of 1846. Early American visitors sensed a unity to the Pacific Northwest because of the isolation, but none anticipated that any benefit to American interests would accrue from owning the land north of the Columbia River.

Then the Fraser River gold strikes occurred and momentarily catapulted British Columbia into the place in American imaginations held by the California gold rush. San Francisco businessmen treated the entire Pacific Coast as part of their sphere of operations, imported Vancouver Island coal, financed steamers on the Fraser River, and speculated in British Columbia land. Henry de Groot traveled in British Columbia for six months as a newspaper correspondent during the gold rush. He reported that Californians saw Britain's projected transcontinental union as a challenge. "The settlement of those territories so contiguous to our own, must speedily insure the great gain of our people by furnishing a steady and lucrative market for almost every species of their surplus products." De Groot saw the West Coast as one demographic and economic unit; a transcontinental railroad through the United States would easily redirect whatever Pacific trade came into British Columbia. The *New York Times* reported that the region possessed a vigorous legal trade as well as open smuggling between Victoria and American coastal towns because conditions were primitive and beyond the easy control of customs officials.[31] Another editor wrote in near mystical terms about the historical forces that produced such linkages regardless of national schemes and interests, "as if with universal consent and the conspiracy of all the secret forces of nature."[32]

Secretary of State Lewis Cass was more sober. Suspicious of monarchism on principle, he worried about British discrimination against Americans in the area. A spirit of reciprocity should prevail. After all, British subjects had freely entered the California gold mines. Expecting British discrimination, Cass sent John Nugent as a special agent to reconnoiter the value of the gold fields, find out how many British and Americans were there, and to see how British authorities were treating the Americans.

Nugent reported that the mineral deposits were disappointing and that British Columbia was unsuited for agriculture because of the soggy climate. Local British officials had indeed been imperious and unfriendly with Americans, whatever the protestations and policies of the home government. As for Vancouver Island and British Columbia, which were separate colonies until united in 1866, "their ultimate accession to the American possessions on the Pacific coast is scarcely problematical—but in the meantime their instrinsic value either of locality, soil, climate, or productions, does not warrant any effort on the part of the American government or the American people towards their immediate acquisition." The

MAP 4. *Far Western Borderlands, ca. 1870*

BRITISH AMERICA

LAKE WINNIPEG

Assiniboine River

(MANITOBA)

Red River colony

Red River

◄— *To* Rockies, 1818

To St. Paul, Minn.

Missouri River

STATES

Fort Laramie

N. Platte River

Fraser River was not open for navigation beyond a few miles. Only Esquimault harbor seemed of value, and the coastal land offered little except forests. Settlement would probably therefore be slow. In closing, Nugent recommended that Pierce appoint a consul to assist Americans who might do business in British Columbia in the future.[33]

Americans always expected the worst from British officials. Such prejudice was rarely dangerous, but as people from both countries moved into the Pacific Northwest, the precise location of the American-provincial border became important. A local clash might produce an Anglo-American crisis. In 1855, Secretary of State William Marcy wrote to the British minister in Washington and to Governor Isaac Stevens of Washington Territory that the United States sought an early and peaceful marking of the boundary through the Strait of Juan de Fuca. Despite these efforts to avoid conflict, a minor dispute threatened to ignite an international incident in 1859.

A few Americans had settled on San Juan Island in the Strait of Juan de Fuca when the gold yields dwindled and disappointed miners had trickled back to the coast. In June of 1859, the American Lyman Cutler shot a Hudson's Bay Company pig that was demolishing Cutler's potato patch. Cutler also brandished arms and threatened British officials who investigated on the ground that the island was British soil. The truculent American military commander of Washington Territory, General William S. Harney, convinced that American annexation of British Columbia was inevitable anyway, concluded that such wanton aggression from British animals and officials had to be stopped. Eventually, British and American warships, United States regulars, and British troops converged on the area. Washington and London reeled.

President James Buchanan rebuked Harney, moved to arrange a compromise with Britain, and dispatched aging General Winfield Scott in a reprise of his role as borderland peacemaker. Scott's instructions noted that "it would be a shocking event if the two nations should be precipitated into a war respecting the possession of a small island."[34] Scott doused the local fires in the Pacific Coast borderland, as he had along the New York frontier in 1837 and in Maine in 1839. The Treaty of Washington ultimately settled the San Juan dispute. The United States betrayed no hint of aggression here. Short-tempered borderlanders and local officials had only temporarily upset the now peaceful relations between the United States and the provinces.

Americans continued to anticipate eventual union with the tiny British colonies on the Pacific Coast. They had supreme confidence in the power of economic interests to effect cultural and ideological conversions among those who became adjuncts to the American economic system. The belief in a causal relationship between economic exchange and political union had always underlain the American faith in the common destiny of the United States and British North America and the dynamics of the dawning age of the new empire only strengthened the convergence thesis. Americans began to see a dynamic commercial future for the area, Nugent's assessment notwithstanding. The Northern Pacific Railroad charter described Puget Sound as "marked out by nature for a great commercial entrepôt." One promoter assured readers that if the United States built this link to the Pacific, the "whole country would soon become so Americanized (as already half the miners in that country are Americans) that they would in a short time be asking for annexation to the United States." Allen Francis, the American consul in Victoria after April of 1863, shortly concluded that the provincials depended utterly on California, Oregon, and Washington. Americans seemed to control half of Victoria's business. When Britain united Vancouver Island with British Columbia in 1866, ending Victoria's status as a free port, unhappy city residents advocated annexation to the United States. "I am satisfied," Francis wrote, "that three fourths of the inhabitants, outside of government officials and those immediately connected with them would hail the measure—could it be effected—as the greatest boon; and look to it as their only hope of political and commercial salvation."[35] It seemed to be 1849, Montreal, and Israel Andrews all over again.

The Alaska Purchase of 1867 suggested a new source for the pressures of Americanization. From 1854 to 1861, Senator William McKendree Gwin of California had lobbied for Russian Alaska as a base for America's Pacific commercial empire and as a way of forestalling future British competition in the region.[36] American economic interests in the Pacific, California, Oregon, and Washington Territory, as well as visionaries with grand imaginations, provided added impetus. Seward and Charles Sumner hoped that after Alaska, British Columbia would succumb voluntarily to American pressure. George Bancroft believed that republicanism would eventually push monarchism out of North America and that Canada would inevitably join the United States as a result. The Chicago *Evening Journal* looked beyond Alaska's strategic and commercial value. British Columbia's "colonists themselves have already taken the initial steps in the direction of annexation and being surrounded by the United States will tend to strengthen and tighten the cords that were already drawing that province into the folds of the American Union." President Andrew Johnson told the nation in his 1868 annual message that "the acquisition of Alaska was made with the view of extending national jurisdiction and republican principles in the American hemisphere."[37] All saw larger ideological principles at stake.

The dispatches from Allen Francis in Victoria reinforced Washington suspicions that provincials were "general and earnest" in their talk of annexation when they learned of the Alaska Purchase. American residents in Victoria hailed Seward's achievement because it paved the way to expanding trade with Asia's millions. Americans both in Victoria and in Washington, however, exaggerated the numbers and political strength of British Columbia annexationists, who were concentrated in Victoria's commercial circles. Like Israel Andrews in Montreal in 1849, Francis generalized from the particulars he knew and drew false conclusions. Economic discontent, not ideological yearnings, produced British Columbia's annexationism and this proved a narrow and transitory base upon which to construct a movement that would need wide popular support to succeed.

Once again, the strong ideological belief that American capital would sweep aside political differences surfaced. The Reverend Burdett Hart of Fairhaven, Connecticut, saw the Northwest as one of the world's great natural highways and identified Puget Sound as the future entrepôt between North America and Asia. The railroad would carry civilization west and as relations with Vancouver Island grew, "the practical absorption by this country of all that region, a conquest of commerce and business," would result. Although the British were on the move, they were "too late. The trade will be grasped; the connections of business will be established; the destiny of the New Northwest will be sealed." But once again John A. Macdonald and his Conservative Party, with their policy of incorporating all British North American colonies into Canada, produced an offer British Columbians found attractive. By 1870, David Ekstein, Francis's successor, reported that "confederation with the Dominion of Canada is regarded as an accomplished fact."[38] The following year, Canada was a political entity, stretching from the Atlantic to the Pacific oceans.

Americans nevertheless persisted in their faith that natural forces would eventually work to merge the provinces with the United States. The ideology of the dawning new empire assured Americans that a united Anglo-Saxon North America would ultimately develop. So even as impatient American annexationists fulminated, no official policy to acquire Canada for the Union ever emerged. American ideology rendered military strength and protective attitudes superfluous. The provincials would eventually become eager and willing recruits to the triumphant republican empire of the future.

Chapter 11.

A New Northern Neighbor and the Treaty of Washington

It is the imperative duty of the people of the United States of America, through their proper representatives, to earnestly protest against the formation of any government in North America not republican in form, and in which the people are not allowed to govern themselves and choose their own rulers; and whereas, this nation has and does assume to maintain this principle upon this continent; and whereas, any attempt on the part of the imperial government of Great Britain to establish a permanent monarchical government in North America . . . would be an infraction of this principle.
—New York Assembly,
March 1867

Amerian consuls maintained a vigorous presence in the provinces in 1835. They observed changes in provincial economic, political, and even social affairs by virtue of their strategic vantage point at the center of provincial activity. But their commercial-minded republicanism always distorted their comments. Even the most sensitive to the provincials, Israel Andrews for example, assumed that British North Americans shared the same assumptions as American citizens. Even though Andrews argued that a semiindependent spirit had emerged among provincials, he doggedly insisted that their future destiny lay in becoming Americans. His pursuit of American-provincial reciprocity rested in part on his faith that closer trade would accelerate ideological and political convergence.

By 1865, the American consul general in Montreal had been given responsibility over all the provincial consuls and their subagents. Consul General William Averell kept a sharp eye on the coming elections in 1867. John A. Macdonald's Conservatives dominated the government and the Liberals toiled under a serious handicap because, as the party out of power, they controlled no patronage. In desperation, some Liberals had solicited Averell for an $100,000 American contribution to help defeat the Tories. Averell had turned them down.

However the voting went, the American consul was convinced that Confederation lacked a popular base. He also insisted that provincial unification was antidemocratic and antirepublican. In his vision, the British had encouraged Confederation only to jettison a dangerous and expensive imperial liability. He, like most Americans and provincials, did not realize that Britain's entire geopolitical orientation was shifting toward Europe, the Mediterranean, and the Middle East because of the rise of India and other Far Eastern possessions as the most important jewels in the imperial crown. Averell's focus led him to see Confederation as a means to allow the "ruling aristocratic class" to preserve its power and wealth. "In these provinces the want of stability in government and the lack of power to resist the progressive liberal tendencies of the people, with other causes, rendered the change necessary to the continued political and social domination of the Tory Party."[1] The provinces suffered from social and political dry rot, and with the customary conceit of a fervent republican, Averell asserted that union with the United States would instantly solve all provincial political problems.

In the meantime, pro-Confederation politicians in the provinces manipulated the widespread fear of potential American aggression to promote their project of provincial unification. The Civil War had heightened this fear. Upper Canada contained the most virulent anti-Americans, who drew upon their heritage of loyalism, their conservative distaste for republicanism and the freewheeling democracy evident in the United States, and their memories of invasion and depredation during the War of 1812. Americans both at home and in the provinces consistently underestimated this deep antagonism.

William Averell, for example, dismissed provincial anti-Americanism as "the extreme ignorance of the great mass of society in Canada regarding the United States." Education would soon dispel false notions about the alleged evils of republican America, although older people retained a "lethargy and prejudice difficult to change." Averell, however, had prejudices of his own. He clipped provincial newspaper articles opposed to Confederation, and put his trust in editors such as Edward Penny in Montreal and Joseph Howe in Halifax who confirmed Averell's suspicions that the Confederation would never succeed.[2] Like some extreme republican ideologues in the past, he wished to purge all traces of monarchy from the western hemisphere.

Averell also shared many of Israel Andrews's convictions. The consul general argued that trade would nurture provincial friendship with the United States and urged Seward to make some gesture to encourage provincial annexationists and undermine Confederation. But he was a one-man conspiracy. The United States had some thirty consuls, consular agents, and customs officers in the provinces, and none of their reports echoed Averell's plea to add the provinces to the union. Seward ignored Averell's recommendations.

Averell ceased to comment much on politics after Confederation in 1867, although he still noted any provincial dissatisfactions and continued to view Canada as a political arm of the aristocratic classes. "In Lower Canada, or Quebec, the Roman Catholic clergy—all of the most violent ultramontane school—composed a powerful electioneering machinery in favor of Confederation." When pro-Confederationists faltered in Nova Scotia elections, Averell again urged Seward to pursue an American-provincial union. Eventually, economics would rectify the failures of common sense and democracy. "Without a reciprocal trade with the United States," he asserted, provincial annexationists, producers, and marketers would "realize their helplessness." If Washington imposed trade regulations, "dissatisfaction with the present state of things sooner or later will prompt them to seek relief" in union.[3]

David Thurston, the American consul in Toronto in 1865, also discounted Canadian Confederation. Perhaps because the businessmen he conferred with wanted closer relations with the United States to open bigger markets, Thurston too exaggerated Canadian annexationist sentiment. The Maritimes would be especially unhappy in the Confederation, he thought and would prefer union with the United States. Economic interests would eventually alter current Canadian political and ideological convictions. But Thurston also emphasized that fear of provincial vulnerability in the event of an Anglo-American war was an added stimulus to union. Unlike Averell, however, Thurston never recommended that Seward try to subvert Confederation. For his part, Seward was clear. As far as relations with Canada were concerned, the United States dealt "only with the Imperial Government of Great Britain, and through the Legations in Washington and London."[4]

Underneath his diplomatic propriety, Seward retained hope for an eventual American-provincial union. He and other American officials nevertheless quietly accepted the birth of the Dominion of Canada in 1867, a name which in itself had made some Americans bristle. As the New York Assembly revealed, the very idea of a kingdom or monarchy as a next door neighbor was a studied insult to the United States.

William Dart, who assumed Averell's post in Montreal, was more penetrating in observation, circumspect in judgment, and guarded in comment than his predecessor. Dart could see that local annexationism rested on special interests, and he also argued that "the conviction largely obtains that while Great Britain would be willing to see her North American provinces independent, she would not be a party to their transfer directly to the United States." Dart nevertheless spoke with "very few who did not admit that the union of Canada with the United States was simply a question of time. Few are so stupid as not to see the impossibility of a separate national existence for a country extending from New-Foundland, to Puget Sound, with an average width of tillable land scarcely exceeding fifty miles."[5] Many Americans simply refused to believe that Canada was either politically or economically viable as a nation.

Geography, climate, economic interests, and American interpretations of history all seemed to sustain the convergence thesis. Dart believed that the United States could afford to wait. In the meantime, Washington policymakers were determined to avoid unnecessary pressure that might disrupt Anglo-American commercial relations or compromise important diplomatic goals, such as sharing the North Atlantic fisheries or settling claims against Great Britain for Civil War damages.

Americans, therefore, were for the most part content merely to observe the arrival of Confederation and the birth of Canada. After all, British officials and their provincial subjects had considered unification since Lord Durham's report on the rebellions of 1837–38. The 1840 Act of Union merged Upper and Lower Canada, but that had created more difficulties than it solved because of the

French-English clash. Most provincials concealed their enthusiasm for similar political experiments until the 1860s. Then, as American newspapers reported, interest in Confederation rose.

The *New York Times* insisted that a "spirit of change" had appeared in the provinces, even among social and political conservatives. A country separate from the United States seemed about to be born. "North America is certainly large enough for the two families, even if they should not wish to board and lodge together." Confederation would not solve provincial economic problems, however, because the population was too scattered. "In the meantime, they will go to that market where they can buy the cheapest and sell the dearest," the *Times* added, implying that economic realities would eventually encourage annexation. Moreover, as Alexander Galt had drawn his proposals for Confederation from the American system, Canada's structure seemed "sensible and practical."

American practices appeared evident elsewhere in the formation of the Confederation. To the west, the Red River colony and British Columbia were "bidding for a North Pacific Railway, and a system of colonization on our American pattern between Lake Superior and Puget's Sound" as the price of union with the projected Canadian nation. The *Times* concluded, "stretching across the continent, and embracing nearly half of North America, is a nascent empire which the world must ere long take notice of."[6]

The *Times* seemed pompous, but Americans often spun grand political tapestries from common historical threads. The provinces had been moving toward independence since the 1837 rebellions. By the mid-1860s, they seemed self-governing in all respects save foreign policy, which the British government still controlled. The *Times* typified American responses in viewing creation of the new country as an instance of natural evolution. The laws of progress had produced an independent, republican United States and would do the same in the provinces given time. Even so, *The Nation* argued that Canadian politicians, such as John A. Macdonald and D'Arcy McGee, had failed to solve their country's problems. And even a token British tie would retard Canada's political and social development.[7]

Despite skepticism, Americans accepted Canada's sovereignty. An 1866 visitor to the provinces concluded that provincials had the prerequisites to become a great nation—natural resources, prosperous agriculture and fisheries, industry, capital, and foreign trade—but noted that an independent Canada would likely move ever closer to the United States. A Rochester daily argued that Canada's government seemed practical, free, and potentially stable, and once released from "the old fogies and leeches from England, Ireland and Scotland . . . would at once spring forward to an eminence equal to that of all the states along the border."[8]

The *National Intelligencer* regularly copied Canadian stories on finance, fires, canal construction, and Fenian activity. Political news alone evoked editorial commentary, but in 1866 only a few items on Confederation appeared. The details of the proposed "Kingdom of Canada" were printed in full and by 21 March 1867, the *Intelligencer* reported, a "New Nation" was about to emerge. Provincial resources guaranteed "future prosperity and power," but Canada should have a federal system, like the United States, not a "kingly government." Canadian independence posed no threat to the United States, for it reduced the likelihood of an Anglo-American clash.[9] Because the *Intelligencer* was an administration outlet, the editor reflected the passive acceptance of the Canadian Confederation adopted by Andrew Johnson's administration.

Some journals, however, frankly disapproved of the Confederation, reflecting the post–Civil War backlash of Anglophobia that plagued Anglo-American diplomacy. One alarmist saw Confederation as "the consolidation of a great power on our borders under the influence and government of a distant and jealous power." The *New York Herald*, owned by expansionist James Gordon Bennett, saw nothing in Confederation to indicate progress because Canada remained so dependent upon Britain.[10]

Some American politicians, outraged over the Confederation, had ulterior motives. In the House of Representatives, for example, Nathaniel P. Banks from Massachusetts, chairman of the committee on foreign affairs, urged passage of a resolution stating that the creation of Canada defied "the traditions and constantly declared principles of this Government." Britain had not consulted the people, he charged, dismissing the agreement of provincial legislatures as inconsequential. The New York Assembly also denounced Confederation as undemocratic and even unnatural in the republican atmosphere of the New World. Maine politicians, by some extraordinary feat of logic, declared that Confederation violated the Monroe

Doctrine and contradicted provincial interests and wishes, over-looking completely that the British had helped to create Canada as part of their disengagement from North America. Such rhetorical posturing ceased quickly. John Chanler of New York City, for example, forced Banks to admit that he had expressed a personal opinion, and not recommended official policy. As for Maine, old grievances held over from the Aroostook War, the Webster-Ashburton boundary award of 1842, and the lumber and coal clauses in the Reciprocity Treaty of 1854 found expression in its denunciations of Confederation.[11]

Overall, American criticism of Confederation was too mild to be taken seriously. The *Boston Daily Advertiser* wondered how Confederation, which married autonomy with continued dependence, might work. Combined, the provinces had "abundant materials for the creation of a second class American power. If, on the other hand, they should choose annexation, they will add to our national domain a territory of great value and capable of vast development." *Frank Leslie's Illustrated News* was refreshingly straightforward. The United States could remain indifferent to Confederation because of an "implicit confidence . . . in our own powers of absorption, and the belief that sooner or later—the exact time being unimportant—all the populations on the continent, whatever their present condition, must gravitate towards our political system, and ultimately be merged in it."[12] Faith in the convergence thesis made the Canadian Confederation seem a temporary phase in North American development. Even if the British and Canadians established a royal ruler, they could scarcely menace the United States. *Leslie's* mocked the righteously indignant and reflected a widespread view among editors and politicians of the future American-provincial relationship.

American commercial interests reacted to Confederation according to their estimation of how it would affect their provincial connections. The *Merchant's Magazine and Commercial Review* spoke for New York City businessmen who argued that trade with the provinces would surge, eliminating awkward pressures for annexation. After Confederation, the editor noted, "on our northern frontier we have a young nationality, rapidly growing in population and rising in commercial importance." The next steps should be total independence and free trade with the United States, for then

Canada would be able to emulate the American example and progress properly. The *American Railroad Journal*, on the other hand, saw a new national rival. "Confederated, the Provinces will be cemented and united, have one commercial system, one spirit, one destiny, and in their renewed force, will become an antagonist such as they have never been before."[13]

Canada remained a mild political curiosity after provincials celebrated Confederation on 1 July 1867. Many Americans believed that Canada would shortly collapse, as foreigners after 1783 had believed would happen to the United States. Having just fought a war for national union themselves, Americans sympathized with what they saw as the provincial search for political stability and social order. The British provincials continued to seem potential republicans who would follow similar stages of historical evolution. Now as Canadians, they were seeking what to American eyes seemed to be American ends—peace, union, liberty, and economic and social progress. Beyond that, nation building was a theme of the times. The North German Confederation emerged the same year, while Prussia continued absorbing other German states. And the Italians had begun their process of unification.

After Confederation, Canada evoked only occasional political commentary. What remarks appeared focused on Canadian problems. The French-Canadians seemed restive, and disgruntled Nova Scotians dispatched a delegation to Washington to meet with the congressional reciprocity committee. But nothing came of these conversations. By 1869, however, the Canadian economy had slumped, the Red River Rebellion erupted, and British Columbia reportedly nurtured annexationist sentiments. Canada's future looked bleak. No wonder George W. Brega arrived in Washington to lobby for trade concessions. Most Americans still believed that Canadian prosperity depended utterly upon open exchange with the United States and that Canadian economic woes flowed from continued dependence on Great Britain. But American politicians were reluctant to extend commercial favors to Canada. Protectionism still dominated Republican circles, and Canada seemed to many a serious rival engaging in unfair competition because her government subsidized industry and carriers heavily.[14]

In January 1869, Israel T. Hatch's study of American-Canadian commerce accompanied the secretary of the treasury's annual report to Congress. The end of the Reciprocity Treaty had not disturbed the flow of goods across the border, Hatch observed, although the United States had increased its trade revenues. But Britain had always used her provinces as proxies to compete with the United States, building canals and improving the St. Lawrence River to undermine the Erie Canal system in New York. American commerce on the Great Lakes would wither without protection from subsidized Canadian competition. British policy had been wrongheaded, spiteful, and a failure, in Hatch's view. And Canadians had been blind and stubborn and had "vainly attempted to exercise a commercial dominion (worthy of imperial ambition) over our western trade, and its transit lines to the Atlantic." The United States had retaliated in abrogating the treaty, and the provincials had suffered a just retribution. Fresh restrictions would force Canadians to realize that their true economic and political interests lay in union with the United States.[15]

Consul William Dart also wanted Congress to leave the tariff on Canadian goods, but he rejected any policy that even looked hostile. "It seems to me, we can afford to stand still and let her revolve around us." In his view, events of the year 1870 suggested the wisdom of the passive policy toward the provinces as crises broke out in Canada. The French in Quebec sympathized with the Métis in the Red River Rebellion. The Canadian government established a banking system that amounted to a forced loan on the public wealth without raising taxes. "In view of the defection of Nova Scotia, and Prince Edward Island, the Red River rebellion, the expenses incurred in protecting against Fenian invasion, and the increasing desire for independence, throughout the Provinces of Quebec and Ontario, the Dominion Government seems to be beset with perplexities which are fast telling in the Canadian mind."[16]

But the factions favoring greater Canadian independence, undoing Confederation, or joining the United States, neither agreed on policy nor formed an alliance. Individually, they could criticize, but not overcome the institutional momentum Confederation developed. John A. Macdonald's government survived its political crises, avoided a nasty clash with the Métis that might have produced open French-English conflict, and maneuvered Manitoba and British Columbia into Canada. Dart, like Averell before him, and others, simply waited. Their anticipation of Canada's imminent collapse counseled a policy of patience. The domestic orientation of Ulysses S. Grant's administration guaranteed that no action would be taken to pursue a hankering for annexation, the Fenian furor notwithstanding.

The Fenian raids, nonetheless, frightened both provincials and British officials. Already jittery about American intentions toward the provinces because of the neutrality issue during the Civil War, British North Americans divined a concerted and hostile design in the apparent reluctance of the Johnson and Grant administrations to police the border or to forestall Fenian incursions. Many in the Northern states, including politicians and editors, grinned at British and provincial alarm. But Northerners were only momentarily angry, and were simply using the occasion to air their sense of injury over the Confederate raids from Canada.

Fenianism grew from Irish hatred of Great Britain, which was transplanted to the United States and the provinces. Irish home independence leaders dispatched organizers to North America, and the Fenian Brotherhood became active in 1857. This expatriate conspiracy concocted extravagant plans to free Ireland from British rule. Local leaders thought to provoke an Anglo-American clash by invading British North America. During the Civil War, the Fenians plotted their raids and exploited Northern anger against Britain for her apparent aid to the Confederacy. As the South teetered on collapse, Fenian activity quickened, and Irish Union veterans volunteered eagerly to fight for their homeland's freedom.

The Irish had formidable political strength that was necessary to the Republican Party in such important states as New York and Massachusetts. Partly because the politics of Reconstruction engulfed the federal government after 1865, Johnson's administration had little time for the Fenian issue. Johnson intended to suppress open raids, but neither he nor Seward believed that the blustering Fenians would prove truly dangerous. Besides, private political organization, moral exhortation, and agitation were scarcely illegal in the United States, as Secretary of State Seward and many others pointed out. Newspaper editors refused to question the Fenians' studied Union patriotism. Both editors and politicians vented anti-British rhetoric freely while Nathaniel Banks, among others, openly courted the Irish for votes. All this convinced the Fenian leaders that they enjoyed popular and even tacit official support in the

United States. And at the same time, the entire circus persuaded the provincials and their British protectors that the United States was a willing accomplice in a Fenian conspiracy that stretched from the United States and the provinces, to Ireland itself, and even parts of England such as Manchester.[17]

Seward, nevertheless, informed the British about Fenian activities. And Seward also assured Canadian envoy Alexander Galt, in Washington to discuss the Reciprocity Treaty, that the United States would enforce neutrality laws if the Fenians took open military action. But administration officials could only guess which of the many Fenian gatherings in the borderland heralded an immediate invasion. The American government had, in short, an intelligence problem. Johnson's administration did dismiss the vocal Fenian leader, Major Thomas Sweeny, from the army in response to British pressure. In the press, the *New York Times* sniffed a Fenian fraud to wring money out of American Irishmen.

In 1866 the Fenians marched. In April, they collected in Eastport, Maine, to assault Campobello Island. But Federal troops prevented an invasion and eventually confiscated Fenian arms and ammunition. Frustrated, the Fenians dispersed from the Maritime borderland. In May, while Federal agents watched, others gathered at Buffalo and on 1 June crossed the Niagara River and captured Fort Erie. Another group mustered at St. Albans, Vermont. Successful against provincial volunteers sent to dislodge them from Fort Erie, the Fenians withdrew to American soil when British regulars advanced. The St. Albans effort, then, disintegrated.

President Andrew Johnson issued a proclamation to enforce neutrality 6 June 1866. Three days earlier, General George Gordon Meade, the Union victor at the Battle of Gettysburg, had ordered his troops to seize any war supplies they found and to prevent armed crossings into the provinces. Twelve hundred federal troops eventually patrolled the borderland. This force arrested Fenian leaders and sent some 7,000 of the rank and file home by the middle of June after extracting a parole that they would not serve against Canada. The government refused to suppress the Fenian Brotherhood, but Seward and his colleagues hoped that time would eliminate the problem.[18]

Many Americans shared the Anglophobia of the Fenians and sympathized with their goal of seeking self-determination for sub-

ject home peoples. Beyond that, British and provincial embarrassment seemed a just punishment for harboring Confederate raiders.
But Americans no longer saw the provinces as an enemy base. Nor
did any expansionist policy lie behind either public opinion or government reluctance to act against the Fenians. The Fenian troubles
were entirely unrelated to the feeble annexationist currents sput-
tering in American political circles during the Reconstruction
period.

American editors and politicians gave only scattered applause to
the Fenian invasions. *The Nation* denounced the Fenian crusade as
a delusion and a swindle, arguing "we are a Christian people, and
no matter what the Canadians have done or left undone, we owe it
to our own souls not to let bands of ruffians leave our soil for the
purpose of killing their young men and desolating their homes."
American consuls in the provinces took fright. John Potter in Montreal complained that Fenian action would sink whatever hopes remained for an American-provincial merger. William Averell agreed.
At first, Seward denied David Thurston government money to defend Fenians arrested for trial in provincial courts, only relenting in
cases where American support was the only source of legal counsel.[19] During 1867, the United States government watched the Fenians more closely, but still remained wary of an Irish political
backlash against Republicans in the 1868 elections.

Undaunted, the Fenians regrouped for renewed efforts in 1869
and 1870. Like the refugee rebels and the Hunters of 1838, they
clung to their delusions. Canada was a target of opportunity in a
larger game. American consuls warned that Canadian authorities
feared the Fenians, and William Dart ventured the guess that Prime
Minister Macdonald exploited the Fenian scare as an excuse to call
up troops to suppress the Red River Rebellion. At the same time,
the apparent American reluctance to act against the Fenians had
exacerbated provincial anti-Americanism and retarded American-
provincial convergence. "Those who have been anxiously working
for the independence and annexation of these provinces to the
United States deplore this invasion and regard it as calculated to
defer their hopes for years."[20]

Ulysses S. Grant's administration proved bolder than its predecessor. The elections were over and the Anglo-American discussions regarding the *Alabama* claims against Great Britain for dam-

ages during the Civil War approached a possible resolution. The new secretary of state, Hamilton Fish, clamped down. He refused to permit the Fenian rabble to sabotage the delicate negotiations on the fisheries. When Fenian leader John O'Neil launched an opéra bouffe invasion on the very day President Grant denounced "sundry illegal military enterprises and expeditions" being formed in the United States to attack Canada, a lone federal marshal arrested O'Neil and several other Fenian leaders.[21]

William B. O'Donoghue, a self-professed Fenian, organized another filibustering expedition in Minnesota in 1871. His motives were shadowy. A sometime advisor to the Red River Métis leader Louis Riel between 1869 and 1870, O'Donoghue had connections with Minnesota expansionists. Although any hopes for exploiting the Red River disturbances evaporated when Riel compromised with the Canadian government, O'Donoghue nevertheless led a small party that captured Fort Pembina, just south of Winnipeg. Four hours later, American regulars under orders from Washington arrived to take the filibusterers into custody. Here, the United States energetically pursued those violating the neutrality acts and arrested their own nationals on foreign soil for breaking the law.[22]

By 1871, Fenianism was spent, but Canadians were angry that American authorities had not stopped Fenian raids before they left the United States and outlawed the Fenian Brotherhood entirely. Grant's government took more vigorous action than Johnson's against the Fenians. It nevertheless arranged what amounted to a sham prosecution of the leaders arrested for violating the neutrality laws. Grant intended to pardon the accused, but waited until after the fishing season was over so that Canadian authorities would not retaliate against Yankee fishermen working provincial waters. The Fenian incidents embittered Canadians toward the United States, as American consuls in the provinces had warned. For their part, the British remained patient, accepting with only mild reservations Seward's and Fish's assurances that the United States would enforce the law. Given the reorientation of imperial policy by 1871, Great Britain wanted good relations with the United States.

American reluctance to apply the letter and spirit of neutrality did not affect the movement toward an Anglo-American accord over issues arising from the Civil War. Although rejected by the Senate, the 1869 Johnson-Clarendon Convention reflected the will-

ingness to settle outstanding issues. So did the treaty of 1870 providing for the mutual rights of expatriation and changing citizen-
ship. This matter had gnawed at Anglo-American relations from
1793 forward and arose now because Irish-Americans were liable for
arrest if suspected of being Fenians when they visited their homeland. Irish interests in Massachusetts and New York had urged the
Johnson administration to raise the matter with the British government.[23] The spirit of accord and the agreement constituted a fitting
introduction to the talks that produced the Treaty of Washington.

Hamilton Fish, part of New York's William Henry Seward–Thur-
low Weed Republican organization, continued Seward's policy of
avoiding Anglo-American confrontations. Fish, too, believed that
the United States was destined to be the dominant power in the
western hemisphere. A rising prosperity, reestablished political stability with the end of the Civil War, and a vigorous people only
added to America's potential. Fish wanted a foreign policy that
would bind New World republics around "American ideas of republican government, of modification of the laws of war, of liberaliza-
tion of commerce, of religious freedom and toleration, and of the
emancipation of the New World from dynastic and balance of power
controversies of Europe." Despite this, he made an effort to reassure
the British about Charles Sumner's truculent Senate speeches de-
manding Canada in exchange for the *Alabama* claims.[24]

Grant and Fish also adopted a conciliatory posture in their failure
to exploit the Red River Rebellion and in allowing Britain access to
the American Sault Ste. Marie canal locks to move troops west to
assert Canada's authority in the region. Fish rejected Minnesota
Senator Alexander Ramsey's idea of giving the rebels a $100,000
bankroll. The American annexationists never presented a unified
opposition to Grant's policy. Ramsey found an opponent in annexationist Senator Jacob Howard of Michigan, who wanted Detroit,
not St. Paul, to be the economic focus of the western borderland.
Such bickering reduced even further any influence such individuals
might have had.

The vast majority of Americans who spoke or wrote on the matter were generally agreed. Eventually Canada would join the Union
voluntarily. In the meantime, there were pressing, practical items
on the Anglo-American agenda. Popular opinion in the United
States therefore welcomed a joint high commission between the

two countries to settle North American problems that had become major issues by 1870—the fisheries, the San Juan boundary, border-land navigation in rivers and canals, and the movement of goods in bond across the American-Canadian border. The delegates generally proved amiable, conciliatory, and willing to trust their counterparts when the talks began in Washington in March of 1871. Canadian prime minister Macdonald, however, suspected that the British intended to sacrifice his fledgling country's interests on the altar of Anglo-American harmony. Macdonald negotiated as much with his British colleagues as he did with the Americans.

The Treaty of Washington would settle much and clear the diplomatic air for future discussions. Although some points of contention remained, the 1871 agreement represented a symbolic American recognition of Confederated Canada's semiautonomy. The commission spent twice as much time on the Canadian issues as on the *Alabama* claims.

The American government was eager to arrange a sharing of the North Atlantic fisheries by 1871. Abrogation of the Reciprocity Treaty had put sharing the fisheries back onto the terms of the Convention of 1818. In keeping with those terms, Canadian officials arrested several American vessels for violating inshore waters and using provincial ports in the 1870 season. Grant noted in his annual message to Congress that "semi-independent but irresponsible" Canada had been hostile to Americans. Congress might wish to retaliate in some way. Boston papers reported Canadian discussions on the fisheries in great detail. Maritime fishermen were the culprits, they believed, lobbying against New England's interests. Some congressmen and senators believed that the provincials were using the fisheries as a lever to force trade concessions from the United States, a tactic they were suspected of before the negotiations that produced reciprocity in 1854. American negotiators responded by separating the fisheries from the *Alabama* claims. The latter went to arbitration, but much haggling ensued over fishing grounds.[25]

The discussions covered trade and reparations as well as boundaries and fisheries. The Americans probed about renegotiating the boundary west of the Rockies, but backed off quickly when the British agreed only to allowing the German Emperor to arbitrate the San Juan boundary. Caleb Cushing, convinced that British Columbia was of little value to anyone, was content with arbitration, and he accepted Canada as America's new northern neighbor. The Americans rejected Macdonald's call for reparations for the Fenian raids and for renewed reciprocity. Talks almost broke down, but minor eleventh-hour American concessions combined with British payments to the Canadians produced an agreement. Several years passed before legislation enacted all the terms, but the treaty generated Canadian-American, as well as Anglo-American, harmony. According to article thirty-three, Great Britain, Canada, Prince Edward Island, and the United States all had equal powers of ratification.[26]

As the diplomatic discussions were held in camera, Americans learned little until the Treaty of Washington was signed on 8 May. Macdonald had fought both the Americans and his British colleagues, and at the signing, he dramatically declared that Canada's fisheries disappeared with the strokes of his pen. Macdonald represented Canada's interests, but the British had a global perspective. Vulnerable communications with the Far East, concern about Russia's future actions, and Prussia's 1870 humiliation of France made an Anglo-American accord important to Great Britain's imperial security in 1871. But at least Macdonald had the salves of a British douceur and rhetorical protest. Benjamin Butler of Massachusetts, reflecting his constituents' rancor over the same section of the treaty, disliked the free entry of Canadian fish into the United States. But on the whole, Americans were generally satisfied with the treaty. Politicians from both parties were eager for a settlement with Great Britain and the Senate ratified the treaty fifty to twelve on 24 May.[27]

Hamilton Fish had carefully laid the groundwork in the Senate before the vote was taken, so there were no surprises. By 4 December, Congress had passed all the necessary legislation on the American side. Cushing concluded that the United States had done well. The American delegates had restored fishing and transit privileges in Canadian waters without yielding to Canadian demands for renewed reciprocity. From Montreal, William Dart recorded Canadian unease. The British had clearly taken another step in their retreat from North America. But for Dart, this meant another step toward the ultimate convergence of Canada and the United States.[28]

The *Boston Evening Transcript* was one among many American

newspapers that viewed the Treaty of Washington as a symbol of Anglo-American peace and progress. Perhaps coincidentally, perhaps deliberately, the *Transcript* ran a series of articles on the provinces while the talks were in process in Washington. These articles provide a summary of American perceptions about Canada during the period. The correspondent traveled widely, praised the beauty of Montreal's environs, and pronounced the Victoria Railway bridge a triumph "over the apparently insurmountable obstacles of nature." Canadians had "all the rights and liberties of a free people," but believed that union with the United States "will come to pass." Canadians also "anticipated, in case of annexation, a greater activity in trade and more enterprise in business. There is a certain atmosphere of dullness and apathy surrounding them that they think would be dissipated by Yankee bustle and goaheadativeness." Canadian winters were dreary, and the French "slow by nature, custom, and principle. Annexation, independence, or any other form of government will never serve to make them an active, reliable people, as long as they are the spiritless servants of the clergy." Quebec seemed quaint, "foreign," a "fossil city" devoid of "life, energy, or enterprise. You can never Americanize a Frenchman as he exists here."[29] Old prejudices among Protestant Americans died hard.

Ontario seemed to offer travelers little except anti-American prejudice. But Toronto was different. It had an American character, a bustle reminiscent of Boston or New York. People were busy, attended schools and theaters, and factories such as the steel plants around Hamilton hammered out the products of the industrial age. Ontario resembled an American state, in short, and Ontarians, unlike Quebeckers, subscribed to American ambitions, attitudes, and values.

Caleb Cushing, diplomat and world traveler, also reveals how Gilded Age Americans perceived their northern neighbor. In his words, Canada "resembles a mathematical line, having length without breadth" and its future prosperity would "never be sufficient to prevent her landowners and her merchants from looking wistfully toward the more progressive population and the more capacious markets of the United States." True Canadian independence was inevitable, but would be a transitory phase rather than an end in itself. Eventually, "America . . . will comprehend, in a mighty and proud Republic, the whole combined British race of North America."[30]

Cushing and the *Transcript's* correspondent reveal the form American expansionism took in regard to British North America by 1871. They assumed that America's ideology, commerce, and values were essential for any people, especially for those as similar to Americans as provincials seemed to be. When Americans looked north in 1871, they saw that the British base had gone and that the Canadian state had arrived. A new northern neighbor had emerged, a product of historical change as Americans understood it. But, in the future, other, even more powerful, economic and ethnic forces would eventually merge Canada and the United States into one republic. Anglo–North Americans were fundamentally the same people, despite the boundary that divided them.

American perceptions of British North America changed dramatically between 1775 and 1871 because of the complex and shifting nature of United States' expansionism. Three phases of expansionism unfolded between 1783 and 1871 that overlapped one another. First came defensive expansionism to 1815. By 1823, the second phase had added a territorial thrust for settlement and mercantile bases for exploitation of the Pacific Ocean Basin. Beginning in 1850, a third phase gradually emerged that looked toward America's global expansion of the late nineteenth and early twentieth centuries.

Manifest Destiny has been used most often to characterize the whole of America's nineteenth-century expansionism. It seems quite broad, but really has a quite specific application. Manifest Destiny refers to the American drive for additional national territory roughly between 1830 and 1860. Manifest Destiny should be seen as distinct from earlier expansionism. From 1783 to 1820, national security provided the main rationale for the decisions that led to the Louisiana Purchase, the acquisition of Spanish Florida, and the limited interest in Upper Canada before and during the War of 1812. The Monroe Doctrine of 1823 declared America's official opposition to Europeans transferring New World territory among themselves or founding new colonies in the western hemisphere. As the principal shapers of the doctrine, James Monroe and John Quincy Adams had summarized the intent of defensive expansionism and were also its last important spokesmen. The generation of the founding fathers and the one immediately following had reacted to their own revolutionary ideology and a hostile world of seemingly malevolent European powers.[31]

After 1815, American expansionism acquired the themes and impulses usually associated with Manifest Destiny. This period of eclectic and malleable expansionism never abandoned entirely the defensive cast of its predecessor and meant different things to Americans depending on time, place, interests, and circumstance. The motivation behind antebellum expansionism was complex, even confused. Before 1850, the push had been dominantly south and west, into the Old Northwest, Mississippi River Valley, and then into Texas. But after 1850, Southerners looked toward the Caribbean and Central America as likely locations to plant slavery, both as a commercial and a cultural institution.[32] Other sections of the United States, however, refused to permit the South to define and direct national expansion.

At the same time, industrialization gained momentum in the United States. This process generated new forces that later dominated the third phase of national expansionism. High policymakers drew ideas and support from manufacturers and financiers, as well as from merchants. William Henry Seward was an archetypal ideologue and policymaker of the third phase. His public career spanned the transition from Manifest Destiny into the industrial-commercial phase of his country's development.[33]

Old and new forms of expansionism coexisted and tugged against each other during this transition period and contributed to sectional rifts, and hence to the Civil War. Throughout, the provinces stood on one side. British power protected them, but so did the nature, character, and goals of American expansionists.

Although it is useful to talk about the rise of the new American empire, imperialism is not the best term to describe what was happening. Imperialism seems best defined as a policy of subduing and ruling alien peoples for strategic, economic, or political purposes. Americans did become imperialistic in this way. Later in the nineteenth century they sought and acquired bases and possessions in the Pacific Ocean that included Hawaii and the Philippines, and part of Cuba, Puerto Rico, and the Panama Canal in the Caribbean and Central America. That was American imperialism. But the term has little meaning if applied to American policies toward British North America between 1783 and 1871.

American expansionism from 1783 to 1871 was a broad phenomenon with cultural, demographic, diplomatic, economic, ideological, political, and territorial manifestations. Isolating a single phase or facet of American policies toward British North America conceals the changing complexity of the phenomenon. No one has attempted to analyze the relationship between American expansionism and the provinces systematically over this entire span. A broad definition of national expansionism down to 1871, however, creates the best framework for understanding this crucial chapter in the history of American-Canadian relations.

A few statistics illustrate the scope as well as scale of this expansionism. The national population of the United States rose from 3.9 million in 1790 to 12.8 million by 1830, to 23.1 million by 1850, and to 38.5 million by 1870. Sixteen states comprised the union in 1800, thirty-one by 1850, and thirty-three by 1870. America increasingly became a pluralistic society during this period when immigrant waves from other than Anglo-Saxon origins began to arrive. In 1790, the urban population was just over 3 percent, using towns of 8,000 to define "urban." This figure reached 16 percent by 1860. Migrants settled in the Ohio and Mississippi River valleys and along the shores of the Great Lakes. Imports averaged $100 million between 1815 and 1820, dipped, and then rose to $284 million between 1851 and 1860. Exports averaged $70 million per year between 1815 and 1820, but $249 million from 1851 to 1860.

Between 1820 and 1860, internal transportation developments produced turnpikes, then canals, and finally a rail network that laced the northern states and some of the southern ones into a national economic web. Mechanical transport reduced a fifty-two-day transit time for goods moving between New York City and Cincinnati in 1817 to a week by 1852. Agricultural production rose as new lands came under cultivation, as regional specialization became possible because of improved transportation, and as machinery appeared on farms. Cotton cultivation in 1801 had not extended past Virginia's western frontier. By 1840, it had spread to the Texas border, and by 1860 well into that state in a belt that ran from southern Kentucky to the Gulf of Mexico. Industrialization began in the 1830s and continued to progress even through the Civil War era. American banking developed, mostly at the state level, although foreign capital fueled much early industrialization.

In all spheres of American life, qualitative and quantitative changes shaped external as well as domestic affairs. The United States was becoming a modern, pluralistic nation. American society intersected in various ways in the external and domestic affairs of other nations, and no single definition of expansionism covers the complexity that this variety of factors produced. Each phase of expansionism represented a shift in emphasis, rather than a sharp break with the past. The defensive reflex about national security never entirely disappeared from United States expansionism. Foreign policymakers in the 1830s and 1840s continued to fear potential British encirclement. At the same time, other responses coexisted with the simple fear of British hostility. Those with territorial ambitions cited revolutionary republican ideology through the 1860s. But because many believed in republicanism as self-evidently a superior way of life, the idea of the American mission could apply in active or passive forms. In addition, new ideas about race complicated American expansionism in a variety of ways as it affected British North America between 1775 and 1871.[34]

Economic ambitions were important, but not completely dominant in this process. New England's commercial interests in new North American and overseas markets became national, not merely sectional, concerns. Productivity, the search for profits, and the conviction that government should support and nurture free enterprise have been fundamental components of the American national ideology. An innate sense of cultural superiority derived from material success, the Protestant religion, and racial bias were also behind America's expansionistic tendencies. These forces combined to produce America's global ambitions.[35] Ideological convictions thus leavened economic assumptions to shape America's social and political behavior in domestic and foreign affairs.[36]

Americans believed that their national values had universal applicability. Their country was at the cutting edge of human progress, a civilization as much as a nation with specific economic and security interests. Belief in a national culture was a dynamic factor, not just a backdrop, in foreign affairs. Commercial, religious, and humanitarian interests became important national concerns. Americans consciously sought to foster social, economic, and political systems distinct from Old World models. This meant that American merchants were agents of social reform even as missionaries preached political change. Both commercial and social elements reflected complementary aspects of a unified American ideology.

A broad definition of expansionism provides a new point of departure for understanding relations between the United States and the British North American provinces between 1783 and 1871. When Americans surveyed, traveled in, did business in, or even just thought about the provinces and their inhabitants during these decades, they reflected shifting cultural characteristics as well as regional, local, and personal perspectives. They were rarely echoing clearly expounded national policies.

After 1783, Americans watched British activity in the provinces with great suspicion. But after 1815, American leaders became progressively less convinced of a British threat from the north. As the nineteenth century wore on and American power and self-confidence grew, the British seemed less and less a likely local menace. So the image of the provinces as an enemy base faded over time. By 1871, it was little more than a memory.

On an ideological level, Americans had jettisoned a monarchy in 1776 and achieved a republican independence. During the era of defensive expansionism, many harbored a deep desire to eject monarchism and the British from their northern frontier. These views became part of the rationale for the War of 1812, yet America's failed invasions and British power left little choice but to share North America with the provincials and their British masters. In the meantime, journalists and politicians in the United States contented themselves with watching the provinces for signs of colonial restiveness. Another facet of American ideology that affected the provinces was Protestant America's suspicions of Roman Catholics, whether as immigrants or as neighbors in Lower Canada. Americans also saw provincials as potential republican recruits, although this perception fluctuated over time, ultimately to become part of the convergence thesis—the faith that historical forces would ultimately bring the United States and British North America into one vast Anglo-Saxon republic. By 1871, Americans generally believed that provincials would decide for themselves when to become part of the United States.

American-provincial ties of kinship developed because of cross-border migrations. These began with the loyalist evacuations between 1775 and 1783. Migration to the Eastern Townships of Lower Canada in the 1790s was the next phase. These links were reinforced by American trade and investment in the provinces from 1783 forward. After 1815, migration patterns along the lake shores and land necks of the inland seas generated new American-provincial interests and contacts. American papers began to report and reprint provincial news. Nova Scotia became part of the American information link with Great Britain and the European continent by the 1850s, and Americans took great interest in the laying of the transatlantic telegraph cable. In short, evolving American views and the relationship of expansion to the British North American provinces developed from a complex of assumptions, interests, and perspectives that changed over time.

As a result, increasing numbers of Americans saw opportunities in the provinces, especially after 1815. Settlers sought land, until the British made immigration more difficult. Merchants sought trade, bankers sought investments, and entrepreneurs contended for the right to build canals, railroads, and lumber mills. Transportation magnates sought to capture a share of the provincial carrying trade. And travelers saw opportunities for relaxation and cultural enrichment on the great northern tour.

Finally, for different reasons and at different times, some Americans found a temporary or permanent refuge in the provinces when conditions in the United States became intolerable for them. Domestic turmoil drove many out. First came the loyalists. Next came small refugee clusters of religious sects, such as Dunkards, or defeated political factions, such as former Whiskey Rebels. Third came free blacks and slaves. Next came Union deserters, who found a ready refuge in the nearby provinces, as did Confederate prisoners escaping Northern prison camps. Other Confederates made their way to the provinces to plan and carry out operations against the North. In 1871, only descendants or scattered remnants remained from these refugee groups. But Canada always represented a potential refuge for Americans seeking to escape their country and live in a familiar society close to home.

American expansionism and the British North American provinces between 1783 and 1871 clearly had commercial, demographic, financial, ideological, political, territorial, and therefore broadly cultural dimensions. American views of the provinces became increasingly complex and interwoven over time, moving away from the simple perception of the provinces as a northern enemy base to the view of Canada as a brother government soon to adopt the republican principles America held dear. But throughout the period, when Americans looked across the border, they saw a vision of their northern neighbor that reflected their own aspirations and desires.

Notes

CHAPTER 1

1. John Mellon, *A Sermon Preached at the West Parish in Lancaster* (Boston: B. Mecom, 1760); *All Canada in the Hands of the English* (Boston: B. Mecom, 1760).

2. Justin Smith, *Our Struggle for the Fourteenth Colony: Canada and the American Revolution* (New York: G. P. Putnam's Sons, 1907), 1:73–77, 82–88, 103–5, 175–77.

3. Hugh Keenleyside, *Canada and the United States: Some Aspects of their Historical Relations* (1929; reprint, Port Washington, N.Y.: Kennikat Press, 1971), pp. 15–19, 33–35; Albert Weinberg, *Manifest Destiny: A Study of Nationalist Expansion in American History* (Baltimore: Johns Hopkins University Press, 1935), pp. 19–20; James Callahan, *American Foreign Policy in Canadian Relations* (1937; reprint, New York: Cooper Square Publishers, 1967), pp. 2–15.

4. Leon Dion, "Natural Law and Manifest Destiny in the Era of the American Revolution," *The Canadian Journal of Economics and Political Science* 23 (1957): 227–47; Walter La Feber, "Foreign Policies of a New Nation: Franklin, Madison, and the 'Dream of a New Land to Fulfill with People in Self-Control,' 1750–1804," *From Colony to Empire: Essays in the History of American Foreign Relations*, ed. William A. Williams (New York: John Wiley & Sons, 1972), pp. 10–37; David Calabro, "Consensus for Empire: American Expansionist Thought and Policy, 1763–1789" (Ph.D. diss., University of Virginia, 1982), pp. 102–3, 108, 110–13.

5. Worthington C. Ford, ed., *The Journals of the Continental Congress* (Washington, D.C.: Government Printing Office, 1934–37), 1, no. 2, p. 101; Gustav Lanctot, *Canada and the American Revolution, 1774–1783*, trans. Margaret Cameron (Toronto: Clarke, Irwin & Company, 1967), pp. 246–56; Charles Thomson to Benjamin Franklin, 1 Nov. 1774, Ford, *Journals of Congress*, 1, no. 2, p. 566.

6. "To the Oppressed Inhabitants of Canada," 29 May 1775, Ford, *Journals of Congress*, 2, no. 1, pp. 68–70; "Boycott," 17 May 1775, ibid., p. 54. New York Provincial Congress, Broadside, 2 June 1775.

7. "Resolution," 1 June 1775, Ford, *Journals of Congress*, 2, no. 1, p. 75; ibid., 3, no. 3, p. 507; President of Congress to George Washington, 28 June 1775, Edmund C. Burnett, ed., *Letters of the Members of the Continental Congress* (Washington, D.C.: Carnegie Institution, 1921), 1:146; Robert McConnell Hatch, *Thrust for Canada: The American Attempt on Quebec in 1775–1776* (Boston: Houghton Mifflin Company, 1979).

8. George Washington to Philip Schuyler, 28 July 1775, John C. Fitzpatrick, ed., *The Writings of George Washington* (Washington, D.C.: Govern-

ment Printing Office, 1931–34), 3:374; "To the Inhabitants of Canada," ibid., 478–80; One of the Virginia Delegates, 30 June 1775, Burnett, *Letters of Congress*, 1:148; R. H. Lee to Mrs. Macaulay, 29 Nov. 1775, James C. Ballagh, ed., *The Letters of Richard Henry Lee* (New York: Macmillan Company, 1911), 1:161–63; "More Fresh News from Canada. Carleton's Defeat and Arnold's Success," Extract from a Letter, 3 Nov. 1775, Broadside.

9. Washington to President of Congress, 4 Aug., 30 Sept. 1775, Fitzpatrick, *Writings of Washington*, 3:398, 485–86, 526; to Philip Schuyler, 15, 20 Aug. 1775, ibid., 470; to John Augustine Washington, 10 Sept. 1775, ibid., 489; to Benedict Arnold, 14 Sept., 1775, ibid., 494–96.

10. Allan Everest, *Moses Hazen and the Canadian Refugees in the American Revolution* (Syracuse, N.Y.: Syracuse University Press, 1976); "Resolution," 8 Jan. 1776, Ford, *Journals of Congress*, 4, no. 1, p. 39; George Washington to R. H. Lee, 27 Nov. 1775, Fitzpatrick, *Writings of Washington*, 4:117.

11. Washington, "General Orders," 5 Nov. 1775, Fitzpatrick, *Writings of Washington*, 3:65; "Resolution," 15 Feb. 1776, Ford, *Journals of Congress*, 4, no. 2, pp. 151–52; "Instructions to Commissioners," 20 Mar. 1776, ibid., 215–18; Robert Morris to Horatio Gates, 6 Apr. 1776, Burnett, *Letters of Congress*, 1:416.

12. Brantz Mayer, ed., *Journal of Charles Carroll of Carrollton, during his Visit to Canada in 1776, as One of the Commissioners from Congress* (Baltimore: Maryland Historical Society, 1845), pp. 8–11, 17; Lanctot, *Canada and the American Revolution*, pp. 124–33; William Goforth (at Trois Riviere) to John Jay, 8 Apr. 1776, Richard B. Morris, ed., *John Jay: The Making of a Revolutionary* (New York: Harper & Row, 1975), 1:248–52.

13. George Washington to General John Sullivan, 16 June 1776, to President of Congress, 20 Jan. 1777, Fitzpatrick, *Writings of Washington*, 5:148–52, 39–40; versions of Canada article, Ford, *Journals of Congress*, 5, no. 2, pp. 554, 688; 9, no. 3, p. 924; "Resolution," 29 Nov. 1777, ibid., no. 4, p. 981, and 25, no. 1, p. 570; Henry Laurens to John Rutledge, 1 Dec. 1777, Burnett, *Letters of Congress*, 1:579.

14. R. H. Lee to Washington, 22 Oct. 1775, to Sam Adams, 7 Feb. 1776, to Landon Carter, 2 June 1776, Ballagh, *Letters R. H. Lee*, 1:153, 168, 199; President of Congress to John Thomas, 24 May 1776, Burnett, *Letters of Congress*, 1:463.

15. "Resolution," 22 Jan. 1778, Ford, *Journals of Congress*, 10, no. 2, p. 84; Gouverneur Morris to Henry Laurens, 26 Jan. 1778, Eliphalet Dyer to William Williams, 17 Feb. 1778, Burnett, *Letters of Congress*, 3:50, 64–65, 88–89; John Jay to Philip Schuyler, Morris, *Jay*, 1:465; Smith, *Fourteenth Colony*, 2:493–549; John Laurens to father, 28 Jan. 1778, *The Army Correspondence of Colonel John Laurens in the Years 1777–8* (New York: New York Times & Arno Press, 1969), p. 113.

16. Henry to Johnson, 10 Mar. 1778, Burnett, *Letters of Congress*, 3:122; John McKesson to John Jay, 8 Feb. 1779, Morris, *Jay*, 1:554.

17. Henry Laurens to John Rutledge, 11 Mar. 1778, Burnett, *Letters of Congress*, 3:124–25; Laurens to Washington, 20 Nov. 1778, ibid., 498–99.

18. "Resolutions," 16 Sept., 5 Dec. 1778, 1 Jan. 1779, Ford, *Journals of Congress*, 12, no. 1, p. 919; no. 5, p. 1191; 16, no. 1, pp. 11–12; John Jay to Marquis de Lafayette, 3 Jan. 1779, Morris, *Jay*, 1:518.

19. John Sullivan, "Proposed Address to Congress," 2 May 1781, Burnett, *Letters of Congress*, 6:75–76; Virginia Delegates to Governor of Virginia, 29 Oct. 1782, ibid., 527.

20. Charles E. Clark, *The Eastern Frontier: The Settlement of Northern New England, 1610–1762* (New York: Alfred A. Knopf, 1970), pp. 335, 354–59; George Rawlyk, *Nova Scotia's Massachusetts: A Study of Massachusetts–Nova Scotia Relations, 1630–1784* (Montreal: McGill-Queens University Press, 1973), pp. 218–21.

21. See John Bartlett Brebner, *The Neutral Yankees of Nova Scotia: A Marginal Colony during the Revolutionary Years* (New York: Columbia University Press, 1937); Wilfred B. Kerr, "The Merchants of Nova Scotia and the American Revolution," *Canadian Historical Review* 13 (Mar. 1932): 20–36; and Kerr, *The Maritime Provinces of British North America and the American Revolution* (Sackville, N.B.: Busy East Press, 1941); John Dewar Faibisey, "Privateering and Piracy: The Effects of New England Raiding upon Nova Scotia During the American Revolution, 1775–1783" (Ph.D. diss., University of Massachusetts, 1972); Rawlyk, *Nova Scotia's Massachusetts*, pp. 215–16, 227–28.

22. Harold Davis, *An International Community on the St. Croix (1640–1930)* (Orono: University of Maine Press, 1950), pp. 41–48; Faibisey, "Privateering and Piracy," chap. 9.

23. George Washington to Committee of the Massachusetts Legislature, 11 Aug. 1775, Fitzpatrick, *Writings of Washington*, 3:415–16, and to the President of Congress, 30 Jan. 1776, ibid., 3:292; "Petition," 2 Nov. 1775, and "Resolutions," 10 Nov. 1775, 8 July 1776, Ford, *Journals of Congress*, 3, no. 1, pp. 316, 348; 5, no. 2, p. 527; Rawlyk, *Nova Scotia's Massachusetts*, pp. 232–35.

24. Rawlyk, *Nova Scotia's Massachusetts*, pp. 236–40; and Brebner, *Neutral Yankees*, pp. 323–34, cover Eddy. See documents in Frederick Kidder, comp., *Military Operations in Eastern Maine and Nova Scotia During the Revolution* (Albany: Joel Munsell, 1867).

25. John Allan, Report to the Council of Massachusetts, 21 Nov. 1776, Kidder, *Military Operations*, pp. 177–79, 180–82; Allan to Board of War, 27 Aug. 1777, and George Stillman to Board of War, 27 Aug. 1777, ibid., pp. 215–17, 222. See also various resolutions, Ford, *Journals of Congress*, 6, no. 2, p. 1056, and 7, no. 1, pp. 18, 20, 30.

26. Faibisey, "Privateering and Piracy," is persuasive. See also Rawlyk, *Nova Scotia's Massachusetts*, pp. 246–48.

27. Allan to Massachusetts Council, 25 Feb. 1777, to Board of War, 27 Aug. 1777, Kidder, *Military Operations*, pp. 180–82, 216–17.

28. Massachusetts Resolution cited in Faibisey, "Privateering and Pi-

racy," p. 231. See Victor Paltsits, ed., *Minutes of the Commissioners for Detecting and Defeating Conspiracies in the State of New York: Albany County Sessions* (New York: Da Capo Press, 1972), 1:163, 225–26, 346, 411; 2:547.

29. Committee of Foreign Affairs to William Lee, 14 May 1778, Burnett, *Letters of Congress*, 3:237; William Whipple to John Langdon, 6 June 1779, ibid., 4:251, 144n. "Ordered," 21 May 1778, Ford, *Journals of Congress*, 11, no. 2, p. 518; 22 Oct. 1778, ibid., 12, no. 3, p. 1041; R. H. Lee to John Adams, 8 Oct. 1779, Burnett, *Letters of R. H. Lee*, 2:156.

30. James Leamon, "The Search for Security: Maine After Penobscot," *Maine Historical Society Quarterly* 21 (Winter 1982): 119–53; Robert Sloan, "New Ireland: Men in Pursuit of a Forlorn Hope, 1779–1784," ibid., 19 (Fall 1979): 73–90.

31. Brebner, *Neutral Yankees*, pp. 34–46, 61–64; H. N. Müller, "The Commercial History of the Lake Champlain–Richelieu River Route, 1760–1815" (Ph.D. diss., University of Rochester, 1969), pp. 18–30.

32. Müller, "Commercial History," pp. 31–41. Information on Franks in Richard B. Morris, ed., *John Jay: The Winning of the Peace, 1780–1784* (New York: Harper & Row, 1980), 2:93–94n. See also Mayer, *Journal of Carroll*, pp. 44, 57, and citation p. 71; Everest, *Moses Hazen*, pp. 67–74.

33. William O. Sawtelle, "Acadia: The Pre-Loyalist Migration and the Philadelphia Plantation," *Pennsylvania Magazine of History and Biography* 51 (1927): 244–85; A. G. Bradley, *Colonial Americans in Exile: Founders of British Canada* (New York: E. P. Dutton & Co., 1932), p. 119; E. A. Cruikshank, ed., *The Settlement of the United Empire Loyalists on the Upper St. Lawrence and the Bay of Quinte in 1784* (Toronto: Ontario Historical Society, 1934).

34. J. Tomlinson, Jr., to Joel Stone, 18 Aug. 1783, cited in Catherine Crary, ed., *The Price of Loyalty: Tory Writings from the Revolutionary War* (New York: McGraw Hill, 1973), p. 400; Gregory Townsend to Daniel Hubbard, 8 July 1783, ibid., p. 399; poem in *New York Morning Post*, 7 Nov. 1783, cited ibid., pp. 391–92. Helpful on the agonies of relocation are Christopher Moore, *The Loyalists: Revolution, Exile, Settlement* (Toronto: Macmillan of Canada, 1984), and Wilbur Siebert, *The Exodus of the Loyalists from Penobscot to Passamaquoddy* (Columbus: Ohio State University, 1914).

35. See Carl Wittke, "Canadian Refugees in the American Revolution," *Canadian Historical Review* 3 (Dec. 1922): 320–33, and Everest, *Moses Hazen*.

36. See 12 Mar., 29 Aug. 1776, Ford, *Journals of Congress*, 4, no. 2, pp. 198–99; 5, no. 3, p. 716; see also 29 Apr. 1777, ibid., 7, no. 3, p. 313; 10 Nov. 1780, ibid., 18, no. 3, p. 1042; 23, 25 Apr. 1783, ibid., 24, no. 4, pp. 218, 273.

37. Richard B. Morris, *The Peacemakers: The Great Powers and American Independence* (New York: Harper & Row, 1965), pp. 219–20, 262–88, 326, 346–77; George W. Brown, "The St. Lawrence in the Boundary Settle-

ment of 1783," *Canadian Historical Review* 9 (Sept. 1928): 223–38; Samuel Flagg Bemis, "Canada and the Peace Settlement of 1782–3," ibid., 14 (Sept. 1933): 265–84; James Cooper, "Interests, Ideas, and Empire: The Roots of American Foreign Policy, 1763–1779" (Ph.D. diss., University of Wisconsin, 1964), pp. 561, 567–68, 584–604; Gerald Stourzh, *Benjamin Franklin and American Foreign Policy*, 2d ed. (Chicago: University of Chicago Press, 1969), pp. 54–65, 208–11, 221, 251–52.

38. Elbridge Gerry to John Adams, 8 Jan. 1777, Adams to James Warren, 26 July 1778, and to Sam Adams, 28 July 1778, Robert Taylor, ed., *Papers of John Adams* (Cambridge, Mass.: Belknap Press of Harvard University Press, 1963), 5:65–66, 6:321, 326. Sam Adams to James Warren, 3 Nov. 1778, Burnett, *Letters of Congress*, 3:476.

39. William Whipple to Josiah Bartlett, 7 Feb. 1779, John Fell, "Diary," 10–11 Mar. 1779, Burnett, *Letters of Congress*, 4:60, 103; "Committee Report," 23 Feb. 1779, Ford, *Journals of Congress*, 13, no. 4, p. 242; and see 24 Mar. 1779, ibid., no. 5, pp. 348–49.

40. George Mason to Thomas Jefferson, 27 Sept. 1781, Robert A. Rutland, ed., *The Papers of George Mason* (Chapel Hill: The University of North Carolina Press, 1970), 2:698; James Lovell to Horatio Gates, 19 Apr. 1779, Burnett, *Letters of Congress*, 4:164; Sam Adams to Samuel Cooper, 29 Apr. 1779, ibid., 184–85 disagreed. See also Richard Henry Lee to George Mason, 9 June 1779, ibid., 256.

41. 20 Aug. 1779, Ford, *Journals of Congress*, 23, no. 1, pp. 491–92; Cooper, "Interests, Ideas, Empire," pp. 584–86. Samuel Cooper to Sam Adams, 14 Mar. 1779, cited ibid., pp. 599–600.

42. James Lovell to John Adams, 1 Dec. 1777, Taylor, *Papers of Adams*, 5:340; Stourzh, *Franklin*, pp. 197–211, 251–52; Sam Adams to Samuel Cooper, 29 Apr. 1779, Burnett, *Letters of Congress*, 4:184–85.

43. George Mason to Richard Henry Lee, 12 Apr. 1779, and to Edmund Randolph, 19 Oct. 1782, Rutland, *Papers of Mason*, 2:499, 754. 20 Aug. 1782, Ford, *Journals of Congress*, 23, no. 1, pp. 475–76, 496; John Jay to Robert Livingston, Sept. 1782, cited by Calabro, "Consensus for Empire," p. 148.

44. John Adams, Benjamin Franklin, Henry Laurens, John Jay to Robert Livingston, 13 Dec. 1782, Morris, *Jay* 2:440–41; Jay's diary, 4 Oct. 1782, ibid.; Morris, *Peacemakers*, pp. 262–63.

CHAPTER 2

1. Hamilton to George Clinton, 1 June 1783, Harold Syrett, ed., *The Papers of Alexander Hamilton* (New York: Columbia University Press, 1960–82), 3:367–72.

2. Hamilton to Clinton, 3 Oct. 1783, ibid., 467; "Speech on Vermont," 14 Mar. 1787, ibid., 4:115–18, citation from 116. See also 28 Mar. 1787, ibid., 134–37, and "Tully No. II," *American Daily Advertiser*, 26 Aug. 1794, in

ibid., 17:149. Hamilton hinted that the Whiskey Rebels had sought British aid in Canada.

3. "Conversations with George Beckwith," Oct. 1789, Syrett, *Papers of Hamilton*, 5:484–85; Benjamin Lincoln to Hamilton, 1 Dec. 1789, 20 Jan. 1790, ibid., 6:28, 191–92, and 192 n. 2; from Timothy Pickering, 3 Jan. 1793, on mail system, ibid., 449–50, and 3 Jan. 1793, ibid., 13:450. On the growing complexity of American-provincial relations see ibid., 375, 489, 499–500; 7:150–53; 9:336–38; 10:390–91; 11:25, 347–48; 14:534n.

4. Hamilton–John Rivardi correspondence, 1799, ibid., 22:518, 566–74; 23:4–5, 183–84; 24:43. Hamilton's "Defence" series on the Jay Treaty appeared July–September of 1795. For American-provincial relations see ibid., 18:404–11, 453; 19:117–18, 146, 174–75, 192–96, 226–31, 240–41.

5. Harold Davis, *An International Community on the St. Croix (1604–1930)* (Orono: University of Maine Press, 1950), pp. 50–100, is one of the few sustained studies of a borderland society. See George Rawlyk, "The Federalist-Loyalist Alliance in New Brunswick, 1784–1815," *Humanities Association Review*, 27 (Spring 1976): 151–52; Arthur J. Mekeel, "The Quaker-Loyalist Migration to New Brunswick and Nova Scotia in 1783," Friends Historical Association, *Bulletin* 32 (Autumn 1943): 65–75; Lorenzo Sabine, "Moose Island," in *Eastport and Passamaquoddy: A Collection of Historical and Biographical Sketches*, comp. William Kilby (Eastport, Maine: Edward E. Skead & Company, 1888), pp. 142–45. Albert B. Hart, ed., *Commonwealth History of Massachusetts* (New York: States History Company, 1929), 3:350–51. See also Marcus L. Hansen and J. B. Brebner, *The Mingling of the Canadian and American Peoples* (New Haven, Conn.: Yale University Press, 1940), pp. 47–64.

6. Walter Hill Crockett, *Vermont: The Green Mountain State* (New York: Century History Company, 1921), 2:499; Paul Evans, "The Frontier Pushed Westward," *History of the State of New York*, ed. Alexander Flick (New York: Columbia University Press, 1934), 5:150–59; Richard Ellsworth, "The Settlement of the North Country," ibid., 197–202; Harry F. Landon, *The North Country: A History, Embracing Jefferson, St. Lawrence, Oswego, Lewis and Franklin Counties, New York* (Indianapolis: Historical Publishing Company, 1932), 1:88–147.

7. E. A. Cruikshank, "Immigration from the United States into Upper Canada, 1784–1812—Its Character and Results," Ontario Educational Association, *Proceedings of the Thirty-Ninth Annual Convention* (1900), 263–83; H. N. Müller, "The Commercial History of the Lake Champlain-Richelieu River Route, 1760–1815" (Ph.D. diss., University of Rochester, 1969), pp. 161–63; Gerald M. Craig, *Upper Canada: The Formative Years, 1784–1841* (Toronto: McClelland and Stewart, 1963), chap. 3; Adam Shortt, "Founders of Canadian Banking," *The Canadian Banker* 30 (Oct. 1922): 34–47; Alfred Leroy Burt, *The Old Province of Quebec* (1933; reprint Toronto: McClelland and Stewart, 1968), 2:78–81, 114–15; Walter Hill Crockett, *A History of Lake Champlain: A Record of More than Three Centuries, 1609–1936* (Burlington, Vt.: McAuliffe Paper Co., 1936), pp. 207–8.

8. Monroe to Jefferson, 1 Nov. 1784 and 12 Apr. 1785, Julian P. Boyd, ed., *The Papers of Thomas Jefferson* (Princeton, N.J.: Princeton University Press, 1950), 7:459–62, 8:78; J. C. A. Stagg, "James Madison and the Coercion of Great Britain: Canada, the West Indies, and the War of 1812," *William and Mary Quarterly* 3d ser., 38 (Jan. 1981): 3–34; Madison to Rufus King, 8 June, 20 July 1802, William R. Manning, ed., *Diplomatic Correspondence of the United States: Canadian Relations* (Washington, D.C.: Carnegie Foundation, 1940–43), 1:157–60. See also Gilbert Imlay, *A Topographical Description of the Western Territory of North America* (London: J. Bebrett, 1797), p. 46.

9. Gallatin to Thomas Jefferson, 25 July 1807, Henry Adams, ed., *The Writings of Albert Gallatin* (1879; reprint New York: The Antiquarian Press, 1960), 1:345–51; Gallatin to Jefferson, on intended negotiation with Great Britain, ibid., 286–87; James Madison to William Pinkney and James Monroe, 17 May 1806, Manning, *Diplomatic Correspondence*, 1:172–73.

10. Charles R. Ritcheson, *Aftermath of Revolution: British Policy Toward the United States, 1783–1795* (Dallas: Southern Methodist University Press, 1969); Edmond Randolph to George Hammond, 20 May, 2 June 1794, *American State Papers: Foreign Relations* (Washington, D.C.: Gales & Seaton, 1832), 1:461, 465–66; Donald Stewart, *The Opposition Press of the Federalist Period* (Albany: State University of New York, 1969), pp. 145, 184, 484; Edmond Randolph to John Jay, 6 May, 18 Aug. 1794, to George Hammond, 23 July, 1 Sept. 1794, Manning, *Diplomatic Correspondence*, 1:65, 73–77, 78, 80–82; Madison to Monroe and Pinkney, 30 May 1806, 30 July 1807, ibid., 174–75, 179–80. Madison to Jefferson, 3, 24 Apr. 1812, James Madison Papers, Manuscript Division, Library of Congress, Washington, D.C. (photocopies, Alderman Library, University of Virginia, Charlottesville, Virginia). Samuel Eliot Morison on the Henry intrigue in *By Land and Sea: Essays and Addresses* (New York: Alfred A. Knopf, 1953). See also E. A. Cruikshank, *The Political Adventures of John Henry: The Records of an International Embroglio* (Toronto: Macmillan of Canada, 1936).

11. St. Clair to Secretary for Foreign Affairs, 13 Dec. 1788, Clarence E. Carter, ed. and comp., *The Territorial Papers of the United States* (Washington, D.C.: Government Printing Office, 1934–75), 2:167–68; St. Clair to the Secretary of State, 10 Feb. 1791, ibid., 331–33; Senator Benjamin Hawkins to the President, 10 Feb. 1792, ibid., 367; Hamilton, "Conversations with George Hammond," 1792, in Syrett, *Papers of Hamilton*, 13:213–14, 326–28, n. 2, 382–83; Medad Mitchell to Hamilton, 27 Aug. 1793, ibid., 16:288–300; James Wilkinson to Hamilton, 6 Sept. 1799, ibid., 23:377–93. William Henry Harrison to Thomas Jefferson, 30 Dec. 1801, and "Petition to Congress by Democratic Republicans of Wayne County," 6 Dec. 1804, Carter, *Territorial Papers*, "The Territory of Indiana 1800–1810," 7:42, 242. Governor William Hull to William Eustis, 15 June 1811, E. A. Cruikshank, ed., *Documents Relating to the Invasion of Canada and the Surrender of Detroit* (Ottawa: Government Printing Bureau, 1912), pp. 2–3.

12. Jerald Combs, *The Jay Treaty: Political Battleground of the Founding Fathers* (Berkeley: University of California Press, 1970); entry of 12 July 1785, and letter of Postmaster General, 26 Feb. 1787, Worthington C. Ford, ed., *Journals of the Continental Congress* (Washington, D.C.: Government Printing Office, 1934–37), 29:528, 32:79–80; Madison to King, 8 June 1802, Manning, *Diplomatic Correspondence*, 1:157–58. See also Daniel Tompkins to Peter B. Porter, 22 Dec. 1810, "Tompkins Papers," *Document Transcriptions of the War of 1812 in the Northwest*, ed. Richard C. Knopf (Columbus: Ohio Historical Society, 1957–59), 2:305–6.

13. Even before 1783, George Clinton referred to Vermont "traitors" and their British connections. See Clinton to William Floyd, 23 Feb. 1783, *Public Papers of George Clinton* (Albany: Oliver A. Quayle, 1904), 8:80. Samuel F. Bemis, "Relations between the Vermont Separatists and Great Britain 1789–91," *American Historical Review* 21 (Apr. 1916): 547–60. Allen's Memorial to Lord Sydney, 4 May 1789, ibid., 553–54, and Allen to Henry Dundas, 9 Aug. 1791, ibid., 555–58. See also John Jay to John Adams, 1 Nov. 1786, and to Thomas Jefferson, 14 Dec. 1786, Manning, *Diplomatic Correspondence*, 1:31, 32. W. A. Mackintosh, "Canada and Vermont: A Study in Historical Geography," *Canadian Historical Review* 8 (Mar. 1927): 9–30.

14. Aleine Austin, *Matthew Lyon: "New Man" of the Democratic Revolution, 1749–1822* (University Park: Pennsylvania State University Press, 1981), pp. 61, 83–89; Müller, "Champlain Route," pp. 146–47.

15. Jeanne Ojala, "Ira Allen and the French Directory 1796: Plans for the Creation of the Republic of United Columbia," *William and Mary Quarterly* 3d ser., 36 (Oct. 1979): 436–48. Timothy Pickering to Rufus King, 6 Apr., 16, 20 June 1797, Manning, *Diplomatic Correspondence*, 1:103, 110–12. Pickering, a high Federalist and militant during the Quasi-War, even suggested that American troops might help control the French in Lower Canada in exchange for naval aid against France. Pickering to King, 2 Apr. 1798, ibid., 136–39.

16. Gerald S. Graham, "The Gypsum Trade of the Maritime Provinces: Its Relation to American Diplomacy in the Early Nineteenth Century," *Agricultural History* 12 (July 1938): 209–23; George Butler, "Commercial Relations of Nova Scotia with the United States, 1783–1830" (Master's Thesis, Dalhousie University, 1934); [Boston] *Independent Chronicle*, 8 Apr., 4 Nov., 2 Dec. 1784, and 10 June 1785. Tristam Dalton to John Adams, 11 Apr. 1785, Boyd, *Papers of Jefferson*, 7:468–69; Timothy Pickering to Thomas Pinckney, 5 Mar. 1786, Manning, *Diplomatic Correspondence*, 1:96.

17. *New England Palladium and Commercial Advertiser*, 13 Jan., 3 Apr., 18 Aug. 1801. Madison to James Monroe and William Pinkney, 17 May 1806, Manning, *Diplomatic Correspondence*, 1:172–73.

18. Lorenzo Sabine, "Moose Island," pp. 142–74; Davis, *International Community*, pp. 91–94; Graham, "Gypsum Trade," 210–14.

19. Lewis Cass Aldrich, ed., *History of Franklin and Grand Isle Coun-*

ties, Vermont (Syracuse, N.Y.: Mason & Co., 1891), pp. 131–39; "From Reading and Danville, Vermont, to Canada," *Vermont Quarterly* 21 (Apr. 1953): 134–36; Kenneth W. Porter, *John Jacob Astor, Businessman* (Cambridge, Mass.: Harvard University Press, 1931), 1:30–35, 50–67, 76–82; Allen Everest, *The War of 1812 in the Champlain Valley* (Syracuse, N.Y.: Syracuse University Press, 1981), pp. 7–10.

20. On the borderland economy see Müller, "Champlain Route," especially data cited pp. 172, 187–91, 204. See also Chilton Williamson, "New York's Struggle for Champlain Valley Trade, 1760–1825," *New York State History* 22 (Oct. 1941): 426–36, and "New York's Impact on the Canadian Economy Prior to the Completion of the Erie Canal," ibid., 24 (Jan. 1943): 24–38. See also Crockett, *Vermont*, 2:499–510, 530–32; H. Walworth, *Four Eras in the History of Travelling Between Montreal and New York, from 1793 to 1892* (Plattsburgh, N.Y.: Republican Office, 1892). *The Act of Incorporation and the Bye Laws of the Boston and Montreal Turnpike Company* (Peacham, Mass.: Samuel Goss, 1806).

21. Landon, *North Country*, 1:103–58; "A Letter from a Gentleman to His Friend Descriptive of the Different Settlements in the Province of Upper Canada," 20 Nov. 1794, in John Cosens Ogden, *A Tour Through Upper and Lower Canada* (Litchfield, 1799), citation p. 15, pp. 59–74; James C. Mills, *Our Inland Seas: Their Shipping and Commerce for Three Centuries* (Chicago: A. C. McClurg & Co., 1910), pp. 67–70; Nellie Herriam, "First Settlement of Ogdensburg," in *Reminiscences of Ogdensburg, 1749–1907* (New York: Silver, Burdett, & Co., 1907), pp. 1–17.

22. James L. Barton, *Address on the Early Reminiscences of Western New York and the Lake Region of the Country* (Buffalo, N.Y.: Jewett, Thomas & Co., 1848), pp. 39, 57, 64–65; R. W. Bingham, *The Cradle of the Queen City: History of Buffalo to the Incorporation of the City* (Buffalo, N.Y.: Buffalo Historical Society, 1931), pp. 65–66, 138, 192, 224–29; Timothy Bigelow, *Journal of a Tour to Niagara Falls in the Year 1805* (Boston: John Wilson & Sons, 1876); Frank H. Severance, ed., "Visit of Reverend Lemuel Covell to Western New York and Canada in the Fall of 1803," *Publications of the Buffalo Historical Society* (1903), pp. 207–16.

23. "Description of the Settlement of the Genessee Country . . . in a Series of letters from a Gentleman to his friend," in E. B. O'Callaghan, *The Documentary History of the State of New York* (Albany: Weed, Parsons & Co., 1849), 2:1149, 1166; John T. Horton et al., *History of Northwestern New York: Erie, Niagara, Wyoming, Genessee and Orleans Counties* (New York: Lewis Historical Publishing Company, 1947), 1:29–30; Frank Severance, ed., *Studies of the Niagara Frontier* (Buffalo, N.Y.: Buffalo Historical Society, 1911), pp. 168–69; Henry Perry Smith, ed., *History of the City of Buffalo and Erie County* (Syracuse, N.Y.: D. Mason and Company, 1884), 1:73–110.

24. Michael Smith, *A Geographical View of the Province of Upper Canada, and Promiscuous Remarks upon the Government* (Hartford: Hale & Hosmer, 1813), pp. 4–40; *Report of the Commissioners to Explore the*

Route of an Inland Navigation from Hudson's River to Lake Ontario and Lake Erie (New York: Prior & Dunning, 1811), pp. 7–9, 29; Clinton's Journal in William W. Campbell, *The Life and Writings of De Witt Clinton* (New York: Baker and Scribner, 1849), pp. 72–203, but especially pp. 112–17, 159, 164, 195–96. Clinton's comments pp. 126–28. Ronald Shaw, *Erie Water West: A History of the Erie Canal, 1792–1854* (Lexington: University Press of Kentucky, 1966), pp. 20–27, 32–35, 41–43.

25. Wayne to Secretary of the Treasury, 4 Sept. 1796, Carter, *Territorial Papers*, 2:570–72; Fred C. Hamil, "The Moravians of the River Thames," *Michigan History* 33 (June 1949): 97–116; and "Fairfield on the River Thames," *Ohio Archeological & Historical Quarterly* 48 (Jan. 1939): 1–19; Henry Utley and Byron M. Cutcheon, *Michigan as a Province, Territory, and State, the Twenty-Sixth Member of the Federal Union* (New York: Publishing Society of Michigan, 1906), 2:162–63; G. N. Fuller, *The Economic and Social Beginnings of Michigan* (Lansing, Mich.: Wynkoop, Hallenbeck, Crawford, 1916), pp. 109–10; Beverly Bond, *The Civilization of the Old Northwest: A Study of Political, Social, and Economic Development, 1788–1812* (New York: Macmillan Company, 1934), pp. 48–50, 67, 207–22, 240–57, 265–72; *Compendium of the History and Biography of the City of Detroit and Wayne County, Michigan* (Chicago: Henry Taylor, 1911).

26. See 9th Cong., 1st Sess., 3 Mar. 1806, Doc. 110, *American State Papers: Commerce and Navigation* (Washington, D.C.: Gales & Seaton, 1831–34), 1:641; Jedediah Morse, *The American Gazetteer* (Boston: Thomas & Andrews, 1810).

27. Louis M. Sears, *Jefferson and the Embargo* (Durham: Duke University Press, 1927); Burton Spivak, *Jefferson's English Crisis: Commerce, Embargo and the Republican Revolution* (Charlottesville: University Press of Virginia, 1979); Dumas Malone, *Jefferson the President: Second Term, 1805–1809* (Boston: Houghton Mifflin, 1974), pp. 472–89, 565–607; Walter Johnston, Jr., *Jefferson and the Presidency: Leadership in the Young Republic* (Ithaca, N.Y.: Cornell University Press, 1978), chap. 8; Bradford Perkins, *Prologue to War: England and the United States, 1805–1812* (Berkeley: University of California Press, 1961), chap. 5. See also Jeffrey A. Frankel, "The 1807–1809 Embargo Against Great Britain," *Journal of Economic History* 42 (June 1982): 291–308.

28. Jefferson to Congress, 18 Dec. 1807, James D. Richardson, ed. and comp., *A Compilation of the Messages and Papers of the Presidents, 1789–1902* (Washington, D.C.: Bureau of National Literature and Art, 1903), 1:433.

29. See note 26 above, and Richard Mannix, "Gallatin, Jefferson, and the Embargo of 1808," *Diplomatic History* 3 (Spring 1979): 151–72; Reginald C. Stuart, "Special Interests and National Authority in Foreign Policy: American-British Provincial Links During the Embargo and the War of 1812," ibid., 8 (Spring 1984): 145–68.

30. Butler, "Commercial Relations," p. 17; Sabine, "Moose Island," pp. 145–56; John D. Forbes, "Boston Smuggling, 1807–1815," *American*

Neptune 10 (Apr. 1950): 144–54; Robin Higham, "The Port of Boston and the Embargo of 1807–1809," ibid., 16 (July 1956): 189–212; Letters of Melitiah Jordan, Collector at Frenchman's Bay, "Correspondence of the Secretary of the Treasury with Collectors of Customs 1789–1833," Treasury Records, RG 56, M-178, roll 35; *New England Palladium and Commercial Advertiser*, 1, 26 Jan., 19 Feb., 18 Mar., 24 June, 1 July, 26 Aug. 1808, reports smuggling and armed clashes with officers.

31. H. N. Müller covers the Champlain Valley in "Champlain Route," pp. 209–39, 242–45; "Smuggling into Canada: How the Champlain Valley Defied Jefferson's Embargo," *Vermont History* 38 (Winter 1970): 5–21. See also Crockett, *Vermont*, 3:9–14; "Ethan Allen," *Vermont Centinel* 15 Apr. 1808; John Henry to Herman Ryland, 13, 17 Feb. 1808, in Cruikshank, *Political Adventures of Henry*, pp. 18–20.

32. Circular to the Collectors, 26 Apr. and 28 July 1808, Circular Letters of the Secretary of the Treasury (T Series) 1789–1878, RG 56, M-735; Treasury Records, Roll 1, 21 Apr. 1795 to 8 Feb. 1833; Gallatin to Jefferson, 28 May 1808, Adams, *Writings of Gallatin*, 1:393; Gallatin to Jefferson, 29 July 1808, ibid., 397.

33. Malone, *Jefferson, 1805–1808*, pp. 603–4; Spivak, *Jefferson's English Crisis*, pp. 163, 223–24; Jefferson, "Proclamation," 19 Apr. 1808, Richardson, *Messages and Papers*, 1:450–51.

34. Gallatin to Jefferson, 17 Aug. 1808, Adams, *Writings of Gallatin*, 1: 406; Richard P. Casey, "North Country Nemesis: The Potash Rebellion and the Embargo of 1807–1809," *The New York Historical Society Quarterly* 64 (Jan. 1980): 31–49; Landon, *The North Country*, 1:156–58; Clinton, "Journal," Campbell, *Writings of Clinton*, p. 82; Richard Ellesworth, "The Settlement of the North Country," in Flick, *History of New York*, 5:199–202; Harvey Strum, "Virtually Impossible to Stop: Smuggling in the North Country, 1808–1815," *The Quarterly* (July 1982): 21–23.

35. William Chazanoff, "Joseph Ellicot, the Embargo, and the War of 1812," *Niagara Frontier* 10 (Spring 1963): 1–18; Ez. Hill to William Duane, 29 July 1808, cited in Sears, *Jefferson and Embargo*, p. 92.

36. Matthew Lyon to Constituents, 26 Apr. 1808, and Wilson Cary Nicholas to Constituents, Mar. 1809, in Noble E. Cunningham, Jr., ed., *Circular Letters of Congressmen to their Constituents, 1789–1829* (Chapel Hill: University of North Carolina Press, 1978), 2:594–95, 670; Reginald C. Stuart, "James Madison and the Militants: Republican Disunity and Replacing the Embargo," *Diplomatic History* 6 (1982): 145–68. Frankel, "1807–1809 Embargo," doubts widespread smuggling, but Jefferson's administration obtained and enforced tighter laws, provoking greater borderland defiance.

37. Circulars to the Collectors, 9 May 1809, 7, 14, 21 Oct. 1811, Circular Letters of the Secretary of the Treasury (T Series) 1789–1878, RG 56, M-735, Roll 1; "Evasions of the Non-Importation Act," 26 Nov. 1811, *State Papers: Commerce*, 1:873–74.

CHAPTER 3

1. Norval Luxon, *Niles' Weekly Register: News Magazine of the Nineteenth Century* (Baton Rouge: Louisiana State University Press, 1947), is a "biography" of the *Register* and the best work on Niles himself. Quotes from *Niles' Weekly Register*, 5 Oct. 1811, 1:88; 9 May, 30 May 1812, 2:164–68, 209.

2. *Niles' Weekly Register*, 27 June 1812, 2:288; 4 July, 29 Aug. 1812, 2:299–300, 425–27. See Dennis A. Taylor, "The American Picture of British North America on the Eve of the War of 1812" (Master's thesis, Queens University, 1965). Ronald L. Hatzenbuehler and Robert L. Ivie, *Congress Declares War: Rhetoric, Leadership, and Partisanship in the Early Republic* (Kent, Ohio: Kent State University Press, 1983), chap. 8.

3. See *Niles' Weekly Register*, 2–7 (1812–14), passim. Reports of smuggling ibid., 31 Oct. 1812, 3:144; 3 July 1813, 4:288; 27 Nov. 1813, 5:282; 28 Jan. 1815, 7:348.

4. See George F. G. Stanley, *The War of 1812: Land Operations* (Toronto: Macmillan of Canada, 1983); Luxon, *Niles' Weekly Register*, pp. 169–71. Post-war coverage referred to here in *Niles' Weekly Register*, Sept. 1815–Sept. 1816, 9–10, passim. By 10 Sept. 1835, 44, Niles believed that ultimate provincial rebellion and union with the United States was a "moral certainty."

5. See C. P. Stacey, "The War of 1812 and Canadian History," in *The Defended Border: Upper Canada and the War of 1812*, ed. Morris Zaslow (Toronto: Macmillan of Canada, 1964). Pierre Berton, *The Invasion of Canada, 1812–1813* (Toronto: McClelland and Stewart, 1980), and *Flames Across the Border: The Invasion of Canada, 1813–1814* (Toronto: McClelland and Stewart, 1982); Stanley, *War of 1812*.

6. Christopher Coleman, "The Ohio Valley in the Preliminaries of the War of 1812," *Mississippi Valley Historical Review* 7 (June 1920): 39–50; Julius W. Pratt, *The Expansionists of 1812* (1925; reprint, New York: P. Smith, 1957); Ellery Hall, "Canadian Annexation Sentiment in Kentucky Prior to the War of 1812," *Kentucky Historical Society Register* 28 (1930): 373–80; William A. Walker, Jr., "Martial Sons: Tennessee Enthusiasm for the War of 1812," *Tennessee Historical Quarterly* 20 (Spring 1961): 20–37; Harrison Bird, *War for the West, 1790–1813* (New York: Oxford University Press, 1971), pp. 98–113; T. Harry Williams, *The History of American Wars: From 1745 to 1918* (New York: Alfred A. Knopf, 1981), p. 96. Reginald Horsman, "On to Canada: Manifest Destiny and United States Strategy in the War of 1812," (Paper delivered at the War of 1812 Conference, Monroe, Michigan, January 1987).

7. Reginald Horsman, *The Causes of the War of 1812* (Philadelphia: University of Pennsylvania Press, 1962); Roger H. Brown, *The Republic in Peril: 1812* (New York: Columbia University Press, 1964), pp. 120–26, 152–55; Hatzenbuehler and Ivie, *Congress Declares War*, summarized historiography in chap. 1.

8. J. C. A. Stagg, "James Madison and the Coercion of Great Britain: Canada, the West Indies, and the War of 1812," *William and Mary Quarterly*, 3d ser., 38 (Jan. 1981): 3–34, and *Mr. Madison's War: Politics, Diplomacy, and Warfare in the Early American Republic, 1783–1830* (Princeton, N.J.: Princeton University Press, 1983), chap. 1.

9. Campbell to Jefferson, 10 Oct. 1807, cited in Horsman, *Causes*, p. 169. Henry Clay, "Speech," 22 Feb. 1810, Mary W. Hargreaves and James Hopkins, eds., *The Papers of Henry Clay* (Lexington: University of Kentucky Press, 1959–), 1:449–50.

10. Madison to Congress, 1 June 1812, James D. Richardson, ed. and comp., *A Compilation of the Messages and Papers of the Presidents, 1789–1902* (Washington, D.C.: Bureau of National Literature and Art, 1903), 1: 499–505; Reginald C. Stuart, *War and American Thought: From the Revolution to the Monroe Doctrine* (Kent, Ohio: Kent State University Press, 1982), chap. 6.

11. Madison to Albert Gallatin, 15 Aug. 1812, Henry Adams, ed., *The Writings of Albert Gallatin* (1879; reprint, New York: Antiquarian Press, 1960), 1:523–24; Madison to Jefferson, 17 Aug. 1812, and to William Dearborn, 7 Oct. 1812, Gaillard Hunt, ed., *The Writings of James Madison* (New York: G. P. Putnam's Sons, 1906), 8:211, 218.

12. John Armstrong to Brigadier-General William Hull, 24 June 1812, E. A. Cruikshank, ed., *Documents Relating to the Invasion of Canada and the Surrender of Detroit, 1812* (Ottawa: Government Printing Bureau, 1912), p. 37; Gerry's speech, 24 May 1813, *The Debates and Proceedings in the Congress of the United States* [hereafter cited as *Annals of Congress*] (Washington, D.C.: Gales & Seaton, 1834), 13th Cong., 1st sess., 12. See also Cruikshank, ed., *The Documentary History of the Campaign upon the Niagara Frontier in the Year 1812* (Welland, Ontario: The Tribune Office, 1912).

13. Monroe to Colonel John Taylor, 13 June 1812, S. M. Hamilton, ed., *The Writings of James Monroe* (New York: G. P. Putnam's Sons, 1901), 5:206–7; Monroe to Jonathan Russell, 26 June 1812, ibid., 212–13; Monroe to Thomas Jefferson, 31 Aug. 1812, ibid., 220; Monroe to Henry Clay, 17 Sept. 1812, ibid., 223; Monroe to George W. Campbell, 23 Dec. 1812, ibid., 231.

14. C. P. Stacey, ed., "An American Plan for a Canadian Campaign," *American Historical Review* 46 (October 1941): 348–58; Monroe to Jonathan Russell, 21 Aug. 1812, William R. Manning, *Diplomatic Correspondence of the United States: Canadian Relations* (Washington, D.C.: Carnegie Foundation, 1940–43), 1:210–11; Monroe to Henry Clay, 17 Sept. 1812, Hargreaves and Hopkins, *Papers of Clay*, 1:726–28; Monroe to Albert Gallatin, John Quincy Adams, James A. Bayard, 15 Apr., 23 June 1813, and 1, 28 Jan., 23 June 1814, Manning, *Diplomatic Correspondence*, 1:212–19; Michael Scheuer, "Who Should Own the Lakes? Negotiations Preceding the Treaty of Ghent," *Inland Seas* 38 (Winter 1982): 236–44.

15. Adams to Thomas Boylston Adams, 24 Nov. 1812, Worthington C.

Ford, ed., *The Writings of John Quincy Adams* (New York: Macmillan Company, 1913), 1:407; see letters by Crawford, 13 May 1814, and Clay, 2 July 1814, in Hargreaves and Hopkins, *Papers of Clay*, 1:907–8, 937–39; Gallatin to Monroe, 13 June 1814, and James A. Bayard and Gallatin to Monroe, 6 May 1814, Records of Negotiations Connected with the Treaty of Ghent, 1813–15, Dispatches of American Commissioners, National Archives, Washington, D.C., RG 59, M-36; See the American No. 2 in answer to the British No. 2, 9 Sept. 1814, American to the British Commissioners, 13 Oct. 1814, *American State Papers: Foreign Relations* (Washington, D.C.: Gales & Seaton, 1832), 3:723–24.

16. The Treaty of Ghent, Canada, Department of External Affairs, comp., *Treaties and Agreements Affecting Canada in Force Between His Majesty and the United States of America with Subsidiary Documents 1814–1925* (Ottawa: King's Printer, 1927), p. 7; Alexander Dallas, *An Exposition of the Causes and Character of the Late War* (Washington, D.C.: Thomas G. Bangs, 1815), pp. 28–30.

17. Secretary of War to Governor Hull, 30 July 1807, Postmaster General to Simon Perkins, 5 Dec. 1807, in *Territory of Michigan, 1805–1820, The Territorial Papers of the United States*, ed. and comp. Clarence Edwin Carter (Washington, D.C.: Government Printing Office, 1934–75), 10:124, 162; Hull to Secretary of War, 1 Feb. 1810, ibid., 305–6. *The Democratic Clarion and Tennessee Gazette*, 28 Apr. 1812; "Thomas Worthington," various letters in 1811 and 1812 in *Document Transcriptions of the War of 1812 in the Northwest*, ed. Richard Knopf (Columbus, Ohio: Ohio Historical Society, 1957–59), 3:4, 18, 24, 63–64, 80, 122, 129, 172, 220; "Return Jonathan Meigs, Jr., & the War of 1812," ibid., 2:8–9, 21, 77, 83, 113. Robert Breckenridge McAfee, *History of the Late War in the Western Country* (Lexington: Worsley & Smith, 1816).

18. Harrison to Secretary of War, 10 Aug. 1812, Cruikshank, *Documents*, pp. 131–35; Harrison to Secretary of War, 11 Oct. 1808, *Messages and Letters of William Henry Harrison*, ed. Logan Easery (Indianapolis: Indiana Historical Commission, 1922), 1:311–12; General Orders, ibid., 2:35–37; Isaac Shelby to Harrison, 4 April 1813, ibid., 414; Harrison to William Eustis, 22, 26 Oct., 12 Dec. 1812, "William Henry Harrison and the War of 1812," Knopf, *Document Transcription* 1:45, 46, 59, 66–67, 101.

19. Harrison and Oliver Hazard Perry, "Proclamation" 17 Oct. 1813, Easery, *Messages of Harrison*, 2:581; Thomas Posey to Legislative Council and House of Representatives, Indiana, 6 Dec. 1813, ibid., 608–9, and Posey to Secretary of War, 18 Feb. 1815, ibid., 688–89. Dorothy Goebel, *William Henry Harrison: A Political Biography* (Indianapolis: Bobbs-Merrill Company, 1926), pp. 130–31.

20. Andrew Jackson, "Division Orders," 7 Mar. 1812; John Spencer Bassett, ed., *Correspondence of Andrew Jackson* (Washington, D.C.: Carnegie Institution, 1926), 1: 222; Colonel Lewis Cass to the Secretary of War, 10 Sept. 1812, Cruikshank, *Documents*, pp. 218, 222; "Proclamation by General Hull, 13 July 1812, ibid., pp. 58–59. McAfee, *War in the Western Country*, pp. 2, 94, 304–5.

21. Coleman, "Ohio Valley in the War of 1812"; Charles M. Gates, "The West In American Diplomacy, 1812–1815," *Mississippi Valley Historical Review* 26 (March 1940): 499–510; Bird, *War for the West*. Philadelphia *Enquirer*, 19 Oct. 1813; "Minutes of Council of War," Sackett's Harbor, 26 Aug. 1813, General Wilkinson to Secretary of War, 18 Oct. 1813, all in John Armstrong, ed., *Notices of the War of 1812* (New York: Wiley & Putnam, 1840), 2:197, 206–7; G. M. Fairchild, ed., *Journal of An American Prisoner at Fort Malden and Quebec in the War of 1812* (Quebec: Frank Carrel, 1909), p. 12.

22. John Stanly to Constituents, 10 May 1810, Noble E. Cunningham, Jr., ed., *Circular Letters of Congressmen to Their Constituents, 1789–1829* (Chapel Hill: University of North Carolina Press, 1978), 2:721; John Lowell, *Mr. Madison's War* (New York: L. Beach, 1812), p. 25; for opposition to the war see Samuel Eliot Morison, "Dissent in the War of 1812," in Morison et al., *Dissent in Three American Wars* (Cambridge, Mass.: Harvard University Press, 1970), pp. 1–31; Myron Wehtje, "Opposition in Virginia to the War of 1812," *Virginia Magazine of History and Biography* 78 (Jan. 1970): 65–86; Sarah E. Lemmon, "Dissent in North Carolina During the War of 1812," *North Carolina Historical Review* 49 (Apr. 1972): 103–18; Edward Brynn, "Patterns of Dissent: Vermont's Opposition to the War of 1812," *Vermont History* 40 (Winter 1972): 10–27; Harvey Strum, "New York Federalists and Opposition to the War of 1812," *World Affairs* 142 (Winter 1980): 169–87; Donald R. Hickey, "A Dissenting Voice: Matthew Lyon on the Conquest of Canada," *Kentucky Historical Society Register* 76 (1978): 45–52.

23. Randolph's most cited speech on the unjust war of conquest was on 16 Dec. 1811, *Annals of Congress*, 12th Cong., 1st sess., 533; Zebulon Shipherd, 17 Jan. 1814, ibid., 13th Cong., 2d sess., 1029; speeches, 8 July 1813, ibid., 1st sess., 408–9, 1072; Massachusetts Remonstrance," 14/15 June 1813, *Historical Register of the United States*, 1:156–57; "Plautus," *New York Evening Post*, 14 Apr. 1812; Rush to Adams, 17 Nov. 1812, John A. Schutz and Douglass Adair, eds., *The Spur of Fame: Dialogues of John Adams and Richard Rush, 1805–1813* (San Marino, Calif.: Stanford University Press, 1966), p. 253; Daniel Sheffey (Va.) to Constituents, Feb. 1813, Cunningham, *Circular Letters*, 2:819; and Richard Stanford to Constituents, 2 Mar. 1813, ibid., 831–32; Webster to Benjamin J. Gilbert, 8 Feb. 1814, Charles M. Wiltse and Harold D. Moser, eds., *The Papers of Daniel Webster: Correspondence* (Hanover, N.H.: University Press of New England, 1974), 1:163; "Conversation between Rufus King and the Secretary of War [John Armstrong], 4 Apr. 1814, in Charles R. King, ed., *The Life and Correspondence of Rufus King* (New York: G. P. Putnam's Sons, 1898), 5:390.

24. Clay, "Speech," 11 Jan. 1812, Hargreaves and Hopkins, *Papers of Clay*, 1:615; Macon, 12 Feb. 1814, *Annals of Congress*, 13th Cong., 2d sess., 1795–96.

25. *Annals of Congress*, 12th Cong., 1st sess., 2354–56; Stagg, "Madison and Canada," pp. 32–34; Donald R. Hickey, "American Trade Restrictions

During the War of 1812," *Journal of American History* 68 (December 1981): 517–38, traces the larger issue of trade control; Treasury Department, "Circular to Collectors," October 1812, *Military Monitor and American Register*, 9 November 1812, p. 97.

26. John D. Forbes, "Boston Smuggling, 1807–1815," *American Neptune* 1 (April 1950): 145–49; Lorenzo Sabine, "Moose Island," in *Eastport and Passamaquoddy: A Collection of Historical and Biographical Sketches*, comp. William Kirby (Eastport, Maine: Edward E. Skead & Company, 1888), pp. 142–74; Walter R. Copp, "Nova Scotian Trade During the War of 1812," *Canadian Historical Review* 18 (June 1937): 141–55; George Butler, "Commercial Relations of Nova Scotia with the United States, 1783–1830" (Master's thesis, Dalhousie University, 1934), pp. 22–24; Harold Davis, *An International Community on the St. Croix (1604–1930)* (Orono: University of Maine Press, 1950), chap. 7. Gore to King, 28 July 1814, King, *Correspondence of King*, 5:403; Gardner Allen, "Massachusetts in the War of 1812," in *Commonwealth History of Massachusetts*, ed. Albert B. Hart (New York: States History Company, 1929), 3:471–500; Barry Lohnes, "The War of 1812 at Sea: The British Navy, New England, and the Maritime Provinces of Canada" (Master's thesis, University of Maine at Orono, 1971), pp. 306–7, 310–11.

27. Walter Hill Crockett, *Vermont: The Green Mountain State* (New York: Century History Company, 1921), 3:53–80; Izard to John Armstrong, 31 July 1814, cited in Allan Everest, *The War of 1812 in the Champlain Valley* (Syracuse, N.Y.: Syracuse University Press, 1981), p. 151; "Smuggling in 1813–1814: A Personal Reminiscence," *Vermont History* 38 (Winter, 1970): 22–26; H. M. Müller, "A 'Traitorous and Diabolical Traffic': The Commerce of the Champlain-Richelieu Corridor During the War of 1812," *Vermont History* 44 (Spring 1976): 78–96; Governor Isaac Clark, "Proclamation, 4 July 1812," *The United States Gazette*, 10 Aug. 1812.

28. Harry Landon, *Bugles on the Border: The Story of the War of 1812 in Northern New York* (Watertown, N.Y.: Watertown Daily Times, 1954), passim; K. W. Porter, *John Jacob Astor, Businessman* (Cambridge, Mass.: Belknap Press of Harvard University Press, 1931), 1:250–83; Strum, "New York Federalists," 177–78; Gerald M. Craig, *Upper Canada: The Formative Years, 1784–1841* (Toronto: McClelland & Stewart, 1963), pp. 70–75; John Howe, *Journal . . . [of] a British Spy* (Concord: Luther Roby, 1827), pp. 28–43 recalls smuggling in New York during the war.

29. Landon, *Bugles on the Border*, pp. 7, 12, 32–36; Harry F. Landon, "British Sympathizers in St. Lawrence County During the War of 1812," *New York History* 35 (April 1954): 131–38, based heavily on the Parish family papers; and Harry F. Landon, *The North Country: A History Embracing Jefferson, St. Lawrence, Oswego, Lewis and Franklin Counties New York* (Indianapolis: Historical Publishing Company, 1931), 1:159–83. See also Daniel Tompkins to Peter B. Porter, 8 July 1812, to John Bullus, 13 July 1812, to John Armstrong, 2 Jan. 1814, Hugh Hastings, ed., *Public Papers of D. D. Tompkins, Governor of New York, 1807–1817* (Albany, N.Y.:

1898–1902), 3:21, 31, 411–13; Philias S. Garand, *The History of the City of Ogdensburg* (Ogdensburg: Manuel Belleville, 1927), p. 195.

30. Louis L. Babcock, *The War of 1812 on the Niagara Frontier* (Buffalo, N.Y.: Buffalo Historical Society, 1927), pp. 29, 33, 115–38, 178–79, 243–44, 251–319; R. W. Bingham, *The Cradle of the Queen City: History of Buffalo to the Incorporation of the City* (Buffalo, N.Y.: Buffalo Historical Society, 1931), pp. 264–65, 280, 349; William Dorsheimer, "The Village of Buffalo During the War of 1812," Buffalo Historical Society, *Publications* 1 (1879): 185–209; Henry P. Smith, ed., *History of the City of Buffalo and Erie County* (Syracuse, N.Y.: D. Mason & Co., 1884), 1:138, 149n, 174–75; Tilly Buttrick, *Voyages, Travels and Discoveries of Tilly Buttrick, Jr.* (Boston, 1831), pp. 43–48.

31. Elbert Jay Benton, ed., "Northern Ohio During the War of 1812: Letters and Papers in the Western Reserve Historical Society," Western Reserve Historical Society, *Annual Reports* (1913), pp. 30–55; William R. Barlow, "Ohio's Congressmen and the War of 1812," *Ohio History* 72 (1963): 175–94, and Barlow, "The Coming of the War of 1812 in Michigan Territory," *Michigan History* 53 (1969): 91–107; Reginald Horsman, "Wisconsin and the War of 1812," *Wisconsin Magazine of History* 46 (1962): 3–15; Beverly W. Bond, *The Civilization of the Old Northwest: A Study of Political, Social, and Economic Development* (New York: Macmillan Company, 1934), pp. 271–76.

32. Clay, "Speech," 11 Jan. 1812, Hargreaves and Hopkins, *Papers of Clay*, 1:615; "Speech," 8, 9 Jan. 1813, ibid., 769–70; to Thomas Bodley, 18 Dec. 1813, ibid., 841–42.

33. John C. Calhoun, "Speech," 25 Oct. 1814, Robert L. Meriwether, ed., *The Papers of John C. Calhoun* (Columbia: University of South Carolina Press, 1959–), 1:256–57; Burwell Bassett to Constituents, 26 Feb. 1809, 14 Feb. 1813, Cunningham, *Circular Letters*, 2:639, 1:813, 814; Charles Ingersoll, 29 June 1813, *Annals of Congress*, 13th Cong., 1st sess., 353; William Bradley, 9 July 1813, ibid., 413–14; Robertson, 15 Jan. 1814, ibid., 13th Cong., 2d sess., 984; Humphreys, ibid., 1357–58.

34. Taylor, "American Picture on Eve of War," sees an ideological imperative behind American policy makers who wanted to wrest the provinces from monarchical control and remove the threat to republicanism posed by the proximity of old-world influence. *Military Monitor and American Register*, 12 Oct. 1812, p. 68; 2 Nov. 1812, p. 94; 28 Dec. 1812, pp. 167–68; 18 Jan. 1813, p. 204; 22 Feb. 1813, p. 14; 21 June 1813, pp. 335–36, 340–41. See also the *Geographical & Military Museum*, 28 Mar. 1814.

35. *New England Palladium and Commercial Advertiser*. For sample issues carrying other than strictly military news, see 24 July, 15 Sept., 18 Dec. 1812, 15 June 1813, 22 Apr., 14, 21 Oct. 1814. *Raleigh Minerva*, 31 Jan. 1812, p. 7, and 12 Feb. 1813, p. 78. See also *National Intelligencer*, 8 Feb., 29 Mar. 1812; Captain Giles Kellogg to James Madison, 1 June 1812, James Madison Papers, Alderman Library, University of Virginia.

36. Adams to Abigail Adams, 30 June 1811, Ford, *Writings of Adams*,

4:128, to James Monroe, 5 Sept. 1814, ibid., pp. 111–17; "Backwoodsman," *Military Monitor*, 21 June 1813, pp. 340–41; speech by John Rhea, 26 Jan. 1814, *Annals of Congress*, 13th Cong., 2d sess., 1145–46; James Monroe to Albert Gallatin, John Quincy Adams, and James A. Bayard, 23 June 1813, Manning, *Diplomatic Correspondence*, 1:215.

37. Michael Smith, *A Geographical View of the Province of Upper Canada* (New York: M. Smith, 1813), pp. 68–69, 82–87, 201–3.

38. Alexander McLeod, "The Ends for Which God in His Providence Permits the Existence of this War," in *A Scriptural View of the Character, Causes, and Ends of the Present War* (New York: Eastburn, Kirk & Co., 1815), pp. 224–25; Adams to Jonathan Russell, 14 Dec. 1815, Ford, *Writings of Adams*, 5:444; David R. Moore, *Canada and the United States, 1815–1830* (Chicago: Jennings & Graham, 1910), pp. 13–18, 53–64; Scheuer, "Who Should Own the Lakes?" pp. 236–44.

39. Henry Clay, "Campaign Speech," 25 July 1816, Hargreaves and Hopkins, *Papers of Clay*, 2:220; John Quincy Adams to Louisa Catherine Adams, 3 Jan. 1815, Ford, *Writings of Adams*, 5:261; William McCarty, *History of the American War of 1812, from the Commencement until the Final Termination Thereof* (1816; reprint, Freeport, New York: Books for Libraries Press, 1970), pp. 9, 165, 250; Samuel Perkins, *A History of the Political and Military Events of the Late War between the United States and Great Britain* (New Haven, Conn.: S. Converse, 1825), pp. 78, 105–17, 241–43, 385, 397, 510–12; Samuel White, *History of the American Troops during the Late War under the Command of Colonels Fenton and Campbell* (Baltimore: B. Edes, 1830); Charles Ingersoll, *Historical Sketch of the Second War between the United States of America and Great Britain* (Philadelphia: J. Lippincott, 1845), 1:14–18, 444–52; 2:14, 347–48, 350–61.

40. See *Annals of Congress*, 14th Cong., 1st sess., 959–99, 1007–10, 1029–32, 1048, 1367.

CHAPTER 4

1. Julius W. Pratt, "John L. O'Sullivan and Manifest Destiny," *New York History* 14 (1933): 213–34.

2. "The Northeastern Boundary Question," *United States Magazine and Democratic Review* 3 (Sept. 1838): 29–49, citation on 49. [Hereafter cited as *Democratic Review*.]

3. "Lord Durham's Report," *Democratic Review* 5 (June 1839): 542–79. In "Hurrah for a War with England," ibid., 9 (Nov. 1841): 411–16, O'Sullivan denounced America's martial spirit and assumption that Canadian liberation would ensue. O'Sullivan ran articles on the American peace movement. See ibid. 10 (Feb. 1842): 107–20, and (Mar. 1842): 211–22.

4. "Annexation," ibid. 17 (July 1845): 5–10, citation on 9. In December 1845, the Whigs disavowed territorial ambitions in response to Polk's corollary to the Monroe Doctrine. Frederick Merk, *The Monroe Doctrine and*

American Expansionism, 1843–1849 (New York: Alfred A. Knopf, 1966); David M. Pletcher, *The Diplomacy of Annexation: Texas, Oregon, and the Mexican War* (Columbia: University of Missouri Press, 1973).

5. R. W. Van Alstyne, "New Viewpoints in the Relations of Canada and the United States," *Canadian Historical Review* 25 (June 1944): 109–30; Albert B. Corey, "Canadian Border Defence Problems after 1814 to Their Culmination in the 'Forties," Canadian Historical Association, *Annual Report* (1938): 11–20; John W. Foster, *Limitation of Armament on the Great Lakes* (Washington, D.C.: Carnegie Endowment, 1914); Howard Jones, *To the Webster-Ashburton Treaty: A Study in Anglo-American Relations, 1783–1843* (Chapel Hill: University of North Carolina Press, 1977). See C. P. Stacey, "The Myth of the Unguarded Frontier, 1815–1871," *American Historical Review* 56 (Oct. 1950): 1–18; Kenneth Bourne, *Britain and the Balance of Power in North America, 1815–1908* (Berkeley: University of California Press, 1967), pp. 9–110.

6. John Hope Franklin, "The Southern Expansionists of 1848," *Journal of Southern History* 25 (Aug. 1959): 323–38 and Robert E. May, *The Southern Dream of a Caribbean Empire, 1854–1861* (Baton Rouge: Louisiana State University Press, 1973).

7. *Argus* cited in *National Intelligencer*, 1 Apr. 1815; "Horace" in ibid., 26 Apr. 1815; *Niles' Weekly Register*, 4 Nov. 1815, 9:159–62, 169; ibid., 7, 28 Sept. and 12 Oct. 1816, 11:30, 77, 108–9. Henry Clay, "Speech," 29 Jan. 1816, Mary W. Hargreaves and James Hopkins, eds., *The Papers of Henry Clay* (Lexington: University of Kentucky Press, 1959–), 2:152. Theodore Burton, "Henry Clay, Secretary of State, Mar. 7, 1825–Mar. 3, 1829," *The American Secretaries of State and their Diplomacy*, ed. Samuel Flagg Bemis (New York: Alfred A. Knopf, 1928), 4:115–58. See also John C. Calhoun, 27 Feb. 1815, Robert L. Meriwether, ed., *The Papers of John C. Calhoun* (Columbia: University of South Carolina Press, 1959–), 1:277; *The Debates and Proceedings in the Congress of the United States* [hereafter cited as *Annals of Congress*], (Washington, D.C.: Gales & Seaton, 1834), 13th Cong., 3d sess., 1133–34, 1204, 1218–33; 14th Cong., 1st sess., 197, 836, 857, 860–61.

8. David R. Moore, *Canada and the United States, 1815–1830* (Chicago: Jennings & Graham, 1910), pp. 1–84, passim. Lewis Cass, "Proclamation," 7 Oct. 1815, *Territory of Michigan, 1805–1820* in *The Territorial Papers of the United States*, ed. Clarence Carter (Washington, D.C.: Government Printing Office, 1934–75), 10:718–19; Cass to Secretary of War [John C. Calhoun], Summer 1819, ibid., 808–9; Cass to Secretary of War [John C. Calhoun], 3 Aug. 1819, 8 Oct. 1819, ibid., 852–55, 867–70. Calhoun to Cass, 11 Feb. 1822, ibid., 11:224–25; "Memorial of the Legislative Council, 5 Aug. 1824, to the Senate and House of the United States," ibid., 11:609. Edgar Bruce Wesley, *Guarding the Frontier: A Study of Frontier Defense from 1815 to 1825* (Minneapolis: University of Minnesota Press, 1935), argued that frontier military policy was to cope with the Indian situation.

9. *National Intelligencer*, 11 Sept. 1817; 30 Oct. 1818; *Niles' Weekly*

Register, 12 July 1817, 12:320; quote from ibid., 20 Nov. 1819, 17:191. Niles reported British efforts to improve provincial fortifications without comment in 1819 and 1820.

10. Charles S. Campbell, *From Revolution to Rapprochement: The United States and Great Britain, 1783–1900* (New York: John Wiley & Sons, 1974), chaps. 3–6; Bradford Perkins, *Castlereagh and Adams: England and the United States, 1812–1823* (Berkeley: University of California Press, 1961), chaps. 9–10.

11. Adams to Monroe, 29 Aug. 1815, and to William Eustis, 29 Nov. 1815, Worthington C. Ford, ed., *The Writings of John Quincy Adams* (New York: Macmillan Company, 1913–17), 5:360, 423; to Russell, 14 Dec. 1815, ibid., 444. Letters on naval limitations, ibid., 497–98, 555; James Monroe to Adams, 21 May 1816, William R. Manning, ed., *The Diplomatic Correspondence of the United States: Canadian Relations* (Washington, D.C.: Carnegie Foundation, 1940–43), 1:244.

12. Contrast the myth of the undefended border in Foster, *Limitation on the Lakes* with Stacey, "Myth of Unguarded Frontier"; Stanley Falk, "Disarmament on the Great Lakes: Myth or Reality?" *United States Naval Institute Proceedings* 87 (Dec. 1961): 69–73. Corey, "Canadian Border Defence Problems"; *American State Papers: Military Affairs* (Washington, D.C.: Gales and Seaton, 1834), 2:671; Cass, 8 Apr. 1836, "On the Means and Measures Necessary for the Military and Naval Defences of the Country," ibid., 4:366–76; J. R. Poinsett, 10 Jan. 1838, "A Plan for the Protection of the North and Eastern Boundary of the United States," ibid., 7:895–98; John Wool to John Eaton, printed in *North Country Notes,* eds. Allen Everest and Charles McLellan, No. 8 (Mar. 1962).

13. Woodward to Adams, 5 Dec. 1818, *Michigan Historical Collections* 36 (1908): 346; Henry Dearborn to Webster, 19 Feb. 1830, Charles M. Wiltse, ed., *The Papers of Daniel Webster* (Hanover, N.H.: University Press of New England, 1974–), 3:17–18; Lorenzo Sabine, "British Colonial Politics," *North American Review* 60 (Jan. 1845): 87–126, citations on 123–25; General T. S. Jesup to Joel R. Poinsett, 21 Mar. 1839, cited by Bourne, *Balance of Power,* pp. 55–56, still saw a British menace in Canada.

14. Petition from Detroit in *Niles' Weekly Register,* 15 Feb. 1845, 66: 375–77; *Baltimore American* reprinted in ibid., 345. And see ibid., 6 Dec. 1845, passim; *New York Evening Post,* 16 May 1845. Matthew Maury in *National Intelligencer,* 20 May 1845.

15. *New York Times,* 23 July 1852.

16. *New York Daily Tribune,* 17 June 1854.

17. The best treatment is Donald F. Warner, *The Idea of Continental Union: Agitation for the Annexation of Canada to the United States, 1849–1893* (Lexington: University Press of Kentucky, 1960). See also Lester B. Shippee, *Canadian-American Relations, 1849–1874* (New Haven, Conn.: Yale University Press, 1939), pp. 16–20; C. D. Allin and G. M. Jones, *Annexation, Preferential Trade and Reciprocity* (1912; reprint, Westport, Conn.: Greenwood Press, 1971). Important background is in Gilbert Tuck-

er, *The Canadian Commercial Revolution* (New Haven: Yale University Press, 1936), pp. 178–96.

18. *Niles' Weekly Register*, 28 Mar., 4 Apr., 2 May 1849, 75:205, 220, 282–84.

19. Vermont Legislature, 1849, cited in Shippee, *Canadian-American Relations*, p. 16 n. 21; New York Assembly cited in Allin and Jones, *Annexation*, p. 379.

20. D. S. Dickinson, 12 Jan. 1848, in *Speeches in Senate Collected and Bound for W. H. Seward*, p. 2.

21. *Washington Union* cited in Allin and Jones, *Annexation*, p. 376; J. A. Turner, "Annexation of Canada," *De Bow's Review* 9 (Oct. 1850): 397–412; Charles Sumner to Richard Cobden, 2 May 1849, Edward Pierce, *Memoir and Letters of Charles Sumner* (Boston: Roberts Brothers, 1893), 3:42–43, and Sumner to Lord Morpeth, 8 Jan. 1850, ibid., 211.

22. *New York Herald* cited Allin and Jones, *Annexation*, p. 383.

23. Franklin Pierce, "Inaugural Address," 4 Mar. 1853, James D. Richardson, ed. and comp., *A Compilation of the Messages and Papers of the Presidents, 1789–1908* (Washington, D.C.: Bureau of National Literature and Art, 1908), 5:198–200, and Pierce, "Second Annual Message," 4 Dec. 1854, ibid., 274–75; William Marcy to James Buchanan, 16 Dec. 1853, Letterbooks, vol. 45, William Learned Marcy Papers, Manuscript Division, Library of Congress, Washington, D.C.; Richard W. Van Alstyne, "Great Britain, the United States, and Hawaiian Independence, 1850–1855," *Pacific Historical Review* 4 (Mar. 1935): 19 ff. Robert W. Johannsen, "Stephen Douglas and the American Mission," in *The Frontier Challenge: Responses to the Trans-Mississippi West*, ed. John G. Clark (Lawrence: University of Kansas Press, 1971), pp. 111–40.

24. *New York Times*, 24, 29 Mar., 2 Apr. 1859. See remarks by Daniel Dickinson of New York, 20 Dec. 1847, 12 Jan. 1848, *Congressional Globe, Containing the Debates and Proceedings* (Washington, D.C.: F. & J. Rives and George Bailey, 1834–74), 30th Cong., 1st sess., pp. 54 ff, 157–60.

25. Reginald Horsman, *Race and Manifest Destiny: The Origins of American Racial Anglo-Saxonism* (Cambridge, Mass.: Harvard University Press, 1981), p. 283 refers to provincials. On the French, see "Canada," *American Quarterly Review* 7 (Mar. 1830): 188–213; Edward Everett, "Lafayette in North America in 1824 and 1825," *North American Review* 30 (Jan. 1830): 235; *Buffalo Commercial Advertiser*, as reprinted in *Niles' Weekly Register*, 4 Apr. 1849, 75:220. R. W. Haskins, "Human Destiny Upon the Theatre of the American Continent," *The Knickerbocker* 30 (Nov. 1847): 399–407, voiced American Anglo-Saxonism. William Duane, *Canada and the Continental Congress* (Philadelphia: Edward Gaskill, 1850), p. 20.

26. Albert Weinberg, *Manifest Destiny: A Study of Nationalist Expansion in American History* (Baltimore: Johns Hopkins University Press, 1935), pp. 109–12, 151–52, 214, 228–32; Johannsen, "Douglas," pp. 113–14, 125–26.

27. Joseph Sansom, *Travels in Lower Canada* (New York: Kirk & Mercein, 1817), pp. 44, 63–64; C. Upham, Introduction to Thomas Chandler Haliburton's "An Historical and Statistical Account of Nova Scotia," *North American Review* 30 (Jan. 1830): 134–35.

28. "Canada," *American Quarterly Review* 7 (Mar. 1830): 188–213; "Bouchette's British North America," ibid., 11 (June 1832): 412–49; Everett, "Lafayette in America," 235–36; Edward Everett, review in *North American Review* 33 (Oct. 1831): 449–55.

29. Godwin cited in Weinberg, *Manifest Destiny*, p. 209.

30. *Proceedings of a Convention of Delegates Assembled at Faneuil Hall, in the City of Boston, to take into Consideration the Proposed Annexation of Texas* (Boston: J.H. Eastburn's Press, 1845), p. 9; Everett, "Speech at the Yellow Springs, Ohio," 29 June 1829, Everett, *Orations and Speeches on Various Occasions* (Boston: Little, Brown and Company, 1865), 1:210; Sabine, "British Colonial Politics," *North American Review* 60 (Jan. 1845): 87–126, and "British Colonial Politics," ibid. 67 (Jan. 1848): 1–26; Duane, *Canada and Congress*, pp. 19–20; and see Winfield Scott to John C. Hamilton, 29 June 1849, in Charles W. Elliot, *Winfield Scott: The Soldier and the Man* (New York: Macmillan Company, 1937), p. 599.

31. See Henry S. Burrage, "The Attitude of Maine in the Northeastern Boundary Controversy," Maine Historical Society, *Collections* (1904): 353–68; Maria Irish, "The Northeastern Boundary of Maine," *Journal of American History* 16 (1922): 311–22; Thomas Le Duc, "The Maine Frontier and the Northeastern Boundary Controversy," *American Historical Review* 53 (Oct. 1947): 30–41; David Lowenthal, "The Maine Press and the Aroostook War," *Canadian Historical Review* 32 (Dec. 1951): 315–36; and Jones, *Webster-Ashburton Treaty*, pp. 12–18, 88–94. Albert Gallatin, *The Right of the United States to the North-Eastern Boundary* (New York: Samuel Adams, 1848), is a revised version of the original American position. Ian C. Pemberton, "Loyalists in the Jackson Era: The Fate of the 'Canadian Party' in the Indian Stream Republic Boundary Controversy of the 1830s," paper delivered at the Canadian Historical Association Annual Meeting, Dalhousie University, Halifax, Nova Scotia, 1981.

32. Levi Lincoln, Governor of Massachusetts, to Henry Clay, Secretary of State, 6 Dec. 1825, and Clay to Lincoln, 15 Dec. 1825, Manning, *Diplomatic Correspondence*, 2:71–73n; Clay to Albert Gallatin, 19 June 1826, ibid., 76–77, 88–90; Clay to Barrell, 19 Nov. 1827, ibid., 141–43, and Barrell's report, 148–60; Clay to Charles Vaughan, 9 Jan. 1829, ibid., 190–91.

33. "Statement from Maine House of Representatives," 29 Mar. 1837, *Register of Debates in Congress* (Washington, D.C.: Gales & Seaton, 1825–37), 25th Cong., 1st sess., Appendix, p. 99; "Speech of Governor of Maine," 28 Apr. 1838, 25th Cong., 2d sess., H. Doc. 354, *U.S. Serials Set* 330; see Winfield Scott correspondence Feb.–Mar. 1839, 26th Cong., 1st sess., H. Doc. 169, *U.S. Serials Set* 366; Winfield Scott, *Memoirs of General Scott Written by Himself* (New York: Sheldon & Co., 1864), 2:333–45. Howard Jones, "Anglophobia and the Aroostook War," *New England Quarterly* 48 (Dec. 1975): 519–39, believes war was possible.

34. Millard Fillmore, "Speech," 1 Mar. 1839, Frank Severance, ed., *Millard Fillmore Papers* (Buffalo, N.Y.: Buffalo Historical Society, 1907), 1:141–43; Webster, "Memorandum on the Northeastern Boundary Negotiations," 9 Mar. 1839, Wiltse, *Papers of Webster: Correspondence*, 4:346–49; quote from Webster to David Ogden, 11 Mar. 1839, ibid., 350–51.

35. Richard N. Current, "Webster's Propaganda and the Ashburton Treaty," *Mississippi Valley Historical Review* 34 (September 1947): 187–200; Frederick Merk, *Fruits of Propaganda in the Tyler Administration* (Cambridge, Mass.: Harvard University Press, 1971), explores Webster's maneuvering to achieve a diplomatic settlement. See also George G. Gill, "Edward Everett and the Northeastern Boundary Controversy," *New England Quarterly* 42 (June 1969): 201–13. The treaty is in Canada, Department of External Affairs, *Treaties and Agreements Affecting Canada in Force Between His Majesty and the United States of America with Subsidiary Documents, 1814–1925* (Ottawa: King's Printer, 1927), pp. 18–22. *Niles' Weekly Register* 56 (2 Mar. 1839). See Norval Luxon, *Niles' Weekly Register: News Magazine of the Nineteenth Century* (Baton Rouge: Louisiana State University Press, 1947), p. 187. Jones, *Webster-Ashburton Treaty*, is the best overall treatment.

36. Webster-Ashburton Treaty, Articles 3, 6, 10. Thomas Le Duc, "The Webster-Ashburton Treaty and the Minnesota Iron Ranges," *Journal of American History* 51 (Dec. 1964): 476–81.

37. Michael Scheuer, "Deadlock: Charting the Canadian-American Boundary on the Detroit River," *Michigan History* 67 (Mar./Apr. 1983): 24–30; John Quincy Adams to Albert Gallatin and Richard Rush, 28 July 1818, Ford, *Writings of Adams*, 6:394–408; Sansom, *Travels*, p. 51; Richard Rush to Henry Clay, 26 Mar. 1825, Manning, *Diplomatic Correspondence*, 2:488–89.

38. R. W. Van Alstyne, "International Rivalries in the Pacific Northwest," *Oregon Historical Quarterly* 46 (Sept. 1945): 185–218 and Howard Kushner, *Conflict on the Northwest Coast: American-Russian Rivalry in the Pacific Northwest, 1790–1867* (Westport, Conn.: Greenwood Press, 1975), provide background. See also H. F. Angus, ed., *British Columbia and the United States: The North Pacific Slope from the Fur Trade to Aviation* (New Haven, Conn.: Yale University Press, 1942), pp. 4–45, to the 1830s. Kenneth Porter, *John Jacob Astor, Businessman* (Cambridge, Mass.: Harvard University Press, 1931), pp. 164–201.

39. John Schroeder discusses early Oregon lobbyists in Congress in "Representative John Floyd, 1819–1829: Harbinger of Oregon Territory," *Oregon Historical Quarterly* 70 (Dec. 1969): 333–46. See also Barbara Cloud, "Oregon in the 1820s: The Congressional Perspective," *Western Historical Quarterly* 12 (Apr. 1981): 145–64.

40. Michael B. Husband, "Senator Lewis F. Linn and the Oregon Question," *Missouri Historical Review* 66 (Oct. 1971): 1–19.

41. Adams to Richard Rush, 22 July 1823, Manning, *Diplomatic Correspondence*, 2:58, 65; see remarks answering John Floyd on the need to occupy Oregon, 21 Dec. 1824, and 26 Feb. 1825, *Register of Debates*, 18th

Cong., 2d sess., 37, 690–95; Albert Gallatin to Henry Clay, 19 June 1826, Manning, *Diplomatic Correspondence*, 2:503–4.

42. Slacum, 11 Nov. 1835, Department of State, Special Agents, C. William Slacum, RG 59, vol. 11, National Archives, Washington, D. C.; Slacum assumed American rights to the Oregon country. Thomas Hart Benton, *Thirty Years' View: or, A History of the Working of the American Government for Thirty Years from 1820–1850* (New York: D. Appleton & Co., 1854), 1:109–10; Robert Greenhow, *Memoir, Historical and Political, on the Northwest Coast of North America and the Adjacent Territories* (Washington, D.C.: Blair and Rives, 1840), pp. 199, 200 for quotes. Merk, *Monroe Doctrine and Expansionism*, p. 75, and see his discussion of party newspapers pp. 78–82.

43. Norman A. Graebner, *Empire on the Pacific: A Study in American Continental Expansion* (New York: Ronald Press, 1955), chap. 2, emphasizes commercial interests and influence; Pletcher, *Diplomacy of Annexation*, is the best treatment. Merk, *Monroe Doctrine and Expansionism*, pp. 92–103, 281–82; William E. Lass, "How the Forty-Ninth Parallel Became the International Boundary," *Minnesota History* 44 (Summer 1975): 209–19. See also *North American Review* 62 (Jan. 1846): 214–52, for an extended review of Robert Greenhow's report, published in book form in 1845. Allen to Cushing, 2 Jan. 1846, Caleb Cushing Papers, Manuscript Division, Library of Congress, Washington, D.C., file 51. Treaty reprinted in *Treaties Affecting Canada*, pp. 28–29. See the letters by John C. Calhoun and James Buchanan to Richard Pakenham, 3 Sept. 1844, and 12 July 1845, and Buchanan to Louis McLane, 12 July 1845, Manning, *Diplomatic Correspondence*, 3:255–63, 281, 285–286.

44. Edwin A. Miles, " 'Fifty-Four Forty or Fight'—An American Political Legend," *Mississippi Valley Historical Review* 64 (Sept. 1957): 291–309; Pletcher, *Diplomacy of Annexation*, pp. 412–20.

45. See "Protocol Relative to Cession of Horseshoe Reef on Lake Erie," 9 Dec. 1850, *Treaties Affecting Canada*, p. 33. James Buchanan to Richard Pakenham, 26 Dec. 1846, and to John F. Crampton, 22 Feb. 1849, Manning, *Diplomatic Correspondence*, 3:340–41, 4:8, 8n. See also Lewis Einstein, "Lewis Cass," in *The American Secretaries of State and their Diplomacy*, ed. Samuel Flagg Bemis (New York: Alfred A. Knopf, 1928), 6:297–384; Campbell, *Revolution to Rapprochement*, pp. 89–93. For a new approach see Kinley Brauer, "Anglo-American Imperial Rivalry, 1815–1860," Paper delivered at the Ninth Annual Meeting of the Society for Historians of American Foreign Relations, Washington, D.C., 1983. I am grateful to Professor Brauer for sending me a copy of this paper in manuscript form.

CHAPTER 5

1. There is no history of borderland smuggling. This material is in T. L. Thompson, a Secret Inspector of Customs, Letters Concerning Appoint-

ments, Removals, and General Activities of Secret Inspectors of Customs 1842–50, Treasury Department, RG 217, E-248, documents 106–164 passim, National Archives, Washington, D.C.

2. Thompson to J. C. Spencer, 21, 29 Aug. 1843, ibid., doc. 111.

3. Thompson to Mr. C. Young, 26 June 1844, and to George Bibb, 24 July, 23 Sept., 18 Dec. 1844, ibid., docs. 142, 146, 152.

4. Fred Landon, *Western Ontario and the American Frontier* (Toronto: Ryerson Press, 1941), pp. 50–59, 69–78, 120–126, 142–48; Gerald M. Craig, *Upper Canada: The Formative Years, 1784–1841* (Toronto: McClelland & Stewart, 1963), chaps. 3–4; Herbert Marshall, Frank A. Southard, Jr., and Kenneth W. Taylor, *Canadian-American Industries: A Study in International Investment* (New Haven, Conn.: Yale University Press, 1936), pp. 3–11.

5. W. S. MacNutt, *The Atlantic Provinces: The Emergence of Colonial Society* (Toronto: McClelland & Stewart, 1957), pp. 107–8, 114, 132–34, 150–53; Harold Davis, *An International Community on the St. Croix (1604–1930)* (Orono: University of Maine Press, 1950), pp. 116–53; J. S. Martell, ed., *Immigration to and Emigration from Nova Scotia, 1815–1838*, Public Archives of Nova Scotia, Publication, no. 6 (1942), pp. 99, 101–11.

6. George W. Brown, "The Opening of the St. Lawrence River to American Shipping," *Canadian Historical Review* 7 (Mar. 1926): 4–12; Dorothy Cleaveland, "The Trade and Trade Routes of Northern New York from the Beginning of Settlement to the Coming of the Railroad," *The Quarterly Journal of the New York State Historical Association* 4 (Oct. 1923): 205–31; Harry F. Landon, *The North Country; A History Embracing Jefferson, St. Lawrence, Oswego, Lewis and Franklin Counties, New York* (Indianapolis: Historical Publishing Company, 1932), 1:189–90, 288–89; Robert J. A. Irwin, "William Hamilton Merritt and the First Welland Canal," *Niagara Frontier* 11 (Winter, 1964): 105–18; P.-Andre Sevigny, *Trade and Navigation on the Chambly Canal: A Historical Overview* (Ottawa: Parks Canada, 1983), pp. 21–24.

7. Russell to Clay, Mary W. Hargreaves and James Hopkins, eds., *The Papers of Henry Clay* (Lexington: The University of Kentucky Press, 1959–), 2:73–74; see also Gallatin to James Monroe, 25 Nov. 1815, Henry Adams, ed., *The Writings of Albert Gallatin* (1879; reprint, New York: Antiquarian Press, 1960), 1:665.

8. V. Dennis Golladay, "The United States and the British North American Fisheries, 1815–1818," *American Neptune* 33 (Oct. 1973): 246–57; Malcom Mercer, "Relations between Nova Scotia and New England, 1815–1867, with Special Reference to Trade and the Fisheries" (Master's thesis, Dalhousie University, 1938); Samuel Flagg Bemis, *John Quincy Adams and the Foundations of American Diplomacy* (New York: Alfred A. Knopf, 1949), pp. 457–61; F. Lee Benns, *The American Struggle for the British West Indian Carrying Trade, 1815–1830* (Bloomington: Indiana University Press, 1923), pp. 36, 65–67, 168–87.

9. "Message from the President . . . transmitting a Report of the Secre-

tary of State . . . Relative to Duties on Imports into Canada, Nova Scotia, and New Brunswick," 18 Apr. 1816 (Washington, D.C.: William A. Davis, 1816); *American State Papers: Commerce and Navigation* (Washington, D.C.: Gales & Seaton, 1832), 2:35, 452–53; see also *American State Papers: Foreign Relations* (Washington, D.C.: Gales & Seaton, 1832), 5:1–2, 12–13; "Commerce of United States," September 1825, *Register of Debates in Congress, 1825–1837* (Washington, D. C.: Gales & Seaton, 1825–37), 19th Cong., 1st sess., Appendix.

10. See 18 Apr. 1816 report of the Secretary of State, "Obstructions to American Commerce in the Provincial and Colonial Possessions of Great Britain," *State Papers: Commerce*, 2:31. John Quincy Adams to Lord Castlereagh, 17 Sept. 1816, Worthington C. Ford, ed., *Writings of John Quincy Adams* (New York: Macmillan Company, 1913–17), 6:80–83; see Rush-Adams correspondence, 3, 23 Apr. 1822, 23 June, 9 Oct. 1823, 12 Aug. 1824, William R. Manning, ed., *Diplomatic Correspondence of the United States: Canadian Relations, 1784–1860* (Washington, D.C.: Carnegie Foundation, 1940–43), 2:23–24, 316–19, 387–88, 433–36.

11. Henry Clay, "Speech," 31 Jan. 1817, Hargreaves and Hopkins, *Papers of Clay*, 2:297–302; "Report of Mr. Russell, 21 Jan. 1823, on a recent act to regulate the trade of Lower and Upper Canada passed 5 Aug. 1822," *State Papers: Foreign Relations*, 5:224–25; "Response to petition from Baltimore Merchants," *Register of Debates*, 19th Cong., 1st sess., 576–84; ibid., 19th Cong., 2d sess., 1419–33; House speeches and quotes, pp. 1454–60, 1470–78, 1493–96, 1507, 1514–31, passim; Senate in ibid., 419, 440–46, 451, 504.

12. See John Quincy Adams to Richard Rush, 30 July 1818, and to Rufus King, 15 Aug. 1822, Ford, *Writings of Adams*, 6:411; 7:293, and to Stratford Canning, 11 Nov. 1822, ibid., 323–37. "Memorial to Congress from Merchants, Shipowners, and Manufacturers of the City of Baltimore," 20 Feb. 1826, 19th Cong., 1st sess., H. Doc. 99, *U.S. Serials Set* 135, 3–4; see Clay-Gallatin correspondence, 8 Aug., 22 Sept., 27, 30 Oct. 1826, Manning, *Diplomatic Correspondence*, 2:106–11, 513, 518–19; "Memorial of Delegates of St. Lawrence County, N. Y.," 24 Jan. 1827, 19th Cong., 2d sess., S. Doc. 40, *U.S. Serials Set* 145, pp. 3–4; Jackson to Congress, 7 Dec. 1831, James D. Richardson, ed. and comp., *A Compilation of the Messages and Papers of the Presidents, 1789–1908* (Washington, D.C.: Bureau of National Literature and Art, 1908), 2:546–48; Benns, *American Struggle*, pp. 168–87; Theodore Burton, "Henry Clay," in *The American Secretaries of State and Their Diplomacy*, ed. Samuel Flagg Bemis (New York: Alfred A. Knopf, 1928), 4:124–26, and John S. Bassett, "Martin Van Buren," ibid., 185–87.

13. Hints that the provinces might prove more valuable than the West Indies are in *Register of Debates*, 22d Cong., 1st sess., Appendix, clxvi-clxxxiii; the "Act to Regulate Foreign and Coasting Trade on Northern, North-eastern, and North-western frontiers of the United States," 2 Mar. 1831, ibid., 65–66. Jackson to Senate, 2 Mar. 1833, ibid., 129–31, 141–43.

14. Correspondence of the Secretary of the Treasury with Collectors, 1789–1833, Treasury Department, RG 56, M-178, National Archives, Wash-

ington, D.C. In Maine, reels 5 for Eastport and Belfast, 35 for Penobscot, and 39 for Bath.

15. Ibid., Burlington, Vermont, and Niagara, New York in reel 34; Champlain, New York, in reel 37; Ogdensburg, New York, in reel 33. Doty to S. Ingham, Secretary of the Treasury, 25 Sept. 1830, ibid., reel 33.

16. Buffalo: Barker to S. Ingham, 24 July 1829, ibid., reel 34. Detroit: Andrew Mack to S. Ingham, 31 Oct. 1829, 16 Mar. 1830, 1 Nov. 1831, ibid., reel 33. Albert H. Porter, *Historical Sketch of Niagara from 1678–1876* (1876), p. 37.

17. "Report of the Land Agent, Commonwealth of Massachusetts, 13 Dec. 1837, Caleb Cushing Papers, Manuscript Division, Library of Congress, Washington, D.C., file 215; "Resolutions of the Legislature of Maine in Relation to the Commercial Intercourse between the United States and the British Provinces of Nova Scotia and New Brunswick," 7 May 1838, 26th Cong., 2d sess., S. Doc. 423, *U.S. Serials Set* 318, 1; "Memorial of a Number of Citizens of Newburyport, Mass.," 28 Dec. 1840, 26th Cong., 2d sess., S. Doc. 31, ibid., 1–2. Jesse Hawley, *An Essay on the Enlargement of the Erie Canal* (Lockport, N.Y.: Courier Office, 1840), pp. 6–8. "Resolution of the Legislature of Michigan Relative to the Transportation of the United States Mail through Canada," 31 Dec. 1849, 31st Cong., 1st sess., H. Misc. Doc. No. 13, *U.S. Serials Set* 581.

18. Consular instructions and dispatches are in the Department of State files, National Archives, Washington, D.C., RG 59. Consular Dispatches, Halifax, RG 59, T-469. See dispatches dated 31 Dec. 1835 and 31 Dec. 1837. The semi-annual general returns broke down tonnages, values of goods landed and shipped, and the numbers of Americans employed in the trade.

19. Andrews to Daniel Webster, 1 Apr. 1843, to State Department, 16 Apr., 5 July 1846, to James Buchanan, 20 Apr. 1846. Consular Dispatches, St. John, T-485. Citation from Andrews to State Department, 15 Jan. 1848, ibid. Buchanan to Andrews, 31 Dec. 1846, *Instructions to Consuls*, ser. 1, 2:271.

20. The Sydney and Pictou reports are in Consular Dispatches, T-479. Letter by Norton, 21 Nov. 1849, ibid., Charlottetown, P.E.I., merchants had supported annexationism privately.

21. James Tallmadge, *Address Before the American Institute* (New York: Hopkins & Jennings, 1841). Tallmadge spoke at the close of its annual fair. James L. Barton, *Commerce of the Lakes* (Buffalo, N.Y.: Courier Office, 1846), p. 37. *Tabular Representation of the Present Condition of Boston in Relation to Railroad Facilities, Foreign Commerce, Population, Wealth, Manufactures; Also a Few Statements Relative to the Commerce of the Canadas* (Boston: J. H. Eastburn's, 1851). This report was given by a Joint Special Committee on the Railroad Celebration, 17–19 Sept. 1851.

22. *New England Palladium & Commercial Advertiser*, 11, 1 Apr. 1815; 4 Sept., 20 Oct. 1818; *National Intelligencer*, 16 May 1815; 2, 19 July 1816, 12 Mar., 3 Apr. 1817; quote on plaster trade 18 July 1817; *Niles' Weekly Register*, 11 May, 30 Nov. 1816, 11:178–80, 228.

23. *Niles' Weekly Register*, 16 Oct. 1819, 17:111; Ronald Shaw, *Erie Water West: A History of the Erie Canal, 1792–1854* (Lexington: University of Kentucky Press, 1966), pp. 72, 80, 101–2, 414–15. *Evening Star*, 29 Jan. 1835 cited ibid., p. 415; Marcy to New York Legislature, 6 Jan. 1835, Charles Lincoln, ed., *Messages from the Governors* (Albany: J. B. Lyon Company, 1909), 3:510.

24. The material in this paragraph comes from *Niles' Weekly Register*, the *New England Palladium and Commercial Register*, the *New York Commercial Advertiser*, the *National Intelligencer*, and the *Albany Argus & Daily City Gazette* for the 1820s.

25. "Canada" article from the *National Advocate* reprinted in *Niles' Weekly Register*, 29 May 1819, 16:237–38; ibid., 9 Jan. 1830, 37:328; J. D. Wallenstein, *North American Review* 27 (July 1828): 12; Edward Everett, "Speech at Yellow Springs, Ohio," 29 June 1829, Everett, *Orations and Speeches on Various Occasions* (Boston: Little, Brown & Co., 1868), 1:209–11.

26. W. E. Greening, "The Lumber Industry in the Ottawa Valley and the American Market in the Nineteenth Century," *Ontario History* 62 (June 1970): 134–36; A. R. M. Lower et al., *The North American Assault on the Canadian Forest: A History of the Lumber Trade Between Canada and the United States* (Toronto: Ryerson Press, 1938), pp. 56–60, 76–84, 90–101, 109–22.

27. Hamilton Hill, *The Trade of Boston* (Boston: J. H. Eastburn's Press, 1871), pp. 133–40. *American Almanac* (1831), p. 261; (1835), pp. 300–302; (1839), pp. 203–4; (1841), pp. 104, 247, provide examples. *Niles' Weekly Register*, 7 Sept. 1833, 45:24; 7 June 1834, 46:244–45, 253–54; 17 Oct. 1835, 48:70, cites "The Spirit of Improvement" in reference to a Portland-Quebec railroad project. John Hayward, *The New England Gazetteer* (Boston: John Hayward, 1839), described St. Albans, Vermont, Eastport, Maine, and the Bay of Fundy as linkages between the states and the provinces. *Daily Albany Argus*, 10 Sept. 1835; 26 May, 15 June–29 July 1837. *Rochester Daily Advertiser*, 8 Aug. 1837.

28. See William J. Wilgus, *The Railroad Interrelations of the United States and Canada* (New Haven, Conn.: Yale University Press, 1937), pp. 37–60; J. Ogden Ross, comp., *The Steamboats of Lake Champlain 1809 to 1930* (Albany: Champlain Transportation Company, 1930), discusses the interrelated growth of borderland steamboat and railway companies. See also *Report of the Directors and Engineers of the Lake St. Louis and Province Line and the Plattsburgh and Montreal Railroad Companies on the Railroad Routes between Montreal and New York* (Montreal: J. Starke & Co., 1852), pp. 28, 34, for citations; Edward Hungerford et al., *Vermont Central–Central Vermont: A Study in Human Effort* (Boston: Railway and Locomotive Historical Society, 1942), pp. 9–10, 19–22; *The Bridge Question* (Montpelier: E. P. Walton & Sons, 1847), pp. 3, 8–16, 26–27.

29. David Stevenson, "Lake Navigation of North America," *Merchant's Magazine & Commercial Review* 3 (1841): 216–26; "Commerce of Que-

bec," 4 (1841): 96–97; 4 (1841): 574–75; see articles on "Canadian Commerce," ibid., 6 (1842): 538–54; and 9 (1843): 182–83; "Commerce and Resources of British America," ibid., 10 (1843): 16–47.

30. *De Bow's Review* 3 (May 1847): 438–39; 6 (Sept. and Nov. 1848): 182, 310–21, 366–67; 7 (Dec. 1849): 542–44. *American Railroad Journal*, 3 June 1848, 357–60; 28 Oct. 1848, 693. *Albany Argus*, 9 Dec. 1845.

31. House Report 258, 29 February 1848, 30th Cong., 1st sess., *U.S. Serials Set* 525.

32. Gilbert Tucker, *The Canadian Commercial Revolution, 1845–1851* (New Haven, Conn.: Yale University Press, 1936), pp. 21–93.

CHAPTER 6

1. Scott, Winfield, *Memoirs of General Scott, Written by Himself* (New York: Sheldon & Company, 1864), 1:301–17; for general studies see Orrin Tiffany, *The Relations of the United States to the Canadian Rebellion of 1837–1838* (Buffalo, N.Y.: Buffalo Historical Society, 1905), pp. 1–147; Wilson Porter Shortridge, "The Canadian-American Frontier during the Rebellion of 1837–1838," *Canadian Historical Review* 7 (Mar. 1926): 13–26; A. B. Corey, *The Crisis of 1830–1842 in Canadian American Relations* (New Haven: Yale University Press, 1941). J. R. Poinsett to Winfield Scott, 5 Jan. 1838, 25th Cong., 2d sess., H. Doc. 74, copy in Public Archives of Canada.

2. Scott to Worth, 12 Dec. 1837, cited in Charles W. Eliot, *Winfield Scott: The Soldier and the Man* (New York: Macmillan Company, 1937), p. 336 n. 14, and pp. 336–44. Scott, *Memoirs*, 1:305–12; James C. Curtis, *The Fox at Bay: Martin Van Buren and the Presidency, 1837–1841* (Lexington: University Press of Kentucky, 1970), pp. 171–74. Howard Jones, "The *Caroline* Affair," *The Historian* 38 (May, 1976): 485–502; the best study is Kenneth Ray Stevens, "The 'Caroline' Affair: Anglo-American Relations and Domestic Politics, 1837–1842" (Ph.D. diss., Indiana University, 1982).

3. N. S. Benton to John Forsyth, 6 Feb. 1838, William R. Manning, ed., *Diplomatic Correspondence of the United States: Canadian Relations, 1784–1860* (Washington, D.C.: Carnegie Foundation, 1940–43), 3: 461–63n. Eliot, *Scott*, pp. 336–44; Tiffany, *Relations to Rebellions*, pp. 37, 50–51, 78–82.

4. *United States Magazine and Democratic Review* 1 (1838): 218 [hereafter cited as the *Democratic Review*].

5. John Duffy and H. N. Müller, "The Great Wolf Hunt: The Popular Response in Vermont to the *Patriote* Uprising of 1837," *Journal of American Studies* 8 (Aug. 1974): 153–69, is well-grounded in newspaper articles. Correspondent of the *New York American*, 17 July 1837, and St. Johnsburg, Vermont, *Caledonian*, nd., in Caleb Cushing Papers, Manuscript Division, Library of Congress, Washington, D.C., file 215. See also H. N. Müller, "Trouble on the Border, 1838: A Neglected Incident from Vermont's Neglected History," *Vermont History* 44 (Spring 1976): 97–102; Eugene P.

Link, "Vermont Physicians and the Canadian Rebellion of 1837," ibid., 38 (Summer 1969): 177–83; Walter Hill Crockett, *Vermont: The Green Mountain State* (New York: The Century History Company, Inc., 1921), 3:281–86; Lewis Cass Aldrich, ed., *History of Franklin and Grand Isle Counties, Vermont* (Syracuse, N.Y.: D. Mason & Co., 1891), pp. 154–60.

6. Douglas Frank, "The Canadian Rebellion and the American Public," *Niagara Frontier* (Winter 1969): 96–104, is the best treatment. See also Harry Landon, *The North Country: A History Embracing Jefferson, St. Lawrence, Oswego and Franklin Counties, New York* (Indianapolis: Historical Publishing Company, 1932), 1, chap. 12; Augustus N. Hand, "Local Incidents of the Papineau Rebellion," *New York History* 15 (1934): 376–87; and Shortridge, "Canadian-American Frontier."

7. *Daily Albany Gazette*, 8–30 Dec. 1837, passim; *Daily Albany Argus*, 26 Aug. 1837–17 May 1838, passim; John T. Horton et al., *History of Northwestern New York: Erie, Niagara, Wyoming, Genessee and Orleans Counties* (New York: Lewis Historical Publishing Company, 1947), 1:76–78.

8. Jones, "Caroline Affair," 492–93; *Albany Argus*, 2 Jan. 1838; Frank, "Canadian Rebellion," makes extensive use of the Buffalo papers; Marcy to General P. Wetmore, 22, 31 Dec. 1837, William Learned Marcy Papers, Manuscript Division, Library of Congress, Washington, D.C., letterbooks, vol. 3; for Marcy's guarded comments to the New York legislature see 2 Jan., 5 May 1838, Charles Lincoln ed., *Messages from the Governors* (Albany: J. B. Lyon Company, 1909), 3:678–80, 683–90.

9. Carl Wittke, "Ohioans and the Canadian-American Crisis of 1837–1838," *The Ohio State Archeological and Historical Quarterly* 58 (Jan. 1949): 21–34; Robert Ross, "The Patriot War," *Michigan Historical Collections* 21 (1892): 509–609; Albert B. Corey, *Canadian-American Relations Along the Detroit River* (Detroit: Wayne State University Press, 1957); Roger Rosentretor, "Liberating Canada: Michigan and the Patriot War," *Michigan History* 67 (Mar.–Apr. 1983): 32–34, and "To Free Upper Canada: Michigan and the Patriot War, 1837–1839" (Ph.D. diss., Michigan State University, 1983).

10. *Albany Argus*, 27 Dec. 1837, citing Buffalo *Daily Star;* and *Albany Argus*, 5, 22 Jan. 1838. *Detroit Advertiser*, 23 Jan. 1838, cited in Rosentreter, "Free Upper Canada," p. 84.

11. Corey, *Crisis of 1830–42*, pp. 19–32; Charles G. Fenwick, *A History of the Neutrality Laws of the United States* (Washington, D.C.: Carnegie Endowment, 1913), pp. 43–44; Curtis, *Fox at Bay*, pp. 171–74. C. J. Ingersoll to Martin Van Buren, 23, 24 Dec. 1837, Martin Van Buren Papers, Library of Congress, Washington, D.C. (microfilm copy, University of British Columbia Library, Series 2, Reel 19).

12. Van Buren to Senate and House, 5 Jan. 1838, James D. Richardson, ed. and comp., *A Compilation of the Messages and Papers of the Presidents, 1789–1908* (Washington, D.C.: Bureau of National Literature and Art, 1908), 3:399; "Proclamation," ibid., 481; N. Ganon, U.S. Marshal, to

Martin Van Buren, 28 Dec. 1837, ibid., 3:399–400. H. W. Rogers, District Attorney for Erie County and United States Attorney, to Martin Van Buren, 30 Dec. 1837, Manning, *Diplomatic Correspondence*, 3:456n; N. S. Benton, U.S. Attorney for Northern District of New York, to John Forsyth, 6 Feb. 1838, ibid., 461–63n. For the Forsyth-Fox correspondence see ibid., 31–34, 44.

13. *The Congressional Globe, Containing the Debates and Proceedings, 1833–1873* (Washington, D.C.: F. & J. Rives and George Bailey, 1834–73), 25th Cong., 2d sess., 79, 83 (Rhett and Menifee), 195 (Loomis), and 215 (Buchanan defending new Neutrality Law). Millard Fillmore of Buffalo opposed "improper interference in the Canadian rebellion," despite concern over the *Caroline* affair. Speech, 12 Jan. 1838, Frank Severance, ed., *Millard Fillmore Papers* (Buffalo, N.Y.: Buffalo Historical Society, 1907), 1:136–37.

14. Thomas Hart Benton, *Thirty Years' View: or, A History of the Working of the American Government for Thirty Years from 1820 to 1850* (New York: D. Appleton & Co., 1854), 2:276–77, 278–79, 281. "Northern Frontier—Defence Estimates," report from Secretary of War, 9, 10 Jan. 1838, 25th Cong., 2d sess., H. Doc. 89, *U.S. Serials Set* 325; Niagara Frontier, expenses, 12 Jan. 1838, 25th Cong., 2d sess., *American State Papers: Military Affairs* (Washington, D.C.: Gales and Seaton, 1832), 7:901, and "Memorial of Oswego County," 14 Feb. 1838, ibid., 970–71.

15. Martin Van Buren to House of Representatives, 20 June 1838, Richardson, *Messages and Papers*, 3:478–79. Oscar Kinchen, *The Rise and Fall of the Patriot Hunters* (New York: Bookman Associates, 1956), is the best single study. The Swanton, Vermont, *North American*, 8 May 1839, defended "Canadian Rights and Independence" and denounced the "affinity between British tyrants & American aristocrats." Its serial "History of Canada" justified rebellion.

16. *North American*, 8 May 1839, pp. 24–37; Shortridge, "Canadian-American Frontier," 19, for citation. E. A. Theller, *Canada in 1837–38* (Philadelphia: Henry F. Anners, 1841), 1:29, 51, quote from 2:277. See also his letters of 19, 22 June 1838, MG 24, B 42, Public Archives of Canada.

17. Thomas Jefferson Sutherland, *A Letter to Her Majesty the British Queen* (Albany, N.Y.: C. Van Benthuysen, 1841), pp. iii, 14–15; Caleb Lyon, *Narrative and Recollections of Van Dieman's Land, during a Three Year Captivity of Stephen S. Wright* (New York: J. Winchester, 1844), collected several statements; Marcus Smith cited p. 47. Linus W. Miller, *Notes of an Exile to Van Dieman's Land* (Fredonia, N.Y.: W. McKinstry & Co., 1846), pp. 2–4, 7–9, 59; Robert Marsh, *Seven Years of My Life, or Narrative of a Patriot Exile* (Buffalo, N.Y.: Paxon & Stevens, 1848), pp. iii, 6, 18, 20, 206–7; "Recollection from *Gleason's Pictorial*," *New York Times*, 5 Oct. 1852. James Doyle, "American Literary Images of the Upper Canada Rebellion," unpublished paper. I am grateful to Professor Doyle for sharing this paper with me. For statements that suggested similar heroic and historical imagery to that found in the narratives, see "Memorial, to the Honorable, the

Senate and House of Representatives," *Ogdensburgh Times & Advertiser,* Extra, 1 Jan. 1839, and "A Letter to a Friend," 26 November 1838, Caleb Cushing Papers, file 215.

18. Kinchen, *Patriot Hunters,* pp. 37–51, 70–84, 94–102, 107–23, Webster to Tyler cited pp. 108–9. On exiles, see also Abel Upshur to Edward Everett, 27 Dec. 1843, Manning, *Diplomatic Correspondence,* 3:233–34, Stevens, " 'Caroline' Affair," pp. 57–71. For American-provincial cooperation, see "Report of the Secretary of State, touching the Territorial Relations of the United States and Great Britain on this Continent," 11 Feb. 1839, 25th Cong., 3d sess., H. Ex. Doc. 181, especially the attached correspondence, such as W. J. Worth to Col. K. Cameron, 24 Feb., 5 Mar. 1838, pp. 110–11; A. Macomb to Sir John Colborne, 21 June 1838, p. 95; A. Eustice to Sir John Colborne, 2 Jan. 1839, p. 109; Stevens, " 'Caroline' Affair," pp. 57–71.

19. *New England Palladium and Commercial Advertiser,* 26 May, 12 June 1818; *National Intelligencer,* 13 Apr. 1815; for comment on Canadians as republicans 8 Nov. 1815; 20 May 1818; on Robert Gourlay, 18–22 June 1818. *Niles' Weekly Register,* 13, 20, 27 June 1818, 14:272, 294, 308. Gourlay's trial covered ibid., 5, 19 Sept. 1818, 15:32, 62. *Advocate* cited ibid., 29 May 1819, 16:237–38.

20. *Niles' Weekly Register,* 2, 16 Mar. 1822, 22:2, 34; *Albany Argus,* 13 Dec. 1825.

21. *Niles' Weekly Register,* 11 Mar. 1826, 30:20–22; *Albany Argus,* 9, 21 Apr. 1827; *Niles' Weekly Register,* 31 Mar., 7, 21 Apr. 1827, 32:85, 107–8, 131; and ibid., 8 Dec. 1827, 33:227. The *Argus* was more restrained in its judgments. See, for example, 25 July 1827. For Niles's coverage of the arrest of provincial editors, see *Niles' Weekly Register,* 9 May 1829, 36:165, and 19 Sept. 1829, 37:53.

22. Reginald Horsman, *Race and Manifest Destiny: The Origins of American Racial Anglo-Saxonism* (Cambridge, Mass.: Harvard University Press, 1981). Winthrop Jordan, *White Over Black: American Attitudes Toward the Negro, 1550–1812* (Chapel Hill: University of North Carolina Press, 1968), is useful. See also John Higham, *Strangers in the Land: Patterns of American Nativism, 1860–1925* (New Brunswick: Rutgers University Press, 1963).

23. Hezekiah Niles stated, "In Lower Canada a very large majority of the people are Canadians proper—that is, descendants of the original French settlers." *Niles' Weekly Register,* 17 May 1834, 46:191. J. D. Wallenstein, "Lower Canada," *North American Review* 27 (July 1828): 1–30, and "Review of Captain Basil Hall's travels in the United States and Canada," ibid., 29 (Oct. 1829): 522–574; "Canada," *American Quarterly Review* 7 (Mar. 1830): 188–213.

24. *Niles' Weekly Register,* 5 Apr. 1834, 46:85, and 19 Sept. 1835 and 13 Feb. 1836, 49:37 and 401; *Albany Argus,* 9 July 1836.

25. *Democratic Review* 1 (1838): 218; *National Intelligencer* citations Jan.–Feb. 1838, passim; *Baltimore American* cited ibid., 23 Jan. 1838. *New York Albion,* Nov. 1837–Jan. 1838, clippings in MG 24, B 157, Public Ar-

chives of Canada; Norval Luxon, *Niles' Weekly Register: News Magazine of the Nineteenth Century* (Baton Rouge: Louisiana State University Press, 1947), pp. 185–87. *Boston Daily Advertiser*, 6 Dec. 1837.

26. Notes for a speech in Congress, and clippings, Caleb Cushing Papers, file 215. Cushing clipped from provincial as well as American papers. "The Canada Question," *Democratic Review* 1 (Jan. 1838): 205–20, passim. See also O'Sullivan's articles "History of the Recent Insurrection in the Canadas," ibid., 4 (June 1838): 72–104, and "The Canada Question," ibid., (Jan. 1839): 8–29. Hugh Keenleyside, *Canada and the United States: Some Aspects of Their Historical Relations* (1929; reprint, Port Washington, N.Y.: Kennikat Press, 1971), pp. 108–11, believes that a majority of Americans in 1835 probably favored annexing Canada and therefore supported filibustering, but the evidence does not sustain his conclusion.

27. Letter from St. Lawrence County, 26 Feb. 1838, printed in *Niles' Weekly Register*, 10 Mar. 1838, 54: 19; for attack on *Robert Peel*, see ibid., 9 June 1838, 54:225–26. The incident is described in Landon, *North Country*, 1:304–9. *Albany Argus*, issues for June 1838, argued for a proper border patrol to deter or punish marauding.

28. See *Niles' Weekly Register*, Sept. 1838–Feb. 1839, 54: passim. Corey, *Crisis of 1830–1842*, pp. 119–20. *Albany Argus*, 21, 24 Nov. 1838, for citations.

29. Zadock Thompson, *History of Vermont, Natural, Civil, and Statistical* (Burlington, Vt.: Chauncey Goodrich, 1842), 2:103; F. B. Hough, *History of St. Lawrence and Franklin Counties* (Albany, 1853), pp. 656–73; Crisfield Johnson, *History of Oswego County, New York, 1789–1877* (Philadelphia: L. H. Everts & Co., 1877), p. 73; *Compendium of the History and Biography of the City of Detroit and Wayne County, Michigan* (Chicago: Henry Taylor, 1909), pp. 115–16.

30. Lord Durham's Proclamation in *Niles' Weekly Register*, 28 July 1838, 54:349–50. "Lord Durham's Report," *Democratic Review* 5 (June 1839): 542–79.

31. Dunkin, "British American Politics," *North American Review* 49 (Oct. 1839): 373–431.

32. Sabine, "British Colonial Politics," ibid., 60 (Jan. 1845): 87–126; Sabine's commentary on other, similar documents in ibid., 67 (July 1848): 1–26.

33. *De Bow's Review* 6 (Sept. 1848): 181–200; *Niles' Weekly Register*, 28 Mar., 4 Apr., 2, 9 May 1849, 75:205, 220, 282–85, 303.

34. *Niles' Weekly Register*, 62 (Mar.–Sept. 1842), and 63 (Sept. 1842–Mar. 1843), 64 (Mar.-Sept. 1843), passim. The *Advertiser* cited ibid., 71 (28 Nov. 1846):194.

35. See Chapter 9, below. *Niles' Weekly Register*, 11 Oct. 1848, 64:228–29, noted that provincials now acknowledged that commerce was "king."

CHAPTER 7

1. Philip Stansbury, *A Pedestrian Tour of Two Thousand Three Hundred Miles in North America* (New York: J. D. Myers & W. Smith, 1822), pp. v–vi.

2. Ibid., pp. 146, 151–55, 159–60.

3. Ibid., pp. 211, 214–16, 233–34.

4. See George Rogers Taylor, *The Transportation Revolution, 1815–1861* (New York: Harper & Row, 1951); Ronald Shaw, *Erie Water West: A History of the Erie Canal, 1792–1854* (Lexington: University Press of Kentucky, 1966).

5. New Yorkers wrote the majority of the travel journals about the provinces published between 1815 and 1871. New Englanders were next in number. And a Philadelphian and a Virginian did one each. Most of the travel guides were published either in New York or New England towns, usually Boston. G. M. Davison, *The Fashionable Tour: A Guide to Travellers Visiting the Middle and Northern States and the Provinces of Canada* (Saratoga Springs, N.Y.: G. M. Davison, 1830), aimed at wealthy southerners escaping the summer heat. Davison had detailed timetables for stage lines and vessels traveling the St. Lawrence from Ogdensburg to Montreal, distances covered, and historic sites, usually with patriotic overtones drawn from War of 1812 battles.

6. *New England Palladium and Commercial Advertiser*, 9 Sept. 1825; *National Intelligencer*, 30 Oct. 1816; *Niles' Weekly Register*, Sept. 1826, 31:29; *Daily Albany Argus*, 10 Oct. 1833, 7 May 1834, 9 July 1835.

7. See Harry Landon, *The North Country: A History Embracing Jefferson, St. Lawrence, Oswego, Lewis and Franklin Counties, New York* (Indianapolis: Historical Publishing Company, 1932), 1:456–80, for northern New York's tourism. *Harper's New Monthly Magazine* 18 (Jan. 1859): 176–95, had a detailed tour of Quebec City, complete with engravings.

8. Roderick Nash, *Wilderness and the American Mind*, 3d ed. (New Haven, Conn.: Yale University Press, 1982), especially chaps. 3–5. See also Russell B. Nye, "The American View of Nature," in Nye, *This Almost Chosen People: Essays in the History of American Ideas* (Toronto: Macmillan Company of Canada, 1966), pp. 256–304; Loren Baritz, "Agrarianism: John Taylor of Caroline," in *City on a Hill: A History of Ideas and Myths in America* (New York: John Wiley, 1964), chap. 4.

9. Henry Gilpin, *A Northern Tour: Being a Guide to Saratoga, Lake George, Niagara, Canada, Boston, &C. &C.* (Philadelphia: H. C. Carey & I. Lea, 1825), pp. 175–84; Davison, *Fashionable Tour*, pp. 263–65; *The Northern Traveller and Northern Tour* (New York: Goodrich & Wiley, 1834), devoted 60 of 400 pages to Canada, but lavished attention on Niagara Falls and Montreal's well-cultivated countryside; Theodore Dwight, *The Northern Traveller* 6th ed. (New York: John P. Haven, 1841), included maps and described alternate routes to Montreal from Niagara and Lake Champlain, pp. 111–22.

10. Timothy Bigelow, *Journal of a Tour to Niagara Falls in the Year 1805* (Boston: John Wilson and Son, 1876), pp. 1–65; Christian Schultz, *Travels on an Inland Voyage 1807 and 1808* (1810; reprint, New York: Gregg Press, 1968), pp. 45–97.

11. *Pictorial Guide to the Falls of Niagara* (Buffalo, N.Y.: Salisbury and Clapp, 1842); T. G. Hulett, *Every Man His Own Guide to the Falls of Niagara*, 5th edition (Buffalo, N.Y.: Faxon & Co., 1845); Joseph Earl Arrington, "Godfrey N. Frankenstein's Moving Panorama of Niagara Falls," *New York History* 49 (April 1968): 169–99; "Niagara," *Harper's New Monthly Magazine* 7 (August 1853): 289–305. See also *Tunis's Topographical and Pictorial Guide to Niagara* (Niagara Falls, N.Y.: W. E. Tunis, 1856); F. H. Johnson, *Every Man His Own Guide at Niagara Falls* (Rochester: D. M. Dewey, 1852); William Burr's, *Descriptive and Historical View of Burr's Moving Mirror of the Lakes* (New York: George Bunce, 1850) was a travelogue spun around pictures. "Great Britain and America: Thoughts at Niagara," *The Knickerbocker* 22 (Sept. 1843): 193–96.

12. *The Ontario and St. Lawrence Steamboat Company's Handbook for Travellers to Niagara Falls, Montreal and Quebec, and through Lake Champlain to Saratoga Springs* (Buffalo, N.Y.: Jewett, Thomas & Co., 1852); John Disturnell, *Disturnell's American and European Railway and Steamship Guide* (New York: J. Disturnell, 1853); William S. Hunter, Jr., *Hunter's Panoramic Guide from Niagara Falls to Quebec* (Boston: John P. Jewett & Company, 1857). See also *The River St. Lawrence in One Panoramic View from Niagara Falls to Quebec* (New York: Alex Harthill, 1859); O. L. Holley, ed., *The Picturesque Tourist: Being a Guide through the Northern and Eastern States and Canada* (New York: Disturnell, 1844); Zadock Thompson, *Northern Guide* (Burlington, Vt.: S. B. Nichols, 1857). Most of these were in a pocket or handbag-sized format.

13. Frederic Cozzens, *Acadia, or, A Month with the Blue Noses* (New York: Derby & Jackson, 1859), p. 199; *Coit Correspondence, or, A Trip to New Brunswick by the Coit Family* (Worcester: Charles Hamilton, 1871), p. 48. Frederick W. Seward, *Seward at Washington* (New York: Derby and Miller, 1891), 1, chap. 49, "A Canadian Journey."

14. "Quebec," *The Knickerbocker* 38 (Dec. 1851): 629–31; "Summer Letters," *New York Times*, 15, 23, 27, 29, 30 August 1853; "Quebec," *Harper's New Monthly Magazine* 17 (Jan. 1859): 176–95; John E. Cooke, "A Glimpse of Quebec," *Lippincott's Magazine* 6 (Sept. 1870): 319–22.

15. "Quebec," *Harper's New Monthly Magazine* 18 (Jan. 1859): 176–95.

16. Ray Allen Billington, *The Protestant Crusade 1800–1860: A Study in the Origins of American Nativism* (New York: Macmillan Company, 1938), chap. 1, and pp. 33–44, 54–76.

17. Bigelow, *Journal*, p. 87; "Halls Travels," *North American Review* 9 (June 1819): 147; Joseph Sansom, *Travels in Lower Canada* (New York: Kirk & Mercein, 1817), pp. 24–26; *A Summer Month, or, Recollections of a Visit to the Falls of Niagara and the Lakes* (Philadelphia: H. C. Carey & I. Lea, 1823), pp. 123, 136–37; Benjamin Silliman, *Remarks Made on a Short*

Tour between Hartford and Quebec in the Autumn of 1819, 2d ed. (New Haven: S. Converse, 1824), pp. 390–91; J. D. Wallenstein in *North American Review* 27 (July 1828): 12; "Quebec," *Albany Argus,* 26 Aug. 1845; Moses Guest, *Poems on Several Occasions* (Cincinnati: Looker & Reynolds, Printers, 1823), p. 131.

18. Billington, *Protestant Crusade,* pp. 53–54, 92–93, 99–108; William Stone, *Maria Monk and the Nunnery of the Hotel Dieu* (New York: Howe & Bates, 1836).

19. J. C. Myers, *Sketches on Tour through the Northern and Eastern States, the Canadas & Nova Scotia* (Harrisonburg: J. H. Wartmann and Brothers, 1849), pp. 216–19; H. D. Thoreau, *A Yankee in Canada* (Boston: Ticknor & Fields, 1866), pp. 23–24, 62.

20. Gilpin, *Northern Tour,* p. 184; *Northern Traveller,* pp. 167–76; Dwight, *Northern Traveller,* pp. 111, 121–22; H. S. Tanner, *The Traveller's Handbook for the State of New York and the Province of Canada,* 2d ed. (New York: T. R. Tanner, 1844), pp. 130–31, 145–46; John Disturnell, *The Eastern Tourist* (New York: J. Disturnell, 1848), pp. 133–35; Charles Lanman, *A Tour to the River Saguenay in Lower Canada* (Philadelphia: Carey & Hart, 1848), pp. 163–64. Lanman's sister did a more conventional tour four years later, but her husband was an angler, like her brother. So her party went to unconventional places in the upper Maritimes. Adeline Lanman, *A Tour Down the St. Lawrence River* (1852); Burr, *Descriptive View,* p. 25; Dana cited in *Yankees in Canada: A Collection of 19th Century Travel Narratives,* ed. James Doyle (Toronto: E.C.W. Press, 1980), pp. 89, 95; Seward, *Seward at Washington,* 1:303, 317.

21. Bigelow, *Journal,* pp. 86, 103, 111; *North American Review* 9 (June 1819): 141–44; Sansom, *Travels,* pp. 16, 68–72; Myers, *Sketches,* pp. 224–32; R. W. Haskins, "Human Destiny Upon the Theatre of the American Continent," *The Knickerbocker* 30 (Nov. 1847): 399–407.

22. Silliman, *Remarks,* p. 391; Thoreau, *Yankee in Canada,* pp. 43, 83–84.

23. Gilpin, *Northern Tour,* p. 184; *Northern Traveller,* p. 162; Dwight, *Northern Traveller,* pp. 121–22; Tanner, *Traveller's Handbook,* p. 130; "Quebec," *Knickerbocker* 38 (Dec. 1851): 629.

24. Bigelow, *Journal,* p. 94; William Darby, *A Tour from the City of New York to Detroit, in the Michigan Territory, Made between the 2d of May and the 22d of September, 1818* (New York: Kirk & Mercein, 1819), pp. 78–79; Sansom, *Travels,* pp. 29, 43; Stansbury, *Pedestrian Tour,* p. 146; *Summer Month,* pp. 95, 140–41; Silliman, *Remarks,* pp. 236–37, 392; William Thompson in Doyle, ed., *Yankees in Canada,* pp. 53–63; for the entire volume, see Thompson, *Major Jones's Sketches of Travel in his Tour from Georgia to Canada* (Philadephia: Carey & Hart, 1848), pp. 181–84; Thoreau, *Yankee in Canada,* pp. 21, 38–41, 101.

25. Darby, *New York to Detroit,* pp. 78–79, 84–85, 99–107, 189; *Northern Traveller,* pp. 81–82, 89–90; Robert Vandewater, *The Tourist, or Pocket Manual for Travellers* (New York: Harper & Brothers, 1834); Samuel De

Veaux, *The Traveller's Own Book to Saratoga Springs, Niagara Falls, and Canada* (Buffalo, N.Y.: Faxton & Read, 1841), pp. 210–13; Cozzens, *Acadia*, p. 95, and see also pp. 139–40, 202–3.

26. Thompson in Doyle, ed., *Yankees in Canada*, pp. 56–57.

27. Myers, *Sketches*, to p. 193, and pp. 298–300; Burr, *Descriptive View*, pp. 14, 27; "Niagara," *Harper's New Monthly Magazine* 7 (Aug. 1853): 303; Sylvester B. Beckett, *Guide Book of the Atlantic and St. Lawrence and St. Lawrence and Atlantic Railroads* (Portland, Maine: Sanborn & Carter and H. J. Little & Co., 1853), p. 144, for Island Pond reference; *Tunis's Topographical Guide*, pp. 73, 94–103; *Hunter's Panoramic Guide*, pp. 18, 21, 42–43; J. Disturnell, *The Great Lakes, or Inland Seas of America* (New York: Charles Scribner, 1865), pp. 21–22, 30–31, 152, and *The Traveler's Guide to the Fashionable Northern Tour through the United States and Canada* (New York: American News Company, 1864), pp. 113–60.

28. Seward, *Seward at Washington*, 1:319.

29. Goldwin Smith, *Canada and the Canadian Question* (1891; reprint, Toronto: University of Toronto Press, 1971). Carl Berger, *The Sense of Power: Studies in the Ideas of Canadian Imperialism, 1867–1914* (Toronto: University of Toronto Press, 1970), deals with Canadian nationalists who supported imperial unity based on an Anglo-Saxon ideology that included Americans. Donald Warner, *The Idea of Continental Union: Agitation for the Annexation of Canada to the United States, 1849–1893* (Lexington: University of Kentucky Press, 1960). Warner's book balances Berger's transatlantic axis. See also Milton Plesur, "The Quest for a Canadian-American Consensus," in his *America's Outward Thrust: Approaches to Foreign Affairs, 1865–1890* (Dekalb: Northern Illinois University Press, 1971), pp. 182–97.

30. Schultz, *Travels*, pp. 50, 55, 95–97. Citation taken from his letter dated 6 Aug. 1807, p. 59.

31. Darby, *New York to Detroit*, pp. 84–86, 99n. Darby traveled for a time with the boundary survey party under Major Joseph Delafield. Sansom, *Travels*, p. 43. Silliman, *Remarks*, p. 397. The 1841 guide is De Veaux, *Traveller's Own Book*, p. 212; Myers, *Sketches*, p. 193.

32. Silliman, *Remarks*, p. 287. On guides, see Vandewater, *The Tourist*; *Pictorial Guide*, p. 184. *Ontario Company Handbook*, pp. 64–65; *Tunis's Guide*, pp. 28–29; *Hunter's Panoramic Guide*, p. 30.

33. Darby, *New York to Detroit*, pp. 150, 189.

34. Sansom, *Travels*, p. 73; Silliman, *Remarks*, pp. 277, 363.

35. Myers, *Sketches*, pp. 296–99; Cozzens, *Acadia*, Chaps. 1, 5; *Coit Correspondence*; *Appleton's Northern and Eastern Guide* (New York: D. Appleton & Co., 1850), pp. 68–69.

36. *Northern Traveller*, pp. 81–82, 89–90, 161; Hulett, *Every Man His Own Guide*, pp. 44–45; Tanner, *Traveller's Handbook*, pp. 139, 145–46; George Thayer, "From Vermont to Lake Superior in 1845," *Michigan Historical Collections* 30 (1906): 549–66.

37. Disturnell, *Eastern Tourist*, pp. 133, 144; and *American and Euro-*

pean Guide, pp. 60–80, for timetables; pp. 126, 128, for telegraph lines; and p. 130 for hotels. *Great Lakes*, pp. 30–33 for lake trade; p. 141 for Pembina; p. 152 for citation.

38. Burr, *Descriptive View*, p. 14; Ontario Company, *Handbook; Times*, 15, 29 Aug. 1853; "Niagara," *Harper's New Monthly Magazine* 7 (Aug. 1853): 303; "A Trip to Newfoundland," ibid., 11 (Dec. 1855): 45–57; Beckett, *Guide Book*, pp. 144–63.

CHAPTER 8

1. Fred Landon, ed., "The Diary of Benjamin Lundy Written during his Journey through Upper Canada, January 1832," *Ontario Historical Society, Papers and Records* 19 (1922): 110–33; Robin Winks, *The Blacks in Canada* (New Haven, Conn.: Yale University Press, 1971), pp. 154–57.

2. "Diary of Lundy," 121.

3. See William H. Pease and Jane H. Pease, *Black Utopia: Negro Communal Experiments in America* (Madison: State Historical Society of Wisconsin, 1963), chaps. 3–4. Fred Landon, "Negro Colonization Schemes in Upper Canada Before 1860," *Proceedings and Transactions of the Royal Society of Canada* 3d ser., 23 (May 1929): 73–80.

4. Winks, *Blacks in Canada*, p. 102; Fred Landon, *Western Ontario and the American Frontier* (Toronto: Ryerson Press, 1941), pp. 204–17.

5. Fred Landon, "When Uncle Tom's Cabin Came to Canada," *Ontario History* 44 (Jan. 1952): 1–5; Landon, "Abolitionist Interest in Upper Canada," ibid., 44 (Oct. 1952): 165–72. Norman MacRae, "Crossing the Detroit River to Find Freedom," *Michigan History* 67 (Mar.–Apr. 1983): 35–39; Larry Gara, *The Liberty Line: The Legend of the Underground Railroad* (Lexington: University of Kentucky Press, 1961), pp. 8, 36–37, 65.

6. Likers in John W. Blassingame, ed., *Slave Testimony: Two Centuries of Letters, Speeches, Interviews, and Autobiographies* (Baton Rouge: Louisiana State University Press, 1977), p. 396. See also comments by ex-slaves pp. 397, 401, 405–6, 410, 411 n. 11, 432, 420.

7. Mary A. Shadd, *A Plea for Emigration; or, Notes of Canada West, in its Moral, Social, and Political Aspect* (Detroit: George W. Pattison, 1852).

8. F. H. Howay, "The Negro Immigration into Vancouver Island in 1858," *Proceedings and Transactions of the Royal Society of Canada* 3d ser., 29 (May 1935): 145–56, citation from 155–56. See also Philip S. Foner, "The Colored Inhabitants of Vancouver Island," *B.C. Studies* 8 (Winter 1970–71): 29–33. Ralph E. Weber, "Riot in Victoria, 1860," *Journal of Negro History* 56 (Apr. 1971): 141–48, links the increase of antinegro feelings in Victoria to the rise in numbers of blacks in the 1850s.

9. See B. B. Thatcher, *North American Review* 35 (July 1832): 128–30; Garrison to Wendel Phillips, 4 June 1829, to Louis Kossuth, Feb. 1852, to Helen E. Garrison, 17 Oct. 1853, Walter M. Merrill and Louis Ruchames, eds., *The Letters of William Lloyd Garrison* (Cambridge, Mass.: Belknap

Press of Harvard University Press, 1971), 2:489, for notes on Wilson, 486 n. 12; 4:172, 274; Gara, *Liberty Line*, pp. 73–75, 85, 93.

10. Clay to Albert Gallatin, 24 Feb. 1827, William R. Manning, ed., *Diplomatic Correspondence of the United States: Canadian Relations, 1784–1860* (Washington, D.C.: Carnegie Foundation, 1940–43), 2:132–33, 135; to Barbour, 13 June 1828, ibid., 181. Fred Landon, "Canadian Negroes and the John Brown Raid," *Journal of Negro History* 6 (Apr. 1921): 174–82.

11. Roman J. Zorn, "Criminal Extradition Menaces the Canadian Haven for Fugitive Slaves, 1841–1861," *Canadian Historical Review* 38 (Dec. 1957): 284–94; Fred Landon, "The Negro Migration to Canada after 1850," *Journal of Negro History* 5 (Jan. 1920): 22–36; Gara, *Liberty Line*, pp. 102–3, 149, 161–63.

12. *New York Times*, 22 July 1852; Henry Bibb's report, 9 Nov. 1852; article on Bibb's problems, 12 Apr. 1853.

13. "An Autobiography of the Reverend Josiah Henson," Robin Winks et al., eds., *Four Fugitive Slave Narratives* (Reading, Pa.: Addison-Wesley Publishing Company, 1969), pp. 69–70, 109; Samuel Ringgold Ward, *Autobiography of a Fugitive Negro* (1885; reprint, New York: New York Times & Arno Press, 1968), pp. 135, 182; Benjamin Drew, *A Northside View of Slavery. The Refugee: or, The Narratives of Fugitive Slaves in Canada* (Boston: J. P. Jewett and Company, 1856), reprints interviews with many blacks living in the provinces by the early 1850s. Samuel G. Howe, *The Refugees from Slavery in Canada West* (Boston: Wright & Potter, 1864), pp. 28, 35–50, 103–4.

14. *New York Herald*, 1 Feb. 1861, *Charlestown Advertiser*, 29 May 1861, in Howard Perkins, ed., *Northern Editorials on Secession* (Washington, D.C.: American Historical Society, 1942), 1:408–13; 2:971.

15. Robin Winks, *Canada and the United States: The Civil War Years* (Baltimore: Johns Hopkins University Press, 1960). Allen P. Stouffer, "Canadian-American Relations, 1861–1871" (Ph.D. diss., Claremont Graduate School, 1971). See also R. F. Sams, "The Congressional Attitude towards Canada during the 1860s" (Master's thesis, Queens University, 1947), pp. 62–101.

16. Executive Order, 21 Nov. 1862, James D. Richardson, ed. and comp., *A Compilation of the Messages and Papers of the Presidents, 1789–1908* (Washington, D.C.: Bureau of National Literature and Art, 1908), 4:125–26.

17. Apart from Winks and Wilfred Bovey, "Confederate Agents in Canada during the American Civil War," *Canadian Historical Review* 2 (Mar. 1921): 46–57, studies on Confederates in Canada are partisan. See, for example, Oscar Kinchen's *Daredevils of the Confederate Army: The Story of the St. Albans Raiders* (Boston: Christopher Publishing House, 1959), *Confederate Operations in Canada and the North* (North Quincy, Mass.: Christopher Publishing House, 1970), and Clayton Gray's lurid *Conspiracy in Canada* (Montreal: L'Atelier Press, 1957).

18. William H. Seward, 4, 24 Oct. 1864, "Diary, or Notes on the War," George E. Baker, ed., *The Works of William H. Seward* (Boston: Houghton,

Mifflin and Company, 1884), 5:155, 158–60; Howard K. Beale, ed., *The Diary of Gideon Welles* (New York: W. W. Norton & Company, 1960), 2:152. Millard Fillmore worried about such attacks in 1862. See "Memorial to Congress," 10 Jan. 1862, and "Memorial to New York Legislature," Frank Severance, ed., *The Millard Fillmore Papers* (Buffalo, N.Y.: Buffalo Historical Society, 1907), 2:407–12. See also 415–16. Horatio Seymour to New York government, 5 Jan. 1864, Charles Lincoln ed., *Messages from the Governors* (Albany: L. J. Lyon Company, 1909), 5:550.

19. On the Joshua Giddings Affair, see "Arrest of the American Consul General to the British Provinces," 16 Feb. 1864, 38th Cong., 1st sess., H. Ex. Doc. 39, *U.S. Serials Set* 1189; Winks, *Civil War Years*, pp. 269–72.

20. M. Harper to Brig. Gen. Thomas Rowley, 26 Aug. 1864. *The War of the Rebellion: Official Records of the Union and Confederate Armies* (Washington, D.C.: Government Printing Office, 1893), ser. 1, 43:929–31.

21. Dix to Stanton, 25 Nov. 1863, *Correspondence Relating to the Fenian Invasion, and the Rebellion of the Southern States* (Ottawa: Hunter, Ros & Company, 1869), p. 35; Giddings to Seward, 12 Jan. 1864, ibid.; J. T. Howard to F. W. Seward, 26 May 1864, ibid., p. 36; Col. R. Hill to Capt. C. H. Potter, 30 July 1864, ibid., p. 36; Union surveillance of these Confederate agents can be partly traced in Instructions to Consuls, Department of State, Ser. 1, 9–11, National Archives, Washington, D.C.

22. Kinchen, *Daredevils* is colorful, but Winks, *Civil War Years*, chap. 14, is a scholarly treatment.

23. Reuben Fenton to New York Government, 3 Jan. 1865, Lincoln, ed., *Messages*, 5:612; Major General Dix to E. M. Stanton, 22 Nov. 1864, *Correspondence Relating to Rebellion*, p. 40; Seward to C. F. Adams, 6 Dec. 1864, ibid., p. 47; Seward, 14, 19, 27 Dec. 1864, and 1 Jan, 27 Mar. 1865, Baker, *Works of Seward*, 5:166–68; Lincoln to Congress, 6 Dec. 1864, Richardson, *Messages and Papers*, 6:246.

24. George Strong, 14 Dec. 1864, Allan Nevins and Milton H. Thomas, eds., *The Diary of George Templeton Strong, 1835–1875* (New York: Octagon Books, 1974), 3:528. "Executive Order," 8 Mar. 1865, Richardson, *Messages and Papers*, 6:282; Seward, 27 Mar. 1865, Baker, *Works of Seward*, 5:179; Harold Davis, *An International Community on the St. Croix (1604–1930)* (Orono: University of Maine Press, 1950), pp. 193–95.

25. Gray, *Conspiracy in Canada*, is weak, but does cover Booth's visit.

26. On escaped Confederates, see Winks, *Civil War Years*, pp. 131–34, 140–45; Letters of Charles Edward Coons, MG 24, B 152, Public Archives of Canada; *New York Times*, 29 June 1864; Wood Gray, *The Hidden Civil War: The Story of the Copperheads* (1942; reprint, New York: Viking Press, 1964), pp. 166–69, 179–85, 206–7, 216.

27. A. J. Clark, "When Jefferson Davis Visited Canada," Ontario Historical Society, *Papers and Records* 19 (1922): 87–89.

28. A. S. Dinen to Col. James B. Fry, 29 June 1863, *Official Records*, ser. 3, 3:425–26; and George Shaw, Third District of Massachusetts, to James

Fry, 13 July 1863, ibid., 485. Ella Lonn, *Desertion During the Civil War* (1928; reprint, Gloucester, Mass.: Peter Smith, 1966), pp. 201–3, 233.

29. Martin J. Havran, "Windsor and Detroit Relations during the Civil War," *Michigan History* 38 (Dec. 1954): 371–89.

30. William F. Raney, "Recruiting and Crimping in Canada for the Northern Forces, 1861–1865," *Mississippi Valley Historical Review* 10 (June 1923): 21–33; Marguerite Hamer, "Luring Canadian Soldiers into Union Lines during the War between the States," *Canadian Historical Review* 27 (June 1946): 150–62.

CHAPTER 9

1. Thomas Le Duc, "Israel Andrews," in *Dictionary of American Biography*, ed. Allan Johnson and Dumas Malone (New York: Charles Scribner's Sons, 1955–77), Supplement 1, pp. 29–30; "I. D. Andrews and the Reciprocity Treaty of 1854," *Canadian Historical Review* 15 (Dec. 1934): 437–38; William D. Overman, "I. D. Andrews and Reciprocity in 1854: An Episode in Dollar Diplomacy," ibid., 15 (Sept. 1934): 248–63; Donald C. Masters, "A Further Word on I. D. Andrews and the Reciprocity Treaty of 1854," ibid., 17 (June 1936): 159–67, are the only works dealing with Andrews's life.

2. Andrews to James Buchanan, 1 Nov. 1848, Department of State, Miscellaneous Documents Relating to Reciprocity Negotiations, RG 59, T-493, vol. 1, 1848–1854, National Archives, Washington, D.C.; 6 July 1849, Instructions and Subsequent Dispatches, Department of State, Special Agents, vols. 16–17. Quotations taken from dispatches of 31 July, 29 August, 20 October, 6 December 1849.

3. Israel Andrews, *Report on the Trade and Commerce of the British North American Colonies with the United States and Other Countries Embracing Full and Complete Tabular Statements from 1820 to 1850* (Washington, D.C.: Government Printing Office, 1851). He also prepared a second volume, *Report upon the Trade and Commerce of the British North American Colonies and upon the Trade of the Great Lakes and Rivers* (Washington, D.C.: Government Printing Office, 1854). Andrews to Webster, 9 July 1851, Department of State, Special Agents 1849, vol. 16.

4. Andrews to William L. Marcy, 3 May 1853, Department of State, Dispatches from United States Consuls, RG 59, T-222, National Archives, Washington, D.C.; Andrews to Marcy, 13 May 1854, Special Agents, Department of State, vol. 16. The idea of the American mission is best handled by Frederick Merk, *Manifest Destiny and Mission in American History: A Reinterpretation* (New York: Alfred A. Knopf, 1963), pp. 261–65, and Russell B. Nye, "The American Sense of Mission," in Nye, *This Almost Chosen People: Essays in the History of American Ideas* (Toronto: Macmillan Company of Canada, 1966), pp. 164–207.

5. Andrews to Lewis Cass, 15 Apr. 1857, Department of State, Dis-

patches from Consuls, Montreal. The State Department investigated his claims but balked at more payments. Overman, "Andrews and Reciprocity"; Le Duc, "Andrews and Reciprocity," 437–38, and "Israel Andrews," and Masters, "A Further Word on Andrews," 159–67 all cover the financial difficulties. Broadsides to President and William L. Marcy, 31 March 1856, Department of State, Special Agents 1849, vol. 16.

6. Background for the provincial perspective can be found in Cephas D. Allin and George Jones, *Annexation, Preferential Trade, and Reciprocity* (1912; reprint, Westport, Conn.: Greenwood Press, 1971); Gilbert N. Tucker, *The Canadian Commercial Revolution, 1845–1851* (New Haven, Conn.: Yale University Press, 1936); Donald C. Masters, *The Reciprocity Treaty of 1854* (1937; reprint, Toronto: McClelland and Stewart, 1963); Lester B. Shippee, *Canadian-American Relations, 1849–1874* (New York: Russell & Russell, 1939), to p. 88; Donald F. Warner, *The Idea of Continental Union: Agitation for the Annexation of Canada to the United States, 1849–1893* (Lexington: University Press of Kentucky, 1960), pp. 30–35.

7. Bancroft to James Buchanan, 29 Jan. 1849, William R. Manning, ed., *Diplomatic Correspondence of the United States: Canadian Relations, 1784–1860* (Washington, D.C.: Carnegie Foundation, 1940–43), 4:245, and Bancroft to John Clayton, 9 Mar. 1849, ibid., 252; Clayton to John F. Crampton, 26 June 1849, ibid., 12; Webster to Crampton, 17 July 1852, and to Andrews, 1 Sept. 1852, ibid., 43, 45. Kenneth E. Shewmaker, " 'Hook and Line, and Bob and Sinker': Daniel Webster and the Fisheries Dispute of 1852," *Diplomatic History* 9 (Spring 1985): 113–29.

8. Marcy to Andrews, 12 Sept. 1853, Manning, *Diplomatic Correspondence*, 4:82. See Marcy to Andrews, 15 Apr. 1854, to James Buchanan, 5 June 1854, to Mr. Rogsen, 12 June 1854, Letterbook, William Learned Marcy Papers, Manuscript Division, Library of Congress, Washington, D.C. These efforts are described in Frederick E. Haynes, *The Reciprocity Treaty with Canada of 1854* (Baltimore: Guggenheimer, Weil & Co., 1892); J. Laurence Laughlin & H. Parker Willis, *Reciprocity* (New York: Baker & Taylor Co., 1903), chap. 2; Charles C. Tansill, *The Canadian Reciprocity Treaty of 1854* (Baltimore: Johns Hopkins University Press, 1922); Ivor Spencer, *The Victor and the Spoils: A Life of William L. Marcy* (Providence: Brown University Press, 1969), pp. 246–49, 257–62, 306–8.

9. Pierce, Second Annual Message, 4 Dec. 1854, James D. Richardson, ed. and comp., *Compilation of the Messages and Papers of the Presidents, 1789–1908* (Washington, D.C.: Bureau of National Literature and Art, 1908), 5:277; C. Dorwin to William L. Marcy, 5 Oct. 1854 and 1 Nov. 1855, Department of State, Consular Dispatches, Montreal, reel 2; Marcy to Israel Andrews, 12 Sept. 1853, Manning, *Diplomatic Correspondence*, 4:82.

10. Andrews to James Buchanan, 1 Nov. 1848, Department of State, Documents on Reciprocity; to John Clayton, 31 July 1849, vol. 1; Department of State, Special Agents 1849, vol. 17; to William L. Marcy, 31 Mar. 1854, and 13 May 1854, ibid.; "Report of the Secretary of the Treasury

on the Trade and Commerce of the British-American Colonies with the United States and other countries since 1829," 6 Feb. 1851, 51st Cong., 2d sess., S. Ex. Doc. 23. Andrews wrote the first part of this bulky document. "Report," 6 Feb. 1851; "Reciprocal Trade with the British American Colonies," 11 Feb. 1853, 32d Cong., 2d sess., H. Rep. 4, *U.S. Serials Set* 687; and "Report on Reciprocity Treaty," ibid. *Congressional Globe, Containing the Debates and Proceedings* (Washington, D.C.: F. & J. Rives and George Bailey, 1834–74), 30th Cong., 1st sess., pp. 391, 398, 723; 30th Cong., 2d sess., pp. 182–85, 327–32; 31st Cong., 1st sess., vol. 1: 238, 261, 701–2, 893; vol. 2: 1908, 31st Cong., 1st sess., Appendix, pp. 600–603; 31st Cong., 2d sess., Appendix, pp. 750–52.

11. *Merchant's Magazine and Commercial Review* 28 (Mar. 1853): 275–88, citation on 280; *American Almanac* (1855), pp. 142, 315; (1856), pp. 151, 342; and especially (1857), pp. 130, 340, 374–75; *Merchant's Magazine* 33 (Aug. 1855): 200–207; "The Reciprocity Treaty," *North American Review* 155 (Oct. 1854): 464–85; *National Intelligencer*, 2 Aug. 1854; *The American Railroad Journal*, 1 Dec. 1855, 28:757; *New York Times*, 8 May 1858; *De Bow's Review* 23 (July 1857): 98, and 26 (Apr. 1859): 450; George A. Rawlyk, "Thomas Coltin Keefer and the St. Lawrence–Great Lakes Commercial System," *Inland Seas* 19 (Fall 1963): 190–94.

12. Laurence Officer and Lawrence B. Smith, "The Canadian-American Reciprocity Treaty of 1855 to 1866," *Journal of Economic History* 28 (Dec. 1968): 598–623. Data from Masters, *Reciprocity*, pp. 117, 121, 124; Allen P. Stouffer, "Canadian-American Relations, 1861–1871" (Ph.D. diss., Claremont Graduate School, 1971), pp. 41–44; E. H. Derby, *A Preliminary Report on the Treaty of Reciprocity with Great Britain* (Washington, D.C.; Treasury Department, 1866), pp. 5, 14, 23, 32, 37, and U.S. Congress, Committee on Commerce, "Report on Reciprocity Treaty with Great Britain," in *Report of Minister of Finance on the Reciprocity Treaty with the United States, also the Memorial of the Chamber of Commerce of St. Paul, Minnesota, and Reports of Congress, U.S., Thereon* (Quebec: Stewart, Derbishire and George Desbarats, 1862), pp. 49–50.

13. Norton to Marcy, 20 Mar. 1854, Manning, *Diplomatic Correspondence*, 4:540; Marcy to Andrews, 25 Nov. 1854, Department of State, Instructions to Consuls, RG 59, E-54, ser. 1, 4:347, National Archives, Washington, D.C.; Dorwin to Marcy, Report 9, 1 Dec. 1854, Dispatch 33, 9 Oct. 1855, Department of State, Consular Dispatches, Montreal; Dorwin to Marcy, 3, 5 Feb. 1857, ibid.; Albert Pillsbury to Lewis Cass, 12 Mar. 1857, Manning, *Diplomatic Correspondence*, 4:676–77; John Babson, 23 May 1859, "Letters and Reports Received by the Secretary of the Treasury from Special Agents, 1854–1861," Department of the Treasury, RG 36, M-177, Reel 2, National Archives, Washington, D.C.

14. Haynes, *Reciprocity Treaty*, pp. 13–14; Laughlin and Willis, *Reciprocity*, chap. 2; Tansill, *Canadian Reciprocity*, pp. 32–78; Roy F. Nichols, *Franklin Pierce: Young Hickory of the Granite Hills*, 2d ed. rev. (Philadelphia: University of Pennsylvania Press, 1958), pp. 263–65, 343–44, 356;

Robert Scribner, "The Diplomacy of William L. Marcy: Secretary of State, 1853–1857" (Ph.D. diss., University of Virginia, 1949), pp. 313–37; Masters, *Reciprocity Treaty*, pp. 29–47.

15. Akira Iriye, *From Nationalism to Internationalism: U.S. Foreign Policy to 1914* (London: Routledge & Kegan Paul, 1977); and "Culture and Power: International Relations as Intercultural Relations," *Diplomatic History* 3 (Spring 1979): 115–28; Morell Heald and Lawrence S. Kaplan, *Culture and Diplomacy: The American Experience* (Westport, Conn.: Greenwood Press, 1977). Also on American foreign policy as a projection of national culture are James A. Field, Jr., *America and the Mediterranean World, 1776–1882* (Princeton, N.J.: Princeton University Press, 1964), and William A. Williams's several books.

16. W. E. Greening, "The Lumber Industry in the Ottawa Valley and the American Market in the Nineteenth Century," *Ontario History* 62 (June 1970): 134–36; A. R. M. Lower, *The North American Assault on the Canadian Forest: A History of the Lumber Trade Between Canada and the United States* (Toronto: Ryerson Press, 1938), pp. 1–122, 129, 132; Masters, *Reciprocity Treaty*, pp. 112, 117, 121.

17. Jesse Hawley, *An Essay on the Enlargement of the Erie Canal* (Lockport, N.Y.: Courier Office, 1840), pp. 6–8; Arthur M. Johnson and Barry Supple, *Boston Capital and Western Railroads: A Study in Nineteenth-Century Railroad Investment Process* (Cambridge, Mass.: Harvard University Press, 1967), pp. 115–21; Peter Baskerville, "Americans in Britain's Backyard: The Railway Era in Upper Canada 1850–1900," *Business History Review* 55 (Autumn 1981): 314–36; John A. Poor, "First Article on the St. Lawrence and Atlantic Railway" for *Portland Advertiser*, 10 Sept. 1844, in *The First International Railway and the Colonization of New England: Life and Writings of John Alfred Poor*, ed. Laura E. Poor (New York: G. P. Putnam's Sons, 1892), pp. 147–53; *Railroad Journal*, 14 Feb. 1852, 25:109, and 6 Mar. 1852, 25:152–54, are two of many articles on provincial railroad affairs this periodical published each year.

18. Officer and Smith, "Canadian-American Reciprocity," 605–6, argue that increased trade after the treaty came from smuggling that surfaced. See also Harold Davis, *An International Community on the St. Croix (1604–1930)* (Orono: University of Maine Press, 1950), pp. 208–35, for the impact of reciprocity on a closely knit segment of the American-provincial borderland.

19. *Albany Argus*, 30 Jan. 1849; "Statement Exhibiting the Trade Between the British North American Colonies and the Districts of Passamaquoddy, Portland, Boston, and New York during the Years ending December 31, 1828 and 1831," Secretary of the Treasury to the House of Representatives, 4 Apr. 1838, 25th Cong., 2d sess., H. Doc. 300, *U. S. Serials Set* 329, pp. 218–19; *American Almanac* (1835), pp. 300–302, and (1849), pp. 218–19; Department of State, Dispatches from Consuls, Halifax, T-469; St. John, T-485. See also letter from Secretary of the Treasury with Report on Reciprocity Treaty, 1 Feb. 1864, 38th Cong., 1st sess., H. Ex. Doc. 32, *U. S.*

Serials Set 1189, p. 6; Walter Johnson, *The Coal Trade of British America* (Washington, D.C.: Taylor & Maury, 1850).

20. Le Duc, "Andrews"; Overman, "I. D. Andrews," pp. 248–63, and letter from T. H. Le Duc, (Dec. 1934), ibid., 437–38; Andrews to James Buchanan, 1 Nov. 1848, Department of State, Miscellaneous Documents on Reciprocity, RG 59, T-493, vol. 1; to John Clayton, 31 July and 1, 29 Aug. 1849, Department of State, Special Agents 1849, vol. 16; Andrews to Clayton, 9 Feb. 1850, Department of State, Consular Dispatches, Montreal, vol. 1, Reel 1; to Daniel Webster, 9 July 1851, Department of State, Special Agents 1849, vol. 16.

21. Norton to John Clayton, 21 Nov. 1849, Manning, *Diplomatic Correspondence*, 4:318–19; C. Dorwin to William Marcy, 1 Nov. 1855, Department of State, Consular Dispatches, Montreal, vol. 2, reel 2; Albert Pilsbury to Lewis Cass, 12 Mar. 1857, Manning, *Diplomatic Correspondence*, 4:676–77.

22. George Bancroft to James Buchanan, 29 Jan. 1849, Manning, *Diplomatic Correspondence*, 4:245; Bancroft to John Clayton, 9 Mar. 1849, ibid., 252; Daniel Webster to John F. Crampton, 17 July 1852, ibid., 43; William Marcy to Israel Andrews, 12 Sept. 1853, ibid., 82; Marcy to James Buchanan, 11 Mar. 1854, Marcy Papers, vol. 48.

23. "Commercial Reciprocity and the American System," *United States Magazine and Democratic Review* 14 (May 1844): 447–64; "Repeal of the British Corn Laws," ibid., 29 (Nov. 1851): 385; "Who Owns British North America?" ibid., 31 (Aug. 1852): 113–33; part 2, ibid. (Sept, 1852): 225–43.

24. *Railroad Journal*, 3 Jan. 1852, 25:5; 6 Mar. 1852, 25:154; 12 June 1852, 25:376; Andrews's report was discussed at length 18 Dec. 1852, 25:801–4; *Philadelphia Gazette* quoted ibid., 25 Dec. 1852, 25:826–27; ibid., 12 Aug. 1854, 27:507; "Comparing American and Foreign Securities," ibid., July 1855, 28:417.

25. "Our Commercial Relations with the British American Colonies," *De Bow's Review* 12 (Mar. 1852): 225–36; "The States of British America and the United States: Freedom of Trade and Union of Interests," *Merchant's Magazine* 26 (June 1852): 660, 681.

26. "Reciprocity with the British Provinces," *Merchant's Magazine* 28 (Mar. 1853): 277–78; 285. Charles Levi Woodbury wrote on a narrow economic theme in "Commerce with the Canadas and with the British North American Colonies," ibid. 30 (May 1854): 561–76; Seymour, "Canada: Its Commerce and Resources," ibid., 33 (Aug. 1855): 200–207.

27. "The Reciprocity Treaty," *North American Review* 155 (Oct. 1854): 464–85; citation on 483.

28. *National Intelligencer*, 26 July 1854 and 2 Aug. 1854.

29. *Albany Argus*, 1846 and 1849 passim, quote on Corn Laws from 10 Mar. 1846. See also 30 Jan. and 13 Feb. 1849.

30. *New York Times*, 27 Sept., 22 Oct. 1851; 31 July, 27 Oct. 1852; Senator Horatio Seymour's speech favoring the Reciprocity Treaty appeared in whole in the 14 Feb. 1853 edition.

31. "Report of Secretary of Treasury," 6 Feb. 1851, 51st Cong., 2d sess., S. Ex. Doc. 23, pp. 22–23.

32. Heald and Kaplan, *Culture and Diplomacy*, pp. 92–123; F. R. Dulles, *Yankees and Samurai: America's Role in the Emergence of Modern Japan, 1791–1900* (New York: Harper & Row, 1965), pp. 55–57, 64–65, 70–73.

33. G. Bhagat, *Americans in India, 1784–1860* (New York: New York University Press, 1970); Field, *America and Mediterranean*, chaps. 7–8.

34. Chicago *Democrat* cited by *New York Times*, 23 July 1852; *Democratic Review* 17 (July-Aug. 1845): 9–10; *New York Daily Tribune*, 17 June 1854; *Niles' Weekly National Register*, 1 Feb. 1845, 66:345, and ibid. 15 Feb. 1845, 375–76.

35. Allin and Jones, *Annexation and Reciprocity*, pp. 374–84; Warner, *Idea of Union*, pp. 23–27.

36. Andrews to Secretary of State, 28 June 1849, Department of State, Special Agents 1849, vol. 16; William Duane, *Canada and the Continental Congress* (Philadelphia: Edward Gaskill, 1850), p. 19.

37. Albert K. Weinberg, *Manifest Destiny: A Study of Nationalist Expansion in American History* (Baltimore: Johns Hopkins University Press, 1935), pp. 224–25.

38. Joseph Sansom, *Travels in Lower Canada* (New York: Kirk & Mercein, 1817), pp. 44, 47–48, 63–64; Reginald Horsman, *Race and Manifest Destiny: The Origins of American Racial Anglo-Saxonism* (Cambridge, Mass.: Harvard University Press, 1981), p. 283; *New York Evening Star*, 29 Jan. 1835.

39. Winfield Scott to John C. Hamilton, 29 June 1849, cited in Charles W. Eliot, *Winfield Scott: The Soldier and the Man* (New York: Macmillan Company, 1937), p. 599; *New York Herald* cited in Allin and Jones, *Annexation and Reciprocity*, p. 383; "Resolutions of the New York Assembly," cited ibid., p. 379.

40. Andrews to William Marcy, 3 May 1853, Department of State, Consular Dispatches, Montreal, Reel 2; Marcy to Andrews, 12 Sept. 1853, Manning, *Diplomatic Correspondence*, 4:82; Nichols, *Pierce*, pp. 343–44; C. Dorwin to Marcy, 1 Nov. 1855, Department of State, Consular Dispatches, Montreal, Reel 2; Albert Pilsbury to Lewis Cass, 12 Mar. 1857, Manning, *Diplomatic Correspondence*, 4:767–77.

41. *Railroad Journal*, 12 Aug. 1854, 27:507; "The Reciprocity Treaty," *North American Review* 155 (Oct. 1854): 483.

42. *National Intelligencer*, 26 July, 2 Aug. 1854; *Frank Leslie's Illustrated Newspaper*, 20 Dec. 1856, pp. 33–34, 41.

43. Masters, *Reciprocity Treaty*, pp. 105–28; Lower, *Assault on Canadian Forest*, p. 129; Officer and Smith, "Canadian-American Reciprocity," 598–623; Boston Board of Trade, *Third Annual Report* (Boston: George C. Rand & Avery, Printers, 1857), pp. 43–46, 129, 264–70; Boston Board of Trade, *Fifth Annual Report* (Boston: T. R. Marvin, 1859), pp. 63–68; *Boston Evening Transcript*, 8 Aug. 1854; James Chapman, "Relations of Maine and

New Brunswick in the Era of Reciprocity, 1849–1867" (Master's Thesis, University of New Brunswick, 1957), pp. 25–33.

44. "Remonstrance," 16 June 1868, H. Misc. Doc. 138, *U.S. Serials Set* 1350, by Pennsylvania collieries; C. Fields to W. P. Fessenden, 26 Oct. 1864, cited in James G. Snell, "The Eagle and the Butterfly: Some American Attitudes towards British North America, 1864–1867" (Ph.D. diss., Queens University, 1971), p. 36; Joshua Giddings to J. A. Giddings, 23 Jan. 1864, William D. Overman, "Some Letters of Joshua R. Giddings on Reciprocity," *Canadian Historical Review* 16 (Sept. 1935): 294; *New York Times*, 17 Jan. 1866; William B. Parker, *The Life and Public Services of Justin Morrill* (Boston: Houghton, Mifflin Company, 1924), pp. 97, 149–51, 320–21.

45. Giddings to his son, 23 Jan. 1864, Overman, "Letters of Giddings on Reciprocity," p. 294; Fields to William P. Fessenden, 26 Oct. 1864, cited in Snell, "Eagle and Butterfly," p. 36. *New York Times*, 17 Jan. 1866; dispatches from American consuls in the provinces noted difficulties the treaty caused merchants in the cross-border trade. See David Thurston to William Hunter, 23, 27 June 1865, Department of State, Dispatches, Toronto, and Cleveland Merchants to Honorable Hugh McCulloch, Secretary of the Treasury, 27 Jan. 1866, ibid. "Trade with Canada," Chamber of Commerce of the State of New York, *Fourth Annual Report* (New York: John W. Amerman, 1862), pp. 289–307.

46. Derby, *A Preliminary Report*, pp. 17–20, 26–28, 65–66. The President submitted this report to the Congress in February of 1867. Senate Speeches, 21 Dec. 1864, 11, 12 Jan. 1865, Charles Sumner, *The Works of Charles Sumner* (Boston: Lea & Shepard, 1870–73), 9:178–91.

47. McCulloch to Seward, 26 May 1868, 40th Cong., 2d sess., S. Misc. Doc. 87, *U.S. Serials Set* 1319, p. 3. See also Joe Patterson Smith, *The Republican Expansionists of the Early Reconstruction Era* (Chicago, 1933), pp. 42–72; Edward Stanwood, *American Tariff Controversies in the Nineteenth Century* (1903; reprint, New York & London: Garland Publishing, Inc., 1974) 2:134–37.

48. Derby, *A Preliminary Report*; Boston Board of Trade, *The Reciprocity Treaty between the United States and Great Britain of June 5, 1854* (Boston: T. R. Marvin & Son, 1865); "The Reciprocity Treaty—Shall it be Abrogated?" *Merchant's Magazine* 50 (May 1864): 376–87; *Boston Courier*, 15 Jan. 1866; Hamilton A. Hill, *Review of the Proceedings of the Detroit Convention* (Boston: J. H. Eastburn's Press, 1866); Masters, *Reciprocity Treaty*, pp. 70–87; Graeme S. Mount, "Maine and the End of Reciprocity in 1866," *Maine Historical Quarterly* 26 (Summer 1986): 22–39; Stouffer, "Canadian-American Relations, 1861–1871," pp. 56–58; Warner, *Idea of Union*, pp. 35–47; Snell, "Eagle and Butterfly," pp. 16–45, 61–64, 80–96; Chamber of Commerce of the State of New York, *Fifth Annual Report of the Chamber of Commerce for the State of New York* (New York: John W. Amerman, 1865), pp. 5–7; R. F. Sams, "The Congressional Attitude towards Canada during the 1860s" (Master's thesis, Queens University, 1947), pp. 73–83

traces consolidating congressional opposition to the Reciprocity Treaty. The vote was 38–8 for abrogation.

49. *Report of the Minister of Finance*, p. 32; *Railroad Journal*, 30 Apr. 1864, 37:417–18; 6 July 1864, 37:683, for citation; *Merchant's Magazine* 50 (May 1864): 376–77; 52 (Jan. 1865): 75; Boston Board, *Reciprocity*, pp. 9–22.

50. Derby, *Preliminary Report*, pp. 6, 20, 47–51, 65–66; *Boston Courier*, 15 Jan. 1866; Chamber of Commerce of the State of New York, *Report of the Select Committee on the Reciprocity Treaty as to Trade Between the British North American Provinces and the United States of America* (New York: John W. Amerman, 1865), pp. 37–38, 44; Chapman, "Maine and New Brunswick," pp. 107–9, 115.

51. J. D. Hayes, "Reciprocity with the British North American Provinces," in *"The Niagara Ship Canal" and "Reciprocity"* (Buffalo: Matthews & Warren, 1865), p. 46.

52. Israel Hatch, "Reciprocity," speech at the Commercial Convention at Detroit 14 July 1865, Hayes, *"Niagara Ship Canal,"* pp. 47–58; J. Johnston, "Speech," in Derby, *Report*, p. 82; Hill, *Proceedings of Detroit Convention*, pp. 38–39, 40–56, 63. Hill wrote widely on mid-nineteenth century commerce and served on the National Board of Trade in the 1860s and 1870s.

53. Sams, "Congressional Attitude," pp. 107–10. Walter La Feber, *The New Empire: An Interpretation of American Expansion, 1860–1898* (Ithaca, N.Y.: Cornell University Press, 1963), chap. 1; Iriye, *Nationalism to Internationalism*, to p. 52, sees several factors behind continuity—geopolitics, ideas, definitions of national and particular interests, and mass culture.

CHAPTER 10

1. Ernest Paolino, *The Foundations of American Empire: William H. Seward and American Foreign Policy* (Ithaca, N.Y.: Cornell University Press, 1973), is the best treatment of Seward in this context. But see also Walter G. Sharrow, "William Henry Seward and the Basis for American Empire, 1850–1860," *Pacific Historical Review* 36 (Aug. 1967): 325–42; Richard W. Van Alstyne, *The Rising American Empire* (New York: Oxford University Press, 1960), pp. 146, 162–77; Hallie MacPherson, "The Interest of William McKendree Gwin in the Purchase of Alaska, 1854–1861," *Pacific Historical Review* 3 (Mar. 1934): 31–33, 38; for an early Seward speech embracing these themes see "The Whale Fishery and American Commerce in the Pacific," 29 July 1862, pp. 6–7, *Speeches in the Senate Collected for William H. Seward* (n.p., n.d.).

2. Seward, "The Destiny of America," 14 Sept. 1853, George Baker, ed., *The Works of William H. Seward* (Boston: Houghton, Mifflin and Company, 1884), 4:123–24. Entire speech runs pp. 121–43.

3. Seward, 21, 22 August 1857, Frederick W. Seward, *Seward at Washing-*

ton (New York: Derby and Miller, 1891), 1:317, 319, for citations. Chapter 49 covers the provincial tour, including the journal.

4. Seward, "Political Equality the National Idea," 18 Sept. 1860, Baker, *Works of Seward*, 4:333; James Grant Snell, "The Eagle and the Butterfly: Some American Attitudes towards British North America, 1864–1867" (Ph.D. diss., Queens University, 1971), pp. 222–37.

5. *Communication of William H. Seward* (Washington, D.C.: Government Printing Office, 1864), p. 22; and see Abraham Lincoln to Congress, July 1861 and Jan. 1862, on participation in the 1862 London industrial exhibition. James D. Richardson, ed. and comp., *A Compilation of the Messages and Papers of the Presidents, 1789–1908* (Washington, D.C.: Bureau of National Literature and Art, 1908), 6:32, 61. See ibid., 128, 135–36, 187, 246, for Lincoln's references to transoceanic telegraphs.

6. Paolino, *Foundations of Empire*, pp. 8–16, and chaps. 3, 5; Seward, "The North Pacific Coast," August 1869, at Victoria, B.C., and "Speech," Sitka, Alaska, 12 Aug. 1869, Baker, *Works of Seward*, 5:570, 568; David Shi, "Seward's Attempt to Annex British Columbia, 1865–1869," *Pacific Historical Review* 47 (May 1978): 217–38. Stephen A. Douglas had also talked of a North American "zollverein" in *An American Continental Commercial Union or Alliance* (Washington, D.C.: Thomas McGill & Co., 1889). His comments were originally written in 1861, just after Southern secession.

7. Donald Marquand Dozer, "Anti-Expansionism during the Johnson Administration," *Pacific Historical Review* 12 (Sept. 1943): 253–75, and Joe Patterson Smith, *The Republican Expansionists of the Early Reconstruction Era* (Chicago, 1933), are the principal general studies. See also W. Stull Holt, *Treaties Defeated by the Senate: A Study of the Struggle between President and Senate over the Conduct of Foreign Relations* (Baltimore: Johns Hopkins University Press, 1933), pp. 107–11, 123–30.

8. Studies of postbellum expansionism and Canada are Theodore Blegen, "A Plan for the Union of British North America and the United States," *Mississippi Valley Historical Review* 4 (Mar. 1918): 470–83; James Callahan, "Americo-Canadian Relations Concerning Annexation, 1846–1871," *Indiana University Studies* 12 (1925): 187–214; A. O. MacRae, "When Annexation Was in Flower," *Dalhousie Review* 9 (Oct. 1929): 282–86; Ronald D. Tallman, "Annexation in the Maritimes? The Butler Mission to Charlottetown," ibid. 53 (Spring 1973): 97–112; Joe Patterson Smith, "American Republican Leadership and the Movement for the Annexation of Canada in the 1860s," Canadian Historical Association, *Annual Report* (1935), 67–75.

9. *New York Daily Tribune*, 4 July 1866.

10. E. H. Derby, "Commercial Relations with British America," report of the Secretary of the Treasury, 14 June 1866, 39th Cong., 1st sess., H. Ex. Doc. 128, *U.S. Serials Set* 1263, passim.

11. "Anglo-Saxon Mind and Its Great Thought," *Harper's New Monthly Magazine* 21 (Sept. 1860): 547–53; John Stahl Patterson, "American Des-

tiny," *Continental Monthly* 3 (Jan. 1863): 79–99, and ibid., (Feb. 1863), 160–68; citation on 162. *New York Daily Tribune*, 7 Apr. 1865; Adams to Seward, 16 Mar. 1865, cited in Snell, "Eagle and Butterfly," pp. 271–72. See also Orestes Brownson, *The American Republic* (1865), as cited in Charles Sanford, ed., *Manifest Destiny and the Imperialism Question* (New York: John Wiley & Sons, 1974), p. 62. See also Alexander Monro, *The United States and the Dominion of Canada* (Saint John, Nfld.: Barnes & Company, 1879), pp. 157–58; W. Fraser Rae, *Columbia and Canada: Notes on the Great Republic and the New Dominion* (New York: G. P. Putnam's Sons, 1879), pp. 313–15.

12. The best treatments of this are Maureen Robson, "The Alabama Claims and the Anglo-American Reconciliation 1865–1871," *Canadian Historical Review* 42 (Mar. 1941): 1–22; Doris Dashew, "The Story of an Illusion: The Plan to Trade the Alabama Claims for Canada," *Civil War History* 15 (Dec. 1969): 332–48.

13. David Donald, *Charles Sumner and the Rights of Man* (New York: Alfred A. Knopf, 1970), pp. 305–10, 392–94, 485–87; Sumner, "The Cession of Russian America to the United States," 9 Apr. 1867, *The Works of Charles Sumner* (Boston: Lee & Shepard, 1870–83), 11:218–23; "Prophetic Voices concerning America," *Atlantic Monthly* (1867), reprinted in *Works of Sumner*, 12:173–75, 181–83 for citation; on Canada for the *Alabama* claims, see "National Affairs at Home and Abroad," speech at Republican State Convention in Worcester, 22 Sept. 1869, ibid., 13:127–29. See also Sumner to John Motley, 11, 15 June 1869, Edward L. Pierce, *Memoir and Letters of Charles Sumner* (Boston: Roberts Brothers, 1894), 4:409, 410.

14. "The Annexation Fever," *The Nation*, 15 Apr. 1869, 8:289–90; J. B. Austin, "Manifest Destiny," *Lippincott's Magazine* 4 (Aug. 1869): 183–86; Henry Tuckerman, "American Diplomacy," *Atlantic Monthly* 22 (Sept. 1868): 348–58; George Bancroft to Hamilton Fish, 8 Oct. 1869, George Bancroft Papers, Massachusetts Historical Society; Brownson as cited in Sanford, *Manifest Destiny*, pp. 63–64.

15. Bennett cited in Albert K. Weinberg, *Manifest Destiny: A Study of Nationalist Expansion in American History* (Baltimore: Johns Hopkins University Press, 1933), p. 233. A. H. De Rosier, "American Annexation Sentiment Toward Canada, 1866–1871" (Master's thesis, University of South Carolina, 1955).

16. Derby, "Commercial Relations"; Israel Hatch, *Report upon the Commercial Relations of the United States with the Dominion of Canada* (Washington, D.C.: Government Printing Office, 1869); Josephus N. Larned, *Report on the State of Trade between the United States and British Possessions in North America* (Washington, D.C.: Government Printing Office, 1871), are the three major reports in this period.

17. Boston Board of Trade, *Report on the Northern Pacific Railroad* (Boston: J. H. Eastburn's Press, 1865), pp. 11–12; *American Railroad Journal*, 38 (1865), 39 (1866), passim.

18. John A. Poor, "The Transcontinental Railway," address at Turland,

Vermont, June 1869, Laura Poor, ed., *The First International Railway: Life and Writings of John Alfred Poor* (New York: G. P. Putnam's Sons, 1892), pp. 224, 244; John A. Poor, *Memorial in Behalf of the European and North American Railway Co.* (Augusta: Stevens & Sayward, 1861), pp. 42–43; Elda Garrison, "The Short Route to Europe: A History of the European and North American Railroad" (Master's thesis, University of Maine, Orono, 1950).

19. Peter Baskerville, "Americans in Britain's Backyard: The Railway Era in Upper Canada, 1850–1880," *Business History Review* 55 (Autumn, 1981): 314–36; Edward Phelps, "Foundations of the Canadian Oil Industry, 1850–1866," in *Profiles of a Province: Studies in the History of Ontario* (Toronto: Ontario Historical Society, 1967), pp. 156–65; J. G. Snell, "H. H. Emmons, Detroit's Agent in Canadian-American Relations, 1864–1866," *Michigan History* 56 (Winter, 1972): 302–18.

20. Department of State, Dispatches from United States Consuls, RG 59, Toronto (1866–71), T-491; see Thurston to Seward, 1 Jan. 1868, vol. 3, reel 3.

21. Sims to Hamilton Fish, 28 Oct. 1869, Department of State, Dispatches from Consuls, Prescott (1865–71), T-481; Montreal (1850–71), T-222. Farther east, B. Hammatt Norton at Pictou, Nova Scotia, believed that the end of reciprocity had devastated the local coal economy, encouraging talk of annexation to the United States to seek relief. Norton to Seward, 8 July, 8 Oct. 1867, Department of State, Dispatches from Consuls, Pictou (1859–71), vol. 8, roll 4.

22. "From the Extreme North-West," *New York Times*, 24 Aug. 1852, on the Métis in the Lord Selkirk settlement; *Harper's* 17 (Sept. 1858): 546–47, on American migration to British Columbia; Burdett Hart, "The New Northwest," *The New Englander* 17 (Nov. 1859): 995–1015; "The People of the Red River," *Harper's* 18 (Dec. 1858): 169–76. See also "To Red River and Beyond," ibid., 21 (Oct. 1860): 581–606, continued 22 (Feb. 1861): 306–22, a travel narrative that described the settlers, hinting at a borderland forming with the people of Minnesota to the south. "Central British America," *Atlantic Monthly* 5 (Jan. 1860): 103–8, noted the potential importance of Vancouver's harbor and the activity of Minnesotans to establish steamboats on the Red River.

23. This borderland has a surprisingly extensive historiography. See Donald F. Warner, "Drang Nach Norden: The United States and the Riel Rebellion," *Mississippi Valley Historical Review* 39 (Mar. 1953): 693–712; and Warner, *The Idea of Continental Union: Agitation for the Annexation of Canada to the United States, 1849–1893* (Lexington: University Press of Kentucky, 1960), pp. 105–22; Ruth Hafter, "The Riel Rebellion and Manifest Destiny," *Dalhousie Review* 45 (Winter, 1965–66): 447–56; Alvin Gluek, *Minnesota and the Manifest Destiny of the Canadian Northwest: A Study in Canadian-American Relations* (Toronto: University of Toronto Press, 1965); Fridley Russell, "When Minnesota Coveted Canada," *Minnesota History* 41 (Summer 1968): 76–79; and James G. Snell, "The Frontier

Sweep Northwest: American Perceptions of the British American Prairie West and the Point of Canadian Expansion (Circa 1870)," *Western Historical Quarterly* 11 (Oct. 1980): 381–400.

24. Background on Taylor in Snell, "Eagle and Butterfly," pp. 208–19, and the introduction in H. Bowsfield, ed., *The James Wicks Taylor Papers* (Winnipeg, 1968), to p. xxxix.

25. James Wicks Taylor, *Northwest British America and Its Relations to the State of Minnesota* (St. Paul, Minn.: Newson, Moore, Foster & Company, 1860), pp. 8–9. This report contained other documents on the potential value of the British prairies. Taylor to Chase, 17 Dec. 1861, Bowsfield, *Taylor Papers*, pp. 21–22.

26. Taylor, "Relations Between the United States and Northwest British America," 20 May 1862, 37th Cong., 2d sess., H. Ex. Doc. 146, *U.S. Serials Set* 1138, p. 85; "Memorial of the Legislature of Minnesota," 11 Feb. 1862, 37th Cong., 2d Sess., S. Misc. Doc. 44, *U.S. Serials Set* 1124, pp. 1–3; George Sheppard to George Becker, 30 June 1865, Bowsfield, *Taylor Papers*, pp. 46–47.

27. Taylor to Seward, 17 May 1867, 27 Feb. 1868, Bowsfield, *Taylor Papers*, pp. 48–49, 56–57, and to Edward Cooper (Assistant Secretary of the Treasury), 23 Nov. 1867, ibid., pp. 51–52; "Resolutions of Mr. Ramsey," 9 Dec. 1867, 40th Cong., 2d sess., S. Misc. Doc. 4, *U.S. Serials Set* 1319. See also "Resolutions of the State of Minnesota" after the purchase of Alaska, in Fridley, "Minnesota Coveted Canada," p. 77.

28. See Warner, "Drang Nach Norden"; Hafter, "Riel Rebellion and Manifest Destiny"; and Gluek, *Minnesota and Manifest Destiny*, chap. 9 for treatments of this episode in relation to the expansionists. Hamilton Fish to James Taylor, 30 Dec. 1869, Bowsfield, *Taylor Papers*, pp. 97–98. For Taylor's letters, which revealed how largely railroad promotion figured in his thinking, see Taylor to Fish, 20, 25 Jan., and 27 June 1879, ibid., pp. 135, 178.

29. *St. Paul Daily Express*, 29 July 1871. The editor wrote that Canadians "will give up the hopeless struggle against the irresistible law of gravitation which impels the heterogeneous and dissolved fragments of the Canadian Confederation into the lap of the Great Republic." Cited in Snell, "Frontier Sweeps Northwest," 392. "Resolutions of the Legislature of Minnesota," 14 Mar. 1870, 41st Cong., 2d sess., S. Misc. Doc. 82, *U.S. Serials Set* 1408.

30. For post-1846 see Henry F. Angus, ed., *British Columbia and the United States: The North Pacific Slope from Fur Trade to Aviation* (1942; reprint, New York: Russell & Russell, 1970), chap. 7ff. See also Howard Kushner, *Conflict on the Northwest Coast: American-Russian Rivalry in the Pacific Northwest, 1790–1867* (Westport, Conn.: Greenwood Press, 1975), pp. 107–54.

31. Franklin Pierce to Congress, 4 Dec. 1854, Richardson, *Messages and Papers*, 5:278, 333–34. A. Mercer, *Washington Territory, The Great Northwest, Her Material Resources and Claims to Emigration* (1865; reprint,

Fairfield, Wash.: Ye Galleon Press, 1971), pp. 22–28; Henry de Groot, *British Columbia: Its Condition and Prospects, Soil, Climate, and Mineral Resources Considered* (San Francisco: Alta California, 1859), pp. 3–4; *New York Times*, 24, 28 Feb. 1859; James H. Hitchman, "The Waterborne Commerce of British Columbia and Washington, 1850–1970," Occasional Paper #7, Center for Pacific Northwest Studies, Western Washington State College, 1976, pp. 4–5, 64; J. M. S. Careless, "The Lowe Brothers, 1852–70: A Study in Business Relations on the North Pacific Coast," *B.C. Studies* 2 (1969): 1–18.

32. "Fraser River," *The Knickerbocker* 52 (Oct. 1858): 331–40.

33. Cass to George M. Dallas, 24 May 1858, William R. Manning, ed., *The Diplomatic Correspondence of the United States: Canadian Relations, 1784–1860* (Washington, D.C.: Carnegie Foundation, 1940–43), 4: 167–68; Dallas to Lord Malmebury, 12 June 1858, ibid., 730. "Report of Special Agent sent to Vancouver Island and B.C.," 31 Jan. 1859, S. Ex. Doc. 29, *U.S. Serials Set* 984.

34. Jarvis Reed, "San Juan Island's Pig War," *Journal of the West* 7 (Apr. 1968): 236–45; background in James Osborne McCabe, *The San Juan Boundary Question* (Toronto: University of Toronto Press, 1964). William Marcy to John F. Crampton, 17 July, and to Isaac Stevens, 14 July 1855, Manning, *Diplomatic Correspondence* 4:120–21, and 121n. Acting Secretary of War W. R. Dinkard to Brigadier General William S. Harney, 3 Sept. 1859, ibid., 188n; to Scott, 16 Sept. 1859, ibid., 190n. Hunter Miller, *San Juan Archipelago: Study of the Joint Occupation of San Juan Island* (Bellows Falls, Vt.: Wyndham Press, 1943), pp. 33–34, 63, 109–11.

35. Department of State, Consular Dispatches, Victoria, B.C. (1862–71), RG 59, T-130, vol. 1, roll 1. Quote from Francis's dispatch of 1 Oct. 1866. "Annexation of Canada," *Puget Sound Gazette*, 25 May 1865. Northern Pacific Railroad Co., *Charter . . . Organization, and Proceedings* (1865), cited in Leonard B. Irwin, *Pacific Railways and Nationalism in the Canadian-American Northwest, 1845–1867* (Philadelphia: University of Pennsylvania Press, 1939), p. 107; Philip Ritz cited ibid., p. 108.

36. McPherson, "Interest of Gwin in the Purchase of Alaska," 23–38; Peter Buzanski, "Alaska and Nineteenth Century American Diplomacy," *Journal of the West* 6 (July 1967): 451–67; Warner, *Idea of Continental Union*, pp. 128–40; Kushner, *Conflict on the Northwest Coast*, pp. 145–54; provide background relating the Alaska Purchase to the larger schemes for American Pacific Empire.

37. Charles Sumner, "Speech," 9 Apr. 1867, *Works of Sumner*, 11:216–32; George Bancroft to William Henry Seward, 15 June 1867, George Bancroft Papers, Massachusetts Historical Society; Chicago *Evening Journal*, cited in Sanford, *Manifest Destiny*, p. 100; Johnson, "Fourth Annual Message," 9 Dec. 1868, Richardson, *Messages and Papers*, 6: 688. Johnson suggested that natural historical forces, not active policies, might bring the West Indies under American control. "Third Annual Message," 3 Dec. 1867, ibid., 580.

38. Francis to Seward, 13 Apr. 1867, Department of State, Dispatches, Victoria; letter from American residents in Victoria to Seward, 20 Apr. 1867, ibid; Ekstein to Hamilton Fish, 5 Oct. 1870, ibid. Hart, "Opening of the New Northwest," 387. James Callahan, "The Alaska Purchase and Americo-Canadian Relations," *West Virginia Studies in History* (1908), Nos. 2 and 3.

CHAPTER 11

1. William Averell to William Henry Seward, 15 Mar. 1867, Department of State, Dispatches from Consuls, Montreal (1850–71), RG 59, T-222, vol. 8, reel 8.

2. Ibid.

3. Averell to Seward, 28 Jan., 17 Feb. 1868, and 6 Jan. 1869, ibid., vol. 9, reel 9.

4. Thurston to Seward, 31 Mar. 1865, ibid., Toronto (1866–71), T-491; Seward to Averell, 30 Mar. 1867, Department of State, Instruction to Consuls, ser. 1, vol. 15, 11 Dec. 1866–15 Nov. 1867, pp. 174–75.

5. William Dart to Hamilton Fish, 14 Sept. 1869, Department of State Dispatches from Consuls, Montreal (1850–71), vol. 9, reel 9, and Dart to Fish, 18 Mar. 1870, ibid., vol. 10, reel 10.

6. *New York Times*, 8 Nov. 1852, 27 Sept., 6 Oct. 1853, 3 July 1854, 17 Apr. 1858, 26 Mar., 4 Apr. 1859; M. J. Hickey, "The Capital of the Canadas," *Harper's New Monthly Magazine* 23 (Sept. 1861): 446–50; *National Intelligencer*, 8 June 1867.

7. "Political Movements in the New World," and "Canadian Policy," *The Nation*, 20 July, 28 Sept. 1865, 1:75, 391–92; "Dominion of Canada," and "French Canada," ibid., 4 July 1867, 5:2, and 13 Aug. 1868, 7:128.

8. A. Pillsbury, "British North America," *De Bow's Review* n.s. 3 (Feb. 1867): 158–66; see also Henry J. Morgan, "The Place British Americans Have Won in History," ibid., 2 (June 1866): 11–12, *Cincinnati Daily Gazette*, 11 July 1867 cited in James G. Snell, "The Eagle and the Butterfly: Some American Attitudes towards British North America, 1864–1867" (Ph.D. diss., Queens University, 1971), p. 117; *Rochester Daily Union and Advertiser*, 25 Sept. 1866, cited in ibid., p. 244.

9. *National Intelligencer*, 26 Feb., 21 Mar., 28 June 1867.

10. *American Railroad Journal*, 21 Apr. 1866, 39:369; *New York Herald*, 16 June 1867; Joe Patterson Smith, *Republican Expansionists of the Early Reconstruction Era* (Chicago, 1933), p. 109 ff.

11. Banks and Chanler spoke on 27 Mar. 1867, *Congressional Globe, Containing the Debates and Proceedings of Congress, 1833–1873* (Washington, D.C.: F. & J. Rives and George Bailey, 1834–73), 40th Cong., 1st sess., p. 392. Alice R. Stewart, "The State of Maine and Canadian Confederation," *Canadian Historical Review* 33 (June 1952), 148–64; New York Assembly Resolution, Mar. 1867, cited in Snell, "Eagle and Butterfly," p. 129.

12. *Boston Daily Advertiser*, 2 July 1867; *Boston Evening Transcript*, 2, 3, 19 July 1867; *Frank Leslie's Illustrated Newspaper*, 16 Mar. 1867, p. 402, and 29 June 1867, p. 226.

13. "Confederation of British North American Provinces," *Merchant's Magazine and Commercial Review* 51 (Nov. 1864): 366–68; "The Dominion of Canada and the Reciprocal Trade," ibid., 57 (Dec. 1867): 409; L. S. Huntington, "The Independence of Canada," ibid., 61 (Nov. 1869): 319–41; "The Reciprocity Movement in Canada," ibid. (Dec. 1869): 428–31; "Confederation of the British North American Provinces," *American Railroad Journal* 39 (June 1866): 537–38, 540.

14. Snell, "Eagle and Butterfly," sampled American opinion on Confederation. "Reciprocity Movement," *Merchant's Magazine*, 61 (Dec. 1869): 428–31; *National Intelligencer*, 7 Aug., 18 Sept. 1868; James Snell, "A Foreign Agent in Washington: George W. Brega, Canada's Lobbyist, 1867–1870," *Civil War History* 26 (Mar. 1980): 53–70.

15. Israel T. Hatch, "Commercial Relations with the Dominion of Canada," 40th Cong., 3d sess., H. Ex. Doc. 36 *U.S. Serials Set* 1372, passim.

16. Dart to Hamilton Fish, 18 Mar., 22 Apr., 4, 5 May 1870, Department of State, Dispatches from Consuls, Montreal, vol. 10, reel 10.

17. E. B. O'Callaghan to John Daly, 30 Mar. 1844, MG 24, B 50, Public Archives of Canada; Brian Jenkins, *Fenians and Anglo-American Relations during Reconstruction* (Ithaca, N.Y.: Cornell University Press, 1969); Lester B. Shippee, *Canadian-American Relations, 1849–1874* (1939; reprint, New York: Russell and Russell, 1970), pp. 215–38; *Chicago Tribune*, 21, 28 Sept. 1866. Richard Wright, "Green Flags and Red-Coated Gunboats: Naval Activities on the Great Lakes During the Fenian Scares, 1866–1870," *Inland Seas* 22 (Summer 1966): 91–110.

18. Homer Calkin, "St. Albans in Reverse: The Fenian Raid of 1866," *Vermont History* 35 (Jan. 1967): 19–34; Jenkins, *Fenians*, pp. 136–71; 4 June 1866, in *The Diary of George Templeton Strong*, ed. Allan Nevins and Milton Thomas (New York: Octagon Books, 1974), 4:89; Andrew Johnson, "A Proclamation," 6 June 1866, James D. Richardson, ed. and comp., *A Compilation of the Messages and Papers of the Presidents, 1789–1908* (Washington, D.C.: Bureau of National Literature and Art, 1908), 6:433.

19. "What the Fenian War Really Is," *The Nation*, 8 June 1866, 2:728; F. W. Seward to D. Thurston, 3, 19 Oct. 1866, Department of State, Instructions to Consuls, ser. 1, vol. 14, pp. 488, 511–12; John Potter to William H. Seward, 7 June 1866; Averell to Seward, 25 Mar. 1867, Department of State, Dispatches from Consuls, Montreal, vol. 7, reel 7, and vol. 8, reel 8.

20. Dart to Hamilton Fish, 26 May 1870, Department of State, Dispatches from Consuls, Montreal, vol. 10, reel 10. Later, Dart changed his mind. See to Fish, 13 June 1870, ibid.

21. U. S. Grant, "Proclamation," 24 May, 1870, Richardson, *Messages and Papers*, 7:85.

22. Jenkins, *Fenians*, pp. 290–310; John P. Pritchett, "The Origin of the So-called Fenian Raid on Manitoba in 1871," *Canadian Historical Review* 10 (Mar. 1929): 23–42: Alvin Gluek, *Minnesota and the Manifest Destiny*

of the Canadian Northwest: A Study in Canadian-American Relations (Toronto: University of Toronto Press, 1965), pp. 258–71. See also Harry Landon, *The North Country: A History Embracing Jefferson, St. Lawrence, Oswego, Lewis and Franklin Counties, New York* (Indianapolis: Historical Publishing Company, 1932), 1:449–55.

23. Rising Lake Morrow, "The Negotiation of the Anglo-American Treaty of 1870," *American Historical Review* 39 (July 1934): 663–81; Adrian Cook, *The Alabama Claims: American Politics and Anglo-American Relations, 1865–1872* (Ithaca, N.Y.: Cornell University Press, 1975), should be read alongside Jenkins *Fenians*. See also Maureen M. Robson, "The Alabama Claims and the Anglo-American Reconciliation, 1865–71," *Canadian Historical Review* 42 (Mar. 1961): 1–22; Doris Dashew, "The Story of an Illusion: The Plan to Trade the Alabama Claims for Canada," *Civil War History* 15 (Dec. 1969): 332–48.

24. "Report by Hamilton Fish on American–Latin American Relations and Commerce," 14 July 1870, Richardson, *Messages and Papers*, 7:71, 73–74, 76–78; Cook, *Alabama Claims*, pp. 124–36.

25. Grant, "Second Annual Message," 5 Dec. 1870, Richardson, *Messages and Papers*, 7:102–3; *Leslie's Illustrated News*, 7 Jan. 1871, pp. 274–75; *Boston Evening Transcript*, 6, 21 Feb. 1871; J. Paris Mansfield, "New Brunswick and the Treaty of Washington" (Master's thesis, University of New Brunswick, 1958), to p. 80 passim; R. F. Sams, "The Congressional Attitude towards Canada during the 1860s," (Master's thesis, Queens University, 1947), pp. 152–55.

26. Caleb Cushing, *The Treaty of Washington: Its Negotiation, Execution, and the Discussions Relating Thereto* (1873; reprint, Freeport: Books for Libraries Press, 1970), p. 224. "Treaty of Washington, 1871," Canada, Department of External Affairs, comp., *Treaties and Agreements Affecting Canada in Force between His Majesty and the United States of America with Subsidiary Documents, 1814–1925* (Ottawa: King's Printer, 1927), pp. 44–47.

27. *Leslie's Illustrated Newspaper* printed pictures of the commissioners and a state banquet in their honor, 1 Apr. 1871, pp. 40–41, 44; *Boston Evening Transcript*, 10, 11 Feb., 15, 27 Apr., 9, 10 May 1871; Mansfield, "New Brunswick and Treaty," pp. 82–99.

28. Cushing, Caleb Cushing Papers, Library of Congress, file 209; William Dart to J. C. B. Davis, 25 May 1871, Department of State, Dispatches from Consuls, Montreal; Cook, *Alabama Claims*, pp. 189–90; James Osborne McCabe, *The San Juan Boundary Question* (Toronto: University of Toronto Press, 1964), pp. 104–32; Shippee, *Canadian-American Relations*, pp. 373–95.

29. Citations from *Boston Evening Transcript*, 12, 15, 19, 26 Apr., 5, 6, 10 May 1871.

30. Cushing, *Treaty of Washington*, pp. 252–53, 255.

31. See John Logan, *No Transfer: An American Security Principle* (New Haven, Conn.: Yale University Press, 1961); Samuel Flagg Bemis, *John*

Quincy Adams and the Foundations of American Diplomacy (New York: Alfred Knopf, 1949); Bradford Perkins, *Castlereagh and Adams: England and the United States, 1812–1823* (Berkeley: University of California Press, 1964).

32. See Robert E. May, *The Southern Dream of a Caribbean Empire, 1854–61* (Baton Rouge: Louisiana State University Press, 1973).

33. On the transition see Ernest Paolino, *The Foundations of American Empire: William H. Seward and American Foreign Policy* (Ithaca, N.Y.: Cornell University Press, 1973); Walter La Feber, *The New Empire: An Interpretation of American Expansion, 1860–1898* (Ithaca, N.Y.: Cornell University Press, 1963), chap. 1.

34. Albert Weinberg, *Manifest Destiny: A Study of Nationalist Expansion in American History* (Baltimore: Johns Hopkins University Press, 1935). Norman A. Graebner, *Empire on the Pacific: A Study in American Continental Expansion* (New York: Ronald Press Company, 1955); Frederick Merk, *Manifest Destiny and Mission in American History: A Reinterpretation* (New York: Random House, 1963); William Goetzmann, *Exploration and Empire: The Explorer and the Scientist in the Winning of the American West* (New York: Alfred A. Knopf, 1966); Charles Sanford, ed., *Manifest Destiny and the Imperialism Question* (New York: John Wiley & Sons, 1974); Reginald Horsman, *Race and Manifest Destiny: The Origins of American Racial Anglo-Saxonism* (Cambridge, Mass.: Harvard University Press, 1981); and Anna K. Nelson, "Destiny and Diplomacy, 1840–1860," Gerald K. Haines and Samuel Walker, eds., *American Foreign Relations: A Historiographical Review* (Westport, Conn.: Greenwood Press, 1981), pp. 49–64.

35. William A. Williams, *Empire as a Way of Life* (New York: Oxford University Press, 1980), but especially *The Contours of American History* (Cleveland: World Publishing Company, 1961).

36. James A. Field, Jr., *America and the Mediterranean World, 1776–1882* (Princeton: Princeton University Press, 1969), p. 245. Akira Iriye, *From Nationalism to Internationalism: U.S. Foreign Policy to 1914* (London: Routledge & Kegan Paul, 1977), to p. 52, and Iriye, "Culture and Power: International Relations as Intercultural Relations," *Diplomatic History* 3 (Spring 1979): 115–28. Sanford, *Manifest Destiny*, pp. 1–12. Morrell Heald and Lawrence S. Kaplan, *Culture and Diplomacy: The American Experience* (Westport, Conn.: Greenwood Press, 1977); Paul Varg, *New England and Foreign Relations, 1789–1850* (Hanover, N. H.: University Press of New England, 1983); James Doyle, *North of America: Images of Canada in the Literature of the United States, 1775–1900* (Toronto: E.C.W. Press, 1983).

Bibliography

PRIMARY SOURCES

ARCHIVES

Library of Congress
  The Caleb Cushing Papers
  The Ulysses S. Grant Papers
  The James Madison Papers (microfilm copy at University of Virginia)
  The William L. Marcy Papers
  The John Mitchell Papers
  The Franklin Pierce Papers
  The Martin Van Buren Papers (microfilm copy at University of British
    Columbia)
Massachusetts Historical Society
  The George Bancroft Papers
National Archives, Washington, D.C.
  Department of State: RG 59
        Dispatches from United States Consuls: Halifax (1833–71), T-469;
          St. John (1835–71), T-485; Montreal (1850–71), T-222; Sydney and
          Pictou (1859–71), T-479; Quebec (1861–71), T-482; Victoria
          (1862–71), T-130; Prescott (1865–71), T-481; Toronto (1866–71),
          T-491; Winnipeg (1869–71), T-24.
        Instructions to Consuls, Vols. 1–6, to 1871, E-54.
        Miscellaneous Documents Relating to Reciprocity Negotiations of
          the Department of State, vol. 1, 1848–54, T-493.
        Records of Negotiations Connected with the Treaty of Ghent,
          1813–15, M-36.
        Special Agents, vol. 11, C. William Slacum (1835); vol. 12, Aaron
          Vail (1836–42); vols. 16–17, Israel Andrews (1849).
        War of 1812 Papers, M-588.
  Department of the Treasury
        Correspondence of the Secretary of the Treasury with Collectors of
          Customs, 1789–1833, RG 56, M-178.
        Letters and Reports Received by the Secretary of the Treasury from
          Special Agents 1854–1861, RG 36 M-177.
        Letters Concerning Appointments, Removals, and General
          Activities of Secret Inspectors of Customs, 1842–1850,
          RG 217, E-248.
        U.S. Tariff Commissioner, Reports Prior to 1871 on U.S.-Canadian
          Trade, RG 46, DW-42670.

PUBLISHED OFFICIAL DOCUMENTS

American State Papers: Commerce and Navigation. 2 vols. Washington, D.C.: Gales and Seaton, 1832.

American State Papers: Foreign Relations. 5 vols. Washington, D.C.: Gales and Seaton, 1832.

American State Papers: Military Affairs. 4 vols. Washington, D.C.: Gales and Seaton, 1832.

Andrews, Israel D. *Report on the Trade and Commerce of the British North American Colonies with the United States and Other Countries Embracing Full and Complete Tabular Statements from 1820–1850.* Washington, D.C.: Government Printing Office, 1851.

———. *Report upon the Trade and Commerce of the British North American Colonies and upon the Trade of the Great Lakes and Rivers.* Washington, D.C.: Government Printing Office, 1854.

Bevans, Charles. *Treaties and Other International Agreements of the United States of America, 1776–1949.* 12 vols. Washington, D.C.: Department of State, 1968.

Canada. Department of External Affairs. *Treaties and Agreements Affecting Canada in Force between His Majesty and the United States of America with Subsidiary Documents, 1814–1925.* Ottawa: King's Printer, 1927.

Carter, Clarence E., comp. and ed. *The Territorial Papers of the United States.* Washington, D.C.: Government Printing Office, 1934–75. Vols. 2–3, *Northwest Territory, 1787–1803.* Vol. 10, *Michigan Territory, 1805–20.* Vol. 11, *Michigan Territory 1820–29.*

Congressional Globe, Containing the Debates and Proceedings, 1833–1873. 109 vols. Washington, D.C.: F. & J. Rives and George Bailey, 1834–73.

Daveis, Charles. *Report of the Committee on the North-Eastern Boundary: Legislature of the State of Maine.* Washington, D.C.: U.S. Senate Document 19, 1841.

Debates and Proceedings in the Congress of the United States, 1789–1824. 42 vols. Washington, D.C.: Gales and Seaton, 1834–56.

Department of State. *Papers Relating to the Treaty of Washington.* 5 vols. Washington, D.C.: Government Printing Office, 1872.

Derby, E. H. *A Preliminary Report on the Treaty of Reciprocity with Great Britain to Regulate the Trade between the U.S. and the Provinces of British North America.* Washington, D.C.: Treasury Department, 1866.

Ford, Worthington C., ed. *The Journals of the Continental Congress.* 24 vols. Washington, D.C.: Government Printing Office, 1934–37.

Greenhow, Robert. *Memoir, Historical and Political, on the Northwest Coast of North America, and the Adjacent Territories.* Washington, D.C.: Blair & Rives, 1840.

Hatch, Israel T. *Report upon the Operation of the Revenue Laws and the Reciprocity Treaty Upon the Northern Frontier.* Washington, D.C.: House Executive Document 96, 28 Mar. 1860.

————. *Report upon the Commercial Relations of the United States with the Dominion of Canada.* Washington, D.C.: Government Printing Office, 1869.

Historical Statistics of the United States. 2 vols. Washington, D.C.: Government Printing Office, 1975.

Journals of the Assembly and of the Senate of the State of New York. Albany: Various publishers to the state, 1830–71.

Larned, J. N. *Report on the State of Trade between the United States and the British Possessions in North America.* Washington, D.C.: Government Printing Office, 1871.

Martell, J. S., ed. *Immigration to and Emigration from Nova Scotia, 1815–1838.* Public Archives of Nova Scotia, Publication no. 6 (1942).

Message from the President . . . transmitting a Report of the Secretary of State . . . Relative to Duties on Imports into Canada, Nova Scotia, and New Brunswick, 18 Apr. 1816. Washington, D.C.: William A. Davis, 1816.

Register of Debates in Congress, 1825–1837. 29 vols. Washington, D.C.: Gales and Seaton, 1825–37.

Relations between the United States and North-West British America. Washington, D.C.: House Executive Document 146, 11 July 1862.

Report of the Commissioners to Explore the Route of an Inland Navigation from Hudson's River to Lake Ontario and Lake Erie. New York: Prior and Dunning, 1811.

Report of the Minister of Finance on the Reciprocity Treaty with the United States, also the Memorial of the Chamber of Commerce of St. Paul, Minnesota, and Reports of Congress, U.S., Thereon. Quebec: Stewart, Derbishire & George Desbarats, 1862.

Report of the Select Committee of the Chamber of Commerce of the State of New York on the Reciprocity Treaty as to Trade Between the British North American Provinces and the United States of America. New York: John W. Amerman, 1865.

State Papers of Vermont. Montpelier: Secretary of State, 1851.

United States Serials Set. Washington, D.C.: Government Printing Office, 1833–1871.

The United States and West Canada. Washington, D.C.: Senate Miscellaneous Document 69, 1870–71.

Walton, E. D., ed. *Records of the Governors and Council of the State of Vermont [1775–1830].* Montpelier: J. &. J. M. Poland, 1873–79.

The War of the Rebellion: Official Records of the Union and Confederate Armies. Series 1, vol. 43. Washington, D.C.: Government Printing Office, 1893.

PRINTED COLLECTIONS OF PERSONAL PAPERS

Adams, Henry, ed. *The Writings of Albert Gallatin*. 3 vols. 1879; reprint, New York: Antiquarian Press, Ltd., 1960.

Baker, George E., ed. *The Works of William H. Seward*. 5 vols. Boston: Houghton Mifflin and Company, 1884.

Ballagh, James Curtis, ed. *The Letters of Richard Henry Lee*. 2 vols. New York: The Macmillan Company, 1911.

Basler, Roy P., ed. *The Collected Works of Abraham Lincoln*. 9 vols. New Brunswick: Rutgers University Press, 1955.

Bassett, John Spencer, ed. *Correspondence of Andrew Jackson*. 6 vols. Washington, D.C.: Carnegie Foundation, 1926.

Bentley, William. *The Diary of William Bentley, D.D.* 3 vols. Salem: Essex Institute, 1911.

Benton, Thomas Hart. *Thirty Years' View: or, A History of the Working of the American Government for Thirty Years from 1820 to 1850*. 2 vols. New York: D. Appleton & Co., 1854.

Bowsfield, H., ed. *The James Wicks Taylor Papers*. Winnipeg: 1968.

Boyd, Julian P., ed. *The Papers of Thomas Jefferson*. 18 vols to date. Princeton: Princeton University Press, 1950–.

Campbell, William W., ed. *The Life and Writings of De Witt Clinton*. New York: Baker & Scribner, 1849. Clinton, George. *Public Papers of George Clinton*. 10 vols. Albany: Oliver A. Quayle, 1904.

Dallas, Alexander J. *The Life and Writings of Alexander J. Dallas*. Philadelphia: J. B. Lippincott, 1871.

Esary, Logan, ed. *Messages and Letters of William Henry Harrison*. 2 vols. Indianapolis: Indiana Historical Commission, 1922.

Everett, Edward. *Orations and Speeches on Various Occasions*. 4 vols. Boston: Little Brown & Company, 1868.

Fitzpatrick, John C., ed. *The Autobiography of Martin Van Buren*. 2 vols. American Historical Association. *Annual Report*. Washington, D.C.: Government Printing Office, 1918–20.

———. *The Writings of George Washington*. 39 vols. Washington, D.C.: Government Printing Office, 1931–4.

Ford, Worthington C., ed. *Writing of John Quincy Adams*. 7 vols. New York: The Macmillan Company, 1913–17.

Hamilton, S. M., ed. *The Writings of James Monroe*. 7 vols. New York: G. P. Putnam's, 1901.

Hargreaves, Mary W., and James Hopkins, eds. *The Papers of Henry Clay*. 8 vols. to date. Lexington: University of Kentucky Press, 1959–.

Hastings, Hugh, ed. *Public Papers of D. D. Tompkins, Governor of New York, 1807–1817*. 3 vols. Albany, N.Y.: 1898–1902.

Hunt, Gaillard, ed. *The Writings of James Madison*. 10 vols. New York: G. P. Putnam's Sons, 1906.

Johnston, Henry P., ed. *The Correspondence and Public Papers of John Jay*. 4 vols. New York: G. P. Putnam's sons, 1890–93.

King, Charles R., ed. *The Life and Correspondence of Rufus King*. 7 vols. New York: G. P. Putnam's Sons, 1898.

Laurens, John. *The Army Correspondence of Colonel John Laurens in the Years 1777–8*. New York: New York Times & Arno Press, 1969.

Meriwether, Robert L., ed. *The Papers of John C. Calhoun*. 8 vols. to date. Columbia: University of South Carolina Press, 1959–.

Merrill, Walter M., and Louis Ruchames, eds. *The Letters of William Lloyd Garrison*. 4 vols. Cambridge, Mass.: Belknap Press of Harvard University Press, 1971.

Moore, John Bassett, ed. *The Works of James Buchanan*. 12 vols. Philadelphia: J. B. Lippincott Company, 1908–11.

Morris, Richard B., ed. *John Jay: The Making of a Revolutionary, 1745–1780*. New York: Harper & Row, 1975.

_____. *John Jay: The Winning of the Peace, 1780–1784*. New York: Harper & Row, 1980.

Nevins, Allan, and Milton H. Thomas, eds. *The Diary of George Templeton Strong, 1835–1875*. 4 vols. New York: Octagon Books, 1974.

Pierce, Edward. *Memoir and Letters of Charles Sumner*. 4 vols. Boston: Roberts Brothers, 1893.

Poor, Laura, ed. *The First International Railway and the Colonization of New England: Life and Writings of John Alfred Poor*. New York: G. P. Putnam's Sons, 1892.

Rutland, Robert A., ed. *The Papers of George Mason*. 3 vols. Chapel Hill: University of North Carolina Press, 1970.

Schutz, John A., and Douglass Adair, eds. *The Spur of Fame: Dialogues of John Adams and Richard Rush, 1805–1813*. San Marino, Calif.: Huntington Library Press, 1966.

Scott, Winfield. *Memoirs of General Scott, Written by Himself*. 2 vols. New York: Sheldon & Co., 1864.

Severance, Frank, ed. *Millard Fillmore Papers*. 2 vols. Buffalo: Buffalo Historical Society, 1907.

Seward, Frederick W. *Seward at Washington*. 2 vols. New York: Derby & Miller, 1891.

Sumner, Charles. *The Works of Charles Sumner*. 15 vols. Boston: Lee & Shepard, 1870–83.

Syrett, Harold, ed. *The Papers of Alexander Hamilton*. 26 vols. New York: Columbia University Press, 1960–79.

Taylor, Robert, ed. *Papers of John Adams*. 10 vols. Cambridge, Mass.: Belknap Press of Harvard University Press, 1963.

Webster, Fletcher, ed. *The Writings and Speeches of Daniel Webster*. 18 vols. Boston: Little Brown, 1903.

Wiltse, Charles M., and Harold D. Moser, eds. *The Papers of Daniel Webster*. Ser. 1, 7 vols.; Ser. 2, 2 vols.; Ser. 3, 1 vol. to date. Hanover: University Press of New England, 1974–.

OTHER PRINTED COLLECTIONS

Armstrong, John. *Notices of the War of 1812.* 2 vols. New York: Wiley & Putnam, 1840.

Benton, Elbert Jay, ed. "Northern Ohio During the War of 1812: Letters and Papers in the Western Reserve Historical Society." Western Reserve Historical Society, *Annual Reports* (1913): 30–55.

Blassingame, John W. *Slave Testimony: Two Centuries of Letters, Speeches, Interviews, and Autobiographies.* Baton Rouge: Louisiana State University Press, 1977.

Brannan, John. *Official Letters of the Military and Naval of the United States during the War with Great Britain in the Years 1812, 1813, 1814, and 1815.* Washington, D.C.: Way & Gideon, 1823.

Burnett, Edmund C., ed. *Letters of the Members of the Continental Congress.* 8 vols. Washington, D.C.: The Carnegie Institution, 1921.

The Campaign of 1860, Comprising the Speeches of Abraham Lincoln, William H. Seward, et al. Albany: Weed, Parsons & Co., 1860.

Correspondence Relating to the Fenian Invasion, and the Rebellion of the Southern States. Ottawa: Hunter, Ros & Company, 1869.

Crary, Catherine, ed. *The Price of Loyalty: Tory Writings From the Revolutionary Era.* New York: McGraw Hill, 1973.

Cruikshank, E. A., ed. *Documents Relating to the Invasion of Canada and the Surrender of Detroit 1812.* Ottawa: Government Printing Bureau, 1912.

———. *The Documentary History of the Campaign Upon the Niagara Frontier in the Year 1812.* Welland, Ontario: The Tribune Office, 1912.

———. *The Settlement of the United Empire Loyalists on the Upper St. Lawrence and the Bay of Quinte in 1784.* Toronto: Ontario Historical Society, 1934.

Cunningham, Noble E., ed. *Circular Letters of Congressmen to Their Constituents, 1789–1829.* 3 vols. Chapel Hill: University of North Carolina Press, 1978.

Everest, Allen S., and Charles McLellan, eds. *North Country Notes*, No. 8 (March 1962).

Gallatin, Albert. *The Right of the United States to the Northeastern Boundary.* New York: Samuel Adams, 1848.

Innis, H. A., & A. R. M. Lower, eds. *Select Documents in Canadian Economic History.* Toronto: Ryerson Press, 1933.

Kidder, Frederic, comp. *Military Operations in Eastern Maine and Nova Scotia During the Revolution.* Albany: Joel Munsell, 1867.

Knopf, Richard, ed. *Document Transcriptions of the War of 1812 in the Northwest.* 6 vols. Columbus: The Ohio Historical Society, 1957–59.

Lincoln, Charles, ed. *Messages from the Governors.* 11 vols. Albany: J. B. Lyon Company, 1909.

Manning, William R., ed. *Diplomatic Correspondence of the United*

States: Canadian Relations, 1784–1860. 3 vols. Washington, D.C.: Carnegie Foundation, 1940–43.

Michigan Historical Collections, 36 (1908).

Morse, Jedediah. *The American Gazeteer.* Boston: Thomas & Andrews, 1810.

O'Callaghan, E. B., ed. *The Documentary History of the State of New York.* 2 vols. Albany: Weed, Parsons & Co., 1849.

Paltsits, Victor, ed. *Minutes of the Commissioners for Detecting and Defeating Conspiracies in the State of New York: Albany County Sessions.* 3 vols. New York: Da Capo Press, 1972.

Richardson, James D., ed. and comp. *A Compilation of the Messages and Papers of the Presidents, 1789–1908.* 11 vols. Washington, D.C.: Bureau of National Literature and Art, 1908.

Speeches in the Senate Collected and Bound for William H. Seward. N.p., n.d.

Taylor, James Wicks. *Northwest British America, and its Relations to the State of Minnesota.* St. Paul, Minn.: Nelson, Moore, Foster & Company, 1860.

PRINTED PAMPHLETS AND REPORTS

The Act of Incorporation and the Bye Laws of the Boston and Montreal Turnpike Company. Peacham: Samuel Goss, 1806.

All Canada in the Hands of the English. Boston: B. Mecom, 1760.

Alvord, Benjamin. "Northwest Boundary Question." *Putnam's Magazine* 6 (July–Nov. 1870): 300–305.

Barber, John, and Henry Howe. *Historical Collections of the State of New York.* 1941. Reprint. Port Washington: Kennikat Press, 1970.

Barton, James L. *Commerce of the Lakes.* Buffalo, N.Y.: Courier Office, 1846.

Boston Board of Trade. *Fifth Annual Report.* Boston: T. R. Marvin & Son, 1859.

———. *Ninth Annual Report.* Boston: Alfred Mudge & Son, 1863.

———. *The Reciprocity Treaty Between the United States and Great Britain of June 5, 1854.* Boston: T. R. Marvin & Son, 1865.

———. *Report on the Northern Pacific Railroad.* Boston: J. H. Eastburn's Press, 1865.

———. *Third Annual Report.* Boston: George C. Rand & Avery, Printers, 1857.

The Boston Committee in Canada: A Series of Eight Letters Reprinted from the Boston Atlas. Boston: Eastburn's Press, 1851.

The Bridge Question. Montpelier, Vt.: E. P. Walton & Sons, 1847.

Chamber of Commerce of the State of New York. *Fifth Annual Report.* New York: John W. Amerman, 1865.

_____. *Fourth Annual Report*. New York: John W. Amerman, 1862.

_____. *Report of the Select Committee on the Reciprocity Treaty as to Trade Between the British North American Provinces and the United States of America*. New York: John W. Amerman, 1865.

Communication of William H. Seward. Washington, D.C.: Government Printing Office, 1864.

Dallas, Alexander. *An Exposition of the Causes and Character of the Late War with Great Britain*. Washington, D.C.: Thomas Bangs, 1815.

Disclosure No. 1. "Violations of the Laws during the late War with Great Britain." Governor King Pamphlet.

Douglas, Stephen A. *An American Continental Commercial Union or Alliance*. Washington, D.C.: Thomas McGill & Co., 1889.

Duane, William. *Canada and the Continental Congress*. Philadelphia: Edward Gaskill, 1850.

Groot, Henry de. *British Columbia: Its Condition and Prospects, Soil, Climate, and Mineral Resources Considered*. San Francisco: Alta California, 1859.

Haller, Granville O. "San Juan and Secession." Paper read at 16 Jan. 1896 Legion Meeting, in University of British Columbia Special Collections.

Hamilton, M. D. *Statement of the Trade and Commerce of Detroit for the Year 1857*. Detroit: Daily Advertiser Press, 1858.

Hawley, Jesse. *An Essay on the Enlargement of the Erie Canal*. Lockport, N.Y.: Courier Office, 1840.

Hayes, J. D. *"The Niagara Ship Canal" and "Reciprocity."* Buffalo, N.Y.: Matthews and Warren, 1865.

Hayward, John. *The New England Gazetteer*. Boston: John Hayward, 1839.

Hill, Hamilton. *Review of the Proceedings of the Detroit Convention*. Boston: J. H. Eastburn's Press, 1866.

_____. *The Trade of Boston*. Boston: J. H. Eastburn's Press, 1871.

Johnson, Walter R. *The Coal Trade of British America*. Washington, D.C.: Taylor & Maury, 1850.

Lowell, John. *Mr. Madison's War*. New York: L. Beach, 1812.

McLeod, Alexander. "The Ends for Which God in His Providence Permits the Existence of War." In *A Scriptural View of the Character, Causes, and Ends of the Present War*. New York: Eastburn, Kirk & Co., 1815.

Mellon, John. *A Sermon Preached at the West Parish in Lancaster*. Boston: B. Mecom, 1760.

Mercer, A. *Washington Territory, The Great Northwest, Her Material Resources and Claims to Emigration*. 1865. Reprint. Fairfield, Wash.: Ye Galleon Press, 1971.

Poor, John A. *Memorial in Behalf of the European and North American Railway Co.* Augusta, Maine: Stevens & Sayward, 1861.

Proceedings of a Convention of Delegates Assembled at Faneuil Hall, in the City of Boston, to take into Consideration the Proposed Annexation of Texas. Boston: J. H. Eastburn's Press, 1845.

Proceedings of the Conventions of the Northern Lines of Railways held at

Boston, in December 1850, and January 1851. Boston: J. B. Yerrinton & Son, 1851.

Report of the Commissioners to Explore the Route of an Inland Navigation from Hudson's River to Lake Ontario and Lake Erie. New York: Prior & Dunning, 1811.

Reports of the Directors and Engineer of the Lake St. Louis and Province Line and the Plattsburgh & Montreal Railroad Companies on the Rail-Road Routes Between Montreal and New York. Montreal: J. Starke & Co., 1852.

Scripps, James E. *Annual Statement of the Trade and Commerce of Detroit for the Year 1860.* Detroit: Daily Advertiser Press, 1861.

Statement in Regard to Bridging Lake Champlain: Showing the Importance of the Canada Trade to Our Canals; Effects of a Bridge Upon that Trade. Troy: MacArthur's Press, 1851.

Stone, William L. *Maria Monk and the Nunnery of the Hotel Dieu.* New York: Howe & Bates, 1836.

Tabular Representation of the Present Condition of Boston in Relation to Railroad Facilities, Foreign Commerce, Population, Wealth, Manufactures; Also A Few Statements Relative to the Canadas. Boston: J. H. Eastburn's Press, 1851.

Tallmadge, James. *Address Before the American Institute.* New York: Hopkins & Jennings, 1841.

Taylor, James W. *Northwest British America and its Relations to the State of Minnesota.* St. Paul, Minn.: Narson Moore, Foster & Company, 1860.

PRINTED PERSONAL NARRATIVES

Barton, James L. *Address on the Early Reminiscences of Western New York and the Lake Region of the Country.* Buffalo, N.Y.: Jewett, Thomas & Co., 1848.

Beale, Howard K., ed. *The Diary of Gideon Welles.* 2 vols. New York: W. W. Norton & Co., 1960.

Beckett, Sylvester B. *Guide Book of the Atlantic and St. Lawrence and St. Lawrence and Atlantic Railroads.* Portland, Maine: Sanborn & Carter and H. J. Little & Co., 1853.

Bigelow, Timothy. *Journal of a Tour to Niagara Falls in the Year 1805.* Boston: John Wilson & Son, 1876.

Burr, William. *Descriptive and Historical View of Burr's Moving Mirror of the Lakes.* New York: George Bunce, 1850.

Buttrick, Tilly. *Voyages, Travels and Discoveries of Tilly Buttrick, Jr.* Boston, 1831.

Coit Correspondence, or, a Trip to New Brunswick by the Coit Family. Worcester, Mass.: Charles Hamilton, 1871.

Cozzens, Frederick S. *Acadia, or, A Month with the Blue Noses.* New York: Derby & Jackson, 1859.

Dalton, William. *Travels in the United States of America and Part of Upper Canada.* Appleby, 1821.

Darby, William. *A Tour from the City of New York to Detroit, in the Michigan Territory, Made between the 2d of May and the 22d of September, 1818.* New York: Kirk & Mercein, 1819.

Davison, Gideon Miner. *The Fashionable Tour: A Guide to Travellers Visiting the Middle and Northern States, and the Provinces of Canada.* 4th ed. Saratoga Springs, N.Y.: G. M. Davison, 1830.

De Veaux, Samuel. *The Falls of Niagara, or Tourist's Guide to this Wonder of Nature . . . and a Complete Guide thro' the Canadas.* Buffalo, N.Y.: William B. Hayden, 1839.

————. *The Traveller's Own Book to Saratoga Springs, Niagara Falls, and Canada.* Buffalo, N.Y.: Faxton & Read, 1841.

"Description of the Settlement of the Gennessee Country, in the State of New York. In A Series of Letters from a Gentleman to His Friend." 1799. Reprinted in *The Documentary History of the State of New York*, edited by E. B. O'Callaghan. 2 vols. Albany, N.Y.: Weed, Parsons & Co., 1849.

Disturnell, J. *Disturnell's American and European Railway and Steamship Guide.* New York: J. Disturnell, 1853.

————. *The Eastern Tourist.* New York: J. Disturnell, 1848.

————. *The Great Lakes, or Inland Seas of America.* New York: Charles Scribner, 1865.

————. *The Northern Traveller.* New York: J. Disturnell, 1844.

————, comp. *The Traveller's Guide to the . . . Fashionable Northern Tour Through the United States and Canada.* New York: The American News Company, 1864.

Doyle, James, ed. *Yankees in Canada: A Collection of 19th Century Travel Narratives.* Toronto: E.C.W. Press, 1980.

Drew, Benjamin. *A Northside View of Slavery: The Refugees: or, The Narratives of Fugitive Slaves in Canada.* Boston: John P. Jewett and Company, 1856.

Dwight, Theodore. *The Northern Traveller.* New York: John P. Haven, 1841.

"Early Pioneer Days." *Vermont Quarterly* 21 (Oct. 1953): 295–97.

Fairchild, G.M., ed. *Journal of an American Prisoner at Fort Malden and Quebec in the War of 1812.* Quebec: Frank Carrell, 1909.

"From Reading and Danville, Vermont, to Canada." *Vermont Quarterly* 21 (Apr. 1953): 134–36.

Gilpin, Henry. *A Northern Tour: Being a Guide to Saratoga, Lake George, Niagara, Canada, Boston, &C &C.* Philadelphia: H. C. Carey & I. Lea, 1825.

Goodrich, Enos. "Pioneer Sketch of Moses Goodrich and his Trip to Michigan in February, 1836, with his Brother Levi." *Michigan Historical Collections* 17 (1892): 480–90.

Guest, Moses. *Poems on Several Occasions: To Which are annexed Extracts from a Journal . . . during a Journey from New Brunswick, New Jersey, to Montreal and Quebec.* Cincinnati: Looker & Reynolds, 1823.

Herbert, Henry W. *Frank Forester's Fish and Fishing of the United States and British Provinces of North America.* New York: Stringer & Townsend, 1850.

Holley, O. L., ed. *The Picturesque Tourist: Being a Guide through the Northern and Eastern States and Canada.* New York: Disturnell, 1844.

Howe, John. *Journal . . . [of] a British Spy.* Concord, Mass.: Luther Roby, 1827.

Howe, Samuel G. *The Refugees from Slavery in Canada West.* Boston: Wright & Potter, 1864.

Hulett, T. G. *Every Man His Own Guide to the Falls of Niagara.* 5th ed. Buffalo, N.Y.: Faxon & Co., 1845.

Hunter, William S., Jr. *Hunter's Panoramic Guide from Niagara Falls to Quebec.* Boston: John P. Jewett & Company, 1857.

Imlay, Gilbert. *A Topographical Description of the Western Territory of North America.* London: J. Brebett, 1797.

Johnson, F. H. *Every Man His Own Guide at Niagara Falls.* Rochester, N.Y.: D. M. Dewey, 1852.

Landon, Fred, ed. "The Diary of Benjamin Lundy Written during his Journey through Upper Canada, January 1832." Ontario Historical Society, *Papers and Records* 19 (1922): 110–33.

Lanman, Adeline. *A Tour Down the St. Lawrence River.* 1852.

Lanman, Charles. *A Tour to the River Saguenay in Lower Canada.* Philadelphia: Carey & Hart, 1848.

Lyon, Caleb. *Narrative and Recollections of Van Dieman's Land, during a Three Years' Captivity of Stephen S. Wright.* New York: J. Winchester, 1844.

McAfee, Robert B. *History of the Late War in the Western Country.* Lexington, Ky.: Worsley & Smith, 1816.

McCarty, William. *History of the American War of 1812, from the Commencement until the Final Termination Thereof.* 1816. Reprint. Freeport, N.Y.: Books for Libraries Press, 1970.

McLeod, Alexander. *A Scriptural View of the Character, Causes and Ends of the Present War.* New York: Eastburn, Kirk & Co., 1815.

Marsh, Robert. *Seven Years of My Life, or Narrative of a Patriot Exile.* Buffalo, N.Y.: Paxon & Stevens, 1848.

Mayer, Brantz, ed. *Journal of John Carroll of Carrollton, during his Visit to Canada in 1776, as one of the Commissioners from Congress.* Baltimore: Maryland Historical Society, 1845.

Melish, John. *Travels in the United States of America, in the years 1806 & 1807, and 1809, 1810, & 1811.* Philadelphia, 1812.

Miller, Linus Wilson. *Notes of an Exile to Van Diemen's Land.* Fredonia, N.Y.: Wartmann & Bros., 1849.

Myers, J.C. *Sketches Made on A Tour through Northern and Eastern States, the Canadas & Nova Scotia*. Harrisonburg, Va.: J. H. Wartmann and Brothers, 1849.

The Northern Traveller and Northern Tour. New York: Goodrich & Wiley, 1834.

Ogden, John Cosens. *A Tour Through Upper and Lower Canada*. Litchfield, 1799.

Ontario and St. Lawrence Steamboat Company's Handbook for Travellers to Niagara Falls, Montreal and Quebec, and Through Lake Champlain to Saratoga Springs. Buffalo, N.Y.: Jewett, Thomas & Co., 1853.

Parsons, Horatio. *A Guide to Travellers Visiting the Falls of Niagara*. Buffalo, N.Y.: Oliver G. Steele, 1835.

Perkins, Samuel. *A History of the Political and Military Events of the Late War between the United States and Great Britain*. New Haven: S. Converse, 1825.

Pictorial Guide to the Falls of Niagara. Buffalo, N.Y.: Salisbury and Clapp, 1842.

Reminiscences of Ogdensburg, 1749–1907. New York: Silver, Burdett and Company, 1907.

The River St. Lawrence in One Panoramic View from Niagara Falls to Quebec. New York: Alex Harthill, 1859.

Roebling, John A. *Report on the Condition of the Niagara Railway Suspension Bridge, 1 Aug. 1860*. Trenton, N.J.: Murphy & Bechtel, 1860.

Russell, John. *The History of the War Between the United States and Great Britain*. Hartford, Conn.: B. & J. Russell, 1815.

Sansom, Joseph. *Travels in Lower Canada*. New York: Kirk & Mercein, 1817.

Schultz, Christian. *Travels on an Inland Voyage 1807 and 1808*. 1810. Reprint. New York: Gregg Press, 1968.

Severance, Frank, ed. "Visit of Rev. Lemuel Covell to Western New York and Canada in the Fall of 1803." *Publications of the Buffalo Historical Society* (1903): 207–16.

Shadd, Mary A. *A Plea for Emigration; or, Notes of Canada West, in its Moral, Social, and Political Aspect*. Detroit: George W. Pattison, 1852.

Silliman, Benjamin. *Remarks Made on a Short Tour between Hartford and Quebec, in the Autumn of 1819*. 2d. ed. New Haven, Conn.: S. Converse, 1824.

Smith, Michael. *A Complete History of the Late War with Great Britain and Her Allies*. Lexington, Ky.: F. Branford, 1816.

————. *Geographical View of the British Possessions in North America*. New York: M. Smith, 1814.

————. *Geographical View of the Province of Upper Canada*. New York: M. Smith, 1813.

————. *Geographical View of the Province of Upper Canada, and Promiscuous Remarks Upon the Government*. Hartford, Conn.: Hale & Hosmer, 1813.

"Smuggling in 1813–1814: A Personal Reminiscence." *Vermont History* 38 (Winter 1970): 22–26.

Snow, Samuel. *The Exile's Return: or Narrative of Samuel Snow, who was Banished to Van Diemen's Land for Participating in the Patriot War in Upper Canada in 1838.* Cleveland: Smead & Cowles, 1846.

Springer, John S. *Forest Life and Forest Trees.* New York: Harper & Brothers, 1851.

Stacey, Charles P., ed. "A Private Report of General Winfield Scott on the Border Situation in 1839." *Canadian Historical Review* 21 (Dec. 1940): 407–14.

Stansbury, Philip. *A Pedestrian Tour of Two Thousand and Three Hundred Miles, in North America.* 1821. Reprint. New York: J. D. Myers & W. Smith, 1822.

A Summer Month, or Recollections of a Visit to the Falls of Niagara and the Lakes. Philadelphia: H.C. Carey & I. Lea, 1823.

Sutherland, Thomas Jefferson. *A Letter to Her Majesty the British Queen.* Albany, N.Y.: C. Van Benthuysen, 1841.

Tanner, H. S. *The Traveller's Handbook for the State of New York, the Province of Canada, and parts of the adjoining States.* 2d ed. New York: T. R. Tanner, 1844.

Thayer, George. "From Vermont to Lake Superior in 1845." *Michigan Historical Collections* 30 (1906): 549–66.

Theller, Edward A. *Canada in 1837–38, showing . . . the Causes of the Late Attempted Revolution and Its Failure.* 2 vols. Philadelphia: Henry F. Anners, 1841.

Thompson, William Tappan. *Major Jones's Sketches of Travel in his Tour from Georgia to Canada.* Philadelphia: Carey & Hart, 1848.

Thompson, Zadock. *Northern Guide.* Burlington, Vt.: S. B. Nichols, 1857.

Thoreau, Henry David. *A Yankee in Canada.* Boston: Ticknor & Fields, 1866.

Tunis's Topographical and Pictorial Guide at Niagara Falls. Niagara Falls, N.Y.: W. E. Tunis, 1856.

Vandewater, Robert. *The Tourist, or Pocket Manual for Travellers.* New York: Harper and Brothers, 1834.

Wallace, Paul A. W., ed. *Thirty Thousand Miles with John Heckewelder.* Pittsburgh: University of Pittsburgh Press, 1958.

Ward, Samuel Ringgold. *Autobiography of a Fugitive Negro.* 1855. Reprint. New York: Arno Press & New York Times, 1968.

White, Samuel. *History of the American Troops During the Late War under the Command of Colonels Fenton and Campbell.* Baltimore: B. Edes, 1830.

Williams, W. *Appelton's Northern and Eastern Traveller's Guide . . . to the Middle States, Canada, New Brunswick, and Nova Scotia.* New York: D. Appleton & Company, 1850.

Winks, Robin, et al., eds. *Four Fugitive Slave Narratives.* Reading, Pa.: Addison-Wesley Publishing Company, 1969.

NEWSPAPERS AND PERIODICALS

Albany Argus
American Almanac
American Quarterly Review
American Railroad Journal
Atlantic Monthly
Boston Daily Advertiser
Boston Daily Evening Transcript
Boston Palladium
The Caroline Almanac and American Freeman's Chronicle
Commercial and Financial Chronicle
Continental Monthly
Daily Albany Gazette
De Bow's Review
Frank Leslie's Illustrated Newspaper
Harper's New Monthly Magazine
Historical Register of the United States
Independent Chronicle
The Knickerbocker
Lippincott's Magazine of Literature, Science, and Education
The Merchant's Magazine and Commercial Review
The Military Monitor and American Register
The Nation
The National Intelligencer
The New England Palladium and Commercial Advertiser
The New Englander
The New York Commercial Advertiser
New York Daily Tribune
New York Evening Post
The New York Evening Star
Niles' Weekly Register
North American Review
Puget Sound Gazette
Rochester Daily Advertiser
The United States Gazette
United States Magazine and Democratic Review
United States Review

SECONDARY SOURCES

BOOKS

Adams, Ephriam D. *The Power of Ideals in American History.* New Haven, Conn.: Yale University Press, 1913.

Aitken, Hugh G. J. *American Capital and Canadian Resources.* Cambridge, Mass.: Harvard University Press, 1961.

Aldrich, Lewis C., ed. *History of Franklin and Grand Isle Counties, Vermont.* Syracuse, N.Y.: D. Mason & Co., 1891.

Allin, C. D., & G. M. Jones. *Annexation, Preferential Trade and Reciprocity.* 1912. Reprint. Westport, Conn.: Greenwood Press, 1971.

Angus, H. F., ed. *British Columbia and the United States: The North Pacific Slope from Fur Trade to Aviation.* 1942. Reprint. New York: Russell & Russell, 1970.

Asher & Adams New Commercial and Statistical Gazetteer of the United States and the Dominion of Canada. New York: Asher & Adams, 1874.

Austin, Aleine. *Matthew Lyon: "New Man" of the Democratic Revolution, 1749–1822.* University Park: Pennsylvania University Press, 1981.

Babcock, Louis. *The War of 1812 on the Niagara Frontier.* Buffalo, N.Y.: Buffalo Historical Society, 1927.

Baritz, Loren. *City on a Hill: A History of Ideas and Myths in America.* New York: John Wiley, 1964.

Barto, Martha Ford. *Passamaquoddy Genealogies of West Isle Families.* Saint John, N.B.: Lingley Printing Company Limited, 1975.

Belohlavek, John M. *"Let the Eagle Soar!" The Foreign Policy of Andrew Jackson.* Lincoln: University of Nebraska Press, 1985.

Bemis, Samuel Flagg. *John Quincy Adams and the Foundations of American Foreign Policy.* New York: Alfred A. Knopf, 1949.

———, ed. *The American Secretaries of State and their Diplomacy.* 10 vols. New York: Alfred A. Knopf, 1928.

Benns, F. Lee. *The American Struggle for the British West Indian Carrying Trade, 1815–1830.* Bloomington: Indiana University Press, 1923.

Berger, Carl. *The Sense of Power: Studies in the Ideas of Canadian Imperialism, 1867–1914.* Toronto: University of Toronto Press, 1970.

Berton, Pierre. *Flames Across the Border: The Invasion of Canada, 1813–1814.* Toronto: McClelland and Stewart, 1982.

———. *The Invasion of Canada, 1812–1813.* Toronto: McClelland and Stewart, 1980.

Bhagat, G. *Americans in India, 1784–1860.* New York: New York University Press, 1970.

Billington, Ray A. *The Protestant Crusade, 1800–1860: A Study in the Origins of American Nativism.* New York: Macmillan Company, 1938.

Bingham, R. W. *The Cradle of the Queen City: History of Buffalo to the Incorporation of the City.* Buffalo, N.Y.: Buffalo Historical Society, 1931.

Bird, Harrison. *War for the West.* New York: Oxford University Press, 1971.

Bishop, Joseph Buddin. *A Chronicle of One Hundred and Fifty Years: The Chamber of Commerce of the State of New York.* New York: Charles Scribner's Sons, 1918.

Bond, Beverly. *The Civilization of the Old Northwest: A Study of Politi-

cal, Social, and Economic Development, 1788–1812. New York: Macmillan Company, 1934.

Bourne, Kenneth. *Britain and the Balance of Power in North America, 1815–1908.* Berkeley: University of California Press, 1967.

Bradley, A. G. *Colonial Americans in Exile: Founders of British Canada.* New York: E. P. Dutton & Company, 1932.

Brebner, John Bartlett. *The Neutral Yankees of Nova Scotia: A Marginal Colony during the Revolutionary Years.* New York: Columbia University Press, 1937.

Brown, Roger H. *The Republic in Peril: 1812.* New York: Columbia University Press, 1964.

Buley, R. Carlyle. *The Old Northwest: Pioneer Period, 1815–1840.* 2 vols. Bloomington: Indiana University Press, 1951.

Burt, A. L. *The Old Province of Quebec.* Toronto: Ryerson Press, 1933.

————. *The United States, Great Britain, and British North America from the Revolution to the Establishment of Peace after the War of 1812.* New Haven, Conn.: Yale University Press, 1940.

Butler, Nicholas Murray. *The Effect of the War of 1812 on the Consolidation of the Union.* Baltimore: Johns Hopkins University Press, n.d.

Callahan, James. *American Foreign Policy in Canadian Relations.* 1937. Reprint. New York: Cooper Square Publishers, 1967.

————. *The Neutrality of the American Lakes and Anglo-American Relations.* Baltimore: Johns Hopkins University Press, 1898.

Campbell, Charles S. *From Revolution to Rapprochement: The United States and Great Britain, 1783–1900.* New York: John Wiley & Sons, 1974.

————. *The Transformation of American Foreign Relations, 1865–1900.* New York: Harper & Row, 1976.

Clark, Charles E. *The Eastern Frontier: The Settlement of Northern New England, 1610–1763.* New York: Alfred A. Knopf, 1970.

Clark, S. D. *Movements of Political Protest in Canada, 1640–1840.* Toronto: University of Toronto Press, 1959.

Coffin, Victor. *The Province of Quebec and the Early American Revolution.* University of Wisconsin Bulletins, Economic and Historical, No. 1. Madison, 1896.

Combs, Jerald. *The Jay Treaty: Political Battleground of the Founding Fathers.* Berkeley: University of California Press, 1970.

Compendium of History and Biography of the City of Detroit and Wayne County, Michigan. Chicago: Henry Taylor, 1909.

Cook, Adrian. *The Alabama Claims: American Politics and Anglo-American Relations, 1865–1872.* Ithaca, N.Y.: Cornell University Press, 1975.

Corbett, P. E. *The Settlement of Canadian-American Disputes.* New Haven, Conn.: Yale University Press, 1937.

Corey, Albert B. *Canadian-American Relations Along the Detroit River.* Detroit: Wayne State University Press, 1957.

_____. *The Crisis of 1830–1842 in Canadian-American Relations.* New Haven, Conn.: Yale University Press, 1941.

Craig, Gerald M. *Upper Canada, 1784–1841.* Toronto: McClelland and Stewart, 1963.

Creighton, Donald. *The Empire of the St. Lawrence.* 1937. Reprint. Toronto: Macmillan Company of Canada, 1956.

Crockett, Walter Hill. *A History of Lake Champlain: A Record of More than Three Centuries, 1609–1936.* Burlington, Vt.: McAuliffe Paper Company, n.d.

_____. *Vermont: The Green Mountain State.* 3 vols. New York: Century History Company, 1921.

Cruikshank, E. A. *The Political Adventures of John Henry: The Record of an International Embroglio.* Toronto: Macmillan Company of Canada, 1936.

Curtis, James C. *The Fox at Bay: Martin Van Buren and the Presidency, 1837–1841.* Lexington: University of Kentucky Press, 1970.

Cushing, Caleb. *The Treaty of Washington: Its Negotiation, Execution, and the Discussions Relating Thereto.* 1873. Reprint. Freeport, N.Y.: Books for Libraries Press, 1970.

Davis, Harold. *An International Community on the St. Croix (1604–1930).* Orono: University of Maine Press, 1950.

Donald, David. *Charles Sumner and the Rights of Man.* New York: Alfred A. Knopf, 1970.

Dowty, Alan. *The Limits of Isolation: The United States and the Crimean War.* New York: New York University Press, 1971.

Doyle, James. *North of America: Images of Canada in the Literature of the United States, 1775–1900.* Toronto: E.C.W. Press, 1985.

Duffy, John J. *An Anxious Democracy: Aspects of the 1830s.* Westport, Conn.: Greenwood Press, 1982.

Dulles, F. R. *Yankees and Samurai: America's Role in the Emergence of Modern Japan, 1791–1900.* New York: Harper & Row, 1965.

Eliot, Charles W. *Winfield Scott: The Soldier and the Man.* New York: Macmillan Company, 1937.

Engelman, Fred L. *The Peace of Christmas Eve.* London: Rupert Hart-Davis, 1962.

Everest, Allan S. *Moses Hazen and the Canadian Refugees in the American Revolution.* Syracuse, N.Y.: Syracuse University Press, 1976.

_____. *The War of 1812 in the Champlain Valley.* Syracuse, N.Y.: Syracuse University Press, 1981.

Everts, L. H., & J. M. Holcomb. *History of St. Lawrence County, New York, 1749–1878.* Philadelphia: L. H. Everts & Co., 1878.

Fenwick, Charles G. *A History of the Neutrality Laws of the United States.* Washington, D.C.: Carnegie Endowment, 1913.

Field, James A., Jr. *America and the Mediterranean World, 1776–1882.* Princeton, N.J.: Princeton University Press, 1969.

Flick, Alexander, ed. *History of the State of New York.* 10 vols. New York: Columbia University Press, 1934.

Foster, John W. *Limitation of Armament on the Great Lakes.* Washington, D.C.: Carnegie Endowment, 1914.

Fuller, G. N. *Economic and Social Beginnings of Michigan.* Lansing, Mich.: Wynkoop, Hallenbeck, Crawford, 1916.

Garand, Philias S. *The History of the City of Ogdensburg.* Ogdensburg, N.Y.: Manuel Belleville, 1927.

Gilpin, Alec. *The War of 1812 in the Old Northwest.* East Lansing: Michigan State University Press, 1958.

Gluek, Alvin. *Minnesota and the Manifest Destiny of the Canadian Northwest.* Toronto: Toronto University Press, 1958.

Goebel, Dorothy Burne. *William Henry Harrison: A Political Biography.* Historical Bureau of the Indiana Library and Historical Department, Indianapolis, 1926.

Goetzmann, William. *Exploration and Empire: The Explorer and the Scientist in the Winning of the West.* New York: Alfred A. Knopf, 1966.

Graebner, Norman A. *Empire on the Pacific: A Study in American Continental Expansion.* New York: Ronald Press, 1955.

Gray, Clayton. *Conspiracy in Canada.* Montreal: L'Atelier Press, 1957.

Gray, Wood. *The Hidden Civil War: The Story of the Copperheads.* New York: Macmillan Company, 1942.

Hansen, Marcus L., and J. B. Brebner. *The Mingling of the Canadian and American Peoples.* New Haven, Conn.: Yale University Press, 1940.

Harris, Wilmer C. *Public Life of Zachariah Chandler.* Lansing: Michigan Historical Commission, 1917.

Hart, Albert Bushnell, ed. *Commonwealth History of Massachusetts.* 4 vols. New York: States History Company, 1929.

Hatch, L. C. *Maine: A History.* 3 vols. New York: American Historical Society, 1919.

Hatch, Robert. *Thrust for Canada: The American Attempt on Quebec in 1775–1776.* Boston: Houghton Mifflin Company, 1979.

Hatzenbuehler, Ronald, & Robert Ivie. *Congress Declares War: Rhetoric, Leadership and Partisanship in the Early Republic.* Kent, Ohio: Kent State University Press, 1983.

Haynes, Frederick E. *The Reciprocity Treaty with Canada of 1854.* Baltimore: Guggenheimer, Weil & Company, 1892.

Headley, John W. *Confederate Operations in Canada and New York.* New York: Neale Publishing Company, 1906.

Heald, Morrell, & Lawrence S. Kaplan. *Culture and Diplomacy: The American Experience.* Westport, Conn.: Greenwood Press, 1977.

Higham, John. *Strangers in the Land: Patterns of American Nativism, 1860–1925.* New Brunswick, N.J.: Rutgers University Press, 1963.

Hill, Hamilton Andrews. *The Trade and Commerce of Boston 1630 to 1890.* Boston: Damrell & Upham, 1895.

History of Niagara Falls County, N.Y. New York: Sanford & Company, 1878.

Holt, W. Stull. *Treaties Defeated by the Senate: A Study of the Struggle between President and Senate Over the Conduct of Foreign Relations.* Baltimore: Johns Hopkins University Press, 1933.

Horsman, Reginald. *The Causes of the War of 1812.* Philadelphia: University of Pennsylvania Press, 1962.

_____. *Expansion and American Indian Policy.* East Lansing: Michigan State University Press, 1967.

_____. *Race and Manifest Destiny: The Origins of American Racial Anglo-Saxonism.* Cambridge, Mass.: Harvard University Press, 1981.

Horton, John T., et al. *History of Northwestern New York: Erie, Niagara, Wyoming, Genesee and Orleans Counties.* 3 vols. New York: Lewis Historical Publishing Company, 1947.

Hotchkiss, William. *The Early Days of the Erie Canal—Adventure in Statesmanship.* Princeton, N.J.: Princeton University Press, 1940.

Hough, F. D. *History of St. Lawrence and Franklin Counties.* Albany, 1853.

Hungerford, Edward, et al. *Vermont Central–Central Vermont: A Study in Human Effort.* Boston: Railway & Locomotive Historical Society, 1942.

Hurd, Duane. *History of Clinton and Franklin Counties.* Philadelphia: J. W. Lewis, 1880.

Hutchinson, Bruce. *The Struggle for the Border.* Toronto: Longmans Green & Co., 1955.

Ingersoll, Charles. *Historical Sketch of the Second War between the United States of America and Great Britain.* 2 vols. Philadelphia: J. Lippincott, 1845.

Innis, Harold A. *The Cod Fisheries: The History of an International Economy.* Toronto: University of Toronto Press, 1954.

_____. *The Fur Trade in Canada.* Toronto: University of Toronto Press, 1956.

Iriye, Akira. *From Nationalism to Internationalism: U.S. Foreign Policy to 1914.* London: Routledge & Kegan Paul, 1977.

Irwin, Leonard Bertram. *Pacific Railways and Nationalism in the Canadian-American Northwest, 1845–1873.* Philadelphia: University of Pennsylvania Press, 1939.

Jacobs, M. C. *Winning Oregon: A Study of An Expansionist Movement.* Caldwell, Idaho: Caxton Printers, 1938.

Jenkins, Brian. *Fenians and Anglo-American Relations During Reconstruction.* Ithaca, N.Y.: Cornell University Press, 1969.

Johnson, Arthur M., and Barry E. Supple. *Boston Capital and Western Railroads: A Study in Nineteenth Century Railroad Investment Process.* Cambridge, Mass.: Harvard University Press, 1967.

Johnson, Crisfield. *History of Oswego County, New York, 1789–1877.* Philadelphia: L. H. Everts & Co., 1877.

Johnson, Emory, et al. *History of the Domestic and Foreign Commerce of the United States.* 2 vols. Washington, D.C.: Carnegie Institution, 1915.

Johnston, Walter, Jr. *Jefferson and the Presidency: Leadership in the Young Republic.* Ithaca, N.Y.: Cornell University Press, 1978.

Jones, Howard. *To the Webster-Ashburton Treaty: A Study in Anglo-American Relations, 1783–1842.* Chapel Hill: University of North Carolina Press, 1977.

Jordan, Winthrop. *White Over Black: American Attitudes Toward the Negro, 1550–1812.* Chapel Hill: University of North Carolina Press, 1963.

Keenleyside, Hugh. *Canada and the United States: Some Aspects of their Historical Relations.* 1929. Reprint. Port Washington, N.Y.: Kennikat Press, 1971.

Kerr, Wilfred. *The Maritime Provinces of British North America and the American Revolution.* Sackville, N.B., 1941.

Kinchen, Oscar A. *Confederate Operations in Canada and the North.* North Quincy, Mass.: Christopher Publishing House, 1970.

_____. *Daredevils of the Confederate Army: The Story of the St. Albans Raiders.* Boston: Christopher Publishing House, 1959.

_____. *The Rise and Fall of the Patriot Hunters.* New York: Bookman Associates, 1956.

Knowlton, Isaac C. *Annals of Calais, Maine, and St. Stephen, New Brunswick.* St. Stephen, N.B.: Print'N Press, 1875.

Kushner, Howard I. *Conflict on the Northwest Coast: American-Russian Rivalry in the Pacific Northwest, 1790–1867.* Westport, Conn.: Greenwood Press, 1975.

La Feber, Walter. *The New Empire: An Interpretation of American Expansion, 1860–1898.* Ithaca, N.Y.: Cornell University Press, 1963.

Lanctot, Gustav. *Canada and the American Revolution, 1774–1783.* Translated by Margaret Cameron. Toronto: Clarke, Irwin & Company, 1967.

Landon, Fred. *Western Ontario and the American Frontier.* Toronto: Ryerson Press, 1941.

Landon, Harry. *Bugles on the Border: The Story of the War of 1812 in Northern New York.* Watertown, N.Y.: Watertown Daily Times, 1954.

_____. *The North Country; A History Embracing Jefferson, St. Lawrence, Oswego, Lewis and Franklin Counties, New York.* 4 vols. Indianapolis: Historical Publishing Company, 1932.

Laughlin, J. Laurence, and H. Parker Willis. *Reciprocity.* New York: Baker & Taylor Co., 1903.

Lewis, Cleona. *America's Stake in International Investments.* Washington, D.C.: Brookings Institution, 1938.

Logan, John A. *No Transfer! An American Security Principle.* New Haven, Conn.: Yale University Press, 1961.

Lonn, Ella. *Desertion During the Civil War.* 1928. Reprint. Gloucester, Mass.: Peter Smith, 1966.

Lower, A. R. M., et al. *The North American Assault on the Canadian For-*

est: A History of the Lumber Trade Between Canada and the United States. Toronto: Ryerson Press, 1938.

Lubec Historical Society. *200 Years of Lubec History, 1776–1976.* Lubec, Maine: Lubec Historical Society, 1976.

Luxon, Norval. *"Niles' Weekly Register": News Magazine of the Nineteenth Century.* Baton Rouge: Louisiana State University Press, 1947.

Lycan, Gilbert. *Alexander Hamilton and American Foreign Policy: A Design for Greatness.* Norman: University of Oklahoma Press, 1970.

McCabe, James Osborne. *The San Juan Boundary Question.* Toronto: University of Toronto Press, 1964.

McFarland, Raymond. *A History of the New England Fisheries.* New York: D. Appleton & Co., 1911.

McInnis, W. L. *The Unguarded Frontier.* New York: Doubleday Doran & Co., 1942.

MacNutt, W. S. *The Atlantic Provinces: The Emergence of Colonial Society.* Toronto: McClelland and Stewart, 1957.

Malone, Dumas. *Jefferson the President: Second Term, 1805–1809.* Boston: Houghton Mifflin, 1974.

Marshall, Herbert, Frank A. Southard, Jr., and Kenneth W. Taylor. *Canadian-American Industries: A Study in International Investment.* New Haven, Conn.: Yale University Press, 1936.

Mason, Philip, ed. *After Tippecanoe: Some Aspects of the War of 1812.* East Lansing: Michigan State University Press, 1963.

Masters, Donald C. *The Reciprocity Treaty of 1854.* London: Longmans Green & Company, 1937.

May, Robert E. *The Southern Dream of a Caribbean Empire, 1854–1861.* Baton Rouge: Louisiana State University Press, 1973.

Merk, Frederick. *Albert Gallatin and the Oregon Problem: A Study in Anglo-American Diplomacy.* Cambridge, Mass.: Harvard University Press, 1971.

_____. *Fruits of Propaganda in the Tyler Administration.* Cambridge, Mass.: Harvard University Press, 1971.

_____. *Manifest Destiny and Mission in American History: A Reinterpretation.* New York: Random House, 1963.

_____. *The Monroe Doctrine and American Expansionism, 1843–1849.* New York: Alfred A. Knopf, 1966.

Miller, Hunter. *San Juan Archipelago: A Study of the Joint Occupation of San Juan Island.* Bellows Falls, N.Y.: Wyndham Press, 1943.

Mills, James C. *Our Inland Seas: Their Shipping and Commerce for Three Centuries.* Chicago: A. C. McClurg & Co., 1910.

Monro, Alexander. *The United States and the Dominion of Canada.* Saint John, N.B.: Barnes & Company, 1879.

Moore, Christopher. *The Loyalists: Revolution, Exile, Settlement.* Toronto: Macmillan of Canada, 1984.

Moore, David R. *Canada and the United States, 1815–1830.* Chicago: Jennings & Graham, 1910.

Morison, Samuel Eliot. *By Land and Sea: Essays and Addresses*. New York: Alfred A. Knopf, 1953.

———. *The Maritime History of Massachusetts, 1783–1860*. Boston: Houghton, Mifflin, 1921.

Morris, Richard B. *The Peacemakers: The Great Powers and American Independence*. New York: Harper & Row, 1965.

Morton, W. L. *The Critical Years: The Union of British North America, 1857–1873*. Toronto: McClelland and Stewart, 1964.

Mowat, Grace Helen. *The Diverting History of a Loyalist Town*. St. Andrews, N.B.: Charlotte County Cottage Craft, 1932.

Murchie, Guy. *St. Croix: The Sentinel River*. New York: Duell, Sloan & Pearce, 1947.

Nash, Roderick. *Wilderness and the American Mind*. 3d ed. New Haven, Conn.: Yale University Press, 1982.

Nichols, Roy F. *Franklin Pierce: Young Hickory of the Granite Hills*. 2d ed. rev. Philadelphia: University of Pennsylvania Press, 1958.

North, Douglas C. *The Economic Growth of the United States, 1790–1860*. 1961. Reprint. New York: W. W. Norton, 1966.

Nye, Russell B. *This Almost Chosen People: Essays in the History of American Ideas*. Toronto: Macmillan Company of Canada, 1966.

Paolino, Ernest. *The Foundations of American Empire: William H. Seward and American Foreign Policy*. Ithaca, N.Y.: Cornell University Press, 1973.

Parker, William B. *The Life and Public Services of Justin Morrill*. Boston: Houghton Mifflin Company, 1924.

Pease, William H. and Jane H. *Black Utopia: Negro Communal Experiments in America*. Madison: State Historical Society of Wisconsin, 1963.

Perkins, Bradford. *Castlereagh and Adams: England and the United States, 1812–1823*. Berkeley: University of California Press, 1964.

———. *Prologue to War: England and the United States, 1805–1812*. Berkeley: University of California Press, 1961.

Piper, Don C. *The International Law of the Great Lakes*. Durham, N.C.: Duke University Press, 1967.

Plesur, Milton. *America's Outward Thrust: Approaches to Foreign Affairs, 1865–1890*. Dekalb: Northern Illinois University Press, 1971.

Pletcher, David M. *The Diplomacy of Annexation: Texas, Oregon, and the Mexican War*. Columbia: University of Missouri Press, 1973.

Poor, Laura E. *The First International Railway: Life and Writings of John Alfred Poor*. New York: G. P. Putnam's Sons, 1892.

Porter, Albert H. *Historical Sketch of Niagara from 1678–1876*. 1876.

Porter, Kenneth W. *John Jacob Astor, Businessman*. 2 vols. Cambridge, Mass.: Harvard University Press, 1931.

Pratt, Julius W. *Expansionists of 1812*. 1925. Reprint. New York: Peter Smith, 1957.

Rae, W. Fraser. *Columbia and Canada: Notes on the Great Republic and the New Dominion*. New York: G. P. Putnam's Sons, 1879.

Rann, W. S., ed. *History of Chittenden County, Vermont*. 2 vols. Syracuse, N.Y.: D. Mason & Co., 1886.

Rawlyk, George. *Nova Scotia's Massachusetts: A Study of Massachusetts-Nova Scotia Relations, 1630–1784*. Montreal: McGill-Queens' University Press, 1973.

Rich, Edwin. *Montreal and the Fur Trade*. Montreal: McGill University Press, 1966.

Rippy, J. Fred. *Rivalry of the United States and Great Britain over Latin America, 1808–1830*. Baltimore: Johns Hopkins University Press, 1929.

Ritcheson, Charles R. *Aftermath of Revolution: British Policy Toward the United States, 1783–1795*. Dallas: Southern Methodist University Press, 1969.

Rohrbough, Malcom. *The Trans-Appalachian Frontier: People, Societies, and Institutions, 1775–1850*. New York: Oxford University Press, 1978.

Ross, J. Ogden, comp. *The Steamboats of Lake Champlain, 1809–1930*. Albany: Champlain Transportation Company, 1930.

Royster, Charles. *A Revolutionary People at War: The Continental Army and American Character*. Chapel Hill: University of North Carolina Press, 1979.

Sanford, Charles, ed. *Manifest Destiny and the Imperialism Question*. New York: John Wiley & Sons, 1974.

Sears, Louis Martin. *Jefferson and the Embargo*. Durham, N.C.: Duke University Press, 1927.

Setser, Vernon G. *The Commercial Reciprocity Treaty of the United States, 1774–1829*. Philadelphia: University of Pennsylvania Press, 1937.

Severance, Frank H., ed. *Studies of the Niagara Frontier*. Buffalo, N.Y.: Buffalo Historical Society, 1911.

Sevigny, P.-Andre. *Trade and Navigation on the Chambly Canal: An Historical Overview*. Ottawa: Parks Canada, 1983.

Shaw, Ronald. *Erie Water West: A History of the Erie Canal, 1792–1854*. Lexington: University of Kentucky Press, 1966.

Shippee, Lester B. *Canadian-American Relations, 1849–1874*. 1939. Reprint. New York: Russell & Russell, 1970.

Siebert, Wilbur. *The Exodus of the Loyalists from Penobscot to Passamaquoddy*. Columbus: Ohio State University Press, 1914.

―――. *The Underground Railroad: From Slavery to Freedom*. 1898. Reprint. New York: Russell & Russell, 1967.

Smith, Goldwin. *Canada and the Canadian Question*. 1891. Reprint. Toronto: University of Toronto Press, 1971.

―――. *The Treaty of Washington 1871*. New York: Russell & Russell, 1941.

Smith, Henry P., ed. *History of the City of Buffalo and Erie County*. 2 vols. Syracuse, N.Y.: D. Mason & Co., Publishers, 1884.

Smith, Joe Patterson. *The Republican Expansionists of the Early Recon-struction Era.* Chicago, 1933.

Smith, Justin. *Our Struggle for the Fourteenth Colony: Canada and the American Revolution.* 1907. Reprint. New York: Da Capo Press, 1974.

Somkin, Fred. *The Unquiet Eagle: Memory and Desire in the Idea of American Freedom, 1815–1860.* Ithaca, N.Y.: Cornell University Press, 1967.

Spencer, Ivor. *The Victor and the Spoils: A Life of William L. Marcy.* Providence, R.I.: Brown University Press, 1959.

Spivak, Burton. *Jefferson's English Crisis: Commerce, Embargo, and the Republican Revolution.* Charlottesville: University Press of Virginia, 1979.

Stagg, John C. A. *Mr. Madison's War: Politics, Diplomacy and Warfare in the Early American Republic, 1783–1830.* Princeton, N.J.: Princeton University Press, 1983.

Stanley, George F. G. *The War of 1812: Land Operations.* Toronto: Mac-millan of Canada, 1983.

Stanwood, Edward. *American Tariff Controversies in the Nineteenth Cen-tury.* 1903. Reprint. New York: Garland Publishing, 1974.

Stewart, Donald. *The Opposition Press of the Federalist Period.* Albany: State University of New York, 1969.

Stourzh, Gerald. *Benjamin Franklin and American Foreign Policy.* Chi-cago: University of Chicago Press, 1969.

Stover, John F. *Iron Road to the West: America's Railroads in the 1850s.* New York: Columbia University Press, 1978.

Stuart, Reginald C. *War and American Thought: From the Revolution to the Monroe Doctrine.* Kent, Ohio: Kent State University Press, 1982.

Swisher, Carl B. *The Taney Period, 1836–64.* Vol. 5 of *History of the Su-preme Court of the United States.* New York: Macmillan Co., 1974.

Tansill, Charles C. *The Canadian Reciprocity Treaty of 1854.* Baltimore: Johns Hopkins University Press, 1922.

Taussig, F. W. *The Tariff History of the United States: A Series of Essays.* New York: G. P. Putnam's Sons, 1894.

Taylor, George Rogers. *The Transportation Revolution, 1815–1861.* New York: Harper & Row, 1951.

Thompson, Zadock. *History of Vermont, Natural, Civil, and Statistical.* 2 vols. Burlington, Vt.: Chauncey Goodrich, 1842.

Tiffany, Orrin. *The Relations of the United States to the Canadian Rebel-lions of 1837–1838.* Buffalo, N.Y.: Buffalo Historical Society, 1905.

Truesdell, L. E. *The Canadian Born in the United States.* New Haven, Conn.: Yale University Press, 1943.

Tucker, Gilbert N. *The Canadian Commercial Revolution, 1845–1851.* New Haven, Conn.: Yale University Press, 1936.

Tuttle, Mrs. George Fuller. *Three Centuries in the Champlain Valley: A Collection of Historical Facts and Incidents.* Plattsburgh, N.Y.: Daugh-ters of the American Revolution, 1909.

Utley, Henry, and Byron McCutcheon. *Michigan as a Province, Territory, and State, the Twenty-Sixth Member of the Federal Union.* 2 vols. New York: Publishing Society of Michigan, 1906.

Van Alstyne, Richard W. *The Rising American Empire.* New York: Oxford University Press, 1960.

Vander Hill, C. Warren. *Settling the Great Lakes Frontier: Immigration to Michigan, 1837–1924.* Lansing: Michigan Historical Commission, 1970.

Varg, Paul A. *New England and Foreign Relations, 1789–1850.* Hanover, N.H.: University Press of New England, 1983.

———. *United States Foreign Relations, 1820–1860.* East Lansing: Michigan State University Press, 1979.

Walworth, H. *Four Eras in the History of Travelling Between Montreal and New York, from 1793 to 1892.* Plattsburgh, N.Y.: Republican Office, 1892.

Warner, Donald F. *The Idea of Continental Union: Agitation for the Annexation of Canada to the United States, 1849–1893.* Lexington: University Press of Kentucky, 1960.

Weinberg, Albert K. *Manifest Destiny: A Study of Nationalist Expansion in American History.* Baltimore: Johns Hopkins University Press, 1935.

Wesley, Edgar Bruce. *Guarding the Frontier: A Study of Frontier Defense from 1815–1825.* Minneapolis: University of Minnesota Press, 1935.

Wilgus, W. J. *The Railway Interrelations of the United States and Canada.* New Haven, Conn.: Yale University Press, 1937.

Williams, T. Harry. *The History of American Wars: From 1745 to 1918.* New York: Alfred A. Knopf, 1981.

Williams, William A. *The Contours of American History.* Cleveland: World Publishing Company, 1961.

———. *Empire as a Way of Life.* New York: Oxford University Press, 1980.

Willoughby, William R. *The St. Lawrence Waterway: A Study in Politics and Diplomacy.* Madison: University of Wisconsin Press, 1961.

Wilson, Harold Fisher. *The Hill Country of Northern New England: Its Social and Economic History in the Nineteenth and Twentieth Centuries.* Montpelier: Vermont Historical Society, 1947.

Winks, Robin. *The Blacks in Canada: A History.* New Haven, Conn.: Yale University Press, 1971.

———. *Canada and the United States: The Civil War Years.* Baltimore: Johns Hopkins University Press, 1960.

Wright, J. Leitch. *Britain and the American Frontier, 1783–1815.* Athens: University of Georgia Press, 1975.

Zaslow, Morris, ed. *The Defended Border: Upper Canada and the War of 1812.* Toronto: Macmillan of Canada, 1964.

ARTICLES AND ESSAYS

Arrington, Joseph Earl. "Godfrey N. Frankenstein's Moving Panorama of Niagara Falls." *New York History* 49 (Apr. 1968): 169–99.

Baldwin, J. R. "The Ashburton-Webster Settlement." Canadian Historical Association, *Annual Report* (1938): 121–33.

Banks, Ronald F. "The War of 1812: A Turning Point in the Movement to Separate Maine from Massachusetts." In *A History of Maine: A Collection of Readings on the History of Maine, 1600–1974*, edited by Ronald F. Banks, pp. 143–47. Dubuque: Kendall Hunt Publishing Company, 1974.

Barlow, William R. "The Coming of War in Michigan Territory." *Michigan History* 53 (1969): 94–108.

———. "Ohio's Congressmen and the War of 1812." *Ohio History* 72 (1963): 175–94, 257–59.

Baskerville, Peter. "Americans in Britain's Backyard: The Railway Era in Upper Canada, 1850–1880." *Business History Review* 55 (Autumn 1981): 314–26.

Bemis, Samuel Flagg. "Canada and the Peace Settlement of 1782–3." *Canadian Historical Review* 14 (1933): 265–84.

———. "Relations between the Vermont Separatists and Great Britain, 1789–91." *American Historical Review* 21 (Apr. 1916): 547–60.

Berger, Carl. "Internationalism, Continentalism and the Writing of History: Comments on the Carnegie Series on the Relations of Canada and the United States." In *The Influence of the United States on Canadian Development*, edited by R. A. Preston, pp. 32–54. Durham, N.C.: Duke University Press, 1972.

Blegen, T. C. "A Plan of Union of British North America and the United States 1866." *Mississippi Valley Historical Review* 4 (March 1918): 470–83.

Bonham, Milledge L., Jr. "Alexander McLeod: Bone of Contention." *New York History* 18 (Apr. 1937): 189–217.

Bovey, Wilfred. "Confederate Agents in Canada During the American Civil War." *Canadian Historical Review* 2 (Mar. 1921): 46–57.

Brown, George W. "The Opening of the St. Lawrence to American Shipping." *Canadian Historical Review* 7 (Mar. 1926): 4–12.

———. "The St. Lawrence in the Boundary Settlement of 1783." *Canadian Historical Review* 9 (June 1928): 223–38.

Brynn, Edward. "Patterns of Dissent: Vermont's Opposition to the War of 1812." *Vermont History* 40 (Winter 1972): 10–27.

Burpee, Lawrence J. "Influence of the War of 1812 upon the Settlement of Western Canada." *Ontario Historical Society Papers and Records* 12 (1914): 114–20.

Burrage, Henry S. "The Attitude of Maine in the Northeastern Boundary Controversy." Maine Historical Society, *Collections* (1904): 353–68.

Buzanski, Peter M. "Alaska and Nineteenth Century American Diplomacy." *Journal of the West* 6 (July 1967): 451–67.

Cady, John F. "Western Opinion and the War of 1812." *Ohio Archeological and Historical Society* 33 (Oct. 1923): 427–76.

Calkin, Homer. "St. Albans in Reverse: The Fenian Raid of 1866." *Vermont History* 35 (Jan. 1967): 19–34.

Callahan, James M. "The Alaska Purchase and Americo-Canadian Relations," *West Virginia University Studies in History* (1908), Nos. 2 and 3.

———. "Americo-Canadian Relations Concerning Annexation, 1846–1871." In *Studies in American History*, pp. 187–214. Bloomington: Indiana University Press, 1926.

Careless, J. M. S. "The Lowe Brothers, 1852–70: A Study in Business Relations on the North Pacific Coast." *B.C. Studies* 2 (1969): 1–18.

Casey, Richard P. "North Country Nemesis: The Potash Rebellion and the Embargo of 1807–1809." *The New York Historical Society Quarterly* 64 (Jan. 1980): 31–49.

Chazanoff, William. "Joseph Ellicot, the Embargo, and the War of 1812." *Niagara Frontier* 10 (Spring 1963): 1–18.

Clark, A. J. "When Jefferson Davis Visited Canada." Ontario Historical Society, *Papers and Records* 19 (1922): 87–89.

Cleaveland, Dorothy K. "Trade and Trade Routes of Northern New York from the Beginning of Settlement to the Coming of the Railroad." *Quarterly Journal of the New York State Historical Association* 4 (Oct. 1923): 205–31.

Cleland, Robert G. "Asiatic Trade and the American Occupation of the Pacific Coast." American Historical Association, *Annual Report* (1911): 283–89.

Cloud, Barbara. "Oregon in the 1820s: The Congressional Perspective." *Western Historical Quarterly* 12 (Apr. 1981): 145–64.

Coleman, Christopher. "The Ohio Valley in the Preliminaries of the War of 1812." *Mississippi Valley Historical Review* 7 (June 1920): 39–50.

Colquhoun, A. H. G. "The Reciprocity Negotiations with the United States in 1869." *Canadian Historical Review* 8 (June 1927): 232–42.

Copp, Walter. "Nova Scotian Trade During the War of 1812." *Canadian Historical Review* 18 (June 1937): 141–55.

Corey, Albert B. "Canadian-American Relations along the Detroit River." Detroit Historical Society (1957).

———. "Canadian Border Defence Problems after 1814 to their Culmination in the 'Forties.'" Canadian Historical Association, *Annual Report* (1938): 111–20.

Craig, Gerald M. "The American Impact on the Upper Canadian Reform Movement Before 1837." *Canadian Historical Review* 29 (Sept. 1948): 333–52.

Cruikshank, E. A. "Immigration from the United States into Upper Canada, 1784–1812, its Character and Results." Ontario Education Association. *Proceedings of the Thirty-Ninth Annual Convention.* (1900): 263–83.

———. "A Study of Disaffection in Upper Canada 1812–1815." Royal Society of Canada, *Transactions* 6 (1912), sec. 2: 11–66.

Current, Richard N. "Webster's Propaganda and the Ashburton Treaty." *Mississippi Valley Historical Review* 34 (Sept. 1947): 187–200.

Curti, Merle. "Young America." *American Historical Review* 32 (Oct. 1962): 34–55.

Dashew, Doris. "The Story of an Illusion: The Plan to Trade the Alabama Claims for Canada." *Civil War History* 15 (Dec. 1969): 332–48.

Davies, Robert B. " 'Peacefully Working to Conquer the World': The Singer Manufacturing Company in Foreign Markets, 1854–1889." *Business History Review* 43 (Autumn 1969): 299–325.

De Rosier, A. H. "The Settlement of the San Juan Controversy." *Southern Quarterly* 4 (1965): 74–88.

Dickey, John. "Both Sides of the Border: Perspectives on two Centuries of Canadian-American Relations." *Vermont History* 44 (Spring 1976): 45–50.

Dion, Leon. "Natural Law and Manifest Destiny in the Era of the American Revolution." *Canadian Journal of Economics and Political Science* 23 (1957): 227–47.

Dorsheimer, William. "The Village of Buffalo During the War of 1812." Buffalo Historical Society, *Publications* 1 (1879): 185–209.

Dozer, D. M. "Anti-Expansionism during the Johnson Administration." *Pacific Historical Review* 12 (Sept. 1943): 253–75.

Duffy, John, and H. N. Müller, "The Great Wolf Hunt: The Popular Response in Vermont to the *Patriote* Uprising of 1837." *Journal of American Studies* 8 (Aug. 1974): 153–69.

Egan, Clifford. "The Path to War in 1812 through the Eyes of a New Hampshire 'War Hawk.' " *Historical New Hampshire* 30 (1975): 147–77.

Falk, Stanley. "Disarmament on the Great Lakes: Myth or Reality?" *U.S. Naval Institute Proceedings* 87 (Dec. 1961): 63–79.

Foner, Philip S. "The Colored Inhabitants of Vancouver Island." *B.C. Studies* 8 (Winter 1970–71): 29–33.

Forbes, John. "Boston Smuggling, 1807–1815." *American Neptune* 1 (Apr. 1950): 145–49.

Ford, Worthington, C. "Goldwin Smith's Visit to the United States in 1864." Massachusetts Historical Society, *Proceedings* 44 (Oct. 1910): 3–12.

Francis, James M. "Montana Business and Canadian Regionalism in the 1870s and 1880s." *Western Historical Quarterly* 12 (July 1981): 291–304.

Frank, Douglas. "The Canadian Rebellion and the American Public." *Niagara Frontier* (Winter 1969): 96–104.

Frankel, Jeffrey A. "The 1807–1809 Embargo Against Great Britain." *Journal of Economic History* 42 (June 1982): 291–308.

Franklin, John Hope. "The Southern Expansionists of 1848." *Journal of Southern History* 25 (Aug. 1959): 323–38.

Fridley, Russell W. "When Minnesota Coveted Canada." *Minnesota History* 41 (Summer 1968): 76–79.

Galbraith, John S. "British-American Competition in the Border Trade of the 1820s." *Minnesota History* 36 (Sept. 1959): 241–49.

Gates, Charles M. "The West in American Diplomacy, 1812–1815." *Mississippi Valley Historical Review* 26 (Mar. 1940): 499–510.

Gill, George. "Edward Everett and the Northeastern Boundary Controversy." *New England Quarterly* 42 (June 1969): 201–13.

Golloday, Dennis. "The United States and British North American Fisheries, 1815–1818." *American Neptune* 33 (Oct. 1973): 246–57.

Graham, Gerald S. "The Gypsum Trade of the Maritime Provinces: Its Relation to American Diplomacy in the Early Nineteenth Century." *Agricultural History* 12 (July 1938): 209–23.

Greening, W. W. "The Lumber Industry in the Ottawa Valley and the American Market in the Nineteenth Century." *Ontario History* 42 (June 1970): 134–36.

Haeger, John D. "The American Fur Company and the Chicago of 1812–1835." *Journal of the Illinois State Historical Society* 41 (1968): 117–39.

Hafter, Ruth. "The Riel Rebellion and Manifest Destiny." *Dalhousie Review* 45 (Winter 1965–66): 447–56.

Hall, Ellery. "Canadian Annexation Sentiment in Kentucky Prior to the War of 1812." *Register of the Kentucky Historical Society* 27 (1930): 372–80.

Hamer, Marguerite. "Luring Canadian Soldiers into Union Lines during the War between the States." *Canadian Historical Review* 27 (June 1946): 151–62.

Hamil, Fred C. "Fairfield and the River Thames." *Ohio Archeological and Historical Quarterly* 48 (Jan. 1939): 1–19.

———. "The Moravians of the River Thames." *Michigan History* 33 (June 1949): 97–116.

Hand, Augustus. "Local Incidents of the Papineau Rebellion." *New York History* 15 (1934): 376–87.

Harvey, D. C. "The Halifax Castine Expedition." *Dalhousie Review* 18 (Spring 1938): 207–13.

Hathaway, Richard J. "From Ontario to the Great Lake State: Canadians in Michigan." *Michigan History* 67 (Mar.-Apr. 1983): 42–46.

Havran, Martin J. "Windsor and Detroit Relations during the Civil War." *Michigan History* 38 (Dec. 1954): 371–89.

Heath, Gary. "The St. Albans Raid: Vermont Viewpoint," *Vermont History* 33 (Jan. 1965): 251–54.

Hickey, Donald R. "American Trade Restrictions During the War of 1812." *Journal of American History* 68 (Dec. 1981): 517–38.

———. "A Dissenting Voice: Matthew Lyon on the Conquest of Canada." *Register of the Kentucky Historical Society* 76 (1978): 45–52.

Higham, Robin. "The Port of Boston and the Embargo of 1807–1809." *American Neptune* 16 (July 1956): 189–212.

Hill, Hamilton. "The Trade, Commerce and Navigation of Boston, 1780–1880." In *The Memorial History of Boston*, edited by Justin Winsor, 4:195–234. Boston: James R. Osgood, 1883.

Horsman, Reginald. "Wisconsin and the War of 1812." *Wisconsin Magazine of History* 46 (1962): 3–15.

Howay, F. W. "The Negro Immigration into Vancouver Island in 1858." *Proceedings and Transactions of the Royal Society of Canada* 3d ser., 29 (May 1935): 145–56.

Husband, Michael B. "Senator Lewis F. Linn and the Oregon Question." *Missouri Historical Review* 66 (Oct. 1971): 1–19.

Inkster, Tom H. "International Storm Over the San Juans." *Montana* 17 (1967): 36–43.

Irish, Maria. "The Northeastern Boundary of Maine." *Journal of American History* 16 (1922): 311–22.

Iriye, Akira. "Culture and Power: International Relations as Intercultural Relations." *Diplomatic History* 3 (Spring 1979): 115–28.

Irwin, Robert J. A. "William Hamilton Merritt and the First Welland Canal." *Niagara Frontier* 11 (Winter 1964), 105–18.

Jarvis, Reed. "San Juan Island's Pig War." *Journal of the West* 7 (Apr. 1968): 236–45.

Johannsen, Robert W. "Stephen Douglas and the American Mission." In *The Frontier Challenge: Response to the Trans-Mississippi West*, edited by John G. Clark, pp. 111–40. Lawrence: University of Kansas Press, 1971.

Jones, Howard. "Anglophobia and the Aroostook War." *New England Quarterly* 48 (Dec. 1975): 519–39.

———. "The Caroline Affair." *The Historian* 38 (May 1976): 485–502.

Kazar, John Jr. "The Canadian View of the Confederate Raid on St. Albans." *Vermont History* 33 (Jan. 1965): 255–73.

Kerr, Wilfred. "The Merchants of Nova Scotia and the American Revolution." *Canadian Historical Review* 13 (Mar. 1932): 20–36.

Kilby, William Henry. "A New England Town Under Foreign Martial Law." *New England Magazine* 14 (Aug. 1896): 685–98.

Kushner, Howard I. "Visions of the Northwest Coast: Gwinn and Seward in the 1850s." *Western Historical Quarterly* 4 (July 1973): 295–306.

La Feber, Walter. "Foreign Policies of a New Nation: Franklin, Madison, and the 'Dream of a New Land to Fulfill with People in Self-Control,' 1750–1804." In *From Colony to Empire: Essays in the History of American Foreign Relations*, edited by William A. Williams, pp. 10–37. New York: John Wiley & Sons, 1972.

Landon, Fred. "Abolitionist Interest in Upper Canada." *Ontario History* 44 (Oct. 1952): 165–72.

———. "The American Civil War and Canadian Confederation. Royal Society of Canada. *Transactions* 21 (May 1927): 55–62.

———. "Canadian Negroes and the John Brown Raid." *Journal of Negro History* 6 (Apr. 1921): 174–82.

———. "Negro Colonization Schemes in Upper Canada Before 1860." *Proceedings and Transactions of the Royal Society of Canada* 3d ser., 23 (May 1929): 73–80.

———. "The Negro Migration to Canada after 1850." *Journal of Negro History* 5 (Jan. 1921): 22–36.

_____. "When Uncle Tom's Cabin Came to Canada." *Ontario History* 44 (Jan. 1952): 1–5.

_____. "The Work of the American Missionary Association among the Negro Refugees in Canada West, 1848–1864." Ontario Historical Society. *Papers and Records* 21 (1924): 198–205.

Lass, William E. "How the Forty-Ninth Parallel Became the International Boundary." *Minnesota History* 44 (Summer 1975): 209–19.

Leamon, James. "The Search for Security: Maine After Penobscot." *Maine Historical Society Quarterly* 21 (Winter 1982): 119–53.

Le Duc, Thomas. "I. D. Andrews and the Reciprocity Treaty of 1854." *Canadian Historical Review* 15 (Dec. 1934): 437–41.

_____. "Israel Andrews." In *Dictionary of American Biography*, Supplement 1, edited by Allan Johnson and Dumas Malone, pp. 29–30. New York: Charles Scribner's Sons, 1955–77.

_____. The Maine Frontier and the Northeastern Boundary Controversy." *American Historical Review* 3 (Oct. 1947): 30–41.

_____. "The Webster-Ashburton Treaty and the Minnesota Iron Ranges." *Journal of American History* 51 (Dec. 1964): 476–81.

Lemmon, Sarah E. "Dissent in North Carolina During the War of 1812." *North Carolina Historical Review* 49 (Apr. 1972): 103–18.

Link, Eugene P. "Vermont Physicians and the Canadian Rebellion of 1837." *Vermont History* 37 (Summer 1969): 177–83.

Longley, R. S. "Emigration and the Crisis of 1837 in Upper Canada." *Canadian Historical Review* 17 (Mar. 1936): 29–40.

Lowenthal, David. "The Maine Press and the Aroostook War." *Canadian Historical Review* 32 (Dec. 1951): 315–36.

Mackintosh, W. A. "Canada and Vermont: A Study in Historical Geography." *Canadian Historical Review* 8 (Mar. 1927): 9–30.

MacPherson, Hallie. "The Interest of William McKendree Gwinn in the Purchase of Alaska, 1854–1861." *Pacific Historical Review* 3 (Mar. 1934): 28–38.

MacRae. A. O. "When Annexation Was in Flower." *Dalhousie Review* 9 (Oct. 1929): 282–86.

MacRae, Norman, "Crossing the Detroit River to Find Freedom." *Michigan History* 67 (Mar.–Apr. 1983): 35–39.

Mannix, Richard. "Gallatin, Jefferson, and the Embargo of 1808." *Diplomatic History* 3 (Spring 1979): 151–72.

Martin, Tomas P. "The Upper Mississippi Valley in Anglo-American Anti-Slavery and Free Trade Relations, 1837–1842." *Mississippi Valley Historical Review* 15 (1928): 204–20.

Masters, Donald C. "A Further Word on I. D. Andrews and the Reciprocity Treaty of 1854." *Canadian Historical Review* 17 (June 1936): 159–67.

Mekeel, Arthur J. "The Quaker-Loyalist Migration to New Brunswick and Nova Scotia in 1783." Friends Historical Association, *Bulletin* 32 (1943): 65–75.

Miles, Edwin. "Fifty-Four Forty or Fight—An American Political Legend."

Mississippi Valley Historical Review 44 (Sept. 1957): 291–309.

Morison, Samuel Eliot. "Dissent in the War of 1812." In *Dissent in Three American Wars*, edited by Samuel Eliot Morison, pp. 1–31. Cambridge, Mass.: Harvard University Press, 1970.

———. "New England and the Opening of the Columbia River Salmon Trade, 1830." *Oregon Historical Quarterly* 28 (June 1927): 116–30.

Morrow, Rising Lake. "The Anglo-American Treaty of 1870." *American Historical Review* 39 (1934): 663–81.

Morton, W. L. "British North America and a Continent in Dissolution, 1861–1871." *History* 47 (June 1962): 139–56.

———. "Canada and Reconstruction, 1863–79." In *New Frontiers of the American Reconstruction*, edited by Harold Hyman, pp. 105–24. Urbana: University of Illinois Press, 1966.

Mount, Graeme S. "Maine and the End of Reciprocity in 1866." *Maine Historical Society Quarterly* 26 (Summer 1986): 22–39.

Müller, H. N. "Smuggling into Canada: How the Champlain Valley Defied Jefferson's Embargo." *Vermont History* 38 (Winter 1970): 5–21.

———. "A 'Traitorous and Diabolical Traffic': The Commerce of the Champlain-Richelieu Corridor during the War of 1812." *Vermont History* 44 (Spring 1976): 78–96.

———. "Trouble on the Border 1838: A Neglected Incident from Vermont's Neglected History." *Vermont History* 44 (Spring 1976): 97–102.

Nelson, Anna K. "Destiny and Diplomacy 1840–1865." In *American Foreign Relations: A Historiographical Review*, edited by Gerald K. Haines and J. Samuel Walker, pp. 49–64. Westport: Greenwood Press, 1981.

New, Chester. "The Rebellion of 1837 in its Larger Setting." Canadian Historical Association, *Annual Report* (1937): pp. 5–17.

Officer, Lawrence E., and Lawrence Smith. "Canadian-American Reciprocity Treaty of 1855 to 1866." *Journal of Economic History* 28 (Dec. 1968): 598–623.

Ojala, Jeanne. "Ira Allen and the French Directory 1796: Plans for the Creation of the Republic of United Columbia." *William and Mary Quarterly* 3d ser., 36 (Oct. 1979): 436–48.

Onuf, Peter. "Liberty, Development and Union: Visions of the West in the 1780s." *William and Mary Quarterly* 3d ser., 43 (Apr. 1986): 179–213.

Overman, W. L. "I. D. Andrews and Reciprocity in 1854: An Episode in Dollar Diplomacy." *Canadian Historical Review* 15 (Sept. 1934): 248–63.

———. "A Sidelight on the Hunters Lodges of 1838." *Canadian Historical Review* 19 (June 1938): 168–71.

———. "Some Letters of Joshua R. Giddings on Reciprocity." *Canadian Historical Review* 16 (Sept. 1935): 289–96.

Phelps, E. "Foundations of the Canadian Oil Industry 1850–1866." In *Profiles of a Province: Studies in the History of Ontario*, pp. 156–65. Toronto: Ontario Historical Society, 1967.

Pratt, Julius W. "John L. O'Sullivan and Manifest Destiny." *New York History* 14 (1933): 213–34.

Pritchett, John P. "The Origins of the So-Called Fenian Raid on Manitoba in 1871." *Canadian Historical Review* 10 (Mar. 1929): 23–42.

Raney, William F. "Recruiting and Crimping in Canada for the Northern Forces, 1861–1865." *Mississippi Valley Historical Review* 10 (June 1923): 21–33.

Rawlyk, George. "The Federalist-Loyalist Alliance in New Brunswick, 1784–1815." *Humanities Association Review* 27 (Spring 1976): 142–60.

———. "Thomas Coltin Keefer and the St. Lawrence–Great Lakes Commercial System." *Inland Seas* 19 (Fall 1963): 190–94.

Robson, Maureen M. "The Alabama Claims and the Anglo-American Reconciliation, 1865–1871." *Canadian Historical Review* 42 (Mar. 1961): 1–22.

Rosentretor, Roger. "Liberating Canada: Michigan and the Patriot War." *Michigan History* 67 (Mar.-Apr. 1983): 32–34.

Ross, Robert. "The Patriot War." Michigan, *Historical Collections* 21 (1892): 509–609.

Russell, Fridley. "When Minnesota Coveted Canada." *Minnesota History* 41 (Summer, 1968): 76–79.

Sabine, Lorenzo. "Moose Island." In *Eastport and Passamaquoddy: A Collection of Historical and Biographical Sketches*, edited by William Kilby, pp. 142–74. Eastport, Maine: Edward E. Skead & Co., 1888.

———. "Moose Island and Its Dependencies: Four Years Under Martial Law." In *Eastport and Passamaquoddy: A Collection of Historical and Biographical Sketches*, edited by William Kilby, pp. 175–219. Eastport, Maine: Edward E. Skead & Co., 1888.

Sawtelle, William O. "Acadia: The Pre-Loyalist Migration and the Philadelphia Plantation." *Pennsylvania Magazine of History and Biography* 51 (1927): 244–85.

Scheuer, Michael. "Deadlock: Charting the Canadian-American Boundary on the Detroit River." *Michigan History* 67 (Mar.–Apr. 1983): 24–30.

———. "Who Should Own the Lakes? Negotiations Preceding the Treaty of Ghent." *Inland Seas* 38 (Winter 1982): 236–44.

Schroeder, John H. "Representative John Floyd, 1817–1829: Harbinger of Oregon Territory." *Oregon Historical Quarterly* 70 (Dec. 1969): 333–46.

Sharrow, Walter G. "William Henry Seward and the Basis for American Empire, 1850–1860." *Pacific Historical Review* 36 (Aug. 1967): 325–42.

Shewmaker, Kenneth. " 'Hook and Line, and Bob and Sinker': Daniel Webster and the Fisheries Dispute of 1852." *Diplomatic History* 9 (Spring 1985): 113–29.

Shi, David. "Seward's Attempt to Annex British Columbia, 1865–1869." *Pacific Historical Review* 47 (May 1978): 217–39.

Shortridge, Wilson P. "The Canadian-American Frontier during the Rebellion of 1837–1838." *Canadian Historical Review* 7 (Mar. 1926): 13–26.

Shortt, Adam. "Founders of Canadian Banking: Horatio Gates, Wholesale Merchant, Banker, and Legislator." *Journal of Canadian Bankers Association* 30 (Oct. 1922): 34–37.

Sloan, Robert W. "New Ireland: Men in Pursuit of a Forlorn Hope, 1779–

1784." *Maine Historical Society Quarterly* 19 (Fall, 1979): 73–90.

Smelser, Marshal. "Smuggling in 1813–14, A Personal Reminiscence." *Vermont History* 38 (Winter 1970): 22–26.

Smith, Joe Patterson. "American Republican Leadership and the Movement for Annexation of Canada in the Eighteen Sixties." Canadian Historical Association, *Annual Report* (1935): 65–75.

————. "United States of North America—Shadow or Substance? 1815–1915." *Canadian Historical Review* 26 (June 1945): 109–18.

Snell, James G. "A Foreign Agent in Washington: George W. Brega, Canada's Lobbyist 1867–1870." *Civil War History* 26 (Mar. 1980): 53–70.

————. "The Frontier Sweeps Northwest: American Perceptions of the British American Prairie West at the Point of Canadian Expansion (circa 1870)." *Western Historical Quarterly* 11 (Oct. 1980): 381–400.

————. "H. H. Emmons, Detroit's Agent in Canadian-American Relations, 1864–1866." *Michigan History* 56 (Winter 1971): 302–18.

Sprague, John F. "The North Eastern Boundary Controversy and the Aroostook War." In *Historical Collections of Piscataquis County, Maine*, pp. 216–81. Dover: Observer Press, 1910.

Stacey, Charles P. "An American Plan for a Canadian Campaign." *American Historical Review* 46 (1941): 348–58.

————. "Britain's Withdrawal from North America 1846–1871." *Canadian Historical Review* 36 (Sept. 1955): 185–98.

————. "The Myth of the Unguarded Frontier 1815–1871." *American Historical Review* 56 (Oct. 1950): 1–18.

Stagg, John C. A. "James Madison and the Coercion of Great Britain: Canada, the West Indies, and the War of 1812." *William and Mary Quarterly* 3d ser., 38 (Jan. 1981): 3–34.

Stewart, Alice R. "The State of Maine and Canadian Confederation." *Canadian Historical Review* 33 (June 1952): 148–64.

Stouffer, Allen. "Canadian-American Relations in the Shadow of the Civil War." *Dalhousie Review* 57 (Summer 1977): 332–46.

Strum, Harvey. "New York Federalists and Opposition to the War of 1812." *World Affairs* 142 (Winter 1980): 169–87.

————. "Virtually Impossible to Stop: Smuggling in the North Country 1808–1815." *The Quarterly* (July 1982), 21–23.

Stuart, Reginald C. "James Madison and the Militants: Republican Disunity and Replacing the Embargo." *Diplomatic History* 6 (Spring 1982): 145–68.

————. "Special Interests and National Authority in Foreign Policy: American-British Provincial Links During the Embargo and the War of 1812." *Diplomatic History* 8 (Spring 1984): 145–68.

————. "United States Expansionism and the British North American Provinces, 1783–1871." In *Arms at Rest: Peacemaking and Peacekeeping in American History*, edited by Joan R. Challinor and Robert L. Beisner, pp. 101–32. Westport, Conn.: Greenwood Press, 1987.

Tallman, Ronald. "Annexation in the Maritimes? The Butler Mission to Charlottetown." *Dalhousie Review* 53 (Spring 1973): 97–112.

Thomson, D. W. "The 49th Parallel." *Geographical Journal* 134 (1968): 209–15.

Trotter, R. G. "Canada as a Factor in Anglo-American Relations in the 1860s." *Canadian Historical Review* 16 (Mar. 1935): 20–27.

Van Alstyne, Richard W. "The American Empire Makes its Bow on the World State, 1803–1845." In *From Colony to Empire: Essays in the History of American Foreign Relations*, edited by William A. Williams, pp. 83–133. New York: John Wiley & Sons, 1972.

_____. "Great Britain, the United States, and Hawaiian Independence, 1850–1855." *Pacific Historical Review* 4 (Mar. 1955): 19–35.

_____. "International Rivalries in the Pacific Northwest." *Oregon Historical Quarterly* 46 (Sept. 1945): 185–218.

_____. "New Viewpoints in the Relations of Canada and the United States." *Canadian Historical Review* 25 (June 1944): 109–30.

_____. "The Significance of the Mississippi Valley in American Diplomatic History 1686–1890." *Mississippi Valley Historical Review* 35 (1949): 215–38.

Vevier, Charles. "American Continentalism: An Idea of Expansion, 1845–1910." *American Historical Review* 65 (Jan. 1960): 323–35.

Walker, William A., Jr. "Martial Sons: Tennessee Enthusiasm for the War of 1812." *Tennessee Historical Quarterly* 20 (Spring 1961): 22–25.

Warner, Donald F. "Drang Nach Norden: The United States and the Riel Rebellion." *Mississippi Valley Historical Review* 39 (Mar. 1953): 693–712.

Weber, Ralph E. "Riot in Victoria 1860." *Journal of Negro History* 56 (Apr. 1971): 141–48.

Wehtje, Myron. "Opposition in Virginia to the War of 1812." *Virginia Magazine of History and Biography* 78 (Jan. 1970): 65–86.

Weigley, Russell F. "The Anglo-American Armies and Peace, 1783–1868." In *Arms at Rest: Peacemaking and Peacekeeping in American History*, edited by Joan R. Challinor and Robert L. Beisner, pp. 113–59. Westport, Conn.: Greenwood Press, 1987.

Williamson, Chilton. "New York's Impact on the Canadian Economy, Prior to the Completion of the Erie Canal." *New York State History* 24 (Jan. 1943): 24–38.

_____. "New York's Struggle for the Champlain Valley Trade, 1760–1825." *New York State History* 22 (Oct. 1941): 426–36.

Winks, Robin. "The Canadian Negro: An Historical Assessment." *Journal of Negro History* 53 (Oct. 1968): 283–300.

Wittke, Carl. "Canadian Refugees in the American Revolution." *Canadian Historical Review* 3 (Dec. 1922): 320–33.

_____. "Ohioans and the Canadian-American Crisis of 1837–38." *Ohio Archeological and Historical Quarterly* 58 (Jan. 1949): 21–34.

Wright, Richard. "Green Flags and Red-Coated Gunboats: Naval Activities on the Great Lakes During the Fenian Scares, 1866–1870." *Inland Seas* 22 (Summer 1966): 91–110.

Zorn, Roman J. "Criminal Extradition Menaces the Canadian Haven for

Fugitive Slaves, 1841–1861." *Canadian Historical Review* 38 (Dec. 1957): 284–94.

THESES, DISSERTATIONS, AND PAPERS

Babcock, Blakely. "The Effects of the Embargo of 1807 on the District of Maine." Master's thesis, Trinity College, 1963.

Brauer, Kinley. "Anglo-American Imperial Rivalry, 1815–1860." Paper delivered at the Ninth Annual Meeting of the Society for Historians of American Foreign Relations, Washington, D.C., August 1983.

Brown, Robert. "Canadian American Relations in the Latter Part of the Nineteenth Century." Ph.D. diss., University of Toronto, 1962.

Butler, George. "Commercial Relations of Nova Scotia with the United States, 1783–1830." Master's thesis, Dalhousie University, 1934.

Calabro, David Joseph. "Consensus for Empire: American Expansionist Thought and Policy, 1763–1789." Ph.D. diss., University of Virginia, 1982.

Chapman, James. "Relations of Maine and New Brunswick in the Era of Reciprocity, 1849–1867." Master's thesis, University of New Brunswick, 1951.

Cooper, James L. "Interests, Ideas and Empires: The Roots of American Foreign Policy, 1763–1779." Ph.D. diss., University of Wisconsin, 1964.

D'Arcy, William. "The Fenian Movement in the United States, 1858–1886." Ph.D. diss., Catholic University of America, 1947.

De Rosier, A. H. "American Annexation Sentiment toward Canada, 1866–1871." Master's thesis, University of South Carolina, 1955.

Doyle, James. "American Literary Images of the Upper Canada Rebellion." Paper courtesy of the author.

Faibisey, John Dewar. "Privateering and Piracy: The Effects of New England Raiding upon Nova Scotia During the American Revolution." Ph.D. diss., University of Massachusetts, 1972.

Gallison, Elda. "The Short Route to Europe: A History of the European and North American Railroad." Master's thesis, University of Maine, Orono, 1950.

Hall, Roger D. "Newspaper Commentary and the San Juan Water Boundary Dispute." Honors thesis, University of Victoria, 1967.

Hammack, James W. "Kentucky and Anglo-American Relations, 1803–1815." Ph.D. diss., University of Kentucky, 1974.

Hitchman, James H. "The Waterborne Commerce of British Columbia & Washington, 1850–1870." Western Washington State College, Center for Pacific Northwest Studies, Occasional Paper #7, 1976.

Horsman, Reginald. "On to Canada: Manifest Destiny and United States Strategy in the War of 1812." Paper presented at War of 1812 Conference, Monroe, Michigan, January 1987, courtesy of the author.

Lohnes, Barry. "The War of 1812 at Sea: The British Navy, New England,

and the Maritime Provinces of Canada." Master's thesis, University of Maine, Orono, 1971.

Long, John W., Jr. "The San Juan Island Boundary Controversy: A Phase of Nineteenth Century Anglo-American Relations." Ph.D. diss., Duke University, 1949.

MacLean, Raymond. "Joseph Howe and British American Union." Ph.D. diss., University of Toronto, 1966.

Mansfield, J. Paris. "New Brunswick and the Treaty of Washington." Master's thesis, University of New Brunswick, 1958.

Mercer, M. J. "Relations between Nova Scotia and New England, 1815–1867, with Special Reference to Trade and the Fisheries." Master's thesis, Dalhousie University, 1938.

Millman, T. R. "The Legal Regulation of Trade between the United States and Canada." Master's thesis, University of Toronto, 1933.

Müller, H. N. "The Commercial History of the Lake Champlain–Richelieu River Route, 1760–1815." Ph.D. diss., University of Rochester, 1969.

Pemberton, Ian C. "Loyalists in the Jacksonian Era: The Fate of the 'Canadian Party' in the Indian Stream Republic Boundary Controversy of the 1830s." Paper delivered at the Canadian Historical Association Annual Meeting, Halifax, Nova Scotia, May–June 1981.

Rosentreter, Roger L. "To Free Upper Canada: Michigan and the Patriot War, 1837–1839." Ph.D. diss., Michigan State University, 1983.

Sams, R. F. "The Congressional Attitude towards Canada during the 1860s." Master's thesis, Queens University, 1947.

Scribner, Robert L. "The Diplomacy of William L. Marcy." Ph.D. diss., University of Virginia, 1949.

Snell, James Grant. "The Eagle and the Butterfly: Some American Attitudes towards British North America, 1864–1867." Ph.D. diss., Queens University, 1971.

Stevens, Kenneth Ray. "The 'Caroline' Affair: Anglo-American Relations and Domestic Politics, 1837–1842." Ph.D. diss., Indiana University, 1982.

Stouffer, Allen P. "Canadian-American Relations, 1861–1871." Ph.D. diss., Claremont Graduate School, 1971.

Taylor, Dennis A. "The American Picture of British North America on the Eve of the War of 1812." Master's thesis, Queens University, 1965.

Index